# Starting Out

## The Complete
## Home Buyer's Guide

**by**
**Dian Hymer**

*Illustrations by*
*Bill Compton*

CHRONICLE BOOKS

SAN FRANCISCO

W9-CHX-323

**Text copyright © 1997
by Dian Hymer.**
Illustrations copyright © 1997
by Bill Compton.

The Standard Residential Purchase
Agreement, Counter Offer, and Seller's
Property Disclosure Statement forms are
reprinted by permission of Professional
Publishing, a Division of McKenney's
Standard Forms, Inc., 122 Paul Drive, San
Rafael, CA 94903; (800) 288-2006, fax
(415) 472-2069.

Library of Congress
Cataloging-in-Publication Data:

Hymer, Dian Davis.
Starting out: the complete home buyer's
guide/by Dian Hymer; illustrations by
Bill Compton.
    p.   cm.
Includes index.
ISBN 0-8118-1272-3 (pbk.)
1. House buying. I. Title.
HD1379.H96 1997
643'.12—dc20
96-31508          CIP

**Acknowledgments**
A debt of gratitude to Bruce Koon and
Brad and Kris Inman—my co-conspirators
in originating and distributing my
"Starting Out" column.

Special thanks to the hundreds of home
buyers and sellers who have put their trust
in me as their agent, and from whom I
learned a book-full; to Bill LeBlond, senior
editor at Chronicle Books, for supporting
my writing projects over the years; and to
my husband, Allan Hymer, whose keen
wit and generous spirit accompanied me
through it all.

Printed in the United States.

Cover Illustration:
    Laura Tarrish
Cover Design:
    Liz Rico
Book Design and Typesetting:
    Mark Jones

Distributed in Canada by
Raincoast Books
8680 Cambie Street
Vancouver, B.C. V6P 6M9

10 9 8 7 6 5 4 3 2 1

Chronicle Books
85 Second Street
San Francisco, CA 94105

Web Site: www.chronbooks.com

# Contents

# Introduction

Buying a home is like getting married. It is an event that most people experience infrequently. It involves making a big commitment. It's exciting, fun, terrifying, gratifying, enlightening, occasionally maddening, often expensive, and sometimes disappointing. It can be immensely pleasurable, or incredibly painful, depending on the circumstances.

Experiencing a bad marriage can be far more devastating than most bad home purchases will ever be. But in some cases it may be easier to get out of a bad marriage than to unload a home you no longer want. This is why you need to do your homework before you buy a home.

Gone are the days when you could buy a home on a whim. It was not a major concern in the 1980s if you paid a little too much. Home prices were rising in most areas, so buyers were sure to make their money back quickly. In fact, making money on homes was taken for granted. Home price appreciation was one of the primary reasons for buying a home. When money comes easy, emotions can rule and the consequences are rarely serious. So what if you bought the wrong home? You could sell it again in a few years, buy a home you liked better, and probably make a profit in the process.

All this changed at the end of the 1980s, when the real estate market suffered a downturn in one area after another around the country. Home prices dropped significantly in some locations. Many homeowners lost mini-fortunes as the economy soured at the same time that home prices plummeted. Some homeowners are still stuck in homes they can't afford to sell because the home is worth less than the amount of the mortgage. The good news is that lower prices opened the door to home ownership for many buyers who were priced out of the more expensive housing markets around the nation. Consequently, home ownership is on the rise in this country once again, after slipping at the end of the 1980s.

Buying a home used to be an easy process. Before 1980, purchase agreements were simple, usually no more than one page long. Deciding on a mortgage was also simple: All home loans had fixed interest rates. The home inspection business was in its infancy and disclosure laws were unheard of in most states. Real estate agents worked for the sellers, although most buyers didn't know it.

Today, home purchase agreements are complicated legal documents. A myriad of mortgage products are on the market. Homes are put through numerous inspections, and disclosure requirements are changing daily. Now the industry has agency disclosure, buyer's brokers, seller disclosures, computerized loan origination, and on-line home shopping services. Staying on top of the changes in the residential real estate business is a full-time job in itself.

Buying a home is no longer an enterprise to be taken lightly. It's a serious undertaking that requires careful planning and pragmatic decision-making. *Starting Out: The Complete Home Buyer's Guide* will help you through what may seem like a daunting process. *Starting Out* will assist you in charting your course and keep you from making the costly mistakes made by other, less informed home buyers. *Starting Out* will help you decide when, what, and where to buy. You will learn how to pick an agent, a mortgage broker, a lawyer, an inspector, a mortgage, and a neighborhood. You will discover how to analyze a floor plan, how to have a home inspected properly, how to shop for a home on the Internet, and how to make sure you do not overpay for a property. Agency relationships and disclosure requirements will be explained, and you will learn the fine art of negotiating a home sale. You will know how to protect yourself in a real estate transaction. There's even a chapter for repeat buyers, those who already own a home but who need to know when and how to buy the next one.

*Starting Out* began as a weekly syndicated real estate advice column in 1992. The column first appeared in the *San Francisco Examiner, Los Angeles Times,* and the *San Diego Union Tribune.* In 1993, the column was picked up by the *Miami Herald,* the *Chicago Sun Times,* the *Hartford Courant,* and numerous other newspapers around the country. For years, readers—both home buyers and real estate professionals—have asked for a *Starting Out* book that would combine years of home buying advice into one resource. And here it is. The weekly columns were updated and expanded into subchapters. Additional resource material was added where necessary.

Charts and checklists are included throughout the book to help demystify the home buying process. You'll find a checklist of questions to use when interviewing real estate agents, and another to use when you are shopping for a loan. There is a checklist for condo buyers, a home comparison checklist, an adjustable-rate mortgage comparison work sheet, a checklist to guide you through making an offer to buy a home, and many more.

You will learn firsthand from "Tales from the Trenches," real-life home buying experiences that illustrate the fine points of home buying (the names have been changed, for the sake of privacy).

Illustrations of different house styles are also included. These are not architectural drawings, but sketches to help you to distinguish one house style from another. You may find, during your home search, that some houses do not fit one style exclusively but encompass features from various styles.

*Starting Out: The Complete Home Buyer's Guide* can be read cover-to-cover for a comprehensive overview of the home buying process. Or, it can be read a little at a time. Repeat home buyers might want to start by reading Chapter 8 first (Strategies for Repeat Home Buyers), then go back to chapters 1 through 7. The best way to use the book is to read it through entirely before you start your home search. Then, refer back to specific sections from time to time as necessary.

*Starting Out: The Complete Home Buyer's Guide* is unique because although I am a real estate journalist, I am also a top-producing real estate broker who has represented home buyers and sellers in more than four hundred transactions during the past twenty years. My advice is based on practical, hands-on experience rather than on a theory about how the real estate business ought to work. *Starting Out* is not a book written by committee, nor is it written by an outsider. You are getting the straight scoop from a real estate expert who knows the ins and outs of the business firsthand. Real estate agents will also find this book useful as a resource.

Be aware that real estate law, custom, and practices vary considerably from one location to another, and they are constantly changing. A "Guide to local real estate custom and practice" is included in Appendix 1. It will help you find out the specifics of how homes are bought and sold in your area. Mortgage programs and lenders' qualifying guidelines also change over time, as do interest rates and market conditions in general. Also, keep in mind that this book is based on the opinions of the author; these opinions do not represent the standard of care of any given realty company. Make sure that you read all contracts, reports, and disclosures carefully, including the fine print. Find out the answers to any questions you have before, not after, you put pen to paper. You should always work with the best professionals you can find. But, even so, take the initiative to protect yourself when buying a home. If something doesn't make sense to you during your transaction, speak up. If you need technical advice, consult an expert. The cost of consulting an attorney, accountant, or engineer is minimal compared with the cost of buying a home.

Owning your own home can be one of the great joys in life. *Starting Out: The Complete Home Buyer's Guide* will help you buy the right home, and buy it on the right terms. So be careful and protect yourself, then relax and have fun. Happy home buying.

## Disclaimer:

The comments, observations, and recommendations in this book are the opinions of the author, and are based on twenty years of experience in the residential real estate field. However, the author is not qualified to render legal, accounting, engineering, financial, architectural, or other professional advice. Consult the appropriate expert for legal, tax, or other professional recommendations, and be aware that real estate practices and customs are constantly changing and differ from one area to the next.

# Starting Out

**1**

## Why buy a home?

To own a home of your own is part of the American dream. Think about home, and visions of comfort, success, and security come to mind. Your home is your sanctuary, your private haven, a refuge from the outside world. If you own your home, you are in control, master of your private domain.

But home ownership is not for everyone. Homes require maintenance to keep them in good shape, with all systems running properly. As a tenant, you're frustrated when the dishwasher breaks or the hot water runs cold, but someone else usually pays the repair bill. As an owner, you not only have the hassle of fixing the problem but also the privilege of paying for upkeep.

Besides fixing home systems when they break and replacing them when they wear out, it is important to keep a home looking its best to preserve your investment. Homes in top condition sell for more money, in less time, than homes that are run-down. Buyers pay a premium for a home they can move right into.

Despite the work a home requires, there *are* compensating benefits; otherwise why would more than 65 percent of the people in this country own their own homes? One benefit of home ownership is that you are never at the mercy of a landlord who could refuse to extend your lease, causing you to move on short notice. Moving is expensive and time-consuming. Moving is also disruptive, particularly for a family with children. Another benefit of owning is that you can decorate, remodel, renovate, and rearrange to your heart's content without needing the owner's permission. And, with proper planning, renovations can add value to your property.

In addition to improvement potential, owning your home has other advantages. Few home buyers pay all cash for a home. Most buyers take out a mortgage. The amount of cash you put into the purchase as a down payment is called your *equity* in the property.

Part of each monthly mortgage payment pays the interest you owe, and part goes to pay back the amount you borrowed (called the *principal*). Over time, your equity in the property usually grows as the mortgage balance declines. This amounts to enforced savings.

Home buyers who purchase using a fixed-rate mortgage have an advantage over renters because their future cost of housing is more predictable. Except for areas where rent control limits increases, renters can anticipate that over the long run their rent will probably go up. Although property taxes can increase over time, the monthly mortgage payment for fixed-rate homeowners never changes.

Owning a home can also save you on your income tax bill. Homeowners are entitled to write off mortgage interest and property taxes. However, you can only take these deductions if you switch from taking the standard deduction, which all taxpayers are entitled to, to making itemized deductions instead. If your itemized deductions, including mortgage interest and property taxes, do not exceed the standard deduction amount (in 1995, $3,900 for a single person and $6,550 for a married couple filing jointly), you are better off taking the standard deduction. In other words, not all homeowners get a tax break from owning their homes, but most do.

Home prices go up and down, like stock market prices. That's why it's wise to plan on owning a home for a reasonable period of time, say five to ten years. On average, Americans move from one home to another every eleven years. But, if you are starting your career, and your future employment path is uncertain, you may be better off renting than buying. Closing costs that you'll owe when you sell a home can add up to 7 or 8 percent of the sale price. If you buy a home one year and sell it a year or two later, you could lose money unless the local real estate market is surging.

Over the long run, homes have tended to increase in value. The increase in property value due to inflation is called appreciation. Home price appreciation adds to a homeowner's equity in the property. This is often referred to as equity buildup. In the past, homeowners have counted on home price appreciation to pay for a child's college tuition, or for their retirement. Since there is no guarantee of home price appreciation, your home purchase should make sense based on other factors, such as how long you plan to live in the home, tax benefits, how much it would cost you to rent an equivalent home, and the desire to own your own home.

Owning your own home usually gives you more control over the neighborhood in which you live. If you buy into a neighborhood populated primarily by other homeowners, you and your neighbors have a vested interest in maintaining the quality of the local community, which has a positive effect on local property values. Also, there is a psychological benefit to owning rather than renting, commonly referred to as "pride of

**The higher your rent, the more it makes sense to own your home.**

**Plan to own your home for at least five years, particularly if you are buying in a down market.**

ownership." A price tag cannot be attached to this subjective value. The need for the sense of security that comes from owning the roof over your head varies from one person to the next. The nesting instinct is stronger in some than it is in others. For those of us who have a strong desire to control our own private retreat from the world, the price of buying, owning, maintaining, and restoring a home is worth it.

# Ten common home buyer mistakes

It's natural to feel ambivalent about buying a home. It's not only a big financial investment, but the home buying process is complicated and, at times, confusing. The mere thought of making a mistake can be enough to stop you in your tracks. But you can take comfort in knowing that these ten mistakes are ones you don't have to make.

*Looking at homes before you are lender-prequalified and know what price home you can afford.*
Unless your idea of fun is test-driving a Cadillac before you buy a Chevy, find out what your budget will support first, then start looking. It is hard to know where to look or what to look at (detached house, condominium, or cooperative) until you know how much you can afford. Looking at homes that are way out of your price range, regardless of whether the price is on the high side or low side, is not only a waste of time, it's discouraging.

*Assuming that if you don't have a 20 percent cash down payment, buying a home is impossible.*
It's easy to fall into the trap of thinking you will never be able to save enough money to buy a home, given that the old-fashioned way to finance a home purchase is with a loan for 80 percent of the purchase price. But don't assume that this is the only financing option available. Most first-time buyers purchase with less than a 20 percent down payment. There are plenty of financing options available for low-cash-down buyers.

**Bungalow**
Bungalows are built low to the ground and they have an informal, space-saving design. They come in many architectural styles, including the Craftsman style pictured here with its wide overhanging roof and deep porch.

☐ *Working with an out-of-area agent who does not know the local market.*
One of the biggest mistakes you can make is hooking up with the wrong agent. Yet it happens all the time, and it happens so innocently. Let's say you have been looking at homes in Our Town with agent Jane. In fact, you have been taking up her Saturday afternoons for months. Then you hear from a friend that homes are much more affordable in Their Town, so you decide to look there. But what about poor Jane, who has wasted so much of her time with you? Maybe Jane can help you find a house in Their Town. "Sure," Jane says, reluctantly. Why is she reluctant? Because she doesn't know the first thing about that market. She will be doing you a disservice and probably waste more of her (and your) time. If you find yourself in this situation, do yourself and your agent a favor and ask to be referred to a good agent who specializes in the other area.

☐ *Failing to read and understand the entire purchase agreement before you sign it.*
Most of us suffer from "fine print phobia." Many home buyers never read their purchase contract and are unclear about what it says. Ask your attorney or real estate agent to give you a sample contract, like the one you will use when you find a home to buy. Read it. If something is confusing, ask your agent or attorney for an explanation. Then you'll be better prepared when you do sit down to write an offer. Be sure to get copies of everything you sign during your real estate transaction.

☐ *Failing to have a property thoroughly inspected.*
You have to be a little bit schizophrenic to be a conscientious home buyer. First, you have to be able to cast caution to the wind and let yourself fall in love with a home. Then, before amour turns into a permanent relationship, you need to detach yourself emotionally from the home and find out if there is any reason why you should not buy it. Don't forego having a home inspected just because you are afraid you will lose it to another buyer. If the home turns out to be a money pit, you are better off losing it.

☐ *Assuming your real estate agent is a mind reader.*
One of the most common complaints buyers have about their agent is that the agent does not show them the right kind of homes. If you are looking at a lot of homes and see nothing that appeals to you, there is a good chance that you haven't communicated clearly with your agent. It helps to put your needs and desires in writing, then give a copy to your agent. Let him or her know what you do and don't like about the home you see.

☐ *Proceeding blindly through the home buying process with a "wake me when it's over" attitude.*
Buying real estate is a complicated endeavor involving the coordination of many critical details before title transfers and the home is yours. Don't assume that someone else is going to take care of it all for you. A really outstanding agent will make your job easier.

But don't make the mistake of waiting until the last minute to find out that someone dropped the ball and your transaction won't be closing on time, if at all. Monitor the transaction closely by keeping in touch with your real estate agent, attorney, and loan broker. Let them know that you are available to help and that you want to know when problems arise. A successful home purchase requires a team effort.

☐ *Underestimating the amount of cash you will need to close the sale.*
This mistake should never happen. Yet it does, which is another reason you need to monitor your real estate transaction carefully. Your real estate agent should supply an estimate of your closing costs at the time you make an offer to buy a home. Then your loan agent or mortgage broker should provide you with another closing cost estimate within three days after you submit a loan application. This is required by law. One reason buyers come up short is that they are not told until the last minute that the lender requires extra cash reserves in the bank if they are making a down payment of less than 20 percent of the purchase price.

☐ *Applying for a loan with a lender who offers the lowest rates in town even though your real estate agent tells you the lender is flaky.*
How many times have you heard horror stories about loan approvals being interminably delayed, or a lender being so slow processing the loan that the sale didn't close on time? Even worse is the bait-and-switch lender who promises a too-good-to-be-true loan that becomes no longer available just before your loan is approved. A low interest rate is important; you could be paying on the loan for a long time. But a lender's performance, service, and trustworthiness are also important. Be sure to check a lender's reputation by talking to recent customers. The best deal in town may not be worth the savings if the lender's ineptness turns your transaction into a nightmare.

☐ *Refusing to make an offer because there are multiple offers on the property from other buyers, and you don't want to be in competition.*
One way to make sure you have no competition is to buy a home that no one else wants. But a home that is hard to sell might not be a good investment. Buyers often shy away from competition because they are afraid the price will be bid way up. Although this can happen, properties rarely sell for more than fair market value. Actually, fair market value is the price a willing and able buyer will pay for a property. So if the price is bid up, the property may have been priced too low to begin with. Also, there is more to an offer than the price. If you can offer the seller a good clean deal that is not contingent on the sale of another home, your offer just might be accepted. You will never know unless you try.

# The home buyer's game plan

There are two basic ways to approach the home buying process. There is the fly-by-the-seat-of-your-pants approach, which works for some but not for most buyers. This involves previewing hundreds of open houses, calling on ads for homes you will never buy, fending off real estate agents who are anxious for your business, and many sleepless nights pondering when the perfect home will come along. This approach is exhausting, not to mention frustrating. Or you can take the sensible approach and treat finding a home as you would any business endeavor. Set a game plan for yourself and follow it. By following a systematic strategy, you will complete your purchase with relative ease, and in reasonable time.

That said, you should realize that buying a home is not a quick process. Buyers are often surprised at the time, energy, and patience that is required to buy a home. Keep this in mind if you are considering taking on other major projects while you are in the midst of home buying. How busy you are will determine how much you will have to rely on others for help during the transaction. If you are extremely busy, you will need the best support team of real estate professionals (real estate agent, loan originator, insurance representative, title officer, inspector, and in some cases, attorney) that you can find—don't even consider doing it alone. Buying a home is a major undertaking.

Here is an overview of the basic home buying strategy. More detailed information about each step is included in the chapters that follow.

The first step is to find out what price house you can afford to buy. The easiest way to do this is to make an appointment with a loan agent (who works for one lender), or a mortgage broker (who is an independent agent who originates loans for many lenders). Ask the agent or broker to prequalify you for a loan, which will tell you what you can afford. Prequalification should not cost you anything, and there is no obligation to apply for a loan with the person who prequalifies you. But this will give you an opportunity to get to know someone on the lending side of the business.

The next step is to figure out what you want and need in a home. This should include both the essentials, such as the number of rooms you need, and those nonessentials that you would like to have. For example, it may be critical that you have a home with three bedrooms and level-in access from the street. You would also love to have a view. But if a home is suitable in all other regards, you might forego the view.

Then narrow down where you want to live. If you have no idea, ask friends and colleagues at work if

**The home buyer's game plan**
- Prequalify: Find out how much you can afford to pay.
- Develop a wish list.
- Shop neighborhoods: Find out where you want to live.
- Find an agent.
- Find a home.
- Negotiate the purchase—with contract contingencies for your protection.
- Inspect the property, get the loan, check the title, line up insurance.
- When all contingencies are satisfied, sign closing documents and close the transaction.

they are happy where they live. Ask the lender who prequalified you to recommend the best areas you can afford to buy into. Drive through neighborhoods and visit open houses in the areas you are considering. Visiting Sunday open houses not only lets you preview the housing stock, it also gives you a chance to meet local real estate agents.

When you know where you want to buy, you are ready to choose a real estate agent to help you find a home. Again, ask colleagues for recommendations. If you are looking in several marketplaces, use one agent for each market. (See Chapter 2 for more information about selecting an agent.) Home buyers who are looking in an area with only new housing projects may not need an agent. You may have no alternative but to use a member of the sales staff for the housing development where you want to buy. Some new homes projects do cooperate with outside agents. If so, your agent will probably have to register you with the sales office.

Your search may go quickly, or it could take months. This will depend on how aggressive you are. You should look at every home that comes on the market that your agent recommends. How long it takes to find a home will also depend on how much inventory there is on the market. Try to be flexible with your search criteria, particularly on the nonessential elements. Stick firm to the essentials on your wish list.

Finding the home is only part of the process. You must then negotiate the purchase contract with the sellers. Your contract should include contract contingencies to protect you. You will need an inspection contingency that allows you to complete inspections of the property. You will also want a financing contingency, unless you are paying all cash. Even if you pay cash, you will probably want a contingency stating that the property must appraise for the purchase price. The purchase contract should also include a clause stipulating that the sellers will deliver clear and marketable title to the property.

When all contingencies have been satisfied and removed from the contract, the closing documents are prepared and signed by the buyers and sellers. If one or more contingencies cannot be satisfied, the buyers' deposit money is usually returned to them, and the contract is canceled. Closing occurs when title to the property transfers from the sellers to the buyers.

# Determining what you can afford

### Home ownership and taxes

One of the benefits of owning rather than renting your home is that some expenses are tax deductible. With certain limitations, the property taxes and mortgage interest you pay on a personal residence are deductible from your income in the year in which they were paid. Since this can amount to a sizable deduction, home ownership is often touted as one of the few remaining tax shelters. Let's say you purchase a home for $250,000 with a mortgage equal to 90 percent of the purchase price. The monthly payment on a thirty-year $225,000 loan with an interest rate of 8.5 percent is $1,730.25. Of this payment, approximately $1,678 per month is applied to interest during the first year of the loan. This amounts to a mortgage interest deduction of more than $20,000 for that year. If you are in the 28-percent tax bracket, your tax savings would be more than $5,500. The higher your tax bracket, the bigger the tax savings.

Some of the costs associated with home buying (called *closing costs*) are tax deductible. For example, the loan origination fee (called *points*) is considered prepaid interest by the IRS and is deductible in the year you purchase a principal residence. Since one point is equal to 1 percent of the loan amount, this can add up to a sizable tax deduction. The interest that is paid to the lender at closing (called *proration of interest*) is also tax deductible in the year of purchase. Lenders collect enough money at closing to cover the interest owed from the closing date until the next payment period. Make sure that you keep a record of this figure. At the end of the year, the lender will send you a 1099 form (for your income tax filing), which indicates the amount of interest you paid for the year. This 1099 form might not include the proration of interest you paid at closing and you'll want to add in this figure on your tax return.

Many of your closing costs cannot be deducted immediately but they can be used to offset taxable gain when you sell the property. A home sale must be reported to the IRS; the sellers then owe tax on the gain they realized during their ownership. Closing costs that can be subtracted from the sale price to reduce capital gain tax liability include transfer taxes, title insurance premium, inspection fees, appraisal and credit fees, attorney's fees, brokerage commission, and notary and recording fees.

While the costs of maintaining a home are not tax deductible, the cost of capital improvements made to the property can be used to offset capital gain when you sell. Adding a security system to a property that does not already have one is a capital improvement; repairing an already existing security system when it breaks would not qualify as a capital improvement. What is and is not a capital improvement is not always clear, so consult a tax adviser if you have a question. Keep good records in case you need to substantiate tax deductions associated with home ownership.

Homeowners can defer paying tax on their gain if they buy another personal residence within twenty-four months of selling the old one. The replacement residence must cost the same or more than the old home. For example, if you bought a home ten years ago for $100,000 and sold it for $150,000 (after deducting your closing costs and any capital improvements), you would have a $50,000 taxable gain. But if you bought another personal residence within two years that cost $250,000, you could postpone paying tax on your gain until a later time.

Recently the IRS ruled that a buyer can deduct points paid at the time of purchase, even if the seller paid them for you. If you bought a home after December 31, 1990, and the seller paid points for you which you did not deduct, you may be entitled to an unexpected refund. If you qualify for a refund, file an amended return on Form 1040X, which you can get from your local IRS office. Write "seller-paid points" in the top right-hand corner of the form and attach a copy of your closing settlement sheet (called a HUD-1). Be aware that if you deduct seller-paid points now, you will need to adjust your capital gain accordingly when you sell. So, if you paid $100,000 for a home, and the seller paid $5,000 in points that you are going to deduct now, the IRS will calculate your capital gain when you sell based on a $95,000, rather than on a $100,000, purchase price.

The tax code is in a constant state of revision. At this writing, mortgage interest paid on a primary residence mortgage, up to a mortgage amount of $1,000,000, is tax deductible. So is the interest paid on a home equity mortgage up to a loan amount of $100,000. But recent changes in the tax code make it increasingly difficult for individuals to itemize deductions. And some politicians favor flat-tax proposals that could eliminate or limit the mortgage interest deduction. Also, whether an item is tax deductible is not always clear. Always seek the advice of a tax professional if you have any questions about how a home purchase, home improvement, or refinance will affect your taxes.

## Determining your ideal price range

Most buyers have a notion of how much they would like to spend per month for a home. This amount is often based on what they are currently paying for rent. Although it is not wise to stretch yourself too thin where finances are concerned, you should take the tax advantages of home ownership into account when determining your ideal price range. Considering the tax savings, you can probably afford to pay about 25 to 33 percent more for a home than you might think you can.

Suppose you want to pay no more than $1,100 per month for a home. This figure must cover the cost of your principal and interest (the mortgage payment), property taxes, and hazard insurance—better known as your *PITI* (principal, interest, taxes, and insurance). Property taxes and insurance vary from one location to the next. For this example, let's say that your property taxes and insurance make up about 15 percent of your PITI. If you subtract 15 percent (or $165) from $1,100, this leaves you with $935 per month to use for a mortgage payment (principal and interest). If you get an adjustable-rate mortgage (ARM) with a starting rate of 7.5 percent, $935 per month will buy you a loan in the amount of about $133,750. If you have enough cash for a 10 percent cash down payment, your budget will allow you to buy a home for approximately $148,500.

Now, let's figure how much you would pay per month if you buy a home for $193,000 (30 percent more expensive), taking the tax savings associated with home ownership into account. If you have 10 percent down, you will need a $173,700 mortgage. Your monthly mortgage payment on a 7.5 percent ARM will be about $1,214. In your first full year of ownership, you will pay

**You must itemize deductions, which means giving up your standard deduction, in order to take advantage of a home mortgage interest deduction.**

$14,569 for principal and interest. Of this amount, $1,564 will go to principal and the balance, $13,005 will pay interest, which is tax deductible. If you are in the 28-percent tax bracket (for federal income tax), multiply $13,005 by .28 to determine the actual income tax saved in the first full year of home ownership. Divide this amount ($3,641) by 12 to find out the amount of tax saved per month ($303). Subtract $303 from $1,214. The result, $911, is your out-of-pocket expense for the higher mortgage.

The above is only an approximation of your tax savings. For example, the calculations do not take into account the loss of your standard deduction when you itemize deductions. But you can write off more than just the mortgage interest. You can also deduct property taxes and points (loan origination fees). You may also have state income tax savings. Your tax filing status and your income level also effect the tax implications of home ownership, so it's a good idea to consult with a tax advisor.

The time of year you buy will effect how much you can write off in the first year. If you buy at the end of the year, the amount of mortgage interest and property taxes you will pay for that year will be minimal. Your deductible home ownership expenses might not exceed the standard deduction, unless you have other deductions to itemize, such as business expenses and charitable donations. If this is the case, you may want to consider a zero-point loan, since you will not get much tax benefit from writing off points in the year of purchase. But there is a trade-off between the points you pay for a mortgage and the interest rate: The lower the points, the higher the interest rate, and vice versa. Regardless of the loan type, in the next year, you will have higher mortgage interest and property-tax deductions, which you can itemize and write off at that time.

The upper limit to your ideal price will be determined by the maximum home price you can qualify for as determined by lender underwriting guidelines, which are explained below. Even so, some buyers choose to pay less than the maximum they can afford. Establishing your ideal price is a personal decision that will depend on various factors. Your present and anticipated income stream is one important consideration. If your income is rising rapidly, you may want to stretch and buy a more expensive home now rather than have to move again soon. Moving is expensive; moving less often is one way to save money.

Other considerations are: Do you have any long-term debts you have to pay off? Do you have enough cash reserves to take care of unanticipated crises, as well as predictable home maintenance expenses? Do you have other investments that you want to pursue, such as starting your own business? How much disposable income do you have? Are you dipping into savings each month in order to make ends meet? Or do you have more than enough cash to take care of all of the above?

Some prospective home buyers find it useful to prepare a financial statement and monthly operating expense budget. To prepare a financial statement, list all your assets (cash in checking and savings accounts, IRAs, stock and bond accounts, retirement funds, automobiles, and other personal property, etc.). Then list your liabilities (debts that will take longer than a month or two to pay off). Subtract the liabilities from the assets to determine your net worth.

To find out how much cash it takes for you to survive each month (your operating expenses), look through your check logs and charge bills. Tally your monthly expenses for food, clothing, personal care (like haircuts, gym dues), child care, alimony, utilities, transportation, debts, rent, and savings. There may be some obvious expenses that you can cut without feeling deprived. Compare your monthly expenses with your monthly income. Can you afford more than you pay now for housing if you factor in the tax break you may receive? Or are you already living well beyond your means?

Potential home buyers often wonder how much they should stretch financially to buy a home. Although there is no simple answer to this question, one important factor to consider is the kind of real estate market you are buying into. If you are buying into a market that is appreciating (that is, home prices are rising), it may be prudent to stretch to buy a bigger, more expensive home. You will earn appreciation on a more valuable asset. This is one way to build wealth. Ten percent appreciation on a $100,000 home is $10,000; on a $200,000 home it is $20,000. In a declining market, where home prices are dropping, you may be better off buying a more affordable home. Since you will not be earning appreciation, at least initially, your equity build up will depend on how much you pay down your mortgage. In a stable, or declining, market, you may be better off to take a fifteen-year mortgage rather than a thirty-year mortgage, if you can qualify for the higher payments. You build equity faster with a fifteen-year mortgage. If, on the other hand, you're looking for the maximum interest write-off, you'll probably want a thirty-year mortgage.

Figuring out where home ownership fits into your long-range financial plan can be complicated. If the decision-making process seems baffling, you may want to consult a tax or financial advisor. Ask friends and associates for recommendations.

## Lender prequalification

Most home buyers take out a mortgage to help them buy a home. To figure out what price you can pay for a home, you need to find out what size loan you will qualify for. Lender prequalification is a preliminary loan qualification process that involves a brief, no-obligation meeting with a loan agent or mortgage broker to determine what size loan a lender is likely to give you. This loan amount, plus the cash you have for a down payment and closing costs, will determine what price home you can afford. You should get yourself prequalified before you start looking at property. This saves time and avoids the frustration of looking at homes that are way out of your price range.

Ask friends and associates who purchased recently and who were happy with their lender for a referral. You may want to talk to more than one person. Make an appointment for a prequalification interview and be prepared to discuss the intimate details of your financial situation. Take information with you about your income, length of time at your job, assets and debts. Be completely candid with the loan agent. Let him or her know where you are getting the money for your down payment if you do not have the cash sitting in your savings account. Lenders do allow buyers to accept money gifts from parents and loans from friends for part of their down payment, but certain restrictions apply.

Lenders are sticklers for good credit, so ask the loan agent or mortgage broker to run a credit check on you. The cost of a credit report varies, but it should cost about $25 to $50 for an individual or married couple. You might be inclined to wait until you are in contract to buy a home to have your credit checked. But it is better to know in advance if there is anything on your credit record that could keep you from being approved for a loan, so take care of this right away. The loan agent can tell you what to do to clear up problems on a credit report. Or he or she can direct you to a lender who might be willing to give you a loan even though your credit history has significant defects. See Chapter 6 for more information on credit reports.

Ask the loan agent or broker to write you a prequalification letter indicating that you have been prequalified for a loan. This letter will carry more weight if it states that your credit has been checked and is satisfactory. Sellers are usually more receptive to offers from buyers who have a prequalification letter from a lender or mortgage broker, which states that they are likely to be approved for the loan they need. This can really work in your favor if there are other buyers bidding against you for the property; the most qualified buyer is often the winner.

Some buyers don't want their prequalification letter to specify the maximum loan amount they can afford. They fear that the sellers will be encouraged to counteroffer back at a higher price if they know that the buyers can afford to pay more. Ask your loan agent or broker to be prepared to write you a letter tailored to the specific offer you are making. It can be faxed to you or to your agent if you need it quickly.

**To qualify for a mortgage, you need:**
- Sufficient income.
- Good credit.
- An acceptable property.

## Lender qualification guidelines

Lenders look at three basic factors when they consider giving you a loan. First, they look at your ability to pay back the loan, that is, your income and employment history. Generally, lenders like to see a stable pattern of employment, with at least two years at your most recent job. If you have changed jobs recently but have been in the same line of work for years, this should not pose a problem. Second, lenders consider your willingness to repay the loan. This is what the credit report is all about. A lender will assume that if you have a good history of repaying other debts, you will probably repay your home loan on time. If you have a bad credit history, this could prevent you from getting a loan. However there are ways to deal with bad credit. (See Chapter 6 for more information.) Finally, the lender looks at the property that will be the security for the loan. This is the lender's collateral. The lender is primarily concerned that the property appraises for the purchase price, and that the sellers can deliver clear and marketable title to the property.

When lenders analyze your ability to repay a loan, they think in terms of two ratios. Each ratio expresses your expenses as a percentage of your income. The first is the ratio between the monthly cost of buying your new home (your monthly housing expense) and your gross monthly income (before deducting for income taxes), often referred to as your front-end ratio. The lender will take into account all your sources of income, including a co-borrower's salary, and interest, dividend, and royalty income. Divide your total annual income by twelve to determine your gross monthly income.

Lenders usually do not want your monthly housing expense to exceed 28 to 33 percent of your gross monthly income. The more cash you can put down, the more flexible the lender will be. Lenders are stricter on their ratios with borrowers who put 10 percent, or less, cash down. If you put 5 percent down, a lender might use a 28-percent ratio. But, if you can make a 30-percent cash down payment, the lender might feel comfortable with a ratio that even exceeds 33 percent. Suppose your gross monthly income is $5,000. If you put 5 percent cash down and the lender uses a 28-percent qualifying ratio, you will be allowed $1,400 per month for your monthly housing expense ($5,000 multiplied by .28). But, if you have 20 percent cash down, you will be allowed $1,650 for your monthly housing expense ($5,000 multiplied by .33). Your monthly housing expense must cover the cost of the mortgage payment (principal and interest), property taxes, hazard insurance, mortgage insurance (if required), and homeowner association dues, if you are buying a townhouse or a condominium.

Most of your monthly housing expense will go to pay the mortgage. After making a minor adjustment for property taxes, insurance, and any association dues, the lender will determine what size loan you qualify for using an amortization table. Amortization tables give the monthly payment necessary to pay off a given loan amount at different interest rates over a period of time (usually 15 or 30 years). See the sample amortization table at the back of this book.

The second ratio the lenders look at is the ratio between your total monthly debt (housing expense combined with other debts) and your gross monthly income. This is called the back-end ratio. The lender will tally your outstanding debts and calculate the minimum amount required each month to pay back these debts. Your debts will include bills that will not be paid off within the next few months, such as car payments, student loans, and charge card accounts. Lenders usually do not want your total monthly debt to exceed 33 to 38 percent of your gross monthly income, depending on the size of your cash down payment. If you have a 20-percent down payment, your total debt, including housing expense, cannot exceed 38 percent of your gross monthly income. For 10-percent down buyers, 33 percent may be used to determine the back-end ratio.

Suppose you have a student loan that you are repaying at $250 per month, and you have 20 percent down. The lender will multiply your gross monthly income ($5,000) by 38 percent (.38), which equals $1,900. Your monthly debt obligation of $250 is subtracted from this amount, which leaves $1,650 for your monthly housing expense. This is within the lender's acceptable guidelines because your back-end and front-end ratios are the same. But if you have a car payment of $300, in addition to the student loan, you would not be able to qualify for as large a mortgage, unless you were willing and able to pay off the car loan before closing on the house. If you subtract the $550 (for the car and the student loans) from $1,900, the balance is $1,350. This is the amount that can be applied to your monthly housing expense. The higher debt level does not mean that the lender will not qualify you for a loan, it just means that you cannot qualify for as large a loan as you could with a lower debt load. Some lenders may make an exception for buyers whose qualifying ratios are too high if they have a history of paying rent that is equal to or greater than their projected mortgage payment.

Your mortgage broker or loan agent may tell you your ratios are 32/38 or 30/33. The first number refers to your front-end ratio, or the ratio of your monthly housing expense to gross monthly income. The second number is your back-end ratio, or the ratio of your total debt (including housing expense) to gross monthly income.

The acceptable ratios quoted above (28/33 for 90-percent loans, and 33/38 for 80-percent loans) apply to loans that will be sold to Fannie Mae or Freddie Mac, two quasi-government agencies that purchase loans to resell to investors. Fannie Mae and Freddie Mac loans are the hardest to qualify for and they usually carry the best rates and terms. If your ratios are marginal and you cannot qualify according to Fannie Mae/Freddie Mac guidelines, talk to a portfolio lender. Portfolio lenders do not sell their loans, so they can be more flexible in their loan qualification guidelines. They often qualify borrowers on a 38 to 40 percent ratio of housing expense to gross income. Also, lenders tend to push their qualifying ratios higher for borrowers who have little debt. But portfolio lenders may charge a higher interest rate or more points.

**The price home you can afford depends on:**
- Current interest rates.
- What kind of mortgage you choose.
- Your income.
- Your debt and credit history.
- Your cash down payment.

The price home you can afford also depends on the amount of cash you have available for your down payment and closing costs. Closing costs vary from one area to the next but they can run about 5 percent of the purchase price. The lender will subtract an amount to cover closing costs from the cash you have available. The balance (called the down payment) will be added to the loan amount you qualify for to determine the price home you can afford.

One way to increase your purchasing power is to reduce the amount of debt you are paying off before you attempt to qualify for a loan. This can be accomplished by paying debts down or by consolidating high-interest rate debts into one lower-interest rate loan. Another way is to buy a home when interest rates are low, or to use an adjustable-rate mortgage (ARM). The initial interest rate on an ARM is often about two percentage points below a fixed-rate loan, so qualifying is easier. Using the example above, let's say you have $1,650 a month you can use for housing expense (assuming you only have a student loan to repay). The lender deducts about 15 percent of this to pay for property taxes and hazard insurance, which leaves you with about $1,402 to cover the mortgage payment. If you take a fixed-rate thirty-year loan with an interest rate of 8 percent, your $1,402 per month will entitle you to a mortgage in the amount of approximately $191,000. On the other hand, if you take an ARM with a starting interest rate of 6 percent, $1,402 per month will entitle you to a $233,666 mortgage.

## Preapproval

Loan prequalification is an informal process. After discussing the prospective home buyers' financial status with them, a loan agent or mortgage broker issues a letter stating that if the information provided is accurate, the buyers should be able to qualify for a loan. Often these letters are form letters. Even if a prequalification letter is personalized, it is usually loaded with disclaimers to protect the loan agent. Consequently, some real estate agents feel prequalification letters are worth little more than the paper they are written on.

Preapproval is a more formal process. And a preapproval letter is a valuable document. To get preapproved, buyers must make a formal loan application to a lender. The borrower's credit is checked, and the borrower's employment and down payment funds are verified. The financial documentation is then reviewed by an underwriter, who determines if granting the loan is a good investment. If the underwriter gives the OK, the lender issues a letter stating that the buyers are approved for a loan subject only to a satisfactory property appraisal and title search.

**If an ARM has an initial starting interest rate that is below 7.5 percent, the lender will often qualify you based on 7.5 percent, not on the lower rate.**

**Twenty-one ways to expand your purchasing power:**
- Pay off debts.
- Consolidate debts into a lower-interest rate loan.
- Borrow from your parents.
- Use an adjustable-rate mortgage (ARM).
- Use a portfolio lender.
- Buy with someone else.
- Ask your parents to give you money for a down payment (requires a gift letter).
- Ask the seller to pay some of your non-recurring closing costs.
- Ask the seller to carry a second mortgage.
- Ask the seller, or lender, to buy down the interest rate on your mortgage.
- Ask your employer to lend you money, pay some of your closing costs, or buy down an interest rate for you.
- Buy when interest rates are low.
- Buy a property that generates rental income.
- Take advantage of a first-time buyer loan program, if you qualify.
- Take advantage of government-assisted financing programs, if you qualify.
- Close late in the month to reduce the interest owed to the lender at closing.
- Reduce the cash you need for closing costs with a zero-point loan.
- Borrow against a 401(k) retirement plan or insurance policy.
- Borrow against or liquidate securities.
- Use a mortgage with a forty-year due date (but watch out for prepayment penalties).
- Ask your parents to co-sign your loan.

Preapproval must come directly from the lender who will issue the loan. A mortgage broker cannot preapprove buyers for loans. But a mortgage broker can help get you preapproved with a lender, as long as the lender accepts brokered loans. See Chapter 6 for more of the pros and cons of working with a mortgage broker.

Preapproval can improve buyers' bargaining power with sellers because preapproved buyers can remove a financing contingency quickly. Usually a financing contingency runs for thirty days from the purchase contract acceptance date. Buyers who are preapproved can often remove a loan contingency within a couple of weeks of acceptance. Some lenders will lock-in an interest rate for preapproved buyers, which adds additional security if interest rates are rising.

When you get preapproved, it is for a specific loan program from a specific lender. Not all lenders offer all loan programs. You may need to get approved with a different lender, or for a different loan program with the same lender, depending on your financing options at the time you actually buy a home. Check with the loan agent or mortgage broker before you write an offer to see if you need to get re-approved for a loan. If so, make sure to allow enough time for this in the purchase contract. You may need more than two weeks, but you should still be able to cut the normal financing time period down.

**TALES FROM THE TRENCHES: EPISODE 1**

*Gaby started looking for her first home in July 1995. She looked at close to fifty houses, but only a few interested her. Two of the houses she considered making an offer on were sold after multiple offers. Gaby's agent recommended that she get preapproved for a loan so that if she found herself competing with other buyers for a house, she would have an edge on the competition. Gaby didn't find her house until mid-December. It was a charming house, and, once again, there were multiple offers. The other buyers were prequalified for loans, but not preapproved. The offers were for the full asking price, and neither was contingent on the sale of another property. In the end, Gaby got the house. The fact that Gaby was preapproved for a loan swayed the sellers. They felt her offer was relatively risk-free.*

You may get preapproved for a loan and then not find a home to buy for two or three months. In this case the lender will have to update your documentation and get you re-approved. If interest rates shoot up during this time period, and you were marginally qualified for a fixed-rate loan when you were preapproved, you may need to change to an adjustable-rate mortgage (ARM) to qualify for the loan amount you need. Or, you may still be able to qualify for fixed-rate financing, but you may not want to pay the higher interest rate. If you think rates will come down again, you might prefer an ARM at this point.

Besides giving you an edge over other buyers, preapproval will also work in your favor if your ability to qualify for a loan is questionable for any reason. For instance, if you have been at your job less than two years, or if you went through a bankruptcy within the last seven years, a letter of preapproval may alleviate any concerns a seller might have about accepting your offer. If you are not completely preapproved by the time you find a home to buy, have your loan agent write a letter to accompany your offer that gives the seller as much information about your creditworthiness and financial capabilities as possible. It should take you anywhere from several days to several weeks to get preapproved, depending on the lender and on how diligent you are about supplying the necessary financial documentation.

## Closing costs

The various fees associated with a home purchase are called closing costs. Both buyers and sellers pay closing costs. Who pays which costs is often dictated by local custom, but it can be subject to negotiation. Ask a real estate agent in your area which costs you can expect to pay. The loan agent or mortgage broker who prequalifies you for a loan can also give you a closing cost estimate. (See the "Guide to closing costs" in Appendix 1.)

Sellers' closing costs typically include such things as charges associated with paying off loans that are secured against the property; the brokerage fee (real estate commission); all or part of a transfer tax; all or part of the title insurance and escrow fees (although this varies from one area to the next); and other fees set by local custom or negotiated during the sale transaction. A home protection plan for the buyer (which is not available in all states) is paid for either by the seller, the buyer, or shared by the buyer and seller. A home protection plan covers the major systems, such as plumbing and electrical, of the home. It helps defray the cost to repair or replace the covered systems during the first year of the buyer's ownership.

Buyers can usually expect to pay the fees associated with getting a home loan; title insurance (depending on the location); transfer taxes, if there are any (although the seller may pay these, or they may be shared fifty-fifty); inspection fees; mortgage insurance (MI), also called property mortgage insurance (PMI), which protects the lender in case the buyer stops repaying the mortgage; attorney's fees (where attorneys are involved in the transaction); and hazard insurance. The amount of your closing costs will vary depending on local custom and what kind of loan you get.

To qualify for a home loan, you must show the lender that you have enough cash for the down payment and closing costs. In addition, many lenders require that you have enough cash reserves to cover a few mortgage payments. Borrowing money at the last minute to cover your cash requirements may not work because lenders usually require that you have had the cash you need in your own bank account for several months (called *seasoned* money).

There are ways to reduce the amount of your closing costs. The loan origination fee, also called *points,* is usually the most expensive buyer closing cost. If you are buying a $250,000 home with a 90-percent loan, your loan amount will be $225,000. If the lender charges two points, this will cost you $4,500. A no-point loan will have a higher interest rate, but the closing cost savings is significant. Another way to reduce the amount of your closing costs is to close your home purchase late in the month. At closing, the lender will collect enough money from you to cover the interest you owe for that month. Let's say your monthly interest payment will be $2,000. If you close the sale on the fifth day of the month, the lender will collect interest for twenty-five days, or approximately $1,666. If you close on the twenty-fifth day of the month, the interest you will owe the lender at closing will be only about $333.

### Credits for nonrecurring closing costs

Most lenders will not allow a seller to credit money toward a buyer's cash down payment, but they will allow a seller to credit money to the buyer at closing to cover some, or all, of the buyer's nonrecurring closing costs. Nonrecurring closing costs are paid by the buyer on a one-time only basis and include points, transfer taxes, and title insurance. Recurring costs are paid on a regular basis and include mortgage interest payments, hazard insurance premiums, and mortgage insurance premiums.

A seller credit will reduce the amount of your closing costs; it also reduces the amount of cash proceeds the sellers realize from the sale of their property. Asking the sellers for a credit amounts to asking them to accept a lower price. One way to compensate sellers for the money they credit you is to increase the purchase price to cover the cost of the credit. For example, if the sellers are asking $275,000 for their home, you might offer $280,000 with a $5,000 credit to you at closing. In order for this to work, the lender will have to appraise the property at the $280,000 price. If the local market's comparable sales do not justify this higher price, the sellers might be nervous about boosting the sale price above a realistic market value, because the property might not appraise and the deal could fall apart.

---

**TALES FROM THE TRENCHES: EPISODE 2**

*Warren made an offer on a house that needed a lot of restoration work. Since he had experience renovating houses, he was willing to tackle the project because the run-down house was located on a wonderful piece of property and had great potential for improvement. He had enough money for the down payment and closing costs, but he wanted to conserve some of his cash for the renovation. He was in a multiple offer competition, so he knew that he had to pay at least full price for the property. He increased his offer price to eight thousand dollars over the seller's asking price, and asked the seller to credit him eight thousand dollars at closing. This was the maximum credit the lender would allow. The seller agreed to the credit and the lender had no problem appraising the property for the purchase price because the property was so special. That there were multiple offers also convinced the lender that appraising the property for more than the list price was realistic.*

Lender's policies vary on how large a credit for nonrecurring closing costs they will allow. Some permit a credit for the total of all the buyer's nonrecurring costs. Others limit the amount a seller can credit to a buyer, usually 3 to 6 percent of the purchase price, even though the buyer's actual nonrecurring closing costs may exceed this amount. For example, if you are buying a $200,000 house and the lender will allow a 3-percent credit from the seller for your nonrecurring closing costs, the seller can credit $6,000 to you at closing—if, that is, your actual closing costs are at least $6,000. If your nonrecurring costs are less, the lender will only allow a credit for the lesser amount.

Some portfolio lenders are more lenient with seller credits. Some will even permit credits for all of the buyer's closing costs, not just the nonrecurring closing costs. These lenders may not offer the best interest rates in town. But for a buyer who is short on cash to close, it may be worthwhile to pay a higher interest rate in exchange for a larger closing cost credit, assuming the seller will pay it.

Sometimes the only alternative is to wait to buy a house until you have enough cash for closing costs, particularly if you are trying to buy in a hot market. If, on the other hand, you are buying in an area where there is a surplus of inventory, particularly of new homes, you can usually find a seller or builder who will be willing to pay for some of your closing costs.

# Improving your purchasing power

## Getting help from the folks

One way parents can help is by giving their children money for a down payment. The lender will require a gift letter that states that the money is a gift and does not have to be repaid. Lenders will not allow the entire down payment to be a gift unless it amounts to 20 percent, or more, of the purchase price. If the gift is for less than 20 percent, most conventional lenders require that at least 5 percent of the purchase price be the borrowers' own money.

Even a gift for 5 to 15 percent of the purchase price can help to make a home purchase more affordable because the more cash you put down, the lower the amount of the mortgage insurance (MI) premium. MI protects the lender from a buyer default, and is usually required when the mortgage amount exceeds 80 percent of the purchase price. MI premiums vary depending on the MI carrier, the type and amount of the mortgage, and the MI premium payment plan. Premiums are higher for ARMs than they are for fixed-rate mortgages. They are also higher on larger loan amounts. Two common MI payment plans are the monthly plan and the annual level plan. With an annual level plan, the buyer prepays the amount of the first-year MI premium at closing. For a 95-percent ARM, the premium is about .89 percent of the loan amount. For a $250,000 loan, the prepaid MI premium for the first year is $2,225. If the buyer chose a monthly MI plan, the annual premium for the same loan would be .92 percent. In this case, the lender will require the buyer to pay a two-month reserve at closing (about $383). After closing, the buyer would pay monthly MI payments of about $192. For a 95-percent fixed-rate loan, the annual level plan MI premium is approximately .75 percent; the monthly plan premium is approximately .78 percent. For a 90-percent ARM, the annual level plan MI premium is about .62 percent; the monthly plan premium is about .65 percent. For a 90-percent fixed-rate mortgage, the annual level plan premium is approximately .49 percent of the loan amount, and .52 percent for the monthly plan. MI is usually not charged on an 80-percent cash mortgage.

Another way parents can help is by loaning you money, which could result in a sizable savings if it enables you to avoid MI. However, be aware that the lender will include the monthly payment on your parents' loan when qualifying you for a mortgage. The lender will also require that the loan have a due date of five or more years. And many lenders will not allow secondary financing (that is, a loan from your parents that is secured against the property) if you only have 5 percent of your own money to put down.

There is another recent restriction to be aware of. For Freddie Mac and Fannie Mae loans for $207,000 and less (called conforming loans), you cannot avoid MI if you have a 10 percent down combined with a 10-percent loan (called 80-10-10 financing). The lender will charge MI unless you can reduce the amount of the new first loan to 75 percent of the purchase price (10-15-75, or 15-10-75 financing). Not all lenders impose this restriction, so check around before choosing a lender. For loan amounts of more than $207,000 (called jumbo loans), 80-10-10 financing without MI should not be a problem.

Equity sharing is an arrangement where parents can purchase property with their children and both parties can realize tax benefits. Usually the parents provide the down payment, or most of it, and the children occupy the property and make the mortgage payments. To qualify for tax deductions, the IRS requires a written equity share contract (see IRS code 280A) and both parents and children must take title to the property. By taking title to the property, the parents are responsible for repayment of the mortgage debt and property taxes if their children are unable or unwilling to do so. It may be difficult to find a lender for an equity share purchase. Portfolio lenders are your best bet.

Another way parents can help their children is to co-sign a loan. A co-signer, like an equity share partner, takes title to the property and is jointly responsible with the children for repaying the debt. A lender will require two years' tax returns and a three-month history of bank accounts from the parent co-signer. Social Security and dividend income can be used for loan qualification purposes. So, a retired parent may be an eligible co-signer.

If your parents are planning to help you buy a home, talk to a lender before you make an offer and get preapproved for the loan you will need. Buyers who are not preapproved at the time they make an offer should get a letter from their parents stating their intention to help with the purchase. A copy of this letter can be included with the purchase offer to the sellers. Parents who are going to actually take title to the property should sign the purchase agreement. Sellers will be more receptive to an offer if they are convinced the parents are firmly committed to helping their children.

There may be strings attached to your parents' assistance that go far beyond money. Carefully consider how this will effect your relationship with them before you enter into a purchase contract.

## Equity sharing: Buying a house with someone else

Some buyers cannot afford to buy a home they would want to live in on their own, so they pool their resources and buy a home with someone else. While this can be an excellent home buying strategy, you should carefully consider the pros and cons of this kind of purchase before going ahead with it.

"Equity sharing" is a fancy term for co-ownership shared by two or more buyers (who are not married to one another). Sometimes an equity share partner is an investor who donates financially to the purchase but who does not occupy the property. This is quite different from an equity sharing arrangement where both purchasers participate financially, and both intend to occupy the property as their primary residence.

In either case, it is imperative that a knowledgeable real estate attorney draft an equity sharing or partnership agreement. This agreement should cover: Who will make what financial contributions (toward the down payment, closing costs, and the ongoing monthly payment)? What percentage of ownership will each co-owner have? How will decisions be made? Who will be the managing partner? How will the tax benefits be shared? What will be the procedure if one of the parties wants out of the partnership? Will one party have the right to buy the other party (or parties) out? How will the parties decide on a fair buyout price? When will the property be sold? How will profits or losses be shared? How will maintenance costs be handled? How will title to the property be held? What happens if one of the co-owners dies?

Buying with another owner-occupant raises further considerations. You will be sharing your living space with your co-owner, and not all homes are conducive to co-owner occupancy. A friendship could be sacrificed if you are not careful. It's a good idea to rent a home for a while with your prospective co-buyer before you actually buy a home with that person. When you buy with another owner occupant, your partnership agreement should include how you will share the physical space in the home. Loss of privacy can become a major issue. If you plan to make major renovations to a home to make it suitable for co-ownership, make sure that the cost is not prohibitive. Also, talk to an architect or contractor to confirm that what you have in mind is feasible. Check with your real estate agent to verify that your modification plans will not diminish the value of the property. Make sure that you do not over-improve the property for the neighborhood.

Co-buyers usually need both incomes to qualify for the mortgage. What happens if your partner decides to get married, and the new couple wants to buy a home of their own? Or, what if your partner is transferred and wants to buy a home in his new location? In either case, your partner may need to be relieved from the obligation of repaying your mortgage. If you do not have the resources to qualify for the mortgage on your own, and you cannot find another suitable partner, you may have to sell the property and make other living arrangements. Your partnership agreement should be structured in such a way that you will not be forced out of your home. Realize that there is no question that you have more control over your domain if you are the sole owner.

### Buying a rent-producing property

Suppose you like living in the place you are currently renting, but there is no way you can afford to buy it. In fact, you can't afford to buy anything in the neighborhood. So you decide that in order to break into property ownership, you will buy a home in a less-expensive neighborhood and rent it out to someone else. Meanwhile, you will continue to rent where you are. Your long-range plan is to sell your rental property in a few years, after it has appreciated, and invest the proceeds in a property that you will occupy. The plan sounds good on paper, but it requires careful scrutiny before deciding if it will work for you.

Given the recent downturn in many real estate markets around the country, it is risky to buy property with the expectation of rapid home price appreciation. Prices may rise quickly in high-demand markets. But it could take several years of ownership just to break even when you take buying and selling costs into account. If property values drop, you could sell at a loss, which defeats your ultimate goal.

Another factor to consider is that properties must be maintained. A new, or newer, home will probably need less upkeep. An older one may eat up your profit if it requires a lot of repair work. Also, it is difficult to find good property managers to take care of small income-producing properties. You may have to take care of the management and maintenance yourself. If so, you will save the expense of hiring a property manager, but management takes time. In addition to repairs, you will have to deal with tenants— finding them, collecting rent from them, fielding their complaint calls, and evicting the bad ones. Are you temperamentally suited to this kind of work?

Conduct your own rent survey before buying a property you expect to rent out. Find out what the going rents are for similar properties. A real estate agent may be able to provide you with this information, or check the "homes for rent" section of a local newspaper. Investigate any rent control laws, taxes, or restrictions that could jeopardize your future income stream.

For tax purposes, the IRS treats rental property and owner-occupied residences differently. When you sell a primary residence, you can defer some or all of your capital gain tax liability if you buy another residence within two years of the time you sell. The IRS also allows property owners to defer capital gain tax liability when they sell rental property if they buy another rental property and meet the requirements of a 1031 exchange. The IRS does not allow property owners to defer their capital gain tax from the sale of a rental property if they use the proceeds to buy a personal residence. The proceeds must be used to buy another rental property. It may be possible to use the proceeds from the sale of a rental property to buy a personal residence if you treat the personal residence as a rental property for awhile before you move in. Before doing this, get the advice of a knowledgeable tax professional to find out what your tax situation will be. You may have a tax liability for any depreciation you claimed on your residence while it was treated as an income-producing property.

Some first-timers buy a property with income-producing potential, part of which they live in, and part of which they rent out. This strategy may allow you to buy a more expensive property, or a property in a better neighborhood. Check to make sure the lender will count the rental income you'll receive in qualifying you for a loan. If the property is a legal multiple-dwelling unit (like a duplex or triplex), the lender should have no problem allowing a portion of the rental income. (The lender may subtract some of the rental income to allow for possible vacancies.) If a rental unit is not legal (nonconforming), the lender may not count the potential income in qualifying you.

Real estate "For Sale" ads sometimes advertise an "in-law" or "granny" unit as one of the selling features. Some ads make reference to a second unit or a rental unit. Others promote "live-in" or "au pair" quarters. Although the meaning of these terms varies, they usually refer to an area in a home that can be occupied by someone other than an immediate family member. "Live-in" or "au pair" quarters are often a bedroom and bath located away from the main living area that allows the occupant to come and go without interfering with the family's activities. It could be a small bedroom and bath behind the kitchen (built originally as maid's quarters), or it might be a bedroom and bath add-on in the basement. An "in-law," "granny," or second unit usually refers to a living space that is completely separate from the main part of the house and that has its own kitchen. The kitchen may be minimal—a hot plate, toaster oven, and mini-refrigerator.

In a neighborhood zoned for single-family residences, a second kitchen in a home, regardless how skimpy it is, may be a violation of the city building code. If this is the case, it may be illegal for someone other than an immediate family member to occupy the unit. How serious a violation could it be to rent out an "illegal" unit in your home? Isn't it done all the time? In some communities, second units are common and they are tacitly accepted even though technically they are illegal. But problems can arise if neighbors complain.

*Lydia lived in a neighborhood zoned for single-family residences. She had a cottage on her property that had a bedroom, a sitting room, a bathroom, and a small kitchenette built into the living-room wall. Friends who were having difficulty finding a place to rent asked Lydia if they could rent her cottage. Lydia was delighted because she needed the extra income. After her friends moved in, Lydia received complaints about congested parking from the neighbor with whom she shared a common driveway. One day, the neighbor hit the roof when she saw several cars parked in the driveway, and she reported Lydia's illegal rental situation to the city zoning department. An inspector arrived at Lydia's property a few days later, without advance warning, and asked to see the cottage. He cited her for the illegal second kitchen. Lydia had to remove the kitchenette which cost her money and eliminated the rental value of the cottage.*

If you do decide to rent out an illegal unit, check with a knowledgeable real estate attorney before signing a lease. Make sure that you will not be liable for tenant damages if you have to ask the tenant to leave because the city stops your rental activities. Also, make sure that you can afford the property without the rental income.

When you are considering purchasing a property that is advertised with a second unit of some sort, find out precisely what this representation means. If the seller is currently renting the unit, is it legal to do so? If the seller is advertising that he receives income from an illegal rental unit, he may be guilty of misrepresentation. It's better to find out if this is the case before you buy. Suing for damages later will almost certainly be a hassle.

Find out if the "live-in" quarters or "granny" unit was added or converted with the necessary building permits. Often the construction of these units is a bootleg operation. If so, the work may be substandard and not up to current building code requirements. Your lender's appraiser may deduct value from the "in-law" unit if the work was not done with the required permits. This could cause the property to appraise for less than the purchase price. So, be sure to include a provision in your purchase contract that states that the sale is contingent on the property appraising for the purchase price. Also, before you buy, check into the tax ramifications of treating part of your home as rental property.

# The cash down payment

One advantage of owning real estate is that it offers the opportunity to make a profit on the money you invest through "leverage." Leverage is using someone else's money to buy an investment. The less of your own money you use to buy an investment, the more highly leveraged you are. If you make a 10 percent cash down payment and get a loan for 90 percent of the purchase price, you are more highly leveraged than you would be if you put 25 percent cash down and borrowed 75 percent.

The higher the leverage, the greater the profit potential. Suppose you buy a $250,000 house. To be conservative, you decide to put 25 percent down ($62,500) and borrow 75 percent ($187,500). If the property appreciates 20 percent over the next three years and you sell at that time, you will sell for $300,000 and make a $50,000 profit (without considering carrying costs, costs of sale, etc.). You will have earned 80 percent on your investment ($50,000 profit divided by your $62,500 initial investment). The reason for this high rate of return is that you earned appreciation on the whole asset, not just on the amount you invested. That is the beauty of leverage.

A more highly leveraged approach would be to put only 10 percent down and take out a 90-percent loan. This means you will only invest $25,000 of your own money. If the property appreciates the same 20 percent over three years and you sell it then for $300,000, you will make the same $50,000 profit. But you will earn 200 percent on your investment ($50,000 profit divided by your $25,000 initial investment). Higher leverage resulted in a bigger return on the investment. However, there is no guarantee that home prices will go up. Prices have dropped more than 25 percent in some areas in recent years. A highly leveraged homeowner who must sell in a down market could end up selling for significantly less than is owed on the mortgage. This can result in a big out-of-pocket loss.

Leverage is not the only consideration when deciding what size down payment to make. Making the lowest down payment possible offers advantages in addition to maximizing leverage. A low down can free up cash for other investments, as well as for unanticipated emergencies. Because a smaller down payment means a larger mortgage, and since home mortgage interest is usually tax deductible, a larger mortgage can be financially advantageous for buyers who are looking for tax deductions. Making a lower down payment as a percentage of the purchase price can allow you to buy a more expensive home. For example, if you have $40,000 for a down payment and you take out a loan for 80 percent of the purchase price, you can buy a $200,000 home. If you use your $40,000 with a 90-percent loan, you can buy a $400,000 house. (You would, of course, need sufficient income to qualify for the higher mortgage payments.)

On the other hand, there are advantages to making a large down payment. Your monthly mortgage payments will be lower. You will pay less interest over the life of the loan, so your financing costs will be lower. It will be easier for you to qualify for a loan because lenders look more favorably on borrowers who have large cash down payments. You may be able to own your home free and clear of any loans sooner because you will have a lower loan balance to pay off.

When you make a large down payment, it amounts to a savings plan of sorts. Money that is tied up in your home is not liquid, so you cannot spend it easily. Also, you won't have to pay mortgage insurance (often required on low down payment loans) if you make a down payment of 20 percent or more.

**Leverage is using someone else's money to buy an investment.**

# Developing a wish list

Buyers often fear that a shifty real estate agent will talk them into buying a home they will end up hating. This rarely happens. Many top real estate agents feel that it is impossible to "sell" someone a home. Good agents "sell" a lot of homes because they are adept at matching people up with appropriate homes. The key to making sure you end up with the right home is to figure out exactly what you need, want, like, and dislike in a home before you start looking.

Some people know instinctively what they want without spending time analyzing their housing needs. Most buyers, however, particularly those looking for the first time, feel overwhelmed by the selection process. If you fall into the latter category, your task will be made easier if you make a list. The list should be divided into three sections. The first is for the features you need in a home, such as the number of bedrooms and bathrooms, a family room, and a yard for children and pets. The second section is for the features that you would like to have but that are not essential. These might include such things as a view, an English Tudor style home, or a big yard. The third section is for the features you definitely do not want, such as a pool, or a home on a busy street.

To figure out what you need, start by considering how much room you need. What is the minimum size home you can live with? How big a place would you like to have if you could afford it? You will probably end up with a home that falls somewhere in between the two. How long you plan to stay in the home should be taken into account. You should anticipate future changes in your space requirements, such as a child on the way.

**English Tudor**
*The English Tudor style features a steeply pitched roof, leaded-glass windows, and French doors. Half-timbering and brick detailing are characteristic of this style.*

Lifestyle is an important consideration. If you do a lot of entertaining, you may need a formal dining room. If you do not, a dining area or eating area in the kitchen may suffice. Buyers who intend to work at home will need a space that can be dedicated to a home office. Lifestyle also influences where you decide to buy. Commute-time and transportation options are important to buyers who buy outside of the community where they work. The quality of local schools are critical to buyers with children. If you do not drive (or don't like to drive), you will want to be located within walking distance to shops, restaurants, and transportation.

Property condition is a significant factor. First-time buyers who have no previous home maintenance experience are usually wise to buy a house, condominium, or cooperative that is in move-in condition. Buyers who are short of cash and who have experience with home renovation might prefer a "fixer upper." You may be willing to take on a property that needs cosmetic work as long as it lacks major structural defects.

It's a useful exercise to think about homes you have seen that you particularly liked. Try to analyze what it was about these homes that attracted you to them. If you warmed up to a home because it had a sunny exposure, you may prefer living in a home that gets good light. It's also helpful to think about what you don't like about where you are now living. Is it close to a noisy hamburger joint that keeps you awake at night? Is it on two levels, which is murder on your arthritic knees? Is the lack of a second bathroom driving you and your partner nuts each morning as you both race to get to work on time?

Your aim at the analysis stage is to list features so that you can filter the inventory and eliminate all those properties that do not fit the bill. Keep in mind that you will not find the perfect home; it probably does not exist. So you will have to make compromises. It will be easier to decide what concessions you will be willing to make after you look at the available housing stock in your price range.

Copy the home comparison checklist included here and use it to develop a list you can take with you on home-hunting forays. After you personalize the list with your wants and needs, make multiple copies so that you can record notes about each property you see. The more definite you can be about what you want, the easier it will be to find a home. Be sure to give a copy of your home shopping list to your real estate agent.

# Timing your home purchase

The ideal time to buy a home is when home prices are healthy (that is, stable or increasing) and when interest rates are low. But, trying to second-guess the real estate market so that you buy at precisely the most opportune time could cause you to miss opportunities. It is impossible to know in advance how the real estate market will behave in the future. However, if you understand a few basic economic principles, you can hope to make prudent decisions about the best time to buy.

# Home comparison checklist

| Listing characteristics: | Listing address: | Listing address: | Listing address |
|---|---|---|---|
| List price: | | | |
| Neighborhood: | | | |
| Commute time: | | | |
| Proximity to shops and transportation: | | | |
| Quality of schools (good, average, poor): | | | |
| Property condition (good, average, poor): | | | |
| Other factors (crime rate, public transportation, etc.): | | | |
| Overall impression of listing: | | | |
| Opinion of price (accurate, high, low): | | | |

| Your housing requirements... | How does this listing compare? | How does this listing compare? | How does this listing compare? |
|---|---|---|---|
| Need to have:<br>    Ideal price:<br>    ___ bedrooms<br>    ___ bathrooms<br>    Other: | | | |
| Want to have: | | | |
| Don't want: | | | |

The principle of supply and demand applies to real estate as it does to any economic market. When there are more buyers than there are sellers, a high demand for homes is created, which usually puts an upward pressure on prices. This is called a seller's market. A buyer's market means there are more sellers than there are buyers, there are plenty of homes for sale, and prices are usually soft.

Buying in a buyer's market has some advantages. If there is a lot of inventory, buyers have more to choose from. Prices are usually lower than they would be in a stronger market. And there is less competition from other buyers. Many of the fees associated with home buying (title fees, transfer taxes, real estate commissions) are calculated based on the purchase price. Lower purchase prices means lower closing costs. In areas where property taxes are based on the purchase price, you will benefit even more if you buy in a soft market.

The main disadvantage of buying when the market is slow is that the value of your new home may actually drop before it rises again. Plan to stay in your new home for five or more years if you are buying in a down market. If you are uncertain about your future employment or if you think that you may be transferred within the next two or so years, you should probably not buy at all if the market is soft.

Why would a buyer want to buy when the market favors the seller? In a low inventory seller's market, several buyers often compete to buy a single home. Multiple offers are commonplace, and properties often sell for close to, or higher than, the asking price. Buyers who pay more than the asking price in such a market can justify doing so because home prices are appreciating. If they pay a little too much, they aren't too concerned because they expect the property will be worth even more within a few months.

Buyers usually feel more comfortable buying homes when all their friends are buying, even though this may mean paying a higher price. You should be wary of following the herd and buying when the market is booming. If the market has had high levels of appreciation for several years, it may not be a good time to buy because the market may be due for a correction in the downward direction. This is what happened in the Northeast and California at the end of the 1980s. In both cases, there was a home buying spree that pushed prices up, followed by a big downturn in the housing market. Unfortunately, there is no way to know that we have passed a high or low point for the cycle until after that point is passed.

A good time to buy may be when home prices have appreciated at a rate less than the rate of inflation for several years. This could indicate that a market is recovering from a down cycle and is ready for a rebound. By the way, it's OK to buy when prices have peaked, as long as you stay in the home long enough to ride out a downturn. What you want to avoid, if possible, is buying high and selling low.

Like home prices, interest rates tend to cycle and they affect a buyer's ability to buy. The lower the interest rates on home loans, the easier it is for buyers to qualify. An increase in demand for financing tends to put an upward pressure on interest rates.

Financial markets can change quickly, so don't let yourself fall into the trap of waiting for an interest rate cycle to bottom out if you can qualify to buy and rates are already relatively low. Higher interest rates can cause a slowdown in the real estate market. A rate increase can also stimulate market activity, as least initially, as buyers race to buy before rates climb further. When fixed-rate mortgages rise to the 9 percent level, buyers tend to prefer adjustable-rate mortgages (ARMs), which improve affordability and make qualifying easier.

Carefully investigate local market conditions when you're considering whether it is a good time to buy. One state can experience a surge in home prices, while another suffers a downturn. Even within a state or region, there can be tremendous variability. For example, a small niche market might be selling well because it has an exceptional school system. The surrounding communities, with marginal schools, could be less in demand, causing their home prices to be soft.

Deciding on the right time to buy depends not only on external economic factors. It is a personal decision that depends on your particular needs, financial situation, and job security. The best time to buy is when you can afford to and you find a home that suits your needs.

## Protecting yourself

It's normal to feel anxious when you decide to buy a home. You want the transaction to go smoothly but you don't want to be taken advantage of. The last thing you want is to end up in a lawsuit. Your best line of defense is to be proactive. Take nothing for granted. Don't assume that someone else will take care of the critical details necessary to close the sale. Follow up yourself and make sure everything gets done.

Start by picking a good cast of professionals to work with. Ask friends and associates for recommendations and interview people before you commit to working with them. This goes for real estate agents, loan agents or brokers, inspectors, attorneys, title and escrow officers, and insurance agents. Work with local, rather than out-of-area, professionals.

Let your team know that you expect to be kept informed each step of the way and that you want to hear about problems if they arise. Real estate professionals sometimes try to insulate their clients from bad news. This can have disastrous consequences. It is best to deal with problems head-on and to resolve them as quickly as possible.

Ask your real estate agent who he or she owes allegiance to. It may be to the seller, not to you. If so, be careful what you divulge to the agent regarding the price you will be willing to pay for the home. Read the next chapter for more information about working with agents and agency relationships.

Your purchase contract should include contingencies to protect you. If you are worried about paying too much, include a contingency that requires that the property appraise for the purchase price. If homeowners insurance is difficult to get, as it has been in Florida and California recently, include a contingency that allows you a certain time period to line up insurance. If you are unable to get insurance or the property doesn't appraise for the price, you can cancel the contract and get your deposit back. Don't rely on someone else to satisfy a contingency that is vitally important to you. For example, if you can only afford to buy a house if you can run a day-care center from the basement, research the legality of doing this yourself.

Most contracts should also include financing, title, and inspections contingencies. Don't remove your financing contingency until you have a written loan commitment from the lender. Make sure to attend the home inspection. A wealth of information can be gathered by walking through the home with the inspector. It is a good idea to get title insurance to protect you from title defects. Be sure you understand what kind of protection you are getting. Ask the sellers if they are aware of defects, of any kind, affecting the property. Get disclosures in writing so that you have a record to show future buyers that a defect was a pre-existing condition.

Keep a transaction log or diary of the events that occur during your home purchase, including a record of important phone conversations. Keep copies of all documents (contracts, reports, closing statements, etc.) pertaining to the purchase. Read all documents, including the fine print. If you do not understand something, ask for an explanation. If your agent is unable to explain an item to your satisfaction, talk to a knowledgeable real estate attorney. Real estate agents cannot provide professional advice, except on real estate matters, unless they have the appropriate license. If you have questions about the legal, tax, structural, or title aspects of your transaction, contact the appropriate licensed professional.

Ask to see a copy of all the documents you will be signing at closing in advance so that you have time to read and understand them. Complete a final walk-through inspection of the property before closing to make sure that it is in the condition promised to you in the purchase contract. Plan to act in good faith and in a timely fashion. If contract deadlines cannot be met on time, get extensions in writing. To be valid a real estate contract and any modifications to it must be in writing.

Finally, be realistic about the home buying process. There are bound to be some unanticipated frustrations along the way. Real estate transactions are rarely hassle-free. Working with good people will help you through the tough spots; so will taking an active role in the process. Protect yourself, keep a sense of humor, demand excellence from your cast of professionals, and have fun. Remember, the hard work is worth it. There's no place like home.

# 2

# Working with Real Estate Professionals

## Working with real estate agents

Most buyers use a real estate agent to help them buy a home. But not all have the same level of success. Choosing the right agent is one of the most important decisions you will make during your home buying quest. Your goal should be to work with the best agent you can find. There is a monumental difference between working with a truly great agent and working with one who is mediocre. A great real estate agent will uncover the hidden treasure and grease the squeaky wheel. A great agent will give you the confidence to forge ahead when you are feeling scared witless. Working with a poor agent, on the other hand, could be worse than having no agent at all.

### Profile of a great real estate agent

- A good listener who responds to your needs and desires.
- Always answers your phone calls promptly and shows up for appointments on time.
- Can establish rapport with anyone.
- A master of the "soft sell" technique of helping people make decisions without pressuring them.
- Has years of experience successfully helping people buy and sell homes.
- Enthusiastic, with boundless energy and stamina.
- Gets the job done, no matter what.
- Honest and caring.
- You always feel at ease in the agent's presence, never hustled.

### Getting your money's worth

Real estate agents are usually paid a commission when they successfully close a sale. The commission is typically a percent of the sale price, which can amount to thousands of dollars. Are real estate agents worth the money they are paid? It all depends on what the agent does for you. An agent who gives diligent and conscientious service may be worth every penny. To ensure you get your money's worth, here's what you should expect from an agent.

Agents must be good communicators. They need to be able to tune into buyers' needs and desires to match them to the right homes. Agents must be able to size up buyers' housing needs as well as their financial situations.

Good agents are a font of information. They are able to answer buyers' questions about the home buying process. Good agents inform buyers of the costs involved, they know the markets where they work intimately, they have years of experience to draw from, and they have good common sense and surefire instincts.

Good agents are a great source of referrals for the various professionals you will need to work with to get the job done: lenders, inspectors, attorneys, title officers, and insurance company representatives. But don't be surprised if an agent recommends three professionals and leaves the choice to you. Agents are increasingly concerned about their potential liability for a bad recommendation.

An agent who is worth the commission will let you know about new listings that come on the market before the rest of the world gets the news. To do this, an agent needs to be well-connected with the local real estate community and have good working relationships with other brokers. A good agent has access to on-line listing services and can expose you to a broader range of properties than you can discover on your own.

Agents who are worth the commission go the extra mile to make sure you are satisfied. They attend property inspections with you. They accompany you to the signing of closing documents. (Or, at the least, they review the closing documents with you in advance.) They arrange to oversee property repairs when necessary. They prepare a comparative market analysis of a property you want to buy if you are uncertain about the value. They calculate an estimate of your closing costs. They make special arrangements for you. Different buyers have different needs. You may want to show the property to your relatives before closing, measure rooms, get painter's estimates, or have a final walk-through meeting with the sellers. A good agent will happily make all this happen, and more.

Top agents go out of their way to try to present your offer in person to the sellers and to the listing agent, rather than simply dropping the offer off at the listing office. They stay on top of every aspect of your real estate transaction. They are available to deal with your real estate needs promptly, no matter how inconvenient it might be to them. If a crisis arises, they work on resolving it diligently until the problem is solved.

Good agents take responsibility for overseeing your real estate transaction so that it proceeds as smoothly as possible. But they know the limits of their professional responsibilities. A top agent never slips into the role of decision-maker. Buyers and sellers are the decision-makers in the real estate transaction, not the agents. If an agent is representing you in a transaction, he or she should advise you but never decide for you. Good agents use the "soft sell" approach, which means that they help buyers decide what they want without imposing their own will.

Good agents know the limit of their professional expertise, and never exceed that limit to the client's detriment.

Real estate agents are qualified in the area of real estate. Unless they also have additional professional licenses, they cannot give legal or tax advice. Good agents will always know when to refer you to another licensed professional to get the advice you need. They will never give you advice outside their area of expertise that could harm you.

Good agents will point out material facts about a property to you, especially those that may not be visible to you. These are facts that could affect your decision to buy a property or the price you would be willing to pay.

Discount real estate agents are available who provide less service for less money. If you don't want or expect full service from a real estate agent, you don't have to pay for it. It's up to you to decide what you want and then find the best agent to suit your needs.

### Realtor, agent, or broker: What difference does it make?

People often use the terms agent, broker, and Realtor interchangeably to refer to someone who sells real estate. However, these three terms have different meanings. Not all real estate agents are Realtors, and only a small percentage of agents are licensed real estate brokers.

People who sell real estate must be licensed by the state in which they work, either as a salesperson or as a broker. Brokers can represent people in real estate transactions and they can work on their own without supervision. Real estate salespeople cannot work on their own. They can only work under the supervision of a licensed real estate broker. That broker can either be an individual or a corporation like Coldwell Banker or Century 21. It is more difficult to get a broker's license than it is to get a salesperson's license. A broker's license usually requires experience, college-level course work, and the satisfactory completion of a broker's licensing exam, although specific requirements vary from one state to the next. Even though real estate brokers can work independently, many choose to affiliate themselves with another broker. A "broker associate" works under the auspices of another broker. For example, your agent may have a broker's license but rather than work on her own, she associates herself with a large realty company as a broker associate (also called an associate broker).

Both salespeople and brokers are called agents. But, technically, if the individual who is helping you buy or sell a home is acting as an agent under the auspices of a real estate broker, that broker (often called the broker of record) is actually the agent. The broker of record has responsibility for supervising the conduct of the salespeople and associate brokers who work under the umbrella of the broker of record's license.

**Consumers have added protection if they work with an agent who is a Realtor.**

You may hear real estate agents refer to "listing" and "selling" agents. The listing agent lists and markets a particular home. The selling agent writes the offer for the buyer who buys that home.

# Guide to working with agents

| Term | What does this mean? |
| --- | --- |
| **Real estate broker** | Licensed by each state to act as agents for principals (buyers or sellers) in real estate transactions. Can be an individual or a large organization like Coldwell Banker or Century 21. |
| **Associate broker** (or broker associate) | Has a broker's license and can work unsupervised, but chooses to work under the auspices of another broker. |
| **Real estate salesperson** (also called "Agent") | Licensed by the state to act as agents for principals in real estate transactions, but must work under the supervision of a broker. |
| **Client** | Represented by an agent, who owes utmost loyalty to the client. |
| **Customer** | Not represented by an agent. Is not owed loyalty, but is owed honesty and fairness. |
| **Exclusive agent** (single agency) | Represents one principal (either buyer or seller) exclusively in a transaction. |
| **Dual agent** (dual agency) | Represents both buyer and seller in a transaction. This must be disclosed and agreed to by buyer and seller in advance to be legal. It is illegal in some states. |
| **Buyer's agent or broker** | Represents the buyers exclusively in the transaction and owes them allegiance. |
| **Listing agent or broker** | Represents the sellers exclusively in the transaction and owes them allegiance. |
| **Selling agent or broker** | Writes the offer for the buyer who purchases the property, but may not represent the buyer. |
| **Subagent** | An agent who is not the listing broker, who writes a purchase offer for a buyer, but who owes a fiduciary duty to the seller, not to the buyer. |
| **Transaction broker** (or facilitator) | Someone who represents neither the buyer nor the seller, but who is employed to help the buyer and seller reach agreement. A mediator who does not owe a fiduciary duty to either the buyer or seller. |
| **Realtor**® | A member of the National Association of Realtors (NAR), a national trade association for real estate agents, with a code of ethics. Not all agents are Realtors. |
| **GRI, CRS, CRB** | Advanced designations issued by NAR to agents who have met performance and educational requirements. |

A Realtor is a member of the National Association of Realtors (NAR), which is a trade organization for real estate agents. Membership in NAR is voluntary, but most of the large real estate companies require their salespeople to join. NAR does not have the authority to license agents, but it does police its members' activities. NAR members subscribe to a strict code of ethics. An agent who is not a Realtor cannot be held to the NAR code of ethics, and cannot be disciplined by NAR. Home buyers and sellers have added protection if they work with Realtors. A consumer can file a complaint with a local subsidiary of NAR against a Realtor who violates the NAR code of ethics. Complaints against non-Realtor agents must be directed to the state licensing bureau. Ask any agent you are considering if he or she is a Realtor. Only about two out of three agents are. If you have any questions about an agent's Realtor status, call your local association of Realtors.

You might run across other designations. The letters GRI (Graduate Real Estate Institute), CRS (Certified Residential Specialist), and CRB (Certified Residential Broker) next to an agent's name indicate that the agent has completed advanced real estate training. The CRS and CRB designation are more advanced than the GRI. In general, the more experience and the more education an agent has, the better. Agents with broker's licenses or with any of the above designations are professionals who take their career advancement seriously. If you are trying to decide between several agents, find one who has invested the time and effort to get advanced credentials.

### Finding the right agent—or agents

To find a good agent, ask friends and colleagues who purchased a home recently if they would recommend their agent to you. Personal references are usually the best way to find an exceptional agent. If you are new to an area and don't know someone to ask, drive around the neighborhoods where you want to live and make note of the agents who list the most property in the area. Visit Sunday open houses and meet some of these agents in person. Sellers usually interview more than one agent before selecting one to list their home. Buyers are well advised to do the same. However, don't feel that you absolutely must talk to several agents before making a choice. Rapport between you and your agent is vitally important to a satisfactory home purchase transaction. So, when you find an agent who is knowledgeable about the area where you want to live, whom you trust implicitly, and with whom you are compatible, search no more.

**One of the biggest complaints made about real estate agents is that they don't communicate often enough during the transaction.**

Conduct your agent interviews in a business-like fashion. Make appointments to meet the agents in their offices. Use the "Agent interview checklist" in this chapter to guide you through the interview process.

# Agent interview checklist

Agent's name:
Phone:

**Does the agent:**

**Comments**

1   Have an active real estate license in good standing? Check with the governing agency in your state if you are uncertain.

2   Have years of experience in the business? If not, does the agent work under the close supervision of an experienced broker who will assist you if necessary?

3   Have a good reputation for trustworthiness? Ask for names of buyers who used the agent recently and talk to them.

4   Know the areas you are interested in and regularly sell homes there?

5   Work full-time as a real estate agent?

6   Have time to work with you?

7   Have a professional demeanor? This person will represent you to sellers, other agents, lenders, etc.

8   Discuss agency relationships with you? Can the agent work with you in an agency relationship that you find acceptable?

9   Have a personality you can relate to?

10  Work with first-time buyers, if you are a first-time buyer?

11  Interview you regarding your housing needs and wants?

12  Listen attentively?

13  Return phone calls promptly?

14  Answer your real estate questions in a manner that you understand?

15  Provide you with a list of the properties he or she is showing you?

16  Show you homes that suit your needs?

17  Show up on time for appointments?

18  Have some knowledge of home construction?

19  Belong to the multiple-listing service and/or on-line home shopping services for the area where you want to look?

20  Qualify you for a loan, or introduce you to a lender or mortgage broker who can?

21  Complete a closing cost estimate for you?

22  Provide you with recommendations of lenders, mortgage brokers, inspectors, insurance agents, title agents, real estate attorneys, movers, etc.?

23  Have any schedule conflicts that will interfere with your home hunt? If so, interview the agent who will fill in.

If you are unable to decide on an agent after one meeting, have him or her show you several homes that might suit you. This will give you a chance to assess the agent's style and to see if it meshes well with yours. Also, the agent's selection of homes will tell you how well he or she listened when you described your housing needs and desires.

Some buyers shy away from working with busy agents. Granted, you do want to work with an agent who has the time and who is enthusiastic about working with you. But there is merit in selecting a hard-working agent. Approximately 20 percent of the agents sell 80 percent of the property. The agents who sell the most property tend to be the best agents because they have the most experience. A well-organized agent who sells a lot of property is probably your best bet, as long as that agent takes a hands-on approach and values customer satisfaction. Once you have selected an agent, don't be shy about letting him or her know that your expectations are high.

In return for quality service, you should commit to work exclusively with that agent as long as the relationship continues to work well for you. Buyers often wonder if they should work with more than one agent. Yes, if you are looking in more than one area. Don't let an agent talk you into using him or her to buy a home in an area he or she doesn't know well. Unfortunately, agents do cover large areas. Across the country, Multiple Listing Services (MLS)—information-sharing networks used by real estate agents to promote their listings—are in the process of combining to create mega-systems encompassing enormous areas. One huge MLS serves agents working all over the East San Francisco Bay Area. It's impossible for one agent to be an expert on properties in every community in that MLS area. But, legally, there is nothing to keep an agent in Concord from representing buyers of a Piedmont property, which is more than a half-hour drive away.

An ethical agent who really puts the buyers' best interests first would refer out-of-area buyers to an agent who specializes in that area. Only a local specialist is going to be able to protect your interests. An out-of-area agent has no way of knowing the subtle nuances about a place that will enable you to decide which home is the best buy. Having access to comparable sales information from the MLS is not good enough. Unless an agent has seen those comparable properties, this data is of limited use. Agents become good judges of local value by touring and previewing local properties on a regular basis.

Generally, you will get the best service in an area by committing yourself to working with one agent for that area. Good agents don't waste their time working with buyers who are not likely to buy a home through them. If, however, you are trying to buy into an area with extremely limited inventory and high buyer demand—where properties are selling before they even hit the MLS—you may need to hook up with several of the top listing agents in the area and let them know what you are looking for. If you end up working with more than one agent, you should commit to using the agent who shows you the home you buy, if possible.

*Matty and Joel were working with an agent from Danville, California. Frustrated that they were not finding what they wanted in the Danville area, they looked at open houses in an older neighborhood in Oakland, a thirty-minute drive away. They fell in love with a house they saw there and called their Danville agent. Instead of referring Matty and Joel to an Oakland agent, the Danville agent decided that she wanted to represent them. Several other buyers were also interested and wrote offers on the Oakland house. Since it was a multiple offer competition, the Danville agent assumed that the property must have been priced too low, so she recommended Matty and Joel increase their offer by $10,000 over the list price. They got the house, and the sellers got more money than they should have. The other two offers, from buyers who had looked at plenty of property in Oakland, were for considerably less than the list price. Matty and Joel didn't have to pay as much as they did, but their agent, who didn't know local market values, didn't know this.*

After you have decided on an agent or agents to work with, let others that you come into contact with know that you have one. You may do a certain amount of hunting for a home on your own: searching classified ads, visiting open houses, surfing the Internet, and driving neighborhoods. When you call a real estate office to inquire about an ad or a "For Sale" sign, the agent who answers the phone may want your business. This is to be expected because real estate agents usually work on commission and only make money when they make a sale. Such an agent may ask if you are working with an agent. You should mention that you have an agent whether you are asked or not. The agent who shows you a property may be entitled to the commission if you buy it. The same goes for public open houses. Let the agent there know that you have an agent. If you want more information about the property, have your agent follow up on this for you. An agent who puts in a lot of work for you, thinking that you don't have another agent, may assume that he or she is your agent. Being clear at the start is always best.

# Agency disclosure: Whom does an agent represent?

How buyers work with real estate agents has changed dramatically in recent years. This relationship is still changing in some states. Traditionally, real estate agents almost always worked exclusively for the seller, often to the dismay of the buyer, under an arcane arrangement called subagency. Subagency is fast becoming the least popular agency relationship, and is now illegal in some states.

Here's how subagency works. The sellers list their home with an agent who will represent them exclusively. The agent then lists the property on the Multiple Listing Service. Through the Multiple Listing Service, the seller's agent (also called the listing agent or broker) invites other real estate agents (who work for different real estate brokers) to attempt to sell the property. If an agent working for another broker is successful in selling the property, the listing agent will split the commission with the selling agent under an arrangement called subagency. The agent writing the offer for the buyers does not represent the buyers; he or she represents the sellers as a subagent. A subagent owes a primary loyalty to the sellers, not to the buyers.

The law of agency governs the relationship between an agent and a client. An agent owes a fiduciary duty of utmost loyalty and care to a client. A fiduciary must put the client's best interests above all others. A fiduciary negotiates and advocates on a client's behalf. So, if your agent is the seller's subagent, then both of the agents in the transaction are representing the seller. Both agents owe allegiance to the seller, who is the client. You, the buyer, are not a client of either agent; you are merely a customer.

Agents are obliged to be truthful and fair to a customer. As a customer, you may get excellent service from an agent. But an agent does not owe the same loyalty and confidentiality to a customer that is owed to a client. There is a big difference between being an agent's client and being an agent's customer. Sellers who are represented by an agent can tell their agent that they will sell for less than their list price, and their agent must keep this information confidential. But suppose you are a buyer working with this same agent. The agent is representing the seller, not you. If you tell this agent that you will pay a higher price for the home than you are offering, the agent is not obliged to keep this information confidential. In fact, the agent is supposed to pass this information on to the sellers because the agent owes an allegiance to the sellers. The agent's job is to get the highest possible price for the seller, not the lowest possible price for you.

It's natural for buyers to assume that the agent who is showing them homes and writing their offers represents them. But in the past this was rarely the case because sub-agency used to be the norm. Most states now have agency disclosure laws that require brokers (and their sales agents) to disclose the kinds of agency relationships that exist in a given real estate transaction, and whom they represent.

Some states, like California, permit a broker to establish a client relationship with the buyer as long as that broker is not already representing the seller. In this case, a listing broker would represent the seller exclusively and the buyer's broker would represent the buyer exclusively. This is called single agency representation. Buyer's brokers owe an allegiance to the buyer, not to the seller. They are duty-bound to keep the buyer's secrets confidential and not disclose them to the seller. Buyer's brokers can advise buyers if they think a seller's property is overpriced; subagents cannot.

You might wonder why buyers would choose to work with an agent who would not represent them exclusively. In some cases, the buyer might not have a choice. In a subdivision of new houses, the builder may insist that the buyer write an offer with one of the development sales associates, who either represents the seller exclusively or represents the buyer and the seller as a dual agent.

Some states permit dual agency representation, which exits if one broker represents both the buyer and seller. Even if two different agents are involved, it could be dual agency if they both work for one broker. If the seller is represented by an agent from XYZ Realty and the buyers are working with a different XYZ Realty agent, it could be a dual agency situation (depending on what state you are in) because there is only one broker of record. Dual agency must be disclosed and consented to by both the buyers and the sellers to be legal. Undisclosed dual agency is grounds for rescinding (undoing) a contract. Although the law differs from one state to the next, a dual agent is often restricted from revealing that the buyer will pay more or that a seller will accept less, without written permission to do so from the respective party.

A seller's subagent who is abiding by the agency rules is not permitted to tell you if a listing is worth less than the seller's asking price. But you can ask a sub-agent to give you a list of comparable properties that have recently sold. And you can also ask to be shown other currently listed comparable properties. Study the comparable sales information and make your offer accordingly. All offers have to be presented to the sellers. If the sellers think your initial offer is low, they can counteroffer back with a price they can live with. Under no circumstances should you reveal the top price you are willing to pay to a subagent who is duty-bound to pass that information along to the sellers.

**Dual agency representation is legal in many states, but only if it is disclosed and agreed to by both buyer and seller.**

Agency disclosure laws vary from one state to another. In Vermont, for example, the agency disclosure law that took effect July 1, 1995, prohibits both subagency and disclosed dual agency. The latter was replaced with "broker's agency" and "limited agency." Virginia passed a law, effective October 1, 1995, which allows agents to represent the buyer and seller as "designated representatives," rather than as dual agents, when both agents work for the same broker. The duties of a designated representative are clearly defined; they do not require the agents to exercise a fiduciary standard of care. There will no doubt be further attempts to refine state laws to keep agents from representing buyers and sellers as dual agents with split loyalties.

In some states, like Colorado, real estate professionals offer their services as "transaction" brokers or "facilitators." Transaction brokers act as mediators and do not represent either the buyer or the seller. They do not advocate for the interests of either party, and they must treat all parties in the transaction equally. Transaction brokers are forbidden from revealing the buyers', or sellers', confidences to the other party.

No matter what agency relationship you establish with your agent, be sure to understand whether you will be a client to whom loyalty is owed or merely a customer. Be aware that some states still play by the old rules, where all agents work for the sellers. If agency disclosure is the law in the state where you are buying, your agent should provide you with an agency disclosure form before you write an offer to buy a home. This form should explain all possible agency relationships. Most state agency laws set a time frame for the agent to disclose agency relationships to you. But not all agents abide by the law and not all states require agency disclosure. Regardless of whether agency disclosure is the law in your state, take the initiative and discuss agency relationships with your agent before you buy. It may be difficult to undo an agency relationship after you are already involved in a contract to buy a home. Also, many agents don't understand agency relationships, so don't feel bad if the subject matter confuses you. Just make sure you understand what your agent's responsibilities will be in the transaction.

## Should you hire a buyer's broker?

The agency laws in your state will influence your decision of whether to hire a buyer's broker. In California, for instance, buyer brokerage has not caught on in a big way because since 1988 buyers can be represented exclusively in purchase transactions as long as their agent and the listing agent work for different brokers. In some states, where facilitators or transaction brokerage is available, buyers are electing to forego agency representation altogether. However, if you live in a state where subagency is still the norm, you will probably want to consider using a buyer's broker to represent you exclusively in the transaction. Why, then, don't more buyers hire buyer's agents? Buyer brokerage is a relatively new concept slowly taking hold around the country. In some places, buyer's brokers may not be readily available. Even when buyer's brokers are available, some buyers choose not to use them because they think they will get a better deal if they use the seller's agent. Some don't want to hire a buyer's broker because they don't want to pay out of their own pockets for buyer brokerage, which could cost as much as 3½ percent of the purchase price.

There are two types of buyer's brokers. One only represents buyers and never represents sellers. The other represents both buyers and sellers but never represents both in a single transaction. The first usually requires that the buyer sign a contract that obligates the buyer to pay a fee to the broker under certain conditions. Typically, if the broker finds the buyer a home within the time frame specified in the contract, the broker is entitled to a fee. Often an up-front retainer is collected

**Make sure that any buyer broker agreement you sign has a provision for canceling the contract if you are dissatisfied with the service.**

from the buyer when the buyer broker contract is signed. If so, the retainer is usually applied toward the entire fee when the sale is made. If the broker does not find the buyer a home, the fee is often retained by the broker. The second type of buyer broker may work under a conventional commission arrangement where he or she is paid a share of the listing broker's commission, which is paid by the seller. Most states allow a buyer's broker to be paid from the listing broker's commission. Under this agreement, the buyer's agent is paid at closing, and the buyer usually does not have to pay an up-front fee.

> **A buyer broker contract should include an expiration date and it should specify the fee, including how and when it will be paid.**

Some buyers don't use buyer's brokers because they fear they won't be exposed to new listings as quickly as they would if they worked with a large real estate firm that lists a lot of homes. In a hot, low-inventory market, listings often sell before they hit the open market. If you are not working with an agent employed in the listing office, you may not have a chance of buying a new listing.

Herein lies a dilemma. Suppose you are working with an XYZ Realty agent in a large forty-five-agent office. In most states, your agent can represent you exclusively as a buyer's agent as long as you don't buy an XYZ Realty listing. But if you buy an XYZ Realty listing, your agent may not be able to represent you exclusively as a buyer's agent. In some states, your agent will either have to work with you as an agent who represents the seller (a subagent) or as a dual agent, who represents both you and the seller, because XYZ Realty already represents the sellers.

How can dual agents represent the best interests of two parties who have opposing interests? The buyer wants the property for the lowest price possible and the sellers want the highest price possible. Some would argue there is a conflict of interest here. Does this mean that you should avoid looking at listings that are listed with the firm your agent

**Pueblo style**
*A massive looking dwelling made of real or simulated adobe. Pueblo style homes often feature a flat roof with projecting roof beams (called viga). The second and third stories are often stepped.*

works for? This hardly seems reasonable because it is often difficult to find a good home to buy. Most buyers want to be exposed to as much inventory as possible. Just understand that you may not be able to have exclusive representation in a transaction if your agent and the seller's agent work for the same broker. If you find yourself in a situation where you don't feel comfortable having your agent act as a dual agent, ask your agent to refer you to another agent or broker outside your agent's office. The agents should be able to work out a commission-sharing arrangement so that your agent is compensated for the efforts performed on your behalf.

---

**TALES FROM THE TRENCHES: EPISODE 5**
*Dick and Kathy walked into a Sunday open house and decided that they wanted to buy the home. However, they didn't want the agent who was holding the open house to write their offer because she represented the seller as a listing agent. They asked friends who had bought a house recently for the name of their agent. This agent agreed to represent Dick and Kathy as a buyers' agent. But, the listing agent felt that she should write the buyers' offer because she had been the person who first exposed the buyers to the property. Dick and Kathy told their agent to inform the listing agent that they would not buy the house at all if they had to buy it through the listing agent. To ensure a good working relationship, Dick and Kathy's agent agreed to pay the listing agent a fee to compensate her for the time she had spent with the buyers. Dick and Kathy were represented by their own buyer's agent, and the sale went through.*

---

Some buyers in a dual agency situation prefer not to be referred to another broker, particularly if they have the utmost trust in their own agent. If you do accept dual agency, understand that you may have to be your own advocate. Take more precautions to protect yourself than you would if you had exclusive representation by your own agent. Also, find out before you enter into the contract how your agent's brokerage firm handles conflicts that arise in dual-agency transactions.

# The real estate brokerage commission

Most real estate agents work on commission. They get paid only when a home sells and closes. If the home never sells, they work for free. But if the home does sell, they often get paid a percentage of the sale price. The higher the price, the higher the commission. Traditionally, sellers pay the brokerage commission. A seller's agent is supposed to try to get the highest price possible for the seller. But a buyer's agent is supposed to work to get a home on the best possible terms for the buyer, which usually means the lowest possible price. Some argue that there is a built-in conflict in having a buyer's agent paid a percentage of the sale price, because the agent would be working at cross-purposes. The buyer wants to pay the lowest price and the agent wants the highest commission.

No doubt there are unscrupulous agents who put their interests above everyone else's. But an intelligent, honest agent representing you exclusively as a buyer in a real estate transaction will put your best interests first, even if it means the agent will earn a lower commission. An ethical agent will advise you not to buy a home at all if it would be risky for you. In this case, the agent would receive no compensation for his or her efforts. Good agents put their client's needs first because they know they will benefit in the long run. Career agents depend on your future business and your referral business for their livelihood. A good agent would rather represent you in the purchase of a less expensive home than not have you as a client at all.

It's illegal for brokerage companies to conspire to fix commissions at one rate. Practically speaking, however, commissions are often in the range of 6 to 7 percent of the purchase price. In a conventional home sale, the sellers pay the commission from their sale proceeds and it is split fifty-fifty between the listing broker and the selling broker. Each broker has a separate commission-sharing arrangement between the brokerage company and the individual agent who represented the buyer or seller. Frequently, the commission is shared four ways: between two brokers and two agents.

A buyer's broker can be paid in a variety of ways, each with its advantages and disadvantages. One option is for the buyer to pay the broker directly. When the buyer pays his or her agent directly, the sellers usually pay a lower commission because their broker doesn't have to split the commission with another broker. So, the sellers can afford to sell for less and the buyer gets a better price. Let's say the sellers are offering to pay a 6 percent commission. You arrange to pay your own broker directly, so the sellers reduce their commission from 6 to 3 percent, which will be paid to the listing broker. Then the sellers can afford to lower the price of their home by 3 percent without reducing their net proceeds from the sale. If your property taxes will be based on the price you pay for the home, paying a lower price will result in an additional savings over time. A disadvantage of paying a buyer broker directly is that the buyer has to come up with the additional cash to pay the fee. Home buyers are often strapped for cash. Some lenders will allow a buyer to finance a buyer brokerage fee, but check into this before you make an offer if your cash is short.

Some buyers prefer to pay their buyer's broker a flat fee rather than a percent of the purchase price. The flat fee eliminates the concern you might have that the agent would put his or her desire for a large commission (as a percent of the sale price) above your desire to get a home at the lowest possible price. The agent's fee will be the same regardless of the sale price. Another possibility is to pay a buyer's broker by the hour, which can be economical as long as the agent works efficiently.

**Real estate brokerage commissions are negotiable.**

Buyers who can't afford to pay a buyer's broker and who can't find a lender to finance the fee might be able to arrange for the sellers to pay the buyer's brokerage commission. The sellers pay their listing broker the commission agreed to in the listing agreement. The seller's broker then splits the commission with the buyer's broker. The commission is included in the price. So if you get a loan for 90 percent of the purchase price, 90 percent of the commission you owe your buyer's broker is financed. Even though the price you pay for the home will be higher if the sellers pay the commission, you can conserve cash by using this payment method. Most states permit this sort of commission sharing between brokers even though the buyer's broker represents the buyer, not the seller.

While real estate commissions are negotiable, most brokers won't offer you a discount unless you ask for it. Even if asked, some brokers refuse to work for less than a certain fee. Although it is illegal for real estate companies to collectively set a commission rate, it is legal for a single brokerage company to have a set commission. How much an agent or broker will reduce a commission below the company rate varies from one company to the next and often depends on market conditions. You'll usually find more commission negotiation in hot, low-inventory markets. Also, commissions tend to be lower on more expensive properties.

Yet another form of commission negotiation is fairly common. Often, brokers will agree to reduce their commission to complete a transaction. Suppose the buyer's home inspection reveals the need for a new roof. The buyer and seller attempt to negotiate a resolution, but end up $1,000 short of the money needed to re-roof the home. The broker agrees to reduce the commission the seller owes by $1,000, so the seller can afford to pay an additional $1,000 for the roof. Brokers are usually more willing to cut their fee to keep a deal together if they have not already reduced their commission up-front.

Discount brokers openly advertise that they work for less. Often, they have a flexible fee structure. You might be able to find an agent who would be willing to represent you for less if you find the property you want to buy on your own. In the future, more real estate companies will probably offer a flexible fee structure. The buyer or seller will decide what level of service they want and pay a fee priced accordingly.

# Dealing with a difficult agent

You might want to change agents for many reasons. Maybe you have looked for months for a home only to find that a lazy agent failed to tell you about a few gems that sold right away. Perhaps you have entered into a contract to buy a home and your agent refuses to return your phone calls. Or your agent may be too pushy and you suspect that he or she is unethical.

Changing agents (or brokers) before you have entered into a contract to buy a home is relatively easy. If you are working with a conventional agent—that is, you haven't signed an exclusive buyer's broker contract—you can simply tell the agent that you will no longer need his or her services. Determination and fortitude may be required on your part; some agents are manipulative and will try any means possible to keep you as a customer. Don't allow such an agent to use guilt to coerce you into staying in the relationship.

A buyer's broker may require that you sign a contract saying that you will work exclusively with that broker. The contract may require you to pay the broker a fee even if you buy a home through another broker. Your buyer agency contract should include a cancellation clause that specifies when and how you can cancel the contract. If not, call the broker and tell him or her that you wish to cancel the agreement. Ideally, you should get a written confirmation from the broker stating that the contract is canceled. Check with a knowledgeable real estate attorney if you have questions about ending an agency contract.

Changing agents once you have entered into a contract to buy a home is difficult. Make a change only if you are not getting good service. If this happens, call the agent and express your concerns. If this does not result in better service, call the managing broker who oversees the agent's work and discuss your dissatisfaction. If the manager can't shape up the agent, ask that another agent in the office be assigned to help you complete the transaction. When all else fails, talk to an attorney and plan on monitoring each step of the transaction yourself to make sure that nothing is overlooked.

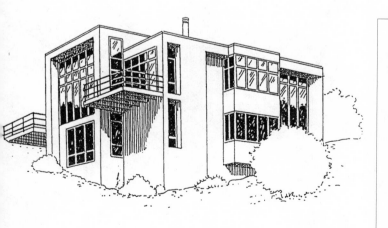

**International style**
A simple architectural design with smooth, uniform wall surfaces, clean lines, and lacking ornamentation. Other features can include: large expanses of windows that appear to be continuous, flat roofs, projecting balconies, and steel pipe railings.

# Buying without an agent

FSBO (pronounced Fizzbo) is shorthand for "For Sale by Owner." A FSBO property is one that is offered for sale by sellers who are not represented by a real estate broker. Sellers might choose to sell their home this way for several reasons. They may have had a horrible experience with the last broker they worked with. More common, however, are FSBO sellers trying to save themselves the cost of a real estate commission, which can be about 6 to 7 percent of the selling price.

The number of FSBOs on the market tends to increase during a seller's market, when a shortage of homes for sale gives a FSBO seller a better chance of selling without the help of a real estate professional. The reverse is true of a buyer's market, where there is plenty of property for sale and relatively few buyers looking to buy homes. In a buyer's market, the number of FSBOs tends to drop as sellers find it harder to sell on their own.

A FSBO listing may be the perfect home for you, but you need to exercise caution when you purchase directly from a seller. First, make sure that the seller's price is right. You can do some legwork on your own by visiting Sunday open houses. Well-priced homes sell quickly, sometimes with multiple offers. If a home sells quickly, you can assume that it was priced right and that it sold for close to the asking price. You usually can't find out the actual selling price until the sale closes, after which the information is public. There are on-line services offering comparable sales information, which you can access over the phone or via modem using your personal computer. (See Chapter 3 for more information

**Prairie Style**
Popularized by American architect, Frank Lloyd Wright, the Prairie style house features a low profile, strong horizontal lines, projecting roof eaves, and an integration with the outdoors through the use of balconies, terraces, walks, and low exterior walls.

about on-line appraisal services.) If this information is too sketchy, try to find a real estate agent who will give you comparable sales information. You might be able to hire an agent to do a comparative market analysis for you. Agents will usually complete a complimentary comparative market analysis for sellers who are considering listing with them. Since there will be nothing in it for the agent (unless you use the agent to represent you), you will probably get the most reliable information if you offer to pay the agent for his or her time. If you decide to hire an agent to represent you, there should be no additional charge for a comparative market evaluation. To be sure you don't overpay for a FSBO listing, include a contingency in your purchase agreement stating that the property must appraise for the purchase price. If you are applying for a mortgage, the lender will insist that the property be appraised as a part of the loan approval process. If you are paying all cash or if you have private financing lined up, pay an appraiser to complete the appraisal for you. A FSBO is not a good deal if you end up paying more than you would if you paid an agent to watch out for your best interests.

Many FSBO sellers are willing to cooperate with a broker who is representing a buyer even though the sellers don't have their own broker. Such sellers will usually pay the buyer's broker a commission from the sale proceeds, as in a conventional home sale. The commission is usually one half the amount the sellers would pay if they had listed the home with a broker. If the sellers absolutely refuse to pay a brokerage fee, you will have to pay the fee yourself if you choose to be represented by an agent.

Hire an attorney or real estate broker to draft and review the purchase contract for you if you decide to buy direct from a seller without using an agent to represent you. Negotiating directly with the seller can be difficult, so consider hiring a professional (again, an attorney or real estate broker) to handle the negotiations for you. Even if you are buying directly from a friend or relative whom you trust and know well, it's a good idea to bring in an intermediary to make sure the transaction goes well. A successful real estate transaction depends on teamwork. If you purchase a home without the aid of a real estate broker, make sure to line up a good loan agent, escrow or closing agent, title officer, insurance agent, home and termite inspectors, and real estate attorney to help you through the process. If you are working with an agent, he or she can help you assemble your team of experts.

Be especially careful if you are buying directly from a seller who purchased at the peak of the market in 1988 and 1989. The housing market then was so competitive in some areas that many buyers paid way over the asking prices and took properties in their "as is" condition. During the economic downturn that followed, many of these home-owners postponed making the necessary repairs. Make sure you don't buy a problem that someone else neglected. Make an inspection contingency a part of the purchase agreement and have the property thoroughly inspected before completing the sale.

# Working with a real estate attorney

Whether you need to hire an attorney to help you through your home purchase depends on the location where you buy and the complexity of the transaction. State and local customs vary considerably. In some states, like California, attorneys rarely handle transactions for home buyers and sellers. Real estate agents, with the help of title and escrow officers, usually take care of all transaction and closing details. They prepare the purchase contract, arrange for property inspections, help the buyers line up financing, arrange for the property appraisal, help the buyers get insurance, and coordinate title and closing matters.

In states where attorneys are not routinely involved in home sales, state law usually permits real estate agents to complete standard-form, fill-in-the-blank purchase contracts. But real estate agents cannot practice law unless they are also attorneys. Agents are allowed to complete standard-form purchase contracts as long as they don't give out legal advice.

But in some areas, attorneys are routinely a part of the home purchase process. How intimately they are involved varies. They may be required to draft the purchase agreement, to research the title history, to check for compliance with government regulations, and to draft and review documents. Your attorney may actually accompany you to a closing, depending on where you buy.

Even if you are buying in an area where attorneys aren't usually part of the process, you may want to hire an attorney. If you are buying a home directly from a seller, and a real estate agent will not be a part of the process, you should definitely hire an attorney to draft, or at least review, the purchase agreement. You may want to pay an attorney to handle the entire transaction.

Purchase contracts are complicated documents, even the preprinted variety. If you have any questions about whether a clause should be included in the contract, you may need to talk to an attorney. For example, a "liquidated damages" clause and a "binding arbitration" clause are optional in some standard-form purchase contracts. Your real estate agent can explain these clauses to you, but your agent cannot advise you whether to include these clauses in your contract. So if you cannot decide on your own, you need to call an attorney for a legal opinion.

You might need to call an attorney during your purchase if you and the seller decide during the transaction that you need to amend the contract with language that can only be drafted by an attorney. Let's say your inspections reveal that there is a serious defect with the property. You decide to proceed with the purchase because the sellers agree to give you a large sum to fix the problem. But the sellers want a "hold harmless" agreement that relieves them of any further responsibility for the problem. The "hold harmless" agreement should be drafted by an attorney.

You should select an attorney with the same care as selecting a real estate agent, an investment adviser, or a doctor. Use an attorney who is knowledgeable in the area of residential real estate law. Attorneys, like doctors, specialize. Because buying a home is a major investment, sound legal advice is imperative. Also, the more knowledgeable the attorney is in the area of law where you need help, the less time he or she will have to spend on your case. Since many attorneys bill by the hour, the less time spent, the less you pay.

Personal recommendations are the best source of attorney referrals. Interview several if you have any questions about an attorney's credentials or about how well you will work together. Make sure the attorney has enough time for you, and make sure you understand up front how much it will cost. Some attorneys work for a set fee. The attorney who will work for you for the lowest fee may not be the best choice. You want the best attorney you can find for the best price. Sometimes it is worth it to pay more for quality service. However, you should find out before you hire an attorney how much it will cost and what services will be included.

Always remember that your attorney works for you. You are the decision-maker, not your attorney. Let your attorney know that you want all documents written in plain language, not in obscure legalized terms. Also, make sure the tone of documents your attorney drafts reflects your true feelings. Review all documents before they are sent off to the other party. It may make sense to be present for important negotiations so that you can make certain that your goals are being accomplished. As with any real estate professionals that you employ, you must monitor your attorney's work. Don't just turn the transaction over to your attorney and walk away. Make sure that you are getting your money's worth.

Nationally, there is a move away from using attorneys to handle real estate transactions. But you should never let someone talk you out of consulting a real estate attorney if you have any questions regarding your real estate transaction that require legal expertise.

# 3

# *Finding a Home to Buy*

## The search is on

Your goal should be to look at as many homes as you can that come close to satisfying the features you listed on your "Home comparison checklist" (see Chapter 1). Start by having your agent show you four or five homes that suit your needs. Looking at more than five properties in one outing can be confusing. Be candid with your agent as you go through each property. Let him or her know your likes and dislikes. The more you communicate with your agent, the easier it will be to find the right home.

Buyers often end up buying a home that is different from what they said they wanted. Often it's impossible to know exactly what you want until you have seen enough homes to know what your options are. In theory, you may want a house with a three-car garage. But if you want to buy a house in an area of older homes, none of which have three-car garages, you have two options. You can either change your priorities to accommodate the available housing stock, which means you settle for a one- or two-car garage. Or you go elsewhere to buy a house. Buying a home always involves compromises. It's hard to know how you will compromise until you know what amenities you can expect to find in homes located in the area(s) where you want to live. Looking at property not only fine tunes your housing needs and wants list, it also teaches you market value. The more homes you see, the more familiar you become with local pricing, and the easier it will be to know how much you should pay for the home you decide to buy.

**Buying a home involves compromises; the perfect home does not exist.**

A neighborhood or city map is a handy home-hunting aid; ask your agent for one. Carry it with you on your shopping forays. Take a copy of your "Home comparison checklist" with you when you look at homes. Make notes about the properties you see as you go.

Pick up descriptive flyers and brochures. Taking photos or videotaping is helpful for some buyers. (If you want to photograph or videotape the interior of a home, ask for the owner's permission in advance. Some sellers are security-conscious, particularly when their home is on the market.)

When you get a call from your agent telling you there is a hot new listing on the market, make arrangements to see it as soon as possible. You may want to take a second, a third, or even a fourth look at a property that interests you. Your agent should be happy to accommodate your wishes. If the home is listed with a broker, you should not contact the seller directly to see it. Your agent should arrange all showings for you.

Some buyers depend 100 percent on their agents to find them a home to buy. They have neither the time nor the inclination to search on their own. Other buyers get far more involved in the search. If you prefer the hands-on approach, you will probably want to hit the Sunday open house circuit, browse the classified ad sections of the local newspapers, and check the Internet for new listings. If you are working with an agent, your agent can and should follow up on any home that interests you.

The home-hunting strategy above works for buyers who are shopping the resale market, that is, homes that have been occupied by another owner. One out of five home buyers buys a new home, which may involve a different strategy. Some new homes are located in neighborhoods of predominantly older homes. You can usually find and negotiate the purchase of one of these the same as you would a resale: Using an agent who has expertise in the area. But if you want to buy into a new-home development, the finding and buying process will differ considerably. You may have to search the new-homes market on your own if the developers won't cooperate with an outside agent. Most developers hire a staff of agents to handle the sale of their new homes. Some developers offer to cooperate with outside real estate agents (advertised as "Broker Coop").

The sales experience in a new-homes development is more focused and intense than that for resales. Resale agents take you from home to home until you find one that is right. Agents at a new-homes project work for the builder and can usually only sell homes in that project. They will be intent on convincing you that their homes are superior to others on the market. Stay focused when looking at homes in new developments. Don't get sidetracked by the fancy decor of a builder's showcase model or by an agent's sales pitch. Make sure that what you are buying is what you want and need. See the section below about buying new homes for more information.

**The home you buy should:**
- Fulfill your housing needs.
- Be well located.
- Satisfy many of your housing wants.
- Be structurally sound.
- Have good resale potential.
- Be affordable.

When markets are rising and housing is in high demand, selling a home is not usually a problem. But when the real estate market stalls, which it does periodically, resale can become difficult or impossible. The best homes tend to sell well in any market, but homes with defects are a different story. A home that is located up a lot of stairs or near a freeway may be relatively easy to sell in a rapidly rising market, particularly if there are few homes for sale and lots of buyers wanting to buy. In this kind of a market, buyers are more willing to make compromises. When the market turns down, however, buyers become cautious and selective, particularly when they have a lot of inventory to choose from. To protect yourself from being unable to sell your home in a slow real estate market, buy a home with broad-based appeal and without major defects, like freeway noise. If you do buy a home that has an incurable defect, you should be able to negotiate a good deal, but you should also expect to sell the home at a discount to the next buyer.

**TALES FROM THE TRENCHES: EPISODE 6**

*Jodie and Brian bought a cute hillside hideaway in a tree-studded, private setting. They were young and healthy; they didn't mind climbing forty steps up from the street to get to the house. They were used to parking on the street at their apartment, so they didn't mind that the house lacked a garage. They were a little concerned about the wavy floors, but an inspector told them not to worry. Two years later, Jodie and Brian were transferred to new jobs and needed to sell. The real estate market in their area had declined since they bought. The defects that Jodie and Brian were willing to overlook when they bought—crooked floors, lots of stairs, and no garage—made their house virtually unsalable. After months on the market, they sold for considerably less than what they had paid for the property.*

From an investment standpoint, a three-bedroom, two-bath home has more appreciation potential than a two-bedroom, one-bath home. But the biggest house on the block is not always the best investment. You are better off buying a moderate-size home in a neighborhood of larger homes. But a home purchase is more than an investment; it's your home. The character of a home and its neighborhood must suit your individual tastes and needs. Subjective factors like charm or coziness will inevitably affect your choice of a home. And since the perfect home does not exist, you will undoubtedly have to make some compromises, like settling for one less bedroom in exchange for a better location, or sacrificing a view for one more bathroom. The choice is yours.

**The biggest house on the block is not usually the best investment.**

# Choosing a neighborhood

You'll often hear that location is the most critical factor affecting a home's value. The most desirable neighborhoods tend to hold their value over time, so it makes sense to buy in the best neighborhood you can afford. The best neighborhoods have some of these features: close proximity to a thriving economic center, good public schools, nearby shopping, good public facilities, convenient commute options, well-maintained homes, and a low crime rate.

Prime neighborhoods are also usually the most expensive neighborhoods, often putting them out of reach for first-time home buyers. You may be wise to sacrifice on amenities, such as an extra bedroom or a remodeled kitchen, to afford a home in a better location. However, the home you buy should suit your housing needs for at least several years because buying and selling homes too frequently is an expensive proposition.

First-time buyers with limited financial resources should look for neighborhoods that are likely to be in high demand in coming years. Finding tomorrow's hot communities requires some research. While there are no guarantees of what the future will bring, some signals indicate a neighborhood on the rise. One is more buyers looking to buy into the area than there are homes for sale. Excess demand tends to put an upward pressure on prices. If you can find a home to buy in a neighborhood that is on the verge of a popularity boom, you can increase your chances of earning home price appreciation in your early years of ownership. A good place to start your search for tomorrow's "hot" spots is on the periphery of the most desirable, well-established neighborhoods in your area. Often these marginal neighborhoods will be the next ones to enjoy a run-up in prices.

Another option for buyers who can't afford a more expensive neighborhood is to buy a home in a good neighborhood on the outskirts of town. There is usually an inverse relationship between housing prices and the commute time to a major metropolitan area. The longer the commute, the lower the price. To maximize your resale potential, choose areas that are close to public transportation suitable for commuters and that have good prospects for future economic growth. Buyers looking for affordable housing who

*Cape Cod Cottage*
*A one-and-one-half-story cottage with a gamble or gambrel roof, clapboard or shingle siding, double hung windows, and the front door at the center of the house. Dormer windows are common.*

don't relish a long commute should consider buying a condominium or townhouse in a desirable neighborhood closer to town. Single family homes usually cost significantly more than condominiums. Buying a condominium is one way to purchase in an expensive area that would otherwise be way out of your price range.

Keep the following factors in mind when you are comparing neighborhoods. A neighborhood with a lot of "pending sale" and "sold" real estate signs is usually in demand. If homeowners in the area are remodeling, they are generally happy with the neighborhood. If homes are selling with multiple offers, this also indicates a healthy interest in the area. Ask your real estate agent to research whether the gap between list prices and sale prices is increasing or decreasing. If the gap is declining, the neighborhood is probably improving. Other positive signs are an increase in the number of out-of-area buyers moving in, an increase in local residents trading up within the neighborhood, an increase in the percentage of owner-occupants (and a decrease in the percentage of renters), and a lot of local community involvement.

Ask about plans to improve local transportation. An area once hard to get to can become a coveted place to live when public transportation becomes available. Property values in the Oakland suburb of Rockridge, located across the bay from San Francisco, shot up when the Rockridge BART (Bay Area Rapid Transit) station opened in 1972. The BART station turned Rockridge into a commuter's haven. Shops and restaurants opened to satisfy a growing demand for services. Rockridge is now one of Oakland's trendiest neighborhoods.

Neighborhood newspapers are a great source of information about what is happening locally. Sensitive topics of concern to the community—plans for zoning changes, freeway and shopping-center construction, demolition of landmarks, etc.—are usually reported in the local newspaper. If the neighborhood has a homeowner's association, this is another good resource. Talk to an association officer and ask to see copies of recent newsletters. Contact the local municipality planning and zoning departments; ask about current zoning and if any changes are proposed. Make sure any property you buy is zoned to permit your intended use. For instance, if your livelihood depends on your running a day-care business from your home, make sure you can do this without violating local laws.

Ask about the intended use for large parcels of vacant land in the neighborhood. If a school will be constructed across the street from the property you are considering, this could have a detrimental effect on the property's value. The noise level may rise, parking may become scarce, and traffic could become a problem. But if a school is going in two blocks away, this could have a positive effect on the value of properties in the area that aren't located directly across the street. Find out about the quality and enrollment in local schools, even if you don't have children yourself. If the local schools aren't used by local homeowners, this can have a negative impact on property values.

Check with the local engineering department about records of any landslides in the area. If you are buying a house that is near a recent slide, you may want a soils engineer to do an analysis of the property.

You should also find out if the property is located near a hazardous waste site. Ask the local planning department or contact the Environmental Risk Information and Imaging Services in Alexandria, Va., for a report of such sites. The report costs $75; call 1-800-989-0403 to order.

By spending some time on the street where you plan to live, you can learn things that you wouldn't otherwise discover until you move in. You might find out that the house is on a cut-through street that gets heavy use from locals. The street will get a lot of traffic, it may be noisy, and it may be less desirable for families with small children. Visit the neighborhood on your own at several different times of day and night. Talk to neighbors. Visit the local schools and shops. Drive from the home to your job a few times during rush hour. If you are dependent on public transportation, find out what is available and how accessible it is. If crime is a concern, visit the local precinct and ask for recent crime statistics.

If you haven't had time to completely investigate a neighborhood before you make an offer to buy a home there, include an inspection contingency in the purchase contract that is broad enough to encompass a neighborhood as well as a home inspection. Such a contingency might state that your offer is contingent upon any and all inspections of the property and neighborhood that the buyers deem necessary. If you only want to buy the home if you can answer a very specific question about the neighborhood, then write this in as a contingency of the contract. For example, the contract might be contingent on the buyers confirming that an apartment house cannot be built next door to the property.

Watch for signs of overbuilding. Developers often flock to high-demand areas. If the area becomes oversaturated with inventory, this can tip the scales so that more homes become available relative to the number of prospective buyers. This tends to create a "soft" market that usually depresses property values.

To sum up, it is impossible to discover everything about a neighborhood before you buy a home, but, at the least, you want to know about local problems: noise, traffic, future construction, rezoning, unreasonable zoning or homeowner association restrictions, as well as contamination, blight and neglect, crime, and vandalism. You cannot count on someone else to enlighten you on these issues. Plan to investigate on your own.

**The quality of local schools usually has an impact on property values in the area.**

# Analyzing the floor plan

Since the floor plan or room layout effects how well you and your family will live in a home, it's important to analyze the floor plan before you buy. Some floor plans are inherently better than others. A home that is made up of a maze of rooms, one connecting to another like cars of a train, can cause endless frustrations. Occupants can't get from one part of the home to another without walking through room after room; lack of privacy becomes a problem.

A classic, good floor plan is the central hall plan. This plan has an entry hall at the center that serves as a hub for the other rooms. Ideally, the living room, dining room, and kitchen are accessible from the central hall without your having to walk through other rooms. Such a plan is said to have good "flow," or circulation.

Your lifestyle needs will set the parameters for your ideal room layout. If you have small children, you will probably want to have bedrooms away from public areas, like the living room or family room. You may also want a family room on the main living level, adjacent to the kitchen. You may want the master bedroom to be on the same level as the children's bedrooms. Families with teenage children, on the other hand, often want the children's bedrooms to be as far away from the master bedroom as possible. You may want a lower-level rumpus room for children well away from the living room, which can be reserved for adult entertaining.

**The room layout affects how your family will live in the home.**

**Georgian**
*A formal and dignified home with balanced proportion, symmetry, and Classical detailing. Other features include: a central hall plan, plaster walls, interior sculptural ornamentation, double-hung windows, and a pitched roof.*

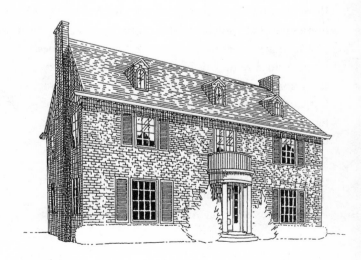

Kitchens are important. Two interior entrances to the kitchen and a door to the outside are best. A kitchen that opens level-out to the yard is a plus, particularly for families with small children. An eating area in the kitchen is desirable. The stove, sink, refrigerator, and countertop workspace should be close to one another.

You can never have too much storage space. A dry basement can provide a good storage area. Storage containers or lofts can often be added to an ample-sized garage. Beware of a home that has neither a garage nor a basement. An attic with a pulldown stair system may be the answer; otherwise you could have a serious storage problem. Take a good look at the seller's furnishings. A master bedroom with beautiful antique armoires and chest of drawers may lack adequate closet space. Likewise, a country kitchen with an enchanting china hutch may be deficient in cabinet space.

Floor-plan features in demand include at least one bathroom on each living level, a formal dining area, a laundry in a convenient location, a master bedroom with its own bathroom (called a suite), at least three bedrooms on one level, easy access from the garage into the home (ideally to the kitchen), plenty of countertop space and cabinets in the kitchen, a pantry, a place to store brooms and cleaning supplies, a fireplace in the living room, lack of wasted space, and updated kitchen and baths.

It may help you to understand a floor plan if you sketch the room layout on a piece of paper. Some buyers find it helpful to draw their furniture onto the floor-plan diagram. This can help you visualize how you will use a home. A furniture diagram will also be a handy guide to furniture placement on moving day. Computer software programs are available that allow you to convert room dimensions into a three-dimensional floor plan into which you can insert pieces of furniture.

Room size is an important consideration. Small rooms and rooms without windows are problematic. Odd-shaped rooms and rooms with windows on several walls can make furniture arrangement difficult. If you have large pieces of furniture, measure them. Take these measurements and a tape measure with you to a home that you are seriously considering. Measure the space you have in mind for the furniture item to make sure it will fit. If a piece of your furniture doesn't fit, don't necessarily exclude the home from your list. Consider replacing the piece of furniture if the home is perfect in all other respects, and you have looked for months for the right place.

**Many defects in a home are correctable, but a truly bad floor plan may be incurable.**

# How important is curb appeal?

Your real estate agent may tell you that a house is "not a drive-by." This means that what you see of the home from the street isn't impressive. It lacks "curb appeal." Curb appeal describes the impression a property makes on people who view it from the street. A building that looks charming, architecturally distinctive, and well-maintained has good curb appeal.

Some buyers won't even look at the inside of a home that lacks curb appeal, although this differs from one buyer to the next. It also depends on the variety and number of homes a buyer has to choose from. Given the choice between a house with an ugly facade and one that's beautiful, most buyers will opt for beauty. But an unlimited choice of homes for sale is rare. Really gorgeous properties usually sell at premium prices, which makes them too expensive for some buyers. But, if you can afford to pay the price, buying a home with curb appeal is probably a good investment. These homes are easiest to resell.

For some buyers, image is the most important factor. Someone who is status-conscious may want a home that has an imposing street presence, perhaps a large two-story house. A retired home buyer, on the other hand, might be motivated to buy an all-level home for health reasons. A retiree who is both status- and health-driven might fall in love with a one-level home in a prestigious neighborhood. The neighborhood would provide the curb appeal that the home lacks.

Neighborhoods have curb appeal. Homes in a run-down neighborhood or in a tract of modest bungalows will sell for less than homes in a prestigious neighborhood of large estates. The curb appeal of a neighbor's house can affect your house, negatively so if that house is poorly maintained. Curb appeal is related to maintenance. Good curb appeal could mean a home that is very well maintained. Conversely, little or no curb appeal might mean that the home suffers from deferred maintenance: peeling exterior paint, a rotting fence, a brown lawn, and a roof that is shot. This sort of curb appeal can be remedied, at a price. Such a home might be a good deal if you can see past the tired facade and if you can buy it at a price that compensates you for the money and effort it will take to restore it.

Curb appeal also refers to architectural pizzazz. An impressive two-story Greek Revival–style home, with tall columns, a second-story gallery, and plantation shutters, will usually sell more quickly and for more money than a similar home with a less imposing street presence. It's possible to improve a home's architectural appeal. Sometimes too much detail can be a problem. Or the exterior colors may be atrocious.

**Greek Revival**
*A two- or three-story home, often with a low-pitched gable roof. The front porch is sheltered by an overhanging roof which is supported by a row of columns. Doors, windows, and frequently a second-story balcony are recessed behind the row of columns.*

A home can be so overgrown with foliage that it has virtually no curb appeal. These defects are all correctable. A home that is too bland can be improved by adding landscaping, fences, shutters, dormer windows, moldings, a good paint job, window boxes, or a front porch. If you can't figure out what to do to improve the curb appeal of a home, ask an architect, color consultant, or landscape architect.

Great curb appeal will never make up for an incurably defective interior. Cosmetics can be changed, but a bad floor plan may be something you will have to live with forever. Don't buy a home based on its curb appeal alone.

# Evaluating property condition

With luck, you will have plenty of inventory to choose from when you decide to look for a home. For some buyers, however, a lot of homes for sale make the selection process tedious and confusing. Remember, you are looking for the best home you can find in your price range. Using your list of housing needs and wants, you will filter through the choice of properties available, eliminating the misfits until you find one you want to buy. One of your selection criteria should be property condition.

Any home you buy should be thoroughly inspected by qualified, impartial professionals. But paying to inspect properties that you don't ultimately buy is a waste of several hundred dollars. Before you make an offer, try to determine whether a home you are considering is one you would never actually buy because of property problems. You will save yourself a lot of time and money, not to mention disappointment.

Novice home buyers usually know little, if anything, about construction and home maintenance. First-timers should make it a high priority to find out as much as possible about what makes a building structurally sound and how to keep it that way. This information will help you make an informed decision about which home to buy. It's also essential information to have as a homeowner. Keeping a home in good repair is the best way to preserve your investment in a property.

You can start learning about home construction by selecting an agent who knows the subject. When you look at properties, have your agent point out examples of good and bad construction, as well as problems relating to deferred maintenance. If you have a friend who is a contractor, architect, or engineer, mention that you are looking for a home and that you would appreciate some advice. Most people love to talk about a subject they know something about. You may want to ask such a friend to take a look at a home you're considering to see if he or she spots any glaring defects.

Find out as much as you can about a property before you make an offer. Ask if the sellers have filled out a seller disclosure statement. If they have, get a copy of it and review it before making a written offer. If defects are disclosed that you are concerned about, have your agent contact the sellers or their agent to get more information. If the sellers haven't completed a seller disclosure statement, ask your agent to find out if the sellers know of any defects.

Find out if there are reports on the property. The sellers may have ordered inspections before listing, or reports could have been done by buyers who decided against buying the property. Ask your agent to get copies of any reports that are available (or get copies directly from the seller if an agent is not involved) and review them. Find out approximately what it will cost to remedy defects that you can't live with. Ask if the sellers will fix these problems, or give you a price break if you purchase the property "as is." If not, you might want to find another home to buy, unless the property is a good buy despite the work required.

**Water is a major cause of structural defects.**

Water should be directed away from structures. Find out if there is any standing water in, under, or around the building. If there is, the property may have a drainage problem, which could be expensive and time-consuming to fix. A musty odor can indicate a drainage problem. So can sloping floors and crooked door and window frames. A leaky roof will be a major expense if it's at the end of its life and needs replacement. Stains on ceilings can indicate that the roof is shot. This kind of evidence may not be visible if the sellers did a fix-up-for-sale paint job before marketing the property. Ask the sellers how old the roof is and if they have had any roof problems.

Find out the age and condition of all the major systems on the property: plumbing, electrical, furnace, air conditioning, hot water heater, spa, pool heater and filter, well and septic system, etc. When were these systems last replaced, serviced, or updated? Is the seller aware of any defects in these systems?

Your personal investigations should never substitute for an inspection by a professional home inspector or inspectors. But your sleuthing should help you decide whether it is worthwhile to make an offer at all—an offer that includes an inspection contingency. See Chapter 5 for more information about inspections.

**Contemporary**
Contemporary is a generic term for modern architectural designs. Contemporaries reflect experimentation with style, shape, scale, and unusual multi-level floor plans. They frequently feature economical designs and energy efficiency, often including active or passive solar systems.

# Deciding what kind of home to buy

## Buying a new home

Owning a new home could be one of the most pleasant experiences of your life—or one of the worst. So exercise diligent care and caution when embarking to the world of new construction.

There are definite advantages to buying a home that's new. Since the home hasn't been lived in, there is no wear and tear or deferred maintenance to worry about. You may be able to have some input on the finishing details. If so, you can avoid the expense and hassle of redecorating to suit your taste. A new home should be built to current code requirements; there should be no need to modernize and retrofit outmoded systems. New homes have up-to-date floor plans and modern amenities. They tend to be more expensive than older homes, but they usually are more energy efficient, which will save you money in the long run. A shortcoming of new-homes projects is a lack of architectural diversity. But even though the homes may lack distinctiveness, new developments offer an appealing lifestyle, often with on-site recreational facilities and security.

A well-built new home will need minimal maintenance for many years. It will hold its value well and be relatively easy to resell. A sloppily built home will be a headache, or worse. It may be difficult to get the builder back to make repairs. A builder who didn't take pride in his work to begin with may not stand behind his shoddy product. Be sure to research the reputation of the builder before you buy into a project. Buying from a developer with a good track record for producing quality homes is one of your best protections.

Visit other, older developments that were constructed by the same builder to check out the quality of workmanship. How do the builder's homes look several years later? Is the project improving with age, or does it look tatty and run-down? Talk to homeowners in some of the builder's older projects. How responsive is the builder to taking care of the inevitable problems that develop? Even a new roof can leak. Does the builder take care of such defects promptly, no questions asked? Or do the homeowners have to hire attorneys to get the builder to do anything?

The best developers are vitally concerned with customer satisfaction. They can't afford to have rumors develop that damage the developer's ability to sell other housing projects. These developers usually have a customer-service department with a staff of employees, who handle customer complaints. Find out if the project you are considering has such a department. If not, how will defects be remedied when they arise?

Investigate the builder's reputation with lenders and materials suppliers. Check at the county courthouse to see if any lawsuits have been filed against the builder. Talk to subcontractors who worked for the builder. Ask if the builder cut corners during construction and if he

**A new home is only as good as its builder.**

paid his bills on time. Contact the local Better Business Bureau and the state contractor's licensing bureau, if you live in a state that licenses builders, to find out if complaints have been filed against the developer. Contact a real estate attorney or the state contractors' licensing agency about the builder's liability for defects. Make sure the builder will give you a written warranty on latent defects for a year or two. The builder's warranty should be included in your purchase agreement.

---

**TALES FROM THE TRENCHES: EPISODE 7**

*Jannie and Bill bought a new house in a small development in a very desirable neighborhood. Demand for houses was high in the exclusive little project, and there was a limited supply, so Jannie and Bill bought quickly without giving a thought to investigating the builder. Bill had owned a new house; it was a hassle-free experience. Jannie had only owned older homes in the past, but she assumed that Bill's positive past experience was a common one for new-homes buyers. Several years after they bought, one house after another in the project developed similar problems. First, the windows and skylights leaked. Then the drainage systems failed. Finally, water began seeping through the exterior walls of some of the units. To make matters worse, the builder had hit financial hard times since he completed the project. Even if the homeowners in the development were able to win a case in court against the builder, it is unlikely they would collect enough money to remedy the problems.*

---

Hire a professional to inspect a new home. Just because a home is new doesn't mean it was built correctly. City inspectors sometimes overlook code violations. Ask the builder for copies of any reports on the property, including the soils report. Have your inspector review these, as well as architectural plans, surveys, engineering calculations, city building inspections, and any other construction documents. The developer may be reluctant to turn over any documentation that is not required by law, but get as much as you can or make arrangements for your representatives to review the documents at the developer's sales office.

You may want to hire someone to check out the construction in progress from time to time. The developer's purchase contract may restrict your access to the project while it is under construction. If so, make sure that the purchase agreement allows you the right to complete inspections periodically. Your final inspection should be about a week before closing so the builder has time to finish up any last-minute details. You may want to have your inspector accompany you on the final walk-through to help you prepare a list of finishing details the builder needs to complete by closing (often called a punch list).

When you buy in a new-homes project, you usually have to use the developer's sales agent and purchase contract. Some projects will permit outside broker cooperation. This means that the builder will share the sales commission with an outside agent, as long as that agent introduced the buyers to the project. The outside agent usually has to physically bring the buyers to the project, or at least, personally register the buyers with the sales office. You may get a slightly better deal if the builder doesn't have to split the commission with another broker, but this will vary from one builder to the next. And, your outside sales agent may have very little to do with the sales transaction, even though he or she might want to. Most developers insist that a project sales agent write the purchase contract and handle the transaction details. Sometimes, the developer has several individuals involved: the sales agent, a design person (who helps the buyers select finishing details), and someone else to handle the financing and closing details.

This doesn't mean that you should not use an outside broker if you are buying into a project that permits it. You may want to look at resales in the area, as well as new homes. An outside agent can show them all to you, and can help you decide where and what to buy. Even though your agent can't write the purchase contract, he or she can review it for you. If you don't have an outside agent to assist you, you may want to hire a real estate attorney to review the purchase contract for you.

Obviously you will want to buy into a successful project, and at the best price you can negotiate. A developer whose project does not sell well may end up auctioning off the unsold units. If the auctioned units sell for considerably less than you paid, the value of your investment will drop.

Location is critical to consider when selecting a new development. If the surrounding community is booming economically, this bodes well for the success of the project. If there are restrictions on future development in the area, this will benefit property owners of already existing homes because the housing supply will be limited.

Location within a project is also important. The best locations sell the fastest and for the most money. Plan on paying more for a prime location. Corner lots tend to have more property, but they can also be noisy. Cul-de-sac locations are often in demand because they are more secluded. The best locations usually have the best views and are always in the highest demand.

Buyers are often frustrated that, unlike the resale market, there may be no room for negotiating the price of a new home. This will vary depending on current market conditions and on how well a project is selling. Most builders would rather upgrade amenities for buyers (light fixtures, floor coverings, bath and kitchen finishes) than lower the purchase price. If a developer agrees to accept a lower price, it may be difficult to sell future homes for higher prices.

**The price on a new home is often non-negotiable, but the builder may make concessions on upgrades and closing costs.**

The value of upgrades can be as much as $10,000 to $20,000—a nice incentive to pay full price. In a slow market, you will get more for your money. But if a project is in high demand, you may have to pay full price, plus the cost of upgrades.

New homes are often sold from models spruced up with designer amenities and upgrades not included in the standard home. Be sure you know what is included in the price. If you negotiate for the builder to include upgrades in the price, check around with outside suppliers to see if the builder's prices for those upgrades are reasonable. Some builders charge an inflated price. For example, the builder may agree to give you $10,000 worth of upgrades that are worth only $5,000 on the open market. If the builder charges a minimal mark up on the upgrades, having the builder do the work may be worthwhile. If not, negotiate to have the developer pay your points or buy down the interest rate on your mortgage instead. In this case, have the home finished with the minimum that is required to get a notice of completion, which your lender will require to close. Then install the upgrades at your own expense after closing.

Be prepared to make decisions about construction finishing details and upgrades according to the builder's time table. You may think it unreasonable when the builder notifies you that you must tell him which kitchen linoleum you want within two or three days. Remember, the builder must stay on a schedule if you are to move into a completed home on time. Try to make many finishing detail decisions well in advance so that you don't feel pressed to make snap decisions.

New homes usually don't have window coverings or landscaping. Some developers put in the front landscaping, but nothing in back. This is a hidden cost that you should factor into the cost of buying a new home. In a slower market, you may be able to negotiate a landscaping allowance from the builder.

An itemized list of finishing details, and who is paying for them, should be made a part of the purchase agreement, and should be signed by you and the builder.

Homes in planned unit developments (PUDs) often have use restrictions, described in the Covenants, Conditions, and Restrictions (CC&Rs). Make sure you read and approve the CC&Rs. Also, know the amount of the homeowner's dues and if there any additional assessments, such as for new roads or a sanitary sewer system. How long are the current association dues expected to be in effect, and how much are they expected to rise in the future? If the dues and the association's reserve account are too low, special assessments will be levied for future repairs, such as repaving roads, driveways, and tennis courts. You should expect that homeowner's dues will rise as the project ages and the general cost of living increases.

There can be unanticipated delays in building a new home. If you are currently renting, don't give a thirty-day notice to vacate your present home until you are sure of the occupancy date on your new home. If you are selling a home to buy the new one, build as much flexibility into your purchase contract as you can. Try to negotiate a rent-back option with your buyer, in case your new home isn't done on time. Find out if the builder will pay the cost of an interim rental (or hotel room) if construction is unexpectedly delayed at the last minute, and you have to move out of your current place.

Be careful about buying when the market is soft. If the development isn't selling well, the builder might not be able to complete future phases. Also, the builder might have to lower prices on newer models to sell them. Developers have been guilty of over-building in some areas. If the market is saturated with new-homes projects, and the housing supply exceeds buyer demand, this will have a negative impact on prices.

Builders used to provide financing for buyers who purchased homes in their developments. This is rarely the case now. However, most builders have at least one lender lined up to provide buyers with home loans. Although you don't have to use this lender, you may find that it makes sense to do so because the lender is familiar with the project. Your loan will probably get processed more quickly and with fewer hassles than if you went to a lender who was unfamiliar with the project.

Home buyers who are shopping the new-homes market exclusively and who will not be working with their own agent can usually find new-homes projects in the classified section of the local Sunday newspaper. Also, check on-line services like America Online, Compuserve, or the Internet for new homes listings. See the section later in this chapter for more information about how to find a home on the Internet.

### Buying an older home

Most buyers purchase older homes, which tend to be less expensive than new homes. That is, when you consider the purchase price alone. But an older house may need refurbishing or retrofitting with new systems, such as heating or plumbing. An older home is usually less energy efficient. Although less expensive to get into, it can end up being more expensive than a new home when all factors are considered.

Many home buyers will buy only an older home, despite these drawbacks. One reason is that older homes tend to have architectural distinctiveness. They are often located in neighborhoods that were developed over a period of time by various builders. They offer a variety of architectural styles, so your home won't look just like the one next door. Buyers who are influenced by curb appeal are often attracted to older homes. Some older homes were built with a level of craftsmanship and a quality of building materials that are hard to find today. For instance, a two-by-four no longer measures a true two by four inches. It's skimpier by about one-half inch in each direction. Home inspectors often deplore the condition of the plumbing and electrical systems in older homes, and they may not be too keen on the state of the foundation, but they frequently prefer the quality of the framing in a 1920s or 1930s home.

Older homes are often loaded with architectural details that are expensive to reproduce today, including high ceilings, decorative moldings, hardwood floors, sun rooms or solariums, French doors and windows, columns and pillars, porches, dormer windows, distinctive roof lines, built-in bookshelves and buffets, and leaded and stained-glass windows, to name a few. Some of the most popular new home styles incorporate these favorite features found in older homes, but usually without the quality of materials and craftsmanship of the past.

Location, of course, is one of the primary reasons for buying a home. A good location is a guarantee of sorts. Homes located in the best locations tend to hold their value better than homes in less desirable locations when the market suffers a downturn. The best locations tend to experience the most appreciation during an upturn. One benefit of buying existing homes is that they were usually built in the best locations available at the time. New-home projects are frequently built in areas that were considered undesirable decades ago. Older neighborhoods are often centrally located, offering good access to freeways, workplaces, theaters, entertainment, cultural activities, and shopping centers. New-home developments are often built on the outskirts of town and are less convenient and may lack facilities. Schools are often better in the more established neighborhoods. When you buy an existing home in an established neighborhood, tree-lined streets are commonplace and yards are usually landscaped, unlike the bare look of many new-home projects.

Maintenance will be higher on an older home if major systems such as the plumbing, heating, electricity, hot water heater, roof, appliances, or drainage have not been renovated or replaced recently. Ask the sellers about the age of these systems. Have they been updated or are they original? Ask for a list of repairs and modifications the sellers have made to these systems, including when they were made. (While you're at it, ask the sellers for copies of utility bills to determine the cost of heating an older home.) Home protection plans (also called home warranties) are available in most states. These cover the major systems of a home for one year. You may want to have one of these plans

### Traditional

*Traditional is a general term used to describe an older style home that does not have a clearly defined style, such as an English Tudor. Traditional style homes often have two stories, a pitched roof, a stucco exterior, hardwood floors, interior floor and ceiling moldings, and a central hall plan.*

in effect at closing. They cost in the range of $250 to $300 per year. Either the buyer or seller can purchase the plan, or the cost can be shared. See chapters 4 and 5 for more about home protection plans.

Another consideration is that most older homes are not built to modern building code requirements. A resale home may not be able to withstand the devastation of a hurricane or a major earthquake as well a new home. Older homes can be modernized to bring them in line with modern codes, but in some cases the cost to do this far outweighs the benefits gained. Older homes often contain materials that are environmentally hazardous, such as asbestos or lead. State laws differ regarding a seller's responsibility for disclosure and removal of environmental hazards on the property. You may need to complete more inspections on an older home than you will on a new home. But it is money well spent.

One benefit of buying an older home is that you can tell how it has withstood the test of time. A defective foundation or drainage system may not be immediately apparent in a new home; years may pass before such problems may develop. Some problems such as soil instability and structural defects are often easier to detect in an old home than they are in a new one.

Owning an older home can be demanding, requiring more maintenance and restoration on an on-going basis. You either have to be prepared to do the work yourself or hire someone else to do it. But there is no disputing that living in a charming older home is immensely pleasurable, if you can afford it.

## Buying a home that needs work

Since the perfect home does not exist, you may decide to settle for one that comes close to your ideal and fix it up over time to more approximate your dream. Or you may find a property that meets your housing wants and needs, except that it is in a state of disrepair. Buyers often shy away from buying homes that need work. Some buyers are not prepared to take on the work and expense of a fix-up project. Others fear that because a property needs work, there is something inherently wrong with it. This is often an irrational fear. Termite infestation, for example, is not usually terminal. Once the infestation is eliminated and the destruction repaired, the building may be like new again. Good home maintenance is the best defense against future termite problems.

A property should not be ruled out just because the termite bill is large, the roof needs replacing, the exterior paint is peeling, and the landscaping has gone to seed. A home suffering from deferred maintenance might be perfect for you once those problems are eliminated. Just make sure before you buy that you know all there is to know about what is wrong. Hire inspectors to check all the systems: foundation, roof, plumbing and heating, drainage, electrical, and appliances. Make sure that any reports provided by the seller are current and complete. If a termite inspector recommends further inspections, have these done to make sure there isn't additional hidden damage. Factor the cost to fix the problems into the price you pay.

A shabby property that isn't selling may be one that you can buy at a discounted price. How and when the fix-up work is done can be negotiated between the buyers and sellers. One approach is to ask the seller to pay for the work, and to have the work completed by closing. Many contractors will agree to take payment for their work at closing, as long as they know there is a bona fide sale in progress. This can present a scheduling problem, however, if you want to close quickly and the work cannot be done in time. Most sellers prefer to sell "as is" and have the buyers complete the work after closing. Buying "as is" can also be beneficial to the buyers because they can deduct the amount of the work and pay a lower purchase price. Some sellers will discount the price even more for an "as is" sale and thus be relieved of the responsibility and hassle of the work. Also, many fees associated with buying a home, as well as property taxes, are based on the purchase price, so your closing costs will be less if you buy "as is," at a lower price. Another benefit of an "as is" purchase is that you may be able to hire contractors to do the work for less than the seller's termite company or roofer will charge.

Buying "as is" requires that you have the extra cash to complete the renovations yourself. If you are cash poor, you may prefer to pay a higher price and have the sellers credit money to you at closing to cover the cost of the repairs. This can work to both the buyer's and seller's advantage. The seller doesn't have to do the work before closing, and it generates cash for the buyer's renovations. This also gives the buyer the option to make changes, such as remodeling a deck or bath that are in need of termite or dry rot repairs. And, the buyer can oversee the work after closing.

### Colonial
*Although there is considerable variability, Colonial homes usually have a square or rectangular shape, a pitched roof, clapboard wood siding, and louvered shutters.*

The buyer's lender may have a say in which of the above approaches you use. A lender might not permit either an "as is" sale or a credit from the seller if the repair work is significant. If the lender's appraiser sees conditions that need repair and notes this in the appraisal, the lender may require that the work be done before closing, particularly if the loan is going to be sold to an investor who might be concerned about purchasing a loan secured by a run-down property. Portfolio lenders may be more lenient regarding "as is" sales.

Sometimes, however, lenders will permit completion of the work after closing. In this case, the lender may require that surplus funds (usually one and one half to two times the cost of the work) be held in an escrow or trust account after closing until the job is complete. The sellers usually provide the extra money, but this is negotiable. Unused funds should be returned to the party that provided the extra money.

Most lenders have a limit on how much money they will permit the seller to credit to the buyer at closing—often no more than 3 to 6 percent of the purchase price. The lender may also want the credit to be called a "credit for buyer's nonrecurring closing costs." (Nonrecurring closing costs are paid for by the buyer one time only, at closing, and can include points, transfer taxes, and title insurance. See Chapter 1 for more information about nonrecurring closing costs.) The amount of the credit usually cannot be more than the actual amount of your nonrecurring costs. So if you are buying a $350,000 house with a $20,000 termite bill and your nonrecurring closing costs total $10,000, the seller will only be able to credit you $10,000. One solution would be to have the seller complete $10,000 worth of termite repairs before closing and credit you the rest of the money. Or the seller could issue a $10,000 check to the contractor to start work, which could be completed after the closing. Another approach is to have the seller give you a certified check made out to the contractor. When you are satisfied that the job is completed satisfactorily, you can release the check to the contractor.

### Fixer-uppers

Some properties need a little work, others need a major overhaul. Those in need of an extensive redo are typically called fixer-uppers or fixers. Renovating fixers was highly profitable for some speculators in the mid- to late-1980s, when home prices in many areas of the country were escalating rapidly. Renovating fixers for profit seemed a quick way to make easy money. You simply had to find a wreck of a house, buy it cheap, slap on a coat of fresh paint, spruce up the bathrooms and kitchen, and resell it mere months later for a handsome mark-up.

What seems too good to be true often is. Renovating fixers is hard work, requiring a lot of time, expertise, and talent. You need to know what to buy and where and how much to pay for it. Market research is critical to the success of a profitable fixer-upper project. Knowing the best locations for fixer projects is not simply an art; it is usually the result of extensive investigation. As with any property, you should buy in the best location you can afford for the best possible price. Research comparable sales in the area to learn market value so you avoid paying too much. Also, find out which properties are in the highest demand. You will want your project to resell as quickly as possible after the renovations are complete, and your renovations must appeal to future home buyers. Creating a visual masterpiece for which there are no buyers could result in financial ruin.

Buying right is not enough. You need to know how much to spend on renovations, which renovations to do, and which not to do. Cosmetic enhancements, like paint and floor coverings, can be relatively inexpensive, and they usually yield a good return on your investment. But they must be selected with the ultimate buyer in mind. If your makeover is done in shades of green but buyers prefer beiges and grays, you may find there is a limited market for your project. Even professional renovators hire interior designers and architects as consultants to keep them from making costly mistakes. If you hire good advisers, your profits should increase.

The best fixer projects are properties with limited appeal in their present condition but that don't have major structural problems or incurable defects—a bad floor plan that cannot be fixed without rebuilding, for example. Correcting an unanticipated structural defect could eat into any profit you might realize when you sell. It's imperative to fully inspect a fixer, even if you have a lot of past experience and think you know it all. Watch out for environmentally hazardous materials on the property. If you miss something that a future buyer insists you remedy when you sell (such as asbestos on furnace pipes, a buried heating oil tank, or lead paint), you could see your profit decline significantly. If your renovations will involve moving walls, consult an architect before you buy to make sure that what you have in mind is feasible.

Working within the parameters of a budget is essential if you hope to profit from your fix-up efforts. Also, keep in mind that if you miscalculate and have to cut corners in areas that are important to today's home buyers, you may have difficulty selling at a profit— or selling at all. Home buyers expect quality and they will pay for it. But they will not overpay for someone else's sloppy improvements. Kitchens, bathrooms, storage space, good lighting, quality finishes in the kitchen and bathrooms, kitchen-family room combinations, home offices, and a spacious master bedroom suite with a private bath and a large walk-in closet are among the features buyers like. Pay a little extra for some of the less expensive finishing items, such as light fixtures, switch plates, hardware (doorknobs, cabinet pulls, and knobs), and bathroom plumbing fixtures. Curb appeal is also important, so plan on improving the landscaping and the front entry.

Financing improvements is a major consideration. Factor into your budget the interest payments you will make during the time it takes to complete the project. When you buy your fixer, the sellers may be willing to provide some financing for you, particularly if they are having difficulty selling the home. A seller who can't carry a first loan may be willing to carry a small second mortgage, say for 10 percent of the purchase price. If a seller will not agree to carry any financing, find a conventional lender who will provide a first mortgage and a line of credit to be used for the improvements. Financing the

# The fixer-upper budget

|  | Profitable fixer-upper project | Unprofitable fixer-upper project |
|---|---|---|
| Purchase price: | $100,000 | $100,000 |
| Renovation costs: | $25,000 | $35,000 |
| Unanticipated costs: | $5,000 | $25,000 |
| Carrying costs during renovation: mortgage interest, taxes, insurance=$1,500 per month | $4,500 (3 months) | $12,000 (8 months) |
| Sale costs: | $11,000 | $11,000 |
| Total cost: | $145,500 | $183,000 |
| Market appreciation/depreciation: | +$3,000 (Market increased 1% per month) | -$5,000 (Market declined after rising for 3 months) |
| Sale price: | $186,000 | $178,000 |
| Profit/loss: | $40,500 profit | $5,000 loss |

purchase of a fixer-upper with a new adjustable-rate mortgage (ARM) that is assumable by a subsequent buyer makes good sense. The interest rate and monthly payment will be lower than on a fixed-rate loan, therefore, the costs of completing the project will be less. If new financing is difficult to obtain by the time you are ready to sell, a buyer can take over your existing loan. The FHA 203K loan program can be used to finance restorations of single-family residences to a maximum of $152,000. For more information, contact a lender or mortgage broker who offers FHA loan programs.

Timing your fixer project can be critical to its success. Try to embark on such a project when home prices are on the rise. This way you not only make a profit by turning an unsalable property into one that is in demand, you also earn some appreciation. Be cautious about the market if prices have been climbing steadily for some time. The market may be poised for a downward correction. If this happens, depreciation in home prices and a soft market could diminish or wipe out any profits you might be counting on.

A less risky fixer project is one you buy to fix up and occupy yourself for a period of time. The longer you occupy the property, the less risk. You can ride out a decline in the market and choose the best time to sell. Also, it's easier for owner-occupants to get financing. However, it can be extremely difficult to live in a property while extensive renovation is going on.

Carefully consider whether you have the temperament to be a successful renovator. Fix-up projects must be carefully supervised to keep them on time and close to budget. It is difficult, if not impossible, to renovate properties for profit if you work full time at another job. A profitable renovator must be well-organized, have a critical eye, be attentive to details, and have the ability to thrive in an environment of total chaos and endless frustration.

**Probate sales**

A probate sale involves a property that is being sold to settle the estate of someone who has died. State law governs probate sales, which may require court approval. Sometimes the sale of a probate property may allow open bidding on the property at the court confirmation hearing, where you could lose the property to another bidder. If you are buying a probate property subject to court confirmation and an over-bid is possible, you may want to delay giving notice to vacate your current home until your offer is confirmed by the court.

Just like foreclosures and fixer-uppers, probates used to have a reputation for being bargain properties. This is rarely the case anymore because most estate sale properties are listed by real estate agents who establish a list price based on the current market value. An estate property that is listed at a comparatively low price may be in need of a lot of work, often because their former owners were elderly or in ill-health, and unable to keep up with necessary maintenance. Given the deferred maintenance, a low list price on a probate might not be a bargain.

**French Provincial**
*A balanced, symmetrical architectural design with a high pitched hip roof, French windows and shutters, and usually two or more floors.*

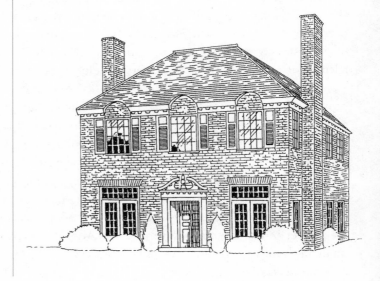

Estate sales are also often sold "as is" to protect the heirs who may have little or no actual knowledge of the property. As with any property, be sure to have it thoroughly inspected by professionals. If court confirmation is a part of the process, you may have to complete inspections before your offer can be approved by the court.

The court confirmation process can be nerve-racking for some home buyers. You don't know for sure that you will get the property until your offer is confirmed in court. In a slow market, over-bidding is less common, particularly if you are paying fair market value. In a rapidly appreciating market, over-bidding is more common. Before you go to court, know the top price you are willing to pay, and don't let yourself get caught up in the frenzy of a bidding competition. Don't pay more than you should.

---

**TALES FROM THE TRENCHES: EPISODE 8**

*Jake was a developer who renovated older homes for profit. He saw a French Provincial house he liked that was being sold as part of a probate. The executor for the estate had already accepted an offer from another buyer. But the sale had to be court confirmed, and over-bidding from other buyers was permitted. Jake hired contractors to inspect the property and he lined up financing. He went to court prepared to pay whatever he needed to secure the house. After several rounds of over-bidding, the first buyer reached his price limit and dropped out of the contest. Jake won the bidding contest by paying $80,000 more than the initial offer price. This was great news for the beneficiaries of the estate. But it was eventually bad news for Jake, who ended up losing a lot of money when he had difficulty selling the property after it was renovated. The real estate market turned sour while he was fixing up the property. In addition, Jake paid way too much for the property to begin with.*

---

Although buying a probate property involves uncertainty, it may be worth the anxiety. Probate properties may need rehabilitation, but some are classic old homes that have not been botched up by tacky remodeling. Buying an old home in original condition is better than undoing someone else's bad renovation, which can be time-consuming and costly.

## Buying a condominium or townhouse

When you buy a single-family detached house, regardless of whether it is new or old, you purchase exclusive ownership rights to the entire property. You become the sole owner. Your property boundary lines distinguish what is yours from what belongs to your neighbors. When you purchase an attached dwelling, such as a condominium or town-house, you acquire exclusive ownership to the interior space of a particular dwelling unit. You share walls, fences, grounds, and facilities, called the common area, with other owners in the condominium or townhouse complex.

As a condo owner, you automatically become a member of a homeowner's association to which you pay monthly or annual dues. Homeowner's dues usually pay for ongoing maintenance of the common areas and for hazard insurance for the complex. The dues may also cover the cost of property maintenance, services such as garbage collection and gardening, and replacement of some building elements (such as boilers and elevators) when necessary. Dues may also fund a reserve account to cover the cost of major expenses, such as repainting the entire exterior of the complex or repairing damage caused by an earthquake or hurricane.

Condo ownership is often recommended for first-time buyers and homeowners who are retiring because the homeowner's association takes care of many routine upkeep chores. This creates a relatively low-maintenance lifestyle. However, to get the most benefit from your homeowner's association, you should plan on devoting time to running its affairs in rotation with your co-owners. Condos and townhouses are generally less expensive than single-family residences in the same area, which appeals to first-time buyers. In terms of resale, a one- or two-bedroom condo is a better investment than a studio, if you can afford it.

Buying a condo or townhouse involves some of the same issues as buying a single-family detached house. You should make sure that the unit suits most of your housing needs and at least some of your wants. You should have it inspected by a home inspector who has experience with the kind of project you are buying into. Ideally, try to find an inspector who has inspected other units in the same project. The inspector should thoroughly inspect the unit you are buying and also look at the quality of construction and condition of the common areas. If common areas and facilities will need major renovation in the near future, this could affect the true cost of your condo. Say that the tennis courts need resurfacing and the swimming pool is badly cracked. If the homeowner's association reserve fund is insufficient to cover these expenses, the individual homeowners are usually assessed for the shortfall.

Unlike buying most single-family houses, attached housing projects are governed by covenants, conditions, and restrictions (called CC&Rs). Read the CC&Rs, bylaws, and articles of incorporation of the homeowner's association carefully. One drawback of living in a planned community development is that you don't have unrestricted ownership privileges. The CC&Rs may spell out restrictions on remodeling, renting, and reselling. They may prohibit pets. If you have difficulty making sense of the CC&Rs and associated legal documents, hire a knowledgeable real estate attorney to review them for you.

You should try to gather as much information about the project as you can before you buy. Ask to see a current financial statement. Attend a homeowner's association meeting and review the minutes of past meetings. Interview residents. Try to buy into a condo development owned predominantly by owner-occupants rather than investors who own units to rent out to tenants. Owners tend to demand a higher caliber of

# Condo buyer's checklist

| Address: | Comments |
|---|---|

Number of units in complex?

Percentage of owner-occupants?

Percentage of unsold units?

Monthly homeowner association dues?
    What do dues cover?
    How often have dues been increased?
    Any anticipated increase in dues?
    How many homeowners are delinquent in paying dues?

Is there a fee for transferring association membership?

What does homeowner's association insurance cover?
    Will you need additional insurance coverage?

Is homeowner association professionally managed?

Amount in the association reserve account?
    Any large expenses anticipated?

Is the association involved in litigation?
(Status and likely resolution?)

Are pets allowed?

Can you rent your unit out?

Are there restrictions that will cramp your style?

How many parking spaces are included?

How many storage spaces are included?

What common facilities are included?

What do current owners like best about the complex?
(Interview a few owners.)

What do current owners like least about the complex?

How is the soundproofing?

How are water pressure, heating systems, etc.?

Does the developer have a good reputation?

Are sale prices going up? Down?

How active are condo sales?

Review past homeowner association meeting minutes.

Attend homeowner's association meeting.

Review CC&Rs (Covenants, Conditions, and Restrictions).

Review bylaws and articles of incorporation, or have an attorney review them.

management and maintenance because they live in the project and observe its condition and operation on a day-to-day basis. A high percentage of renters can indicate that the original developer was unable to sell the project when it was new. Find out how many units are still owned by the original developer. Some lenders won't approve new mortgages for buyers purchasing a unit in a condo development with a large percentage of renters.

Find out specifically what the homeowner's association fee covers, how much it costs, when it is due, and how often and by how much it has been raised in the past. Homeowner's dues projections listed at new construction sites are sometimes unrealistically low. Anticipate that they will go up in the future and budget for this increase. Older projects will tend to have higher monthly dues than newer projects. If the association fee seems high, find out why. In an older building, a high fee might be needed to cover an elevator operator or to replace worn-out building facilities. Ask about anticipated increases in the association dues in the near future. How many homeowners are delinquent in making their dues? A high percentage of delinquencies might indicate dissatisfaction with the association's management. What recourse does the association have when an association member defaults on the dues payments? Find out all you can about the association reserve account. How big is it? Are any major projects planned that will deplete the reserve account? If you are buying a resale condo, find out the amount of the homeowner's association transfer fee and who is responsible for paying the fee. State law may set limits on how much an association can charge for a membership transfer. Double check to be sure you are not being unlawfully overcharged.

Your homeowner's dues will probably help pay the hazard insurance for the entire project. Get a copy of the policy and make sure that there is adequate coverage. For example, if your complex burns down, will the association policy cover the cost to rebuild? Find out precisely what the policy covers. In California, you might want earthquake insurance, which requires an additional endorsement to the policy. After the Loma Prieta earthquake in 1989, the Watergate Condominiums in Emeryville, California, suffered damage. Since the homeowner's association did not have earthquake coverage, the individual association members had to pay an extra assessment in addition to their monthly dues, to pay for the repairs. You will probably need to buy a condo owner insurance policy on your own to cover your personal possessions, liability, and perhaps even the interior finishes of your individual unit. Be aware that your lender may want a copy of the association insurance policy.

**Homeowner's association dues are taken into account by the lender in qualifying you for a loan: they are not tax-deductible on a primary residence.**

Perhaps you have heard horror stories about condominium owners who end up suing the developer over shoddy construction. A condo that seems like an incredible buy may be in a complex that's involved in litigation. Find out if the homeowner's association is suing the builder for structural defects. If the association loses and cannot afford to repair defects, what is the potential amount individual owners will have to pay to remedy the problems? In some litigation-plagued condo projects, resale activity is at a virtual standstill until the litigation is resolved.

Some buyers object to large condo projects because they seem too much like the apartment complexes where they have been renting. A large project may seem impersonal to you, but the owners often hire a management company to take care of the maintenance and financial details, such as collecting delinquent homeowner's dues. In a smaller, more intimate complex you may have to be more involved personally in handling the association's affairs. Disputes can be more difficult to resolve in a small complex because there are fewer voting members. If you want to minimize home maintenance and management concerns, you may be better off buying in a large, well-run complex.

Find out about parking privileges. Will you have a dedicated garage or parking space, or is parking on a first come, first served basis? Is there adequate parking for visitors? Is additional storage provided or available if needed? Also, find out if the building is adequately soundproofed. Talk to several owners who currently live in the complex about the quality of the soundproofing, and if there are any ongoing problems that you should be aware of. Ask current owners what they like—and don't like—about the condo or townhouse complex.

### Row House
A row house usually has two or more floors and is attached on at least one side to another similar dwelling. Row houses are built in a variety of architectural styles. The Italianate style pictured here features curved windows, robust wrought iron stair rails, a high stoop, an ornate door, and a bracketed roof cornice.

An offer to purchase a condo or townhouse should include a contingency for the buyers to read and approve the CC&Rs, bylaws and financial statement, a declaration of any pending litigation, and any other relevant documents.

> Be sure to read and understand the CC&Rs of the homeowner's association yourself—don't delegate this important task to someone else.

Some lenders will not fund loans for buyers of units in new condominium and townhouse developments until a certain percentage (usually 50 to 70 percent) of the units in the development are pre-sold. Also, if you are buying into a new project, there can be completion delays. If you are renting, don't give your landlord a thirty-day notice until you know that the lender will give you financing and that the development will be completed on time. If you are selling another residence to buy a condo or townhouse that is being constructed, try to negotiate a flexible closing or possession date with your buyers in case of unexpected delays.

### Buying a cooperative

Buying a cooperative (also called a co-op or apartment) is similar to buying a condo because in both cases you are buying a home in cooperation with a community of other homeowners, and you and your fellow co-owners share the responsibilities of managing and maintaining the property. But there is a very important difference between the two types of ownership. When you buy a condo, you own your interior living space, and you share the ownership of the common areas with the other co-owners. When you buy into a cooperative, you buy shares of stock in a corporation; the corporation owns the property. The corporation, of which you are a shareholder, leases your individual unit to you. As a cooperative owner, you are simultaneously an owner, a landlord, and a tenant.

Shares of stock in a cooperative are divided according to the relative value of the units. For example, the owner of a dark basement studio will have fewer shares of stock than the owner of a two-bedroom penthouse with a river view. The more shares of stock an owner has, the more clout he or she has when issues affecting the cooperative are put to the vote of the shareholders.

Learn as much as possible about how a cooperative is run before you buy. Any offer should include a contingency for your satisfactory review of the cooperative's documents, including the articles of incorporation, the by-laws, the house rules, and the proprietary lease. If you have difficulty understanding any of these documents, have them reviewed by an attorney who specializes in cooperatives. Some co-ops prohibit renting; others don't allow pets. Make sure that you can live with the restrictions before you buy.

You should carefully review the co-op's financial statements and operating budget. Ask to see copies of financial statements for the past five years so you can determine how well the cooperative has been managed financially. How much does the co-op pay for salaries? Does the co-op hire a professional management company? If so, how good is the company? The financial statement should give you information about the underlying mortgage. A cooperative with a high mortgage balance relative to the property value could be a risky investment. The financial statement should also tell you if any shareholders are delinquent on their maintenance fees, and if the cooperative maintains an adequate reserve fund to take care of major maintenance and renovations. If you have difficulty making sense of the financial statements, consult a CPA who has expertise in cooperative finances.

Like a condo, a cooperative shareholder pays a monthly maintenance fee. Unlike a condo, part of the maintenance fee usually pays a portion of the cooperative property taxes and underlying mortgage, for which cooperative owners can take a tax deduction. But according to IRS code section 216, cooperative owners lose this tax write-off if more than 20 percent of the cooperative's annual income for the year came from sources other than the shareholders. This could occur if the cooperative leased part of the building to nonshareholders, such as in a mixed-use building.

Financing a cooperative can be difficult, particularly in areas where cooperative ownership is uncommon. In one cooperative project in Oakland, California, where cooperative ownership is rare, the only way owners could sell was to provide seller-financing. Conventional lenders would not lend on the project. In New York City, however, financing cooperatives is relatively easy because cooperative ownership is common. Some lenders consider cooperative lending risky because they can't foreclose on a defaulting borrower and take back the property. If a cooperative borrower defaults, the lender may end up with shares of stock in the cooperative corporation rather than with the property itself.

Another way cooperative ownership differs from condo ownership is that the co-op's board of directors has the power to approve or disapprove any buyer. The board cannot turn down a prospective buyer for a reason based on illegal discrimination. But the board can disapprove a buyer for any other reason, or for no reason at all. For example, the board may require a minimum net worth. Or the board might turn down buyers who intend to do a major renovation of their unit because it would be too disruptive for other cooperative members. Prospective buyers from the entertainment industry are routinely turned down at some prestigious co-ops because they are entertainers. At this writing, it is not illegal to discriminate based on profession.

Your fellow share-owners can wield a lot of power over you, so learn as much as you can about them before buying. Meet the board of directors. Talk to co-op owners to find out how much they like living there, and to find out if you like them. The doorman and the maintenance manager can be a wealth of information. Ask if there are any pending assessments or litigation against the project.

As with buying any kind of property, investigate the physical condition of a cooperative. Have property professionally inspected and ask to see the cooperative's prospectus. If the cooperative was converted from an apartment building, which is often the case, there should be an engineer's report on the physical condition of the property.

If so, hire an engineer or an architect who is familiar with cooperatives to review the report for you. What major renovations have been done and are any planned in the future?

Part of your maintenance fee will cover the cost of insurance for the cooperative. Check into the coverage and make sure the project is adequately insured. As with a condo, you will probably need additional insurance coverage for the contents of and improvements to your individual unit. Upgrades you make to your unit may not be covered by the co-op insurance policy.

Be sure to explore the neighborhood carefully. If there is a vacant lot or a building under construction next door to your unit, find out what is planned. A high-rise may interfere with the natural light in your dwelling. Investigate crime rates, traffic patterns, proximity to shops and transportation, just as you would when buying any kind of property.

Find out what percentage of the shares are still owned by the cooperative developers. Ideally, you want to buy into a cooperative with a low percentage of developer-owned (also called sponsor-owned) units. Ask how well the cooperative has been selling. The resale value of a cooperative will depend on its location, how well run and financially solvent it is, and on the services provided.

Buying into a cooperative takes careful investigation. However, the benefit is that you can buy a home of your own in an area where single-family residences may be prohibitively expensive.

# Short sales and foreclosures

In a conventional home sale, the property is sold for enough money to pay off the existing mortgage or mortgages, and to pay the sellers' closing costs (real estate broker commission, transfer taxes, property tax proration, etc.). When the mortgage amount plus closing costs equal more than the selling price, the sellers are "short" the amount needed to close the sale.

Sellers with sufficient financial resources can use money from other sources, such as savings, to pay the amount they are deficient and complete the sale. Sellers unable to do this may convince their lender to accept a loan payoff that is less than the amount owed. A "short sale" refers to a sale where the lender agrees to accept a reduced loan payoff. Some lenders call this a "workout."

You may wonder why a lender would agree to accept less than full payment. Many lenders won't. But some lenders would prefer to clear the loan from their books, even at a loss. When a borrower becomes delinquent on loan payments the lender is often faced with a foreclosure procedure, which is costly.

The number of short sales has increased in recent years in some areas of the country where home prices have declined from their peak levels at the end of the 1980s. Suppose you bought your home in 1989. Since then your home has dropped 20 percent in value. If you bought with a mortgage for 90 percent of the purchase price, your current loan balance could exceed the current market value of your home. If you are transferred and have no alternative but to sell your home and move, you could find yourself needing a short sale to sell at all.

A disclosure should be made to prospective buyers if the sellers need a short sale. The purchase contract may need to include a contingency for the sellers to secure the lender's agreement to accept less than a full loan payment. Many lenders won't consider doing a short sale until the property is marketed and the sellers are sure that they cannot sell for enough to pay the loan off completely. Buyers should insist that the contract specify a time frame for the sellers to obtain permission from the lender to do a short sale. Thirty days should be sufficient, unless MI (mortgage insurance) approval is required. In this case, the approval process could take forty-five to ninety days. Make sure the sellers get the lender's written consent to take a short loan payoff.

You'll need an extra pound of patience to buy a home that is being sold subject to the lender agreeing to a short sale. The process usually takes time. It also requires persistent, savvy negotiation on the part of the sellers and/or their agent. If an agent isn't involved in the transaction, the seller would be wise to hire a knowledgeable real estate attorney to help negotiate a short sale agreement with the lender.

Your purchase contract to buy any property should include a requirement for the sellers to provide you with clear title to the property. If a title search reveals loans secured against the property in excess of the purchase price, the sellers may need permission from their lenders to do a short sale. But this is not always the case. A title search could show many loans secured against the property because the sellers refinanced, perhaps several times. When old loans are paid off through a refinance, they are supposed to be reconveyed. A reconveyance removes a loan that has been paid off from the title record. Sometimes when loans are paid off they aren't reconveyed because of an oversight. This is usually easy to fix, and it should not stop a deal. As soon as you discover that the property you are buying is overencumbered, give the sellers written notice that you object, and that you expect them to remedy the situation before closing. If the sellers can't do this, you may not be obligated to complete the purchase.

Make sure to have a short sale property thoroughly inspected. Lenders will usually only consider accepting a short loan payoff if the sellers are in a hardship situation. The lender will probably insist that the sale be "as is" with respect to property defects and will probably not allow any credits from the sellers to the buyers for repairs. Sellers who lack enough extra money to pay off their loan deficiency may have neglected maintenance and repairs.

You may have more difficulty negotiating the price on a short sale property than on a property where the sellers are making a profit. But even though these sellers will want the highest price possible to minimize their losses, they usually have a strong motivation to sell. If they didn't have an urgent need to sell, they would wait for the market to improve before selling.

## Foreclosures

Sellers who are selling short may still be current on their mortgage payments. A foreclosure sale, on the other hand, is a distressed sale that occurs after the owners stop making mortgage payments. Several types of foreclosure proceedings exist, and state law governs the specifics of how foreclosures are handled. Often foreclosure properties are sold to the highest bidder. Those properties not sold off to a new owner revert to the lender and are called REOs, industry jargon for "Real Estate Owned." REOs are often listed for sale through a real estate broker, but sometimes lenders have an inventory of REOs that are not actively marketed.

You may get a good deal by buying a foreclosure property, but buying foreclosures, like fixer-uppers, requires hard work and thorough research. Often touted as a quick way to get rich, you can just as easily lose your shirt on foreclosures. They are not recommended for first-time home buyers. If property values have dropped since the property was purchased, the remaining loan balance could exceed the market value of the property. So you may not get a great break on the price. To avoid overpaying, you need to know current market values in the area.

Some foreclosure sales require a contingency-free offer for all cash and the purchase must be "as is" regarding property condition. If this is the case, make sure to have the property thoroughly inspected before you make an offer. A distressed sale property might be in bad condition. If you have to pay all cash without the benefit of a financing contingency, you will need to arrange for a mortgage ahead of time, before making an offer. This means incurring costs—for appraisals, loan processing fees, and inspections—before you know if you will be the successful bidder. If you are negotiating directly with a lender's REO department, you may be able to include contract contingencies for financing and inspections in a purchase contract. If you are bidding on a property at a foreclosure sale, your offer will probably have to be contingency-free.

Another problem with foreclosures is that it is difficult to find truly good deals. In some states, lenders record a notice of default after a borrower becomes delinquent on loan payments. Some newspapers print these notices of default, or you may be able to research them at the County Recorder's Office. Some foreclosure experts research notices of default and try to buy properties directly from the defaulting owners before foreclosure happens. But buying a property directly from an owner in default can be risky. An owner who is in jeopardy of losing a property because of financial hardship may have judgments and other outstanding debts secured against the property. If these are not cleared by the time the sale goes through, the creditors may be able to make claim to the property, or look to you for debt satisfaction. Conduct a thorough title search to ensure that you don't buy someone else's bad debts.

**Buying foreclosure properties requires a lot of research and is not recommended for novice home buyers.**

Foreclosure sales are usually advertised in local newspapers, or on-line. The Federal Housing Administration (FHA) and Veterans Administration (VA) periodically announce the availability of their foreclosure properties, usually in newspaper ads and now on the Internet. Some lenders do not tend to aggressively market their REO properties. You may be able to uncover a hidden treasure by contacting lenders' REO departments directly for a list of their available inventories.

Novice buyers who are intent on including foreclosures in their home search should engage the services of a real estate agent or attorney who has expertise in buying and selling foreclosure properties. Your local association of Realtors may be able to recommend such an agent. Or ask a lender's REO officer for the names of local agents who handle a lot of foreclosures.

# Lease options

Leasing with an option to buy is one way for cash-strapped or marginally qualified buyers to become homeowners. A lease option is used by some transferring home buyers who have a home to sell in another location. The lease period provides the optionees time to sell their existing home before buying another one. Here's how it works: The prospective buyers (optionees) lease the property from the seller (optioner) for a period of time. The lease option contract gives the optionees/buyers the right to buy the property at the end of the lease period or earlier at the price agreed to in the contract. In exchange for this privilege, the optionees pay a sum (called option money) to the seller. The option money is applied to the purchase price if the optionees complete the purchase; otherwise, the option money is forfeited to the seller. For a minimal investment, optionees/buyers are able to tie up a property at today's prices, and live in it for a time before deciding to complete the purchase. During the lease period, the sellers cannot sell the property to another buyer. If the sellers do receive another offer and accept it in a backup position, the optionees have the first right to buy the property according to the terms of their lease option contract. During the lease period of the option agreement, the buyers hope to have enough time to accumulate the cash necessary for the down payment so they can complete the sale if they want to. It's a good idea to get prequalified and preapproved (if possible) with a lender before you enter into a lease option agreement so that you know exactly how much income and cash you will need to complete the purchase at the end of the lease.

As with any purchase contract, all the terms of a lease option are negotiable: the length of the lease, the purchase price, the amount of the option money, and the amount of rent. Often a portion of the rent is credited to the purchase price if the buyers exercise the option and complete the purchase. For example, the lease could run for one year, with the optionees paying rent of $1,500 a month. The option agreement might specify that if the optionees complete the purchase, $500 of each month's rent will be applied to the purchase price. If the optionees rent for a full year before they exercise their option and complete the purchase, they will have a credit toward the purchase price of $6,000. You may have to pay higher than market rent for a lease option that includes a credit toward the purchase price of a portion of the rent. Some lenders restrict how much of the rent credit can apply to the purchase price. If the lender won't allow all of your rent credit to apply toward the purchase price, ask if the rent credit can be used to offset your nonrecurring closing costs.

The lease option contract has two parts. The first deals with the particulars of the lease option. The second is the actual purchase agreement that will take effect if the optionees decide to buy the property at the end of the lease period. The terms of the purchase agreement should be negotiated at the time the lease option is signed and should include contingencies for the buyers to inspect the property, obtain financing, and inspect title to the property. It's a good idea to inspect the property and get preapproval for financing before you move in. A cursory title check is also advisable, but you would want this checked again before closing to make sure no changes have occurred. For more information about purchase contracts and contingencies, see Chapter 4.

Buyers are often disappointed to discover that there aren't many lease option listings on the market. But relatively few sellers are able to consider selling on a lease option. If the sellers need all their cash from the sale to purchase another home, a lease option usually won't work. Lease options are more common in a slow market when sellers can't sell. In this situation, a seller might be happy to have rental income from a lease optionee to cover the mortgage payment for a time. Usually, only properties that are not selling for one reason or another are offered on a lease option basis. The best properties are snapped up by motivated buyers who can complete the purchase within a short time. Buyers who restrict their home search to lease options may be disappointed in the selection.

You may have heard that real estate agents don't like to negotiate lease option agreements because they don't make as much money as on a sale. This is not entirely true. Agents who assist in putting lease option deals together usually make the same amount of money as they would on a conventional sale; they just have to wait longer to get paid. The agent usually receives a lease commission when the lease goes into effect; if the sale is completed, the lease commission amount is often subtracted from the sale commission. It is true that some agents have limited experience with lease options because most homes are sold outright. If you are working with an inexperienced agent, make sure to have a knowledgeable real estate attorney review or draft the agreement.

Since lease option listings represent a small percentage of the residential sale market, you may have to create your own lease option opportunities by searching the "homes for rent" ads in a local newspaper. Some landlords who are not intending to sell might be convinced to give you a lease with an option to buy. If you are already renting a home that you would like to own, you can approach your landlord/owner to see if a lease option arrangement is possible. If there is no agent involved, the lease option agreement can be drafted by an attorney or real estate broker (in many states) for a fee.

Although a lease option may seem like the ideal way to buy with a small cash investment, it is a waste of money if you never complete the purchase. A lease option is usually only a good deal for the buyers if they do complete the purchase. But studies show that most lease option buyers never exercise the option and close the purchase. Don't pay option money to lease a property that you know you will never buy. You're better off renting without an option and saving the option money for a down payment on a home you want to buy. If you have any reservations about purchasing a property you are leasing with an option to buy, try to negotiate the smallest amount of option money possible.

# Buying a home long distance

Moving to a new location involves a similar game plan to that described at the beginning of this chapter. The major difference is that much of the research and follow-through must be done from a distance. Technology makes this easier all the time. But buying in a location where you have never lived and about which you know little usually adds additional stress and uncertainty to the already challenging home buying experience.

Find an agent to represent you who will cut your workload and look out for your best interests. You should work with an agent who has experience helping transferring home buyers—one who will understand your specialized needs. Such an agent can anticipate potential problems and resolve them swiftly. He or she will help you select a neighborhood and reduce the amount of research you have to do from a distance. He or she will take care of arranging financing and other closing details so that you can attend to the monumental task of physically moving from one place to the next.

You can find an agent several ways. If you are moved by the company you work for, the company may have a relocation specialist who can help you find an agent or agents. If not, ask friends or associates in the new location for agent recommendations. You may be selling a home to buy a new one. If so, ask your listing agent to find an agent for you in the new location. Many agents work for large real estate companies that have relocation divisions or that are associated with a relocation company. If your agent is a Certified Residential Specialist (CRS), he or she will have a national directory of CRS agents and should be able to find you a CRS agent who specializes in your new locale.

Relocation companies have coordinators who put home buyers and sellers in touch with agents who specialize in the appropriate locations. You can even contact a relocation company yourself and ask to be referred to an agent. If you do work through a relocation company, ask the coordinator to send you a relocation package on your destination location with information about local schools, recreation and cultural facilities, the local economy, commute times to major metropolitan centers, and the climate.

The Internet and other on-line services like America Online and Compuserve can be useful to transferring home buyers. General information about your new community is on the Internet: schools, weather, the local economy, cultural and sporting activities, etc. You can also search for listings in the new location. Many real estate companies and individual agents have home pages on the Internet that describe properties they have listed for sale. You may actually find an agent you want to work with. Just make sure that you carefully screen the agent before committing to working with him or her. (See page 94 for more information about shopping for a home on the Internet.)

Most people will make a fact-finding visit to a new location before deciding to make the move. Whether this is at your own expense or not, you will probably have a lot to accomplish in a short amount of time. To avoid wasting time looking at properties that will never suit your needs, make sure that you carefully screen the agents you are considering before you make the trip. Ask the agents to send you copies of their résumés. These should specify the length of time they have been in the business. If the agent wasn't referred to you by someone whose opinion you respect, ask for references and check them. You can tell a lot about an agent in several phone interviews. If you build an easy rapport, this is a good sign. If you feel that the agent and you are not on the same wavelength, look for another agent.

Make sure that you work with agents who specialize in the areas you are considering. You may need to work with several agents if you are looking in several market areas. Carefully review your list of housing wants and needs with each agent. The more you can tell each agent in advance about what you want and need in a home, the easier it will be to eliminate homes that won't work. Looking at the wrong properties or the wrong neighborhoods is a waste of your valuable time.

**TALES FROM THE TRENCHES: EPISODE 9**

*Martha and Tom were moving from California to New York, where Tom was offered a lucrative position as CEO of a company with headquarters on Long Island. A colleague at work referred his real estate agent to Tom. Tom talked briefly with the agent, and she set up an appointment to show property to him and Martha in the Huntington area. Tom told the agent their price range and that they wanted a light, airy house. The agent never talked to Martha before the day the three met to look at property. Consequently, Martha wasted a day looking at thirteen houses she hated. The agent had interpreted "light and airy" to mean a contemporary house with an open floor plan. However, Tom and Martha wanted a traditional-style home with good natural light, similar to the home they owned in California. Had the agent talked to Martha and asked Tom more specific questions about what they were looking for, she would have saved everyone a lot of time.*

Home prices vary significantly from one place to the next. In 1995, for example, the National Association of Home Builders Housing Opportunity Index survey found that the median home price in San Francisco was $283,000—the highest in the nation. The same survey found that the lowest median price in the nation that year was about one-fifth that, in Jamestown, New York, with a median home price of $56,000. (See the section in this chapter on pricing for more information about median home prices.) Find out how much housing will cost in the new location before you commit to making the move. Also, find out what your current home is worth. Determine how much more or less you will have to pay in the new location for a home that is equivalent to yours.

In the mid-1990s, many California homeowners who accepted transfers out of state got a rude awakening when they discovered that the value of their homes had dropped 20 percent or more. In some cases, they couldn't sell their homes for enough to pay off their mortgages and closing costs. These transferees had to either arrange a short sale with their lender or use savings to make up for the amount they were short. Some employers may be willing to help out financially in a situation like this, but many will not. A wonderful new job opportunity may or may not be worth taking a one-time loss on a home. Know in advance how the transfer will impact you financially.

Once you decide where you want to live, subscribe to the local paper to find out more about the community. Many newspapers are on-line; if so, you can save the cost of a subscription. Your agent may be willing to send you the paper from time to time, or at least pertinent articles. Large newsstands often carry out-of-area newspapers.

If you can't find a home to buy in the short time period you have to look, consider renting initially. Renting for a while gives you the opportunity to learn more about the new location before you buy. This is a great strategy if you are uncertain about where you want to live. It also can give you time to sell your home, if you need to do so to buy a new one. If you are selling one home and buying another and you will have gain from the sale, you will need to buy a new home within two years of selling the old one to defer paying tax on the gain. (See Chapter 8 for more information on capital gain taxes.)

Transferees who think they will be moved again soon may want to postpone buying until after their next transfer. Whether buying makes sense for the short term depends on whether home prices are stable, rising, or falling. Suppose you buy at the peak of the market, just before a downward correction. If you are transferred in a couple of years before the market corrects upward again, you could end up selling at a loss. It's usually risky to buy for a period of less than five years, unless home prices are on the upswing.

# Shopping for a home on the Internet

Thanks to the marvels of modern technology, you can view pictures of homes for sale across the nation (and in some cities abroad, too) in the comfort of your own home. You don't have to be a computer expert to take advantage of the many home-shopping and information sources available on the Internet. All you need is a personal computer (with at least a 386 central processor and 4 megabytes of memory—the more megabytes, the better), a modem (with a baud rate of at least 14.4—the faster, the better), and a subscription to an on-line service like America Online (AOL) or Compuserve, one of the many local Internet-access providers, or to a larger provider such as Netcom or PSI. You will also need a browser like Netscape Navigator, Netcruiser, or Microsoft's Internet Explorer. Browsers allow you to surf the Internet with ease.

Information about buying real estate is available on the Internet from many sources: real estate brokerage companies, multiple listing services, lenders, consumer advocate groups, newspapers, universities, and chambers of commerce, among others. Information sources have sites (also called home pages). Each site or home page has an Internet address, which starts with the prefix http://. This prefix is followed by more detailed location specifics, including the name or an abbreviated name of the site promoter. The Internet address for the National Association of Realtors (NAR) is http://www.realtor.com. The Department of Housing and Urban Development, where you'll find information about FHA loans, is at http://www.hud.gov. "www" refers to the World Wide Web, a massive part of the Internet that connects more than fifty thousand Internet sites. "com" at the end of an Internet address means the site is commercial, "edu" designates an educational entity, and "gov" is a government site.

To connect to the NAR Internet site, simply type the address (http://www.realtor.com) into the site locator line or space on your browser and press the enter key on your keyboard. The NAR home page appears. Each home page you visit will have highlighted words (called links), often underlined in blue or graphically enhanced to look like buttons. Each link you select gives you access to additional information.

More than 4,000 real estate home pages are on the Internet. Obviously, you can't look through each to find the information you need. To simplify your search, browsers give you access to search engines like Yahoo! and Alta Vista. Search engines are sophisticated tools that allow you to hunt for information by subject. When you find home pages that contain relevant information, it's easy to return to these sites because browsers include a site-marking feature, often called a bookmark, that tags a site so you can return to it quickly without going through another time-consuming search.

**You may not find the home you buy on the Internet, but you can use on-line home-shopping services to gather information quickly.**

Let's say that you are moving to Miami, Florida, and you know nothing about the cost of housing, the local schools, property taxes, the weather, recreational activities, or where to live. One way to start your research is to access the Internet and use a search engine to conduct a general search. Type in "Miami homes for sale." This will generate a list of Internet sites containing information about the Miami residential real estate market—both general information about the area and listings of homes for sale. You can browse through these, noting sites you would like to revisit in the future and tagging them with a bookmark.

Hasten your search by visiting real estate home pages that link information from many real estate sites together in one place. For example, the International Real Estate Directory (http://www.ired.com) provides a directory of thousands of sites from around the world, as well as general information about buying and selling real estate. The International Real Estate Directory (IRED) locates listings of homes for sale anywhere in the United States. Go to the IRED Directory and then to U.S. property listings, which are grouped by state. To find Miami listings, select Florida. This will generate a list of home pages that specialize in Florida real estate, including the Florida Living Network, which is the Florida Association of Realtors home page. You can narrow your search further by selecting the South Florida option for access to realty home pages with listings in Miami and Palm Beach.

HomeScout (http://www.homescout.com) includes information on hundreds of thousands of home listings from numerous Internet sites in the United States and Canada. After you connect to the HomeScout home page, simply type in the name of the city and state, the maximum sale price, and the minimum number of bedrooms. Listing Link is another site with listings of homes for sale from multiple listing services around the country (http://www.listinglink.com). The NAR site, also called RIN (Realtor Information Network), is another good place to search for property listings and general real estate information (http://www.realtor.com). You no longer have to go through a real estate agent to access multiple listing service information about properties listed for sale. At this writing, some multiple listing services are still in the process of putting their listing inventories on-line. But many of the larger multiple listing services, like that in Miami, are already on-line.

One problem: you can't go to one site for all the multiple listing service listings from across the country, at least not yet. Listing Link and RIN are competing with one another. In southern California, the San Diego multiple listings are on RIN (http://www.realtor.com). But San Francisco Bay Area listings are on Listing Link (http://www.listinglink.com). To save time, call the local association of Realtors in an area where you want to look for homes and ask where you can find their listings on the Internet. Or ask your agent, if you have one.

**Call a local association of Realtors, a real estate company, or a knowledgeable agent to find out where you can find local property listings on-line.**

Let's say you want to peruse the Miami Association of Realtor multiple listings. One way is to connect to IRED and then link up with the Florida Living Network. Once connected, you can search for Miami listings. Or you can connect to the RIN site. This home page will give you access to a national map. The states with listings on-line are highlighted. Select Florida on the map and a list of counties and cities pops up. For each locale you can search for properties by price range, number of bedrooms and baths, and other features. One caution: Don't limit your search parameters too much. For the best results, keep your search general. For instance, if you are looking for a home in the $200,000 to $250,000 price range with three bedrooms and two bathrooms, search for all properties in the $200,000 to $300,000 price range that have at least one bedroom. This will generate a larger selection of listings. When you select a listing, you will usually be able to see at least one photo (usually the exterior shot) of the property, a description of the property's amenities, and the listing agent or company to contact for more information. For some listings, four or five interior shots are also provided. When you find a listing that looks interesting, you can e-mail, fax, or phone the listing agent for more specifics.

Large real estate companies have home pages that will, in time, include all their listings across the nation. For example, if you want to preview Coldwell Banker's listings anywhere in the U.S. or Canada, go to http://www.coldwellbanker.com. For REMax listings, http://www.remax.com. To find listings offered by smaller local real estate companies, you will probably have the most success by using a site like the International Real Estate Directory (http://www.ired.com), from which you can generate a list of realty home pages for an area.

Remember when you are searching for listings that realty home pages are advertising vehicles for real estate companies, like classified ads in the newspaper. Real estate companies put their listings on-line to generate business for themselves. Be aware that Internet real estate ads are not yet regulated. Make sure to double check any vital information you find on the Internet for accuracy.

If you want more information about a listing but you don't want the listing real estate agent's services, let the agent know that you already have an agent. This is particularly important if you have a contract with a buyer's broker to whom you may have to pay a fee regardless of who sells you a home. If you are looking for an agent, however, you may find one to work with while searching the Internet. Some agents advertise themselves along with their listings. When you pull up information about a listing, you may also have access to the listing agent's résumé, as well as to other listings the agent is representing. Just make sure to check references before using an agent you meet on-line.

Linking up to the local newspaper is another way to search for information about homes for sale in Miami or any other city. Many newspapers around the country have Internet sites that include their real estate classified ad listings. Some realty companies who advertise in the local paper will also have their own Internet sites. If so, their Internet addresses may be included in their newspaper classified ads. Realty companies usually don't advertise all of their listings in the newspaper because it's too expensive. But advertising on the Internet is relatively cheap, so you'll probably find more inventory advertised on-line than you will in the paper.

By the way, you need to enter the Internet site address accurately. For example, if the address is all lowercase letters, you may only be able to link up to the site if you type all lowercase letters. The Internet can be unforgiving in this regard. Don't give up if you don't immediately connect to a site.

Internet addresses must be typed in correctly to connect with the site.

For busy home buyers, viewing home listings on-line may be the most time-effective way to weed out homes that would never work for you. If you are very busy, however, you may need to rely on an agent to screen inventory for you. Many good listings sell before they even reach the Internet, so a good agent is vital to your search. Also, if you are buying into a soft or declining real estate market, you may want to personally preview a lot of property before making an investment to avoid making a foolish decision. The Internet is a tool many buyers find helpful used with, not instead of, a real estate agent's services.

There will always be home buyers, however, who prefer to do it themselves. These buyers may find the various for-sale-by-owner home pages, available in many locales, useful. One such site is at http://www.owners.com. In the future, you may even be able to shop on-line for a home and contract separately for real estate services that have traditionally been available only under the conventional commission fee structure. Real estate companies may one day offer a menu of real estate brokerage services to their clients and customers, enabling home buyers and sellers to negotiate fees for specific realty services rather than simply paying a full commission. You may be able to locate the property you want to buy yourself and contract with a broker to negotiate the sale and settle the transaction for a lower fee. The conventional commission agreement will probably still be available for people who feel more comfortable delegating as much of the real estate transaction work as possible to qualified professionals.

The Internet can be used for more than finding homes to buy or searching for agents to assist you. Information about mortgages and interest rates are readily available. Banks and other lending institutions have home pages that you can visit to find out about their loan products and current interest rate quotes. Some even enable you to apply for a mortgage on-line. For general information about current interest rates, contact Mortgage Market Information Services, Inc. (MMIS) at http://www.interest.com. Two other mortgage information providers are HSH Associates at http://www.hsh.com/today.html and Bank Monitor at http://bankrate.com. For information about comparable home sales, contact Dataquick Information Systems at http://www.dataquick.com. Information about home-owner's insurance and title insurance is available at the Insurance News Network (http://www.insure.com). The United Homeowner's Association (UHA) site offers information about many aspects of the home buying process (http://www.uha.org), as does Inman News Features (http://www.inman.com).

Using the Internet to search for home listings or for general real estate information can be frustrating. Finding the information is one source of frustration; another is the time it takes to connect to a site. During peak hours when the Internet is heavily used, you'll find that information may come to you at a snail's pace. A faster modem will help. A dedicated Internet line (called an ISDN line) moves information along even faster, but it costs more. Also, keep in mind that the on-line real estate industry is in its infancy and will be changing dramatically over the next few years. You will no doubt find home pages appearing and disappearing and site addresses changing. One day, however, you may be able to preview homes from the comfort of your living room using a phone or cable line to connect your television to the Internet. But no matter how advanced or convenient on-line home-shopping services become, don't buy a home without first carefully inspecting it yourself personally. The characteristics of a home that are not transferred to you on-line may be vitally important to your home buying decision.

## Understanding pricing

The value of residential properties is based on a number of criteria. An investor might set a value on an apartment building based on how much income it produces. An insurance agent who is insuring for loss will value a home according to the cost to replace it if it's destroyed (called replacement cost value). The market value of a property may differ significantly from its income or its replacement cost value. Market value is the price that a ready, willing, and able buyer will pay for a property.

The market forces that determine home prices are the basic economic principles of supply and demand. When the supply of homes for sale is limited and buyer demand is high, the market price for homes goes up. When demand is low and there is a surplus of homes for sale, prices drop. Market conditions are constantly changing. The present market value of a home may differ from its market value at another point in time, when economic pressures are different.

**Market value is the price a ready, willing, and able buyer will pay.**

Sellers list their homes for sale at a price called the listing, list, or asking price. The list price is an amount the sellers will accept for their home. When a seller or the seller's agent says there is flexibility in the price, this usually means the sellers are willing to look at offers that are less than the list price. Most sellers build at least a little room for bargaining into the list price. Ideally, the list price is based on a thorough analysis of current market demand for the property. A well-priced listing is one priced close to what present market forces indicate the property should sell for. An overpriced listing is one priced considerably above what current buyers will pay for it.

Housing reports in the news media often talk about increases and decreases in home prices as changes in the median price of homes sold during a period of time. This is misleading because changes in the median price do not necessarily indicate how much actual home prices have increased (appreciated) or decreased (depreciated). The median price is the price that is midway between the least expensive and most expensive homes sold in an area at any given time. During that time, half the buyers purchased homes that were more expensive than the median price, and half bought homes for less than the median price.

Changes in median price measure changes in market activity. When more buyers are purchasing less expensive homes, the median price for the period falls. Conversely, when more buyers are buying larger, more expensive properties, the median price increases. The median price indicates which price range is most active. Not all price ranges will necessarily experience the same amount of market activity at any given time. Just because the median price drops by 5 percent does not mean that property values have depreciated by this amount. In fact, they may have dropped more. In California, for example, the median sale price of existing single-family homes dropped from approximately $202,000 in May 1989 to about $185,000 in April 1994. But during this time, the actual market value of houses in some areas of Southern California dropped a whopping 40 percent. Similarly, if you read that the median price of homes sold jumped 5 percent, this does not mean that the value of homes increased by this amount. It may indicate a big increase in the number of trade-up buyers in the market.

Calculating actual rates of appreciation and depreciation in home prices is difficult. If homes resold on a regular basis, without being remodeled in between sales, figuring out the actual change in a property's value over time would be easier. Your best sources of information about how much home prices are rising or falling are local real estate agents who have worked actively in an area for some time.

Statewide statistics are misleading because micro-niches of the market can experience very different rates of appreciation and depreciation. During the recent California recession, Orinda and Piedmont home prices dropped less than prices in other communities east of San Francisco. The reason for this is that Orinda and Piedmont are both upscale neighborhoods with desirable school systems. Another contributing factor was the Oakland firestorm of 1991, which left thousands of families homeless. Many of these people chose not to rebuild; instead, they used their insurance money to buy replacement homes. This created a high market demand for homes in nearby Orinda and Piedmont during a time when demand for homes in general was very low.

Experienced local agents can usually give you approximate rates of home price increases and decreases for a period of time. They have the benefit of seeing hundreds of homes sell and resell. It's not too often that they see the same property sell over and over, but they can tell you what a home similar to one you are interested in and in the same neighborhood might have sold for three, four, or five years ago.

Buyers often want to know what sellers paid for a property and what improvements they made since they bought. Value is then added or subtracted to the purchase price for any increase or decrease in home prices that has occurred since the seller purchased. Price adjustments are made to account for the seller's improvements. By so doing, the buyers arrive at an approximate current market value for the property. This approach is subjective at best, dependent on a rate of appreciation or depreciation that may or may not be accurate. And although remodeling usually adds value to a property, a poorly done job can actually lower its value.

No matter what past appreciation or depreciation rates tell you a property should be worth today, markets can change quickly. The true value of a property today is what a ready and able buyer is willing to pay for it. Make sure that you don't lose out on a property you really want just because your subjective calculations suggest it should not be worth what it is in today's market.

### How much should you pay?

Deciding how much you should pay for a property will be easier in some cases than it will be in others. If you buy in a tract or condominium development where there are a limited number of home styles and models, you will find more consistency in pricing than in an older established neighborhood with lots of housing variability. The best way to learn the market value in either case is to look at a lot of property. Visiting Sunday open houses is one way to start the education process. Keep track of homes that you see by collecting flyers and brochures. Then ask your agent to let you know when a home that you have seen sells. You will want to know the selling price, how long it took to sell, and if the sale price included any concessions to the buyers from the seller. The sale price is usually public. You may have to ask an agent for information about the details of the transaction.

Knowing the sale price of a property without knowing the terms of the sale can be misleading. A property might sell for $200,000 in its "as is" condition with the buyers paying to correct deferred maintenance at their own expense. Or the same property could sell for $200,000 with the seller paying for a new roof and the termite work and giving the buyers a $5,000 credit for their nonrecurring closing costs. The buyers in the second example are actually paying far less than $200,000 when the seller's concessions are taken into account.

**To avoid overpaying:**
- Look at a lot of listings that are similar to the home you want to buy.
- Keep track of the selling prices of similar properties you have seen.
- Ask your real estate agent to prepare a comparative market analysis of the home you want to buy.
- If you don't have an agent to help you, gather information about comparable properties; hire an appraiser.
- Do a "drive by" analysis of the comparable sales that you did not see.
- Include a contingency in your purchase agreement for the property to appraise for the purchase price.

Ask a real estate agent to prepare a complimentary comparative market analysis (CMA) of the property you are interested in buying before you make an offer to buy it. This analysis should include sales information about properties that sold within the last six months. These properties should be similar in size, condition, and amenities to the one you are considering buying, and they should be located in the same neighborhood. The more recent the sale, the closer it will be to current market value. If you are not using an agent for your home purchase, you might find one who will provide you with comparable sales information, either for a fee or in exchange for your future referral business.

The comparative market analysis should also include a list of pending sales in the neighborhood. A property with a pending sale is one where a buyer has agreed to purchase but where title to the property has not yet transferred. You probably won't be able to find out the selling price or terms of the agreement until the transaction closes because this information is confidential. But it is realistic to assume that if the property sold quickly it probably sold for close to the list price. Once a sale is complete and title passes to the buyer, the sales information is a matter of public record. If you have not seen the comparable properties on your home-hunting forays, be sure to at least drive by them and have a look at the exteriors.

Buyers often wonder if they should hire a licensed appraiser to appraise a property before they make an offer. In most cases this is not necessary because a good real estate agent can provide you with all the information you need to make an intelligent decision. However, if you don't have an agent's help you may want to hire an appraiser. And if you have any doubts about the value of the property, include a provision in the purchase contract that requires the property to appraise for no less than the purchase price. If the lender's appraisal comes in too low, you have a legitimate way out of the contract or you may be able to renegotiate the price with the seller. If you're buying all cash, without a mortgage, you will want to hire an appraiser yourself to appraise the property. This will cost from about $250 to $500.

## Paying a premium for move-in condition

The homes that sell quickly and for the most money are those that are in the best condition. Most buyers do not have the financial means, time, or inclination to renovate an outdated home. So listings that are in "move-in" condition tend to be in highest demand. These properties can sell well even in a depressed market. In a hot market, they often sell with multiple offers.

**Selling prices, not listing prices, are the true indicators of current market value.**

You should expect to pay a premium for a home that is in excellent condition, but you should avoid the temptation to overpay. Sellers will often try to justify a

# Comparative sales analysis worksheet

|  | Listing 1 | Listing 2 | Listing 3 |
|---|---|---|---|
| Sale Date: | | | |
| Property address: | | | |
| List price: | | | |
| Property description:<br>(# of bedrooms, baths,<br>additional features) | | | |
| Square footage<br>(if available): | | | |
| Property condition: | | | |
| Sale price: | | | |
| Date sold: | | | |
| Days on the market: | | | |
| Any seller concessions<br>included in the price? | | | |
| How does the property<br>compare with the home<br>you're considering? | | | |

high price for a home that they have renovated extensively. But in most cases sellers cannot expect to recoup dollar-for-dollar on their renovations.

Renovations that add the most value are remodeled kitchens and bathrooms, returning from 75 to 100 percent of the investment at the time of sale. This is not a guaranteed return, however. How much a buyer will pay for a renovation will depend in part on how well the job was executed and the quality of the materials used. Buyers will pay more for granite, tile, or Corian kitchen countertops than they will for Formica. Another key element is how well the remodel integrates with the overall style of the home and the neighborhood. A remodel that looks out of place can actually diminish the value of a property.

A third bedroom addition to a home that only had two bedrooms will pay back well. So will the addition of a second bathroom to a home that only had one before. But a seller can't expect to recoup as much from the addition of a fifth bedroom to a four-bedroom home, or from adding a fourth bathroom to a home that had three since fewer home buyers need such luxuries. Renovations that improve the indoor/outdoor living of a home usually have a high return value, such as adding French doors or a deck off the kitchen of a home that has no direct yard access. Master bedroom suite renovations and family room additions are also usually good investments.

A swimming pool or spa addition might return only half what it costs. Many buyers with small children don't want pools. Some buyers have been known to fill in a pool in order to create a larger, more usable yard. In this case, a pool might be a detriment and value could actually be subtracted from a property for the cost of getting rid of the pool. A pool will have more value in hot climates than in cooler climates where it won't get much use.

How much you should pay for the seller's improvements is ultimately determined by the market value of the property. It's conceivable that a seller's improvements might create a property that is worth more than what the seller paid for the property, plus the cost of the improvements. This would be the case if a functionally obsolete property is turned into a high-demand home. In addition to making sure that you don't overpay for a renovated property, make sure that you are getting your money's worth for the improvements. Ask for copies of the city building permits and for copies of architectural plans and invoices, if they are available. These will come in handy when the time comes for you to resell. Additions that were done without permits can cause problems. Even if the work was done by licensed contractors, your lender's appraiser might not give full value for the improvements if they were done without permits. If this happens and the appraisal comes in lower than the purchase price, the lender might not approve the loan amount you need. In this case, you might ask the seller to obtain a permit for the remodel as a condition of removing your financing contingency from the contract. It's usually possible to get a permit after the fact, although penalties might be charged and walls might have to be opened up for city building inspectors.

The best buys are usually remodeled houses where the sellers did a top-notch job for themselves, as opposed to renovations completed by a developer. Contractors who buy a property to fix up and resell will include a profit margin to the list price, and they often use cheaper materials.

# Should you buy the first home you see?

Consider yourself lucky if you find a home you like well enough to buy soon after you start your search. Some buyers look for months and occasionally even for years before they find the right home.

One problem with falling in love with the first home you see is that you probably will not know if the property is priced right. You might wonder if other homes on the market would suit you just as well, or perhaps even better. Buyers who have searched for months for a home have the benefit of knowing the inventory. They have seen everything in their price range that might work for them. They have seen properties that subsequently sold, so they have acquired some expertise about prices. Buyers who have looked at a lot of property know a well-priced home when they see it. Another benefit of seeing a lot of property before deciding on one to buy is that you develop a sense for how realistic your wish list is. You have a better sense of what compromises you are willing to make.

But don't automatically rule out buying the first home you see. If you do find the right home early in your search, have your agent give you a crash course in market value. Have your agent prepare a comparative market analysis of the property you are interested in. The next step—and this will require time and energy for both you and your agent—is to look at as many pending sales as you can. Many sellers of pending listings will continue to show the property to prospective buyers with the hope that a buyer may be willing to make a backup offer. Also, have your agent show you all the properties currently on the market in your price range that may suit your needs so you'll know if there is anything else currently on the market that may work for you. Looking at more homes should confirm whether the home you are evaluating is the right one for you.

Try to get a sense of how unique the home you are interested in might be. Ask your agent to provide you with a list of similarly priced homes with similar amenities that have sold during the past year or so. Are there many homes like the one you are interested in or is there a shortage of this type of home? If there are plenty of similar homes, there is less urgency to make an immediate decision. If there is a shortage, however, you may need to move quickly. Include a clause in your purchase contract that makes the contract contingent upon the property appraising for the purchase price to avoid overpaying.

Don't make the mistake of passing up one of the first homes you see just because it's one of the first. You may be kicking yourself later for not acting quickly if you search for months and find nothing you like as well.

**Victorian**
*Victorians feature elaborate architectural detailing, decorative exterior painting (particularly in the West), and bay windows. The Queen Anne Victorian style, for example, is characterized by odd roof lines. There is a great variety of Victorian styles, from San Francisco row houses (pictured here) to sprawling Southern plantations.*

# 4

# *Negotiating the Purchase*

Once you find the home you want to buy, you'll want to pay the lowest price possible. This presents a challenge because sellers invariably want to get the highest possible price for their home. You should be prepared to negotiate.

Not everyone feels comfortable negotiating. It can trigger feelings of vulnerability. What if the other party is more astute and takes unfair advantage of you? Negotiating conjures up visions of haggling or bickering. But this is just one way to look at negotiating. To negotiate also means to "confer" and to "settle." Most of us confer with others—colleagues, children, spouses, friends—and settle differences every day. Even though we may not think of this as negotiating, it is. If the idea of negotiating for a home makes you uneasy, try to think of it a process during which you and the sellers will confer to see if you can settle on a purchase agreement.

A home purchase negotiation typically starts with the buyers, who make a written offer to purchase the property including the price and terms acceptable to them. The sellers either accept the offer or they propose a counter offer. The written counter offer modifies the buyers' offer with a price and terms that are acceptable to the sellers. The ball is then in the buyers' court. They can either accept the sellers counter offer, or counter back to the sellers with further modifications. The process usually involves a give and take on the part of both parties. Finally, if the buyers and sellers are able to meet on price and conditions, the deal is done. The purchase contract is then said to be "ratified."

The ratified purchase contract is a legally binding contract. If all the terms of the contract are satisfied, the sellers transfer title to the buyers and the home sale is complete. If negotiations break down before the contract is ratified and the buyers and sellers are unable to reach a mutual agreement, both parties are free to go their separate ways. The buyers find another home to buy; the sellers find other buyers for their home.

Negotiations can proceed as quickly as a day or two, or they can take considerable time, sometimes weeks. Each home sale negotiation is unique, so it's impossible to know in advance how long the process will take. You are bound to feel nervous until you know the result of the negotiations. Try not to get frustrated if the process takes longer than you would like it to. The best approach is to maintain a flexible attitude; rushing these matters is difficult—and not usually desirable.

# Deciding what to offer

Although there are no set rules to tell you how much to offer, the price you decide on should not be a product of mere guesswork. A number of factors come into play. First, consider the local market conditions. Ask you agent for a market update. Find out how fast homes are selling and if they are selling for close to their asking prices. In hot markets, well-priced homes sell for very close to the list price, usually within a 5-percent range. In slower-paced markets where prices are soft, the gap between the list and sale price may be considerably more than 5 percent. A low offer on a well-priced listing in a strong seller's market may not be worthy of the seller's response. However, in a slow buyer's market, an offer for as much as 10 percent under the asking price may be considered reasonable and worthy of the seller's attention.

It helps to do your homework. By making an uneducated offer, you could overpay for a property that is priced too high for the market. Or you could make a mistake in the other direction and make a ridiculously low offer. You might offend the seller, who then becomes a tough negotiator. Or you could even lose the home to another buyer who is better informed and who makes a more reasonable offer.

Consider how much you can afford to pay for the property. By the time you make an offer to buy a home, you should be at least prequalified for a mortgage. If you are not, talk to a loan agent or mortgage broker before you make an offer to make sure that you can qualify for the financing you need to complete the purchase. Sellers are more eager to negotiate with buyers whose offer is accompanied by a prequalification letter. They will be even more impressed with a preapproval letter. Ask your mortgage broker or loan agent to draft a prequalification or preapproval letter for the price you are offering, not for the maximum amount you can afford. You don't want to tip the sellers off that you might pay more.

Buyers who are stretching to buy a home will be able to afford to pay a higher price if they use an adjustable-rate rather than a fixed-rate mortgage. If you are short on

> If you offer within 5 percent of the list price, you are letting the sellers know that you want to buy their home.
>
> If you offer 10 percent or more below the list price, you are telling the sellers that you think their price is too high.

cash, consider asking the seller or builder to credit you an amount to cover some or all of your nonrecurring closings costs. A motivated seller might be willing to buy down the interest rate on your mortgage. (See Chapter 6 for more information about buy-down mortgages.) A buy-down will lower your monthly payments for a period of time, which makes it easier to qualify for the loan. Realize that when you ask sellers to make concessions to make it easier for you to buy their home, it is the same as asking them to accept a lower price. From the sellers' point of view, a $205,000 sale price that includes a $5,000 credit to pay for the buyer's nonrecurring closing costs or to buy down an interest rate is the same as a $200,000 sale price.

Property condition affects affordability. For example, a $200,000 house that has a $5,000 new roof is more affordable than a $200,000 house that needs a $5,000 new roof. It's wise to find out as much as you can about the condition of a property before you make an offer to buy it. Ask if there are any existing reports, such as a termite, home, or roof inspection report. Find out if the sellers plan to complete any work as a part of a sale agreement. Make sure to budget for major repairs that must be undertaken immediately but that the sellers are unwilling to correct.

Sometimes sellers take property condition into account when negotiating a sale. They may be willing to sell at a lower price if they don't have to complete any work. Or they may agree to complete work before the closing if the buyers compensate them by paying a higher price for the home. This can make a big difference for cash-strapped buyers. Suppose you don't have an extra $5,000 to pay for the new roof a house needs, and at a $200,000 sale price, the sellers refuse to pay for the roof. In this case, you may be better off paying $5,000 more for the house and having the sellers replace the roof, at their expense, before closing. By adding the cost of the roof onto the price of the house, you finance most of the cost of the roof and pay it off over time as you pay off your mortgage. For example, if you are getting a mortgage for 90 percent of the purchase price, you will finance 90 percent of the cost of the new roof. By increasing the cost of the house from $200,000 to $205,000, you raise your loan amount from $180,000 to $184,500 (.90 X $205,000). But you will only have to come up with 10 percent of the cost of the roof in cash or $500 by the closing.

**Regardless of what a property may be worth, you should not pay more than you can afford.**

**Find out as much as you can about the seller's situation before you make an offer.**

While preparing to make an offer, research as much as you can about the sellers and about the market history of their property. Find out why they are selling. If you're working with an agent, he or she can gather this information for you. If not, ask the sellers' agent or the sellers directly if they don't have an agent. Are they transferring, divorcing, or selling to settle an estate? Have they bought another home, or do they need to sell before they can buy one? In each circumstance, the sellers' needs and motivations will be a little different. If the sellers have already bought another home, they may be willing to accept a lower price if the buyer can close quickly. If the sellers are buying a home that is under construction, they may accept a lower price from buyers who will let them stay in their old home until the new one is complete. Is there anything unusual about the sellers' reason for selling that might effect the selling price? This information may be difficult to come by; if the sellers are selling because they have an urgent need for cash, they probably have instructed their agent not to reveal this to anyone.

How long has the property been on the market? Is the current list price the original price? Have there been price reductions? How long ago was the price reduced? If the price was lowered a while ago with no results, the sellers may be considering another reduction. In this case, your best strategy may be to make an offer just before the sellers reduce their price again. If you wait until the price drops, you may encounter competition from other buyers. Find out if there are any other written offers. Is the property being shown a lot or barely at all? If you are making an offer without the threat of a competing offer, you will adopt a very different negotiation strategy than if other buyers are breathing down your neck. Have there been any offers in the past? If so, why were they rejected? Are the buyers still interested in the property or did they buy something else? Be sure to ask if there is flexibility in the sellers' price. You may not get a straight answer to this question, but it is always worthwhile to ask.

## Negotiation strategies

There are many ways to negotiate a home sale. Some strategies work better than others, depending on the circumstances. It's hard to generalize, because each transaction is unique. But there are a few guidelines that apply in most cases. Successful negotiations usually involve give and take. The ideal negotiation happens when both the buyers and sellers come away feeling like winners. Strive for a win-win negotiation, because a lot of emotions are involved in a home sale transaction. Sellers often find it difficult to be unbiased and detached when selling something as personal as their home. You want the sellers to feel good about selling their home to you because you will need their cooperation during the transaction. You may have further negotiations with them after the inspections are done. Problems could arise, even after closing. If you have built a good rapport with the sellers, you will have an easier time later.

**In a win-win negotiation, both parties come away feeling like winners.**

# Purchase offer worksheet

**Listing information**
Address?
List price?
Original list price?
Price reduced when?
Market value (based on comparables)?
How many days on the market?
Have there been any offers?
   Why were offers unacceptable?
Are any other buyers interested?

**General market conditions in the area**
Average time from listing to selling?
What is ratio of sale price to list price?
How many similar properties for sale?
Is it a buyer's or seller's market?
Are multiple offers common?

**Property condition**
Any existing reports?
How much termite work is needed?
Any major systems in need of work?
Approximate cost for required work?
   Will the sellers pay for work?
   Will the sellers negotiate repair costs?
Any outstanding assessments?
   Who pays the assessment?
   How much is the assessment?

**Sellers' motivation**
Why are the sellers selling?
Have the sellers bought another home?
Anything unusual affecting the sale?
When do the sellers want to close?
Is there flexibility in the sellers' price?
Are there any restrictions on the sale?

**Affordability**
Is full asking price affordable for me?
Will the sellers credit for closing costs?
Will the sellers buy down an interest rate?
Will the sellers carry financing?
Are the sellers offering any concessions?
Can the sellers consider a lease option?
Are all appliances included in the sale?
Are any appliances/fixtures excluded?
Is any personal property included?

Buyers want to buy for the lowest price and on the most favorable terms, without turning the seller into an adversary in the process. However, most buyers, like sellers, have a difficult time remaining detached when negotiating a home purchase. This is one reason many people use real estate agents to present their offers and negotiate their purchase agreements. If you don't have an agent, you might consider hiring a real estate attorney to negotiate on your behalf. Even if you do have an agent or attorney helping you, try to keep your ego from interfering with the negotiation process. Decide in advance what you want to accomplish. Determine the top price you can and will pay. Make a pact with yourself to walk away from the property if you have to overpay significantly to get it. But also promise yourself that you will not lose the property if a minor concession on your part will make the deal work. Remember that all elements in the purchase contract are negotiable, not just the price. Some elements will be more important to you than others. Use elements that are less crucial to you but that are important to the other party to bargain with for what you want.

Here are eleven negotiation techniques to consider:

### Bid low and jump up.

This approach is most effective in a slow market where you have the luxury of fishing for the seller's lowest price. Keep in mind that an offer more than 10 percent below the seller's asking price may be considered a low-ball offer by the seller. Whether it is a low-ball offer depends on how overpriced the property is. If the property is way overpriced, your offer may not be low at all in relationship to the market. However, it may be low in terms of the seller's expectations.

Some sellers refuse to counter a very low offer. A good seller's agent should be able to convince the sellers that it is worthwhile to counter an offer from a qualified buyer. Be sure to accompany your offer with a prequalification or preapproval letter to show that you are financially qualified. If the sellers counter back at a price you can live with, your deal is done. More likely, they will counter back at a price that is still above what you are willing to pay. If you think the property is worth it, make a sizable price increase when you counter back to the sellers. They may be so pleasantly surprised that they might accept your counteroffer with no further negotiations. Let's say the home you want to buy is listed for $175,000 and you think it's worth $150,000. You make an initial offer of $140,000. The sellers counter you at $160,000. You jump up $10,000 and counter back at $150,000. They accept. The sellers would be far less likely to accept your counter offer if you increased your price a modest amount, say $2,000.

☐ *Take it or leave it.*

Many buyers would prefer to avoid the negotiation process altogether and present the sellers with the top price they will pay right from the start. There are some problems with this approach. One is that most sellers will counter a low price even if they are told that the offer is your best and final price. Some sellers cannot accept a price without trying to get a little more, just as most buyers cannot pay the sellers' price without first trying to buy it for less. Another problem with making your best offer initially is that there is no room for further negotiation. Before making an offer that represents your best possible price, ask the sellers' agent if he or she thinks the sellers will be receptive to this approach. Some sellers may actually prefer this approach. But if your agent discovers that the sellers are likely to counter any offer for less than their asking price, you are better off starting with a price that allows you to move up some.

A "take it or leave it" approach may be the best strategy, however, if your offer is low and you truly cannot afford to pay more. The alternative is to make an even lower offer to start with, which could alienate the sellers. In this situation, if you start with your best offer, have your agent explain that you would love to pay more for the property but you simply cannot afford to. It might be wise to give the sellers a relatively long time, such as several days to a week, to respond to your "take it or leave it" offer. Given time and no other offers the sellers might decide to take your offer. However, you wouldn't want to leave your offer open for a long time if there are other offers in the works. The sellers could use your offer to get better offers from other buyers.

☐ *Bid high; yield little.*

This approach can be effective in buying a property that you think is well-priced. An offer that is close to the asking price will be very tempting to the sellers. Will they risk losing a good buyer for a few thousand dollars? Say a house is listed for $250,000 and you think it is well-priced, you might offer to pay $245,000. The sellers could decide that your offer, although a little low, is too good to pass up. However, if they do not take your offer but counter back at $248,000, you could come back at $245,500 or $246,000. A deal this close should not fall apart, particularly if the property is well-priced and you want it. Don't get so caught up in the negotiation game that you overlook the bigger picture, which is that you want to buy the property. Don't bargain for the sake of bargaining. Your negotiations should move you closer to making the deal, not further away from it. Remember that in a hot market well-priced listings can sell for the asking price, or more.

☐ *Mimic your opponent.*

This strategy can result in a successful negotiation with both parties feeling that each gave equally, even if they did not. Let's say that the property is listed for $260,000 and you start the negotiation 10 percent below the asking price at $234,000. The sellers counter you back at $255,000, a $5,000 drop from their asking price. You follow the leader and counter back at $239,000, which is $5,000 more than your initial offer price. The sellers counter back at $250,000—another $5,000 drop. And you come up another $5,000 to $244,000, which the sellers accept. Countering in the same increments as your opponent lends a sense of order and predictability to the negotiations. The parties feel they can depend on each other to negotiate fairly.

☐ *Save some bargaining chips.*

Nothing can cause a negotiation to sour faster than a feeling of mistrust. However, this does not mean that you have to lay all your cards on the table at once. This strategy requires that you know as much about the sellers' situation as possible so that you know how best to play your hand. Let's say that you know the sellers want the shortest close possible. You also know that the house has $5,000 of termite work to be done, which the sellers are willing to pay for. But the sellers would rather credit money to the buyers than actually complete the repairs by closing. You could start your negotiations at a low price with a long closing, and ask the sellers to complete the termite work before closing. Then, during negotiations, you can trade off a shorter close for a price concession from the sellers. You might be able to get another price break if you offer to take a credit for the termite work so that the sellers are relieved from the ordeal of having to get the work done quickly.

☐ *Give up something to get something.*

You may even be able to give up something that is relatively unimportant to you in exchange for getting something you want from the sellers. For example, you offer to buy the property at a price that is lower than the sellers will accept. You also ask the sellers to include their washer, dryer, and refrigerator in the sale. The sellers counter back that they want more money for their home and they want to take the appliances with them. You don't really care about the appliances, which are old and in questionable condition. So you agree to exclude the washer, dryer, and refrigerator, but ask the sellers to accept a lower purchase price. You each give up something to get something.

☐ *Inch along.*

When you and the sellers are miles apart in terms of price, it may take many rounds of countering back and forth to reach an agreement. If the sellers' property is priced way too high, it may take time for the sellers to warm up to selling at a more reasonable price. By increasing your price in small increments with each counteroffer, you keep the negotiation going without giving up a lot. To be successful, this negotiation strategy requires that you adopt the proper frame of mind. Patience is essential. You must resign yourself to the process taking some time. It is best not to force the sellers to respond too quickly to each of your counteroffers. This is a slow and steady approach that will hopefully result in success. But it can be risky. You could lose the property if another buyer presents the sellers with a much better offer at some point during your drawn-out negotiation. Also, if the sellers get impatient and feel the process is futile, they could refuse to respond to your counter. If this happens, give the negotiation a break. If no other offers materialize after awhile, make the sellers another offer.

☐ *Introduce an element of surprise.*
Suppose that you are inching along in your negotiations, moving at a snail's pace. Your agent tells you that the sellers' agent feels the sellers are nearing the end of their rope. They are beginning to think that either you don't like their home well enough or that you are not a serious buyer. You decide that you really do want the property. So rather than counter back with another small price increase, which is what the sellers are expecting you to do, counter with a sizable increase in price. The sellers are pleasantly surprised and they accept your price.

☐ *Split the difference.*
This strategy has an incredibly high success ratio. Again, it is an approach that leaves all parties feeling like winners. You decide to buy a home that is listed for $230,000. You make an initial offer of $175,000, which the sellers counter with a $225,000 price. You counteroffer to the sellers with a $200,000 price, and the sellers come down to $215,000. You decide to split the difference between the two prices and counter back to the seller at $207,500, which is halfway between $200,000 and $215,000. This strategy often works well when the buyers and sellers are at a stalemate after several rounds of negotiating. Settling in the middle, price-wise, can make both parties feel they are compromising an equal amount and that neither party is coming out ahead at the expense of the other.

☐ *Either/or.*
With this strategy, you present the other party with two options rather than one. Let's say that you and the sellers have been negotiating back and forth for a while. You want to buy the property for about $5,000 less than the sellers will take. You also know that the sellers would prefer to sell their property "as is" without a seller warranty clause. (Seller warranty clauses vary, but usually give the buyer an assurance that the home systems are operative and the roof is free of leaks.) So you give the sellers a choice: Either you will pay $250,000 with a seller warranty clause as a part of the agreement or you will pay $245,000 "as is" without it. The sellers can choose. Or let's say that you have a home to sell. You can afford to buy another home without selling yours first but you would prefer not to. So you give the seller an either/or proposal. You will either pay $250,000 without a contingency for the sale of your home, or $260,000 with a contingency for the sale of your home within sixty days of acceptance. The trick to this negotiation strategy is to make the option that you prefer attractive enough to the sellers so they select that option.

☐ *Stand firm.*

There are times in negotiations when it is best to stand firm. Perhaps you have negotiated to the point that you have made your best and final offer. You have no more room to move upward in price. You lay your cards on the table and let the other party know that you have reached the end of the line. Even though you have made it clear that this is it, the sellers may counter your final offer with yet another proposal. Your final offer might be unacceptable to the sellers. Or maybe they think you are bluffing. It's perfectly acceptable in this situation to counter back again with the same price that you presented on the last round of the negotiation. This should get your message across. By the way, don't say that an offer is your best and final offer if it is not. This can backfire if the sellers take you seriously and stop the negotiations. Or if there are multiple offers, you could lose out to other buyers who indicate they are willing to negotiate further.

# The purchase contract

It's easy to focus entirely on the price when you're ready to make an offer on a property. But the purchase price is only part of an offer. A purchase offer (also called a purchase agreement, a purchase contract, a binder, a deposit receipt, an earnest money contract, or a sales contract) includes all the terms and conditions of your property purchase, not just the price you will pay. The terms and conditions include the closing date, the size of your cash down payment, the good-faith deposit amount, financing and inspection contingencies, who will pay which closing costs, and who will pay for termite work. When the buyers and sellers agree on a price and on all the terms and conditions that will apply to the transaction, the purchase agreement becomes a ratified, legally binding contract. A purchase agreement is a complicated legal document. It should be drafted carefully and it should accurately reflect your intentions and capabilities. Finally, it must be written to be enforceable; oral agreements to sell real estate are not binding.

Purchase contracts vary depending on the type and location of the property. The purchase agreement may be a preprinted form completed by your real estate agent. Or it may be an original document drafted by an attorney. (See the sample preprinted purchase agreement in Appendix 2. Although the sample contract is designated for purchasing of a resale home, many of the same contract clauses will apply to a new home purchase.) It's a good idea to review a copy of the actual purchase agreement that will be used in your transaction before you sit down to fill in the blanks with your agent. If an attorney will be drafting the agreement for you, ask him or her to provide you with sample contract language to review before you make an offer. If you don't understand something in the purchase contract, get a satisfactory explanation from your agent or attorney.

Be aware that real estate agents, who are not attorneys, cannot give legal advice. Consult a real estate attorney for legal advice, even if you are buying a home in a state where attorneys are not typically part of the residential sale transaction. Whenever the terms of a purchase are complicated, the agreement should be drafted by an attorney.

## The good-faith deposit

The purchase agreement is often called a deposit receipt or an earnest money contract because buyers offer a good-faith deposit on a property at the time they make an offer. The purchase agreement specifies the amount of the deposit and who will hold the deposit money during the transaction. A third party, such as an escrow company, real estate broker, or attorney, usually holds the money until the contract is completed or canceled. If the sale is completed, the buyers' deposit is applied to the purchase price at closing; it becomes part of the buyers' cash down payment. If the sale is canceled, the buyers' deposit is either refunded or forfeited depending on the terms of the contract and the circumstances of the cancellation.

The amount of the deposit is subject to negotiation between the buyers and sellers. It could be $1,000 to $10,000, or more, depending on where and what you are buying. Local custom often prevails. However, in the case of an estate or probate sale the deposit amount may be set by state law. Generally, the more expensive the property, the larger the deposit. One way to make your offer more attractive to the sellers is to offer a substantial deposit. If you do this, make sure you are protected with contingencies. (See below for more information about contract contingencies.) Sometimes the deposit is made in two stages. An initial deposit is made at the time the contract is ratified, then the deposit is increased by an additional amount at a time specified in the purchase agreement. This increase can either occur a certain number of days after acceptance or when contract contingencies are removed. By making the deposit in two steps, you don't tie up a lot of money until you are sure that the deal is going through.

Deposits are refundable. If the buyers are unable to satisfy their contract contingencies, their deposit money is usually returned to them. Suppose that the buyers' inspections reveal that the property has a serious drainage problem. If neither the sellers nor the buyers are willing or able to correct this, the contract may be voidable. If the contract was contingent on satisfactory inspections, the buyers' deposit would probably be returned to them. But if the buyers back out for a reason that is not provided for in the contract, they could risk losing all, or part, of their deposit to the sellers.

**The basic elements of a purchase agreement**
- Identification of the property, the buyers, and the sellers.
- Purchase price.
- Good-faith deposit amount.
- Financing terms and financing contingency, if a new loan is involved.
- Prorations, such as for property taxes and rent.
- Closing date.
- Possession date.
- Provision for transfer of clear title to the property.
- Attached and personal property that is included and excluded.
- Disclosures and compliance obligations that are required by law.
- Inspections contingencies (home, termite, roof, drainage, etc.).
- Final walk-through provision.
- Additional terms and contingencies (such as sale of another property, seller warranties, arbitration, risk of loss, condition of property, home warranty plan).
- Agency relationship confirmation, where required by law.
- How closing costs will be shared.
- Time period for the seller's response.

The buyers' deposit is usually made by a personal check, cashed by whoever is responsible for holding the deposit (broker, attorney, escrow officer). Make sure that you have enough money in your account. Find out if the deposit money can be put into an interest-bearing account. This won't happen automatically. First, you'll have to complete a tax-reporting form for the IRS, since the interest you earn is taxable income. Don't expect a high rate of interest. You will probably earn the current rate on passbook accounts. If you are buying a probate property and you are required to make the deposit directly to the estate, the estate may be entitled to collect interest on the money, not you.

### Contract contingencies

A contingency is a provision included in a real estate purchase agreement that must be satisfied for the transaction to go through. Buyers commonly include contingencies for financing, inspections, and satisfactory title review. If part or all of the buyers' down payment is coming from the sale of another property, the buyers might include a contingency for the sale of that property. Sometimes it is difficult to find homeowner's insurance for some types of properties. If so, the contract might include a contingency for the buyers to obtain acceptable insurance. Seller contingencies might include approval of the contract by the seller's attorney or accountant, or approval of the buyers' financial documents, if the seller is carrying financing.

Local point-of-sale ordinances or state and national laws, may require that additional contingencies be included in a purchase agreement. For instance, a seller must disclose if a property is located in a special flood hazard area designated by the Federal Emergency Management Agency (FEMA). If applicable, the contract should specify a number of days for the sellers to make this disclosure to the buyers. If the property is a condo, townhouse, cooperative, or a detached dwelling that is part of a planned unit development (PUD), the purchase contract should provide a contingency for the buyers to read and approve the Covenants, Conditions, and Restrictions (CC&Rs), articles of incorporation, bylaws, and associated legal documents. Federal law requires sellers of homes built before 1978 to give buyers a lead hazard disclosure pamphlet and disclose any known lead hazards such as the presence of lead-based paint. The contract should also include time periods for the buyers to investigate the ramifications of these disclosures to their satisfaction.

Buyers often assume that if their purchase contract contains a contingency they have an automatic way out of the contract. However, most contracts imply or state explicitly that the parties to the contract will act in good faith. This means that you should not use a contingency to back out of a contract for a reason other than that provided for by the contingency. For example, if your contract includes a financing contingency and you are able to get the financing, you should not disapprove your financing contingency because you find another home you like better. If you do, the sellers might be entitled to some or all of your deposit because you failed to act in good faith. However, if you use good-faith efforts to get financing but cannot, you should be able to withdraw from the contract and have your deposit returned.

Your purchase contract should provide a procedure for satisfying contingencies, either passively or actively. With a passive method, a contingency is satisfied unless the party who benefits from the contingency notifies the other party in writing that the contingency is not satisfied. In this case, silence is considered approval. The active method provides that all contingencies must be approved or disapproved in writing. This method is preferred because it removes any confusion about whether a contingency is satisfied.

Each contract contingency should include a deadline for the contingency to be satisfied. Contingencies should not simply run until the transaction closes. Your purchase contract may include a provision stating that time is of the essence. This means that the buyers and sellers must complete contract requirements within the time specified. If you cannot remove a contingency on time, ask the sellers for an extension before it comes due. Any extension or other modification to the contract should be in writing.

Occasionally, buyers have not completely satisfied a contingency by the deadline but they want the sellers to know they are making progress. In this situation, you can partially remove the contingency and request an extension for a few days to satisfy any remaining conditions. Let's say the general home inspection is satisfactory but the inspector recommends that you have the chimney inspected. The inspection contingency is due and the chimney contractor isn't available for several days. The sellers might agree to an extension if it is combined with a conditional approval. Remove your inspection contingency, excepting the chimney, and have the sellers sign an addendum to the contract granting you five days to inspect the chimney.

When contingencies cannot be satisfied and the contract is canceled, a release of contract form should be signed by both the buyers and sellers. This relieves the parties of any further obligations specified in the contract. The release should also instruct the deposit holder how to disperse the funds. The buyers are then free to buy another property and the sellers are free to sell to another buyer. (See the "Guide to contract contingencies" in Appendix 1.)

### The financing contingency

Most buyers cannot afford to pay all cash for a home; they need a mortgage. Even those who can pay all cash often prefer to buy with a mortgage because home mortgage interest is usually tax deductible. Most purchase contracts include a financing contingency that makes the offer contingent on the buyers obtaining a loan commitment from a lender. This contingency protects the buyers from losing their deposit money if they are unable to find a lender to give them a loan.

Your financing contingency should be very specific. It should include the maximum interest rate and loan fees (points) you are willing to pay. It should also state the loan amount you need, the maximum monthly payment you will accept, and whether you are applying for a fixed or adjustable-rate mortgage. If interest rates rise during the transaction and the loan you specified in your contingency is no longer available, you are protected. If you can no longer qualify at the higher interest rate, you can withdraw from the contract and have your deposit returned. Or if you can still qualify at the higher rate but you don't want to buy under the new financing conditions, you have a legitimate way out of the contract.

You should specify reasonable terms in your financing contingency. If you include rates and points that are lower than what is currently available, the sellers will probably be less than enthusiastic about dealing with you. Why should they take their home off the market for buyers who will only buy if interest rates drop to an acceptable level? In a rising interest-rate environment, you can use a financing contingency to your advantage in negotiations. If you are willing to accept an interest rate that is higher than the going rate and you can qualify, this will ease the sellers' fears that you might back out if rates increase further. In a multiple-offer situation, your willingness to be flexible here could sway the sellers to favor your offer.

There are two parts to any home loan approval process. First, the buyers must prove they have the means to repay the loan. Second, the property must be appraised by an appraiser who is acceptable to the lender to confirm that the purchase price represents fair market value for the property. Make sure that the financing contingency states that both the buyer and the property must qualify for the loan.

It is quite common for buyers to be undecided about what kind of home loan they want at the time they make a purchase offer. Even if you are preapproved for a loan, you may not have made a final decision about which mortgage product you want. It's harder to qualify for a thirty-year fixed rate loan than for an adjustable-rate mortgage (ARM). If you are undecided at the time you write an offer and you think you might want a thirty-year fixed-rate loan, make the contract contingent on this loan. Switching from a fixed rate to an ARM will be no problem, if you want, because it's easier to qualify at lower ARM interest rates. But if you write the contract contingent on getting an ARM and later decide you want a fixed loan, you might not qualify. You would be obliged to accept the ARM or risk losing your deposit if you back out of the contract.

**A financing contingency should state that both the buyer and the property must qualify for the loan.**

Your financing contingency should include a time period for you to obtain a written loan commitment from a lender. Thirty days from contract acceptance should be sufficient, unless the home financing and refinancing market is hot. Buyers who are preapproved for a loan can shorten the contingency time period, perhaps to two weeks or so. Check with your real estate agent or lender to make sure the time period for your financing contingency is adequate. If lenders are backlogged with loan applications, request a forty-five-day time period.

**Don't remove your financing contingency without a written loan commitment from a lender.**

Before you remove your loan contingency from the contract, be sure you have an unconditional loan approval from the lender. Otherwise you could risk losing your deposit. Many loan commitments are contingent on the buyer providing additional documentation, such as a signed copy of last year's tax return, a current bank statement, or a termite clearance on the property. You need to be able to satisfy any loan conditions or convince the lender to waive them for the loan to go through. See Chapter 6 for more information about financing and the loan approval process.

**The inspection contingency**

An inspection contingency gives the buyers a period of time, usually ten to fourteen days following acceptance, to have the property inspected for defects. An inspection contingency should allow the buyers to select their own inspectors and it should permit them to complete any inspections they deem necessary. The inspection fees are usually paid for by the buyers.

It's always advisable to include an inspection contingency in your purchase agreement, but sometimes this might not be possible, such as in a foreclosure or estate sale. You should make arrangements to have these properties inspected before you make an offer. In some areas, it may be local custom to inspect all properties before making an offer, rather than using an inspection contingency.

An inspection contingency can be worded in various ways. In the sample contract provided in Appendix 2, the inspection contingency is either approved or disapproved of by the buyers in writing. If the buyers disapprove, they can terminate the contract and have their deposit returned. The contingency also stipulates that the buyers will provide the sellers with copies of the inspection reports, if the sellers so request. Some inspection contingencies give the sellers the option of fixing problems uncovered during the buyers' inspections. In this case, if the sellers agree to fix the problems, the buyers would not have the right to terminate the contract. They could only cancel the contract if the sellers did not agree to fix the problems. If your inspection contingency gives the sellers the right to remedy defects and you want the right to disapprove the inspections (regardless of whether the sellers will fix problems), write this provision into the contract.

You may be using a preprinted purchase agreement that includes an inspection contingency clause as part of the boilerplate copy. If so, make sure that you read this contingency clause carefully and that you understand it. State and local customs vary significantly regarding inspections, seller disclosures, seller warranties, and the condition of the property at the time of the sale. Don't take anything for granted, and if you have any questions about your rights to inspect the property and the seller's disclosure obligations, ask your real estate agent or attorney.

Inspections are among the main reasons home sale transactions fall apart. However, in most cases, buyers and sellers are able to negotiate a mutually acceptable solution to inspection defects. The sellers may agree to share the cost of repairs, or they might lower the purchase price to compensate the buyers for repairs they will have to complete after closing. Any agreement that modifies the original terms of the purchase agreement should be in writing.

## The closing date

The closing date is the date that title to the property transfers from the sellers to the buyers. The time period for closing varies from one transaction to the next, and is not set by law or custom. The closing date is mutually agreed upon by the buyers and sellers. Like all aspects of the purchase agreement, the closing date is negotiable.

Practically speaking, it's difficult to close a sale in less than thirty days if the buyers need to line up a mortgage. It usually takes thirty days or so to get a loan approved. After a loan is approved, the loan documents are drawn up and all the closing documents are signed. This can take another week or so. Also, other factors can affect the closing date. The sellers may be purchasing another home. They may already be locked into a closing date by the time you make an offer to purchase their home. Or the seller could be turning fifty-five in a couple of months. If he closes before his fifty-fifth birthday, he will lose his $125,000 one-time capital gain exemption, so he'll want to negotiate a close after that. (See Chapter 8 for more information about the $125,000 capital gain exemption.) Buyers who are short of cash might prefer to close later rather than earlier in the month. The later you close, the less "proration of interest" you pay at closing. "Proration of interest" is the amount of money collected by the lender to cover the interest you owe from the closing date to the next payment period (usually the first day of the month).

It's customary for the buyers to propose a closing date in their initial offer. The sellers will counter back with an alternate date if the buyers' date is unacceptable. Buyers who can be flexible on closing may have an advantage when negotiating other elements of the contract, such as the price, particularly if the sellers have an unalterable deadline they are trying to meet.

**One way to lower the amount of your closing costs is to close late in the month.**

The closing date is usually specified in one of two ways, either stated as a certain number of days from acceptance of the offer (such as sixty days following acceptance) or as a specific date (such as December 18, 1997). Using a specific date has some advantages. It eliminates the confusion that can arise when the closing date is a number of days following acceptance. Suppose you propose to close sixty days following acceptance, and it takes two weeks to negotiate the purchase contract. By the time you have an agreement, the closing is two weeks later than you wanted it to be. Another problem can occur if you and the seller use different methods for counting the number of days and you each come up with different closing dates. You might count the acceptance date as day one; the seller could use the day after acceptance as day one.

**The usual way to determine contract contingency and closing deadlines is to count the day following acceptance as day one.**

When you specify a closing date, you can make sure it is a business day. If the closing date is stated as a number of days from acceptance, you could end up with a Saturday or Sunday, days when closings can't be accomplished. If this happens, you might have a dispute with the sellers at the last minute about whether to close the Friday before or the Monday after the contract closing date. It is usually in the buyers' best interest to avoid a Monday closing. Lenders often fund their home loans the day before closing and start charging interest from that date. If the loan is funded on Friday for a Monday closing, the buyers could pay interest for three days before they own the home.

Buyers who are renting and who have to give their landlord thirty-days notice before vacating may want to negotiate a closing that is thirty days after the date their last contingency is to be removed. Buyers then won't have to give their landlord notice that they are vacating until they are sure they are going ahead with the purchase.

## Possession and rent-backs

The purchase contract should be very specific about when the buyer is to take possession of the property. The contract should state the date and time of the day that the buyers will be given keys to locks, alarms, and garage door openers and controls. When the buyers take possession, they can physically move in. But even if they don't move in at that time, they usually take over responsibility for paying the utilities and maintenance of the property.

But possession doesn't have to occur at closing. Sometimes sellers don't want to deliver possession until they have received confirmation that title to the property has transferred or until they have received their proceeds from the sale. In some states sellers attend the closing and receive their proceeds then. In other states, closing occurs days after the sellers sign their closing papers. Closing doesn't occur until the deed granting title to the property is recorded at the county recorder's office. Say the recording is at nine in the morning and confirmation that the recording has occurred is not available until several hours later; the sellers might not want to deliver keys to the buyers until noon.

Occasionally, several home purchase transactions are linked together. You may be buying a home from sellers who are buying another home. The sellers of that property could be buying yet another property. Since it's logistically impossible for buyers to take possession at the same time the sellers are moving out, closing and possession often occur on different days. The buyers can either allow the sellers to stay in possession after closing at no cost to the sellers, or the buyers can ask the sellers to pay rent. You may wonder why a buyer would let a seller stay on rent-free; sometimes such a buyer is trying to negotiate other, more important, issues with the sellers. If the sellers do pay rent, it's customary for the rent to be equal to the buyers' PITI (principal, interest, taxes, and insurance) prorated on a per diem (daily) basis. How long the sellers stay in possession after closing and the amount of rent they pay is negotiable. An interim occupancy agreement should be made a part of the contract. But this does not set up a typical landlord-tenant relationship. The agreement should specify who pays for utilities, maintenance, and any damage that might occur. The buyers' insurance probably will not cover the sellers' possessions. So the sellers should be advised in writing to obtain their own insurance coverage.

Sometimes sellers who are buying another home need a rent-back for longer than a few days. They could be purchasing a new home that is under construction, or they might not know at the time they negotiate the sale of their home when they will be able to give possession to the buyers. If this is the case, the contract should require the sellers to give written notice to the buyers thirty days before they vacate. This way the buyers can give a thirty-day notice to their landlord. Such a rent-back clause might be worded like this: "Sellers have the option to rent-back from the buyers for up to sixty days following closing. Sellers will give buyers a thirty-day written notice prior to vacating the property." In this case, a full sixty-days rent should be collected from the sellers. The unused portion can be returned to them when they vacate. Be careful, though; some lenders object to a seller rent-back for longer than thirty days.

Often, buyers of a vacant home request permission to take early possession so they can start doing fix-up work. This is almost never a good idea. Granted, it is easier to refinish hardwood floors and paint when a property is vacant. But, until you own it, you are spending your money to fix up a property that belongs to someone else. What if the transaction does not close for some unforeseen reason? It is better to wait to do your refurbishing until you own the property.

**Don't spend money fixing up a property before it is yours.**

## Personal property and fixtures

Disagreements often develop over what is and is not included in the sale. The purchase contract should be clear on this issue. Defining a few real estate terms may help you determine what is included in the sale if the contract is vague. *Real property* is the land and anything that is permanently attached to it, such as a house, trees, shrubs, and a fence. *Personal property* refers to movable items that are not permanently attached, such as furniture and clothing. A *fixture* is an item of personal property that has been converted to real property by permanently attaching it to the real property. A furnace is personal property when it is sitting in a contractor's warehouse waiting to be installed; it becomes real property when it is installed in (that is, permanently attached to) a house. A sink is personal property when it is displayed in a plumbing fixture store; it becomes real property when it is set into the countertop of a bathroom in a condominium.

Preprinted real estate purchase contracts usually include clauses describing what is included in the sale. Real property is usually included. Fixtures are also usually included unless they are specifically excluded. Personal property is excluded unless it is specifically included. The "fixtures" clause may require the sellers to include such things as window coverings (including drapes), attached fireplace screens, pool and spa equipment, built-in appliances, television antennas, light fixtures, and attached floor coverings. But these clauses vary so read the one in your contract carefully.

Sometimes sellers will exclude fixtures from the sale of their property. The most common exclusions are light fixtures and built-in shelving units. A seller may have a chandelier that belonged to a family member. It could be extremely valuable or it might have sentimental value. A built-in bookcase may be an integral part of the sellers' bedroom or office furniture set. Ask the sellers to patch holes and paint after they remove the items they are excluding. If an excluded light fixture is the only source of light in a room, you may want to ask the sellers to replace the fixture with another one, or credit you an amount of money so that you can buy a replacement.

There is no harm in being redundant in the purchase contract if it removes ambiguity and prevents after-closing disputes. Suppose the master bedroom drapes match the sellers' bedspread. The sellers have not excluded the drapes and the boilerplate in the contract requires the sellers to include window coverings. Regardless, the sellers may assume that because the drapes match their bedspread they will take them when they leave. If you want the drapes, state so in the contract, even though this point is covered in the fine print. This way, you will not be unpleasantly surprised when you move in and find your bedroom doesn't have any window coverings.

Most contracts include a space for the buyer to write in items of personal property they would like the sellers to include in the sale. Be warned: requesting furniture items can annoy a seller. Ask your agent to check with the sellers or their agent before you start asking for personal property other than appliances. Built-in appliances are usually included in the sale. Sellers may include freestanding appliances such as a washer, dryer, refrigerator, or stove (which are technically personal property), if the buyers request them and the sellers don't need them in their new home. Freestanding appliances are usually included in their "as is" condition and without warranty. It's a good idea to ask about the condition of the appliances before purchasing them.

Don't assume that freestanding appliances will be included in the sale. If the sellers specified in the multiple listing service information on their property and in their listing agreement that they would include these appliances, they should be included. Even so, it's a good idea to include them in the purchase agreement if you want them. If the sellers or their agent have not told you they are including freestanding appliances and they are not included in the written purchase agreement, the sellers are not obligated to leave them for you. Sometimes sellers offer to leave old freestanding appliances that you don't want. If there are such appliances on the property (like a heavy old freezer in the basement) and you think the sellers will leave them, be sure the contract stipulates that the sellers will remove the items by closing.

## Other contract conditions

The purchase contract should include clauses that describe the sellers' responsibilities to the buyers. Such clauses include passing clear title to the property, maintaining the property in its present condition until closing, delivering the property "broom clean" and without personal possessions or debris, complying with local transfer ordinances and disclosure requirements, and making any agreed-upon repairs to the property. In states where agency disclosure is the law, the purchase contract should include a disclosure outlining which agency relationships will be in effect for the transaction.

A termite inspection contingency is often made a part of the purchase agreement, although this varies from one location to the next. The sellers often pay to correct termite damage that has occurred during their ownership, but this can be a negotiable item.

The purchase contract should also specify who is responsible for paying which closing costs. Closing costs include real estate brokerage commission, loan origination fees, title insurance, and transfer taxes. Who pays these charges is usually dictated by local custom but they can be negotiated. (See Appendix 1 for more information on closing costs.)

Mediation and arbitration clauses can be made a part of the purchase agreement in most areas. These clauses provide methods for resolving disputes, which are alternatives to suing in court. In some places, a liquidated damages clause might be made a part of the contract. This clause sets a limit on the damages that could be awarded to the sellers if the buyers default. If you have any questions about whether or not to include these clauses in your contract, contact an attorney. Real estate agents are not qualified to advise on these clauses.

If a maintenance reserve is part of the purchase contract, the sellers agree to pay a sum of money, perhaps $500, to cover the cost of fixing things that are supposed to work at closing but that are found to be defective after the buyers move in. Unused funds are returned to the sellers. Sometimes a maintenance reserve can be used by the buyers to clean up after messy sellers who leave debris behind. Precisely what the maintenance reserve covers depends on how the clause is written. Some contracts don't have maintenance reserve clauses but you can add one if you want to.

Home protection plans (also called home warranties) are service contracts that cover some home systems (such as plumbing, heating, electrical, and major appliances) for a period of time after closing. Home protection plans are available in most states and they can be paid for by either the sellers or the buyers. Sometimes buyers and sellers share the cost. Who pays and how much is negotiable. If a home protection plan is part of the agreement, it should be in the purchase contract and include the name of the warranty company, who will pay for the plan, and how much will be paid. If you don't know which company to use, state that it will be "a company of the buyers' (or sellers') choice."

A final walk-through provision gives the buyers the right to inspect the property before closing and to confirm the property is in the same general condition that it was when they agreed to buy it. A walk-through can also be used to confirm that the sellers completed repairs they agreed to do or that a home still under construction when it was purchased is finished.

You should include a contingency in your contract for any condition that must be met before you will go ahead with the purchase. Say that you only want to buy a particular home if you can complete an extensive renovation. Your architect walks through the property with you before you make an offer and says he needs to do some research before telling you if the renovation is feasible. Your offer, in this case, should be made contingent upon your architect's approval of your remodel plans within seven or so days of acceptance. If your architect nixes the project, you have a legitimate way out of the deal.

Buyers of new homes will want to add contract provisions that are specific to new construction. For example, you may want the builder to provide you with a Home Owner's Warranty (HOW), which is a type of insurance coverage developed by the National Association of Home Builders that covers construction defects. You will also want the builder to provide you with his or her personal warranty for at least one year from closing. This warranty should include an agreement from the builder to correct, at the builder's expense, any major structural defects, defects in the home systems (plumbing, electrical, heating, cooling, etc.), and defects due to workmanship and materials. If the home is part of a new subdivision, the contract should require the builder to provide a copy of the subdivision public report.

Not all preprinted contracts are the same. In one market area you can find a variety of purchase contracts used by different real estate companies. Some contracts are written in such a way that they are biased in favor of the seller. This is often the case when you are buying into a new development and you are required to use the developer's contract. Make sure that you read and understand the completed purchase agreement before you sign it. Most buyers and sellers do not read the contract completely, especially the fine print. This can result in an unpleasant surprise if you discover during the transaction that you agreed to a condition that you did not fully understand. Don't hesitate to ask questions about any aspect of the contract that is confusing. There are no stupid questions when it comes to buying real estate. Consult a real estate attorney if you have any legal questions about the purchase contract.

## Purchase contract addenda

Today's purchase contracts are long—five to eight pages in many cases, with lots of fine print and convoluted legalese. But even though a contract may look impressive, it may not include everything you want your purchase contract to say. Let's say your agent is using a contract that does not include a maintenance reserve clause. The sellers of the last home you bought left the place looking like a tornado hit it and moved out of state. Instead of going through the hassle of trying to track them down, you paid for the junk in the yard to be hauled away and for the house to be professionally cleaned. If you are wary of being burned a second time, include a provision in the contract requiring the sellers to leave several hundred dollars in an escrow or trust account until you can confirm that they left the property in reasonable condition.

To make changes to your purchase agreement, add a contract addendum. This can be a preprinted form or you can create one yourself. Most purchase contracts have a space where you can indicate that an addendum is attached and made a part of the contract. The addendum should be dated and it should include the purchase contract date, the buyers' and sellers' names, and the property address.

An addendum can be used to add conditions to your purchase agreement. Some contracts include sufficient blank spaces for any provisions or modifications you might want to make but you'll often need more space. An addendum can also be used to amend or remove clauses and conditions that are included in the preprinted contract. For example, your preprinted contract might include a "seller warranty" clause that makes guarantees about what condition the property will be in at closing. You may have decided to buy the property in its "as is" condition without any seller warranty. This can be stated on an addendum. It's better to write out the contract modification on an addendum than to simply cross out clauses on the original contract.

## Giving the seller time to respond

Your purchase contract should include a clause that specifies a time period for the seller to respond to your offer. Typically, such a clause states that if your offer is not accepted by the seller in writing by a certain date and time, the offer will expire. In most cases, the clause also requires that written acceptance must be delivered to you or to your agent by the contract deadline.

> Modifications to the purchase contract must be in writing to be legally binding.

Real estate agents often advise their buyers to have their offer expire "upon presentation." However, this is not a good idea. Technically, "upon presentation" means that the offer has expired by the time it is presented. Understandably, many sellers object to being asked for an immediate response, but allowing too much time for a seller to respond can also work against you. In active real estate markets, several days may be enough time for other buyers to make offers on the property you are trying to buy. You could lose out to another buyer or pay a higher price.

Buyers often feel vulnerable when they are waiting for a seller's response to their offer. The biggest fear is that their offer will by "shopped" around to other agents and buyers in the hopes of generating multiple offers. No doubt there are times when this happens. But it is equally as likely that your written offer will discourage other buyers from making offers. Many buyers won't write an offer on a property when an offer is already written. In a low-inventory market, you are more likely to run into competitive bidding than in a market where there are plenty of homes for sale.

Buyers do have some clout when they present an offer. Until the offer is accepted by the seller, it can usually be withdrawn by the buyer. It is in the seller's best interest to respond to an offer in a timely fashion. Buyers can change their minds or find another home they like better if the sellers take too long to reply. Find out when the seller will be able to review your offer and how much time they will need to make a decision. If you set the response date too early, the offer could expire before it is even presented. If this happens, amend the contract in writing to extend the time period for the seller's response. Sometimes it's impossible to know when an offer will be reviewed by the seller. In this case, you can require a response from the sellers within twenty-four or forty-eight hours after they receive the offer, rather than by a specific date.

It's rare to have an offer accepted exactly as the buyers write it, even when the price is acceptable. Sellers usually propose changes to the buyers' offer in the form of a counter offer. The counter offer will include a new deadline for the buyers to respond in writing to the sellers. Make sure that your agent knows how to reach you when you are in the offer and counteroffer stage of a contract negotiation. If you cannot be available in person, your offer should say that facsimile and counterpart signatures are binding. When a document is signed in counterpart, copies of the document are signed by the parties, and the original is signed at a later date.

**All offers must be presented to the sellers—even if they are verbal or for a low price.**

Buying and selling homes can be stressful. Responding to the other party as promptly as possible can minimize uncertainty and stress. Your contract should include the phrase "time is of the essence." This establishes a mutual agreement between you and the seller to act in a timely fashion throughout the transaction.

# Presenting the offer

Offer presentations vary with the type of property and local custom. In a new subdivision, the seller may be a corporation, not an individual. Prices are often preset and if sales activity is brisk, there may be no room for negotiating the price. Making an offer in this situation usually means sitting down with a member of the sales staff and filling out the subdivision purchase contract forms. Making an offer to buy a resale home from a private individual is a different story. Ideally, the buyers' agent presents the offer in person to the seller and the seller's agent, out of the presence of the buyers. Buyers may want to be present when their offer is presented. But this can make the seller feel uncomfortable and hinder negotiations. If you are buying directly from a seller, you may want to hire a real estate broker or attorney to present your offer for you.

The best place for an offer presentation is usually at the broker's office, away from household distractions. Sellers often have an easier time negotiating a reasonable sale when they are in a neutral environment like a real estate office, particularly if the sellers have a strong emotional attachment to the home they are selling.

A buyers' agent should not divulge the terms of the offer to the other agent or to the seller until he or she sits down in person to present the offer. Sellers may refuse to attend a presentation if they hear that the offer price is low. But sellers may decide to counter a low offer if they have the opportunity to hear the whole offer and discuss it with their agent.

---

**TALES FROM THE TRENCHES: EPISODE 11**

*Matt found the home he wanted to buy but he thought that the sellers' price was too high for the market. He was a financially well-qualified buyer who didn't have to sell a home to buy and who could close quickly. When Matt's agent called the sellers' agent to make an offer appointment, the sellers' agent said that if the offer was for less than the asking price, the sellers did not want to be bothered with an in-person presentation. The sellers' agent encouraged Matt's agent to simply drop the offer off at the listing office. Matt's agent refused and insisted on presenting Matt's offer personally to the sellers. The offer was not for full price and the sellers did not accept it. However, they did counter the offer and Matt bought the property.*

---

There are times when it is impossible to present an offer in person. Perhaps the sellers are out of town and will not be back soon. It's usually best in this situation to schedule a phone presentation, which is similar to an in-person presentation. The buyers' agent and the sellers' agent meet at the listing broker's office. The offer is presented over the phone with both agents and the sellers on the line. Or a conference call can be arranged between the four parties. Then fax the contract so that all parties have copies to review.

Some agents go to the offer presentation armed with comparable sales information, hoping to persuade the sellers to accept a lower price. While this can be an effective strategy, it also can alienate the seller unless the agent is extremely tactful. Calling the sellers' price into question can be insulting to sellers who think they have priced their home right. It is sometimes safer to blame a low offer price on an impersonal external factor, like market conditions.

After the offer presentation, the sellers talk in private with their agent, then either accept, reject, or counter the offer. The listing agent relays the sellers' response to the buyers' agent. An important part of the negotiation process is to keep the momentum going. Lethargy and game-playing can result in a stalled transaction, so try to respond without too much delay to any counteroffer from the sellers.

An aggressive or combative posture rarely generates positive results. A spirit of cooperative negotiation usually produces the biggest payoff. Even though you and the seller are at cross-purposes in terms of price—you want it lower, the sellers want it higher—you are both working toward accomplishing the same goal: completing a home sale. All options should be explored before calling a halt to the negotiations. Can you pay more if the sellers are willing to carry some financing for you? Are the sellers prepared to take less if you close quickly? Can you pay more if the sellers pay some of your nonrecurring closing costs or if they buy down the interest rate on your loan?

### The fine art of counter offering

Given the complexity of residential purchase agreements, details in the agreement invariably need fine-tuning. If any terms or conditions of the buyers' offer need to be modified by the sellers, this modification constitutes a counter offer. In most cases, the modifications are written up on a counter offer form attached to the original purchase agreement. In some areas, however, a whole new contract is written by the sellers that includes the original terms of the buyers' offer and the sellers' modifications.

The counteroffer, like the original offer, will include a time period for a response. If the sellers give the buyers one day to respond to the terms proposed in the counter offer and the buyers sign the form within this time frame, the contract is ratified. This means that the buyers and sellers have agreed on the terms of the purchase agreement; they have entered into a legally binding contract.

Often buyers and sellers counter offer back and forth to one another repeatedly before reaching an agreement. Each counter offer changes the terms and constitutes a new offer to the other party, including a new time period for response. If the other party doesn't respond within the specified time, the deal is off. Neither party is obliged to proceed.

There is a lot of psychology in negotiating a home purchase. Although it is easy to get wrapped up the emotional aspects, it is best to remain as detached as you can and to focus on the elements that are most important to you. For instance, if you need to get into a home by the beginning of the school year, it may be worth it to pay a little more in exchange for an early occupancy date.

Patience can be your ally in a home purchase negotiation. If you and the sellers bounce counteroffers back and forth a few times and end up in a logjam, it may be helpful to take a break from negotiating. If another buyer does not come along, you may be able to pick up the negotiations weeks later and find the seller more responsive.

An agent's personality can effect how the negotiations proceed. Some agents explore every possible avenue before they let a negotiation die. Others allow themselves to get too emotionally involved in the process. If an agent adopts a righteous posture and cannot accurately convey the other party's point of view, further negotiations might be stymied. Buyers and sellers whose negotiations come to a halt should find out why they bogged down. If you are still interested in trying to make the deal work, let your agent know. Have your agent call the other party's agent to see if something can be worked out. Verbal negotiations can sometimes help, particularly if the parties have counteroffered back and forth so many times that they are wary. But make sure to put any agreements in writing. Verbal agreements to sell real estate are not binding.

It is better to write out the counter offer terms than to cross out and initial parts of the original contract. Also, counter offer in plain language rather than delete numbered contract clauses. For example, if the sellers will not include their washer and dryer in the sale, it is better to state that the washer and dryer are excluded than it is to state that clause #XYZ is deleted. Clarity in a contract is essential.

## Withdrawing an offer

You can withdraw an offer to purchase property at any time until the offer has been accepted by the seller and the signed acceptance has been delivered back to you or to your agent. The delivery aspect is critical. Let's say you make an offer on a property. The seller takes several days to decide, then signs your offer. Meanwhile, you find another home you like better and decide you don't want to buy the first one. If your agent notifies the seller's agent that you are withdrawing your offer before that seller's signed acceptance is delivered to you or your agent, then your offer is withdrawn.

To avoid any confusion, it is best to give written notice that you are withdrawing an offer. When the withdrawal notice is delivered to the sellers, their agent, or the agent's realty office, make sure that someone gives you or your agent a receipt for the notice. This can simply be a copy of the withdrawal notice with a notation that says "received," along with a date, the signature of the person who received it, and time it was received.

While it is easy to withdraw an offer before it has been accepted, withdrawing from a binding contract is a different matter. The purchase contract should indicate the terms under which either party can withdraw. If either party withdraws for a reason that is not provided for in the contract, there can be serious repercussions. Buyers who withdraw may risk losing their good-faith deposit. The seller might be able to bring a lawsuit against the buyers, depending on the terms of the contract. Sellers who withdraw from a binding contract could be sued by the buyers, either for damages or for specific performance. If a buyer wins a suit for specific performance, the court will require the sellers to abide by the terms of the contract.

Even if you think you know what's at risk if you withdraw from a binding contract, consult a knowledgeable real estate attorney before doing so.

# Multiple offers

Buyers often shy away from making an offer on a property if there are rival offers from other buyers. Of course, you would rather buy without competition. But you should not rule out a property just because other buyers are interested. A property that is in demand will probably be a good investment, and could be easy to sell again when you decide to move on.

Although protocol will differ from one area to the next, your agent should tell you if there are other offers on the property. Find out how the multiple offers will be presented. Ideally, each buyer's agent should present his or her buyer's offer to the sellers and the listing agent in private. This way each buyer's offer is confidential. A listing agent who writes an offer for one of the buyers should enlist the help of another agent, perhaps the office broker or manager, to represent the seller during a multiple offer presentation. This way the buyer working with the listing agent will not have an unfair advantage over the other buyers.

It is rare that an offer is accepted exactly as it is written, so you can expect to see counteroffers when there are multiple offers. If there is one offer that is far superior to the others, the sellers will probably counter that offer. (This offer is in what's called primary position.) They may also counter the remaining offers for backup positions (backup offer number one, backup offer number two, and so on). Sometimes none of the offers are acceptable to the sellers. The sellers might choose to counteroffer with one offer countered in primary position and the others ranked behind it. If the primary counter offer is not accepted within the designated time frame, then the next buyer in line can move into primary position.

It can be risky for sellers to counter more than one offer for primary position, although this is sometimes done. The risk is that the sellers could sell one property to more than one buyer if two or more buyers accept a counte roffer at the same time. To keep this from happening, multiple counter offers for primary position will usually specify that acceptance of the counter offer is subject to the seller's written approval.

Even though you would rather be countered for primary position, it may be worthwhile to accept a counter for a backup position. Hasty decisions are sometimes made in the frenzy of a multiple offer competition. If buyer number one suffers severe remorse and backs out, the property would go to the first backup buyer without being re-marketed to the public.

First-time buyers often find themselves in multiple offer competition because there is usually a high demand for housing at the entry level. Keep in mind that there is more to an offer than the price. Sometimes the highest price in a multiple offer competition is not the winning bid. A well-qualified buyer can be the successful bidder against buyers who offer to pay more but who are only marginally qualified financially. To give yourself a competitive edge, get preapproved for the loan you will need to complete the purchase.

The biggest risk you take in a multiple offer competition is disappointment. Some buyers fear they will pay too much if they get involved in a bidding war. Prices can get bid up in a multiple offer competition, so make sure that you set your price limit in advance. Also, to protect against overpaying, include a provision in the contract that makes the sale contingent on the property appraising for the purchase price. If the property does not appraise, you have a legitimate way out of the contract.

## Escape clauses and backup offers

An escape clause (also called a release or "kick out" clause) allows cancellation of the contract under certain conditions. To protect the sellers, this clause is often included in purchase contracts that are contingent upon the sale of the buyers' property.

Here's how an escape clause works if it is included in a contract that's contingent on the sale of the buyers' home. The contract allows the sellers to continue to market their home until the buyers sell their home or until they remove their home sale contingency. If the sellers receive a satisfactory offer from another buyer while the escape clause is in effect, they can accept the second offer in backup position, subject to the collapse of the first offer. The sellers then notify the first buyers that they have the time specified in the contract (often seventy-two hours, but it's negotiable) to remove their sale contingency. If the first buyers do so, they stay in contract and proceed with the purchase. But if they can't remove the contingency, they must release the sellers from the contract so that the backup offer can be elevated to primary position. In this case, the first buyers' deposit is returned to them.

When you hear that a listing is sold "pending release," this means the sellers have accepted an offer that contains a release (or escape) clause. The sellers can challenge the buyers to either remove the condition in question or step out of the deal if another buyer comes along with an acceptable offer. Agents often don't show listings that are "pending release." They assume that the first buyers will perform, so showing these properties is a waste of time. In some cases, the first buyers will perform. But many buyers can't perform until their home is sold.

If you are considering making an offer on a "pending release" listing, find out as much as possible about it. When did the sellers accept the offer? If it is a relatively new contract, there is a good chance the buyers haven't had sufficient time to sell their home. If the contract was accepted months ago and the buyers are still trying to sell their home, the sellers might be growing impatient and could be receptive to another offer, even at a lower price. Do the first buyers have the ability to perform without having their home sold? If they don't and you want the home, make an offer. Your offer is then called a backup offer, one accepted by the sellers in case the other, already accepted offer, falls apart.

A backup offer is negotiated just as if it were a primary offer. It moves into primary position only when all offers senior to it have been canceled. The time periods for removing contingencies and for closing usually start on the day the buyers are notified in writing that their offer has been elevated to primary position. The buyers' deposit check usually isn't cashed until this happens.

There is no limit to the number of backup offers a seller can accept. But few buyers are going to wait in a long line for the privilege of buying a home. Backup offers tend to be more common in a hot seller's market when the inventory is low and the buyer demand is high.

The benefit of being in backup position is that if the primary offer is canceled, your offer automatically moves into primary position without the property being formally marketed to the public again. The downside is that it is difficult to continue to look seriously for another home when you have your heart set on the one you have the backup offer on. You should continue to look, however, and you should include a clause in the contract that allows you to withdraw your offer with written notice to the seller if you find another home you want to buy. Watch out that you don't get into contract to buy two properties at the same time. This could happen if you are in backup position to buy one home and you enter into contract to buy another home before withdrawing your backup offer.

One reason buyers don't like backup offers, and agents dislike writing them, is that a backup offer tends to solidify the first buyer's resolve to proceed when unanticipated problems arise, like defects discovered during an inspection. An alternative to being in backup position is to have your agent let the seller's agent know you want to make an offer if the primary offer falls apart. The risk of this approach is that another buyer could make a backup offer that is accepted by the seller; you will then miss your chance to make an offer if the primary deal collapses.

## Canceling a contract

Most purchases depend on the satisfaction of certain contingencies (such as financing and inspections). Good faith is an element of most home purchase contracts. This means that you will exercise diligence to satisfy your contract contingencies, and that you will not simply try to use your contingencies as a way to back out of the deal.

A contract to purchase a home is a bilateral agreement between the buyers and sellers. A bilateral contract can only be modified or canceled by mutual agreement of both parties. Problems arise when one party wants to cancel the contract for a reason not provided for in the contract, and the other party does not want to cancel. This is called a breach or default. Buyers and sellers can agree to include several provisions in the purchase contract, in addition to standard contract contingencies, which may help resolve disputes if they arise.

So what happens to the buyers' deposit money if a contract is canceled? The contract should spell this out. Usually, the buyers' deposit is returned if contingencies cannot be satisfied. A liquidated damages or forfeiture clause may enable the sellers to retain the buyers' deposit if the buyers default. Buyers and sellers must mutually agree to make this a part of the contract. If the contract does not include a liquidated damages clause and the buyers default, the sellers can try to recover actual damages, which could be more or less than the deposit amount. But even with a liquidated damages clause, the buyers' deposit money may not be automatically released to the sellers if the buyers default. The buyers and sellers may need to sign a release of contract form, which stipulates that the contract is canceled and who is entitled to the deposit. If there is a dispute over the deposit, the buyers and sellers may have to resort to the court system to solve their problem. Some contracts include mediation and/or arbitration clauses that provide mechanisms for solving deposit and other contract disputes without having to go to court.

Sellers who back out of a contract because they are unable to satisfy a contingency are usually within their rights to do so without penalty, just as a buyer who tries to get financing but cannot get a loan. But if sellers back out (that is, default) after all their contingencies are removed and refuse to go through with the sale, the buyers have several options. Before taking any action, discuss your options with a knowledgeable real estate attorney who can review your contract and advise you. If the seller's default is a nuisance but you aren't damaged significantly, you may want to simply agree to cancel (or rescind) the contract without penalizing the sellers. You would, of course, want your deposit returned. If the seller's default caused you to be seriously damaged, you may want to consider a lawsuit for specific performance. If you were to win, the court would force the sellers to abide by the contract and complete the sale. You might also be able to sue for damages. If you are damaged minimally, you might consider a small claims court suit to recoup any expenses you incurred trying to buy the property.

Your best line of defense against a defaulting seller is to buy from a seller who is truly motivated to sell, one who would have no interest in backing out of a legally binding contract. Also, do not enter into a binding contract to buy a property unless you are sure you want to buy it. Even though contingencies are included in a purchase contract to protect you, your deposit could be at risk if you fail to close the transaction.

Always seek an attorney's advice before backing out of a contract for a reason other than that provided for in the contract. Also, if you have any questions about contract clauses such as liquidated damages, arbitration, or mediation, or about who is entitled to the deposit, consult a knowledgeable real estate attorney. Only an attorney is qualified to advise you on these contract technicalities.

# Buyer's remorse is rarely fatal

Did I buy the right house? Will I be able to afford the monthly payments? What if I lose my job? What if home prices drop? Did I overpay? If these or similar worries plague you, don't despair. You are probably suffering from a common home buyers' malady called buyer's remorse.

Buyer's remorse is an emotional response many if not most home buyers suffer during a real estate transaction. Feelings of regret, fear, depression, or anxiety are common. Typically buyer's remorse sets in after buyers have entered into an agreement to buy a home. But it can strike even before an offer is written. If you find yourself searching for reasons not to buy a home that you have searched for months to find, you may be suffering an early onset of buyer's remorse.

For some home buyers, these feelings are probably related to the uncertainty that results from relinquishing control. Your present home may no longer suit your lifestyle. In fact, you may be sick to death of it. But it is home; it feels comfortable and secure. When you decide to buy a new home, you are forced to step outside your current comfort zone and confront the unknown. Your mind may try to compensate psychologically for feelings of uncertainty by mentally undoing the event. In other words, you may try to talk yourself out of buying your dream home. Couple feelings of uncertainty with the fear of making a long-term commitment, and it is easy to understand why home buyers can suffer bouts of anxiety. Some home buyers won't suffer remorse at all. Most people will experience feelings that fall somewhere in between the two extremes.

The first thing to do if you suffer from remorse is to remind yourself these feelings are normal. The uncomfortable moments will pass. Don't attach more significance to these feelings than is warranted. For example, just because you are regretting your decision to buy a home does not mean you should back out of the purchase. Some people think that if their decision to buy was a good one, they would feel no anxiety. To the contrary, people who are prone to buyer's remorse probably feel uncomfortable about making any major commitment.

The best way to cope with buyer's remorse and minimize its disruptiveness is to make sure you are as informed as possible about the home buying process, local home prices, and home mortgages. Be as certain about the price you are paying for a home as possible; this will increase your comfort level. For some buyers this means continuing to look at open houses and new listings that come on the market for a few weeks after entering into a purchase contract. Ask your agent to keep you informed about other sales in the area and any new listings that might interest you. If your agent did not prepare a comparative market analysis for you on the home you are buying, get one done now.

It's a good idea to study a sample purchase agreement before you buy. If you failed to complete this step, read your contract carefully—including the fine print—to make sure that you understand it and that it says what you think it should. Talk to your agent or real estate attorney if you have any questions about the agreement.

Have the home you are buying thoroughly inspected to make sure you are not buying unwanted problems. You may want to review your finances to confirm that you can afford to make the purchase and that you are not getting in over your head. You will have opportunities during the transaction to return to the property you are buying, for inspections or to measure for furniture. But you may feel more comfortable about your decision if you revisit the property soon after ratifying the contract.

The transaction process itself can cause bouts of remorse, often when the going gets tough, such as when inspections reveal defects or if there is a glitch in your mortgage approval. If you find yourself getting anxious and remorseful during the transaction, remember that your feelings are quite common. Home buying is stressful, even though the results of the process are immensely pleasurable. Moving ranks at the top of the most-stressful-events list, right behind divorce, death of a loved one, and loss of a job. Expect to feel stressed-out at times.

Let your agent know when you are feeling unsettled about the transaction. A good agent can help you deal with anxiety and remorse. Make sure that your agent knows that you will feel better about the entire home buying process if you are kept well informed throughout the transaction.

**Spanish Mediterranean style**
A generic term used for a home with a tile roof, stucco exterior, plaster walls, and arched windows and doorways. Some Spanish Mediterranean–style homes have floor tiles, exposed ceiling beams, balconies, and terraces.

# 5

# Home Inspections

Home buyers usually order inspections after they have negotiated a purchase agreement with the sellers. However, in some parts of the country and with some types of property, inspections may be done before the purchase contract is ratified—sometimes even before a contract is drafted. For example, a foreclosure property that is being sold on the courthouse steps may require a contingency-free, all cash offer. In this case, inspections should be done before the offer is made.

Buyers don't like to pay to have homes inspected before they have successfully negotiated the purchase agreement. Professional inspections can cost from $200 to $500, or more. With a ratified contract, at least the buyers know that they are in agreement with the sellers on the terms and conditions of the sale. Of course, inspections may uncover defects in the property that will result in cancellation of the contract. If so, the buyers will have spent money for inspections on a home they don't buy. But this is money well-spent. Property defects can be expensive to correct, particularly if they are not discovered until after closing.

**Any home you buy—old or new, house, condo, cooperative, or townhouse—should be thoroughly inspected by qualified professionals.**

Your purchase agreement should include an inspection contingency that allows you to complete any inspections of the property that you want. If the results of the inspections don't meet your satisfaction, your deposit money should be refunded, unless you and the seller can agree on an acceptable alternative. See Chapter 4 for more information about the inspection contingency.

# Ensuring a complete inspection

## Choosing the right inspector(s)

The inspection phase of the home purchase transaction is vitally important. You need to know as much as possible about the condition of the home before, not after, you own it. To ensure that you get complete and accurate information, you should choose your inspector (sometimes you'll need more than one) with the same care that you selected your real estate agent or attorney.

Most buyers start by hiring a home inspector to complete a general home inspection. This is an examination of the site and all the major building components and systems: the roof, attic, foundation, basement, garage, drainage, electrical, plumbing, heating and cooling systems, walls, floors, fireplaces and chimneys, windows, doors— the works. If the home is in exceptionally good condition, you may not need to order additional inspections. But sometimes the general inspection turns up problems that should be investigated by specialists, such as a foundation, electrical, or drainage contractor. Your inspection contingency should include a time frame (usually ten to fourteen days) for you to complete all necessary inspections. Order the general inspection as soon as possible after your purchase contract is ratified so that you have time to complete any additional inspections.

The first step is to hire the best home inspector you can find. Your real estate agent can recommend some. Try to get a list of three inspectors' names and telephone numbers and then start investigating. Home inspectors are also listed in the Yellow Pages of the phone book. Make sure that you check references before using an inspector who was not personally recommended to you. Ask friends who purchased recently if they would recommend their home inspector. An inspector who is recommended by both your agent and by a friend whose opinion you trust is probably a good bet. But you should only select an inspector that you feel comfortable with and who you think is the most qualified to inspect the property.

Interview each inspector by phone before you decide on one. Ask how long the inspector has been inspecting homes in the area and how many inspections he or she completes in a year. Do not use an out-of-area inspector who may not be familiar with local conditions. As with most professions, the more experience, the better. A good, active home inspector will inspect at least two hundred homes a year. He or she should work full-time doing home inspections. Make sure that the inspector you use is not also in the business of contracting to fix defects discovered during an inspection. There is a potential conflict of interest if you use an inspector who is also bidding for work.

Ask the inspectors which professional licenses they have. At the least, an inspector should be a licensed contractor or engineer. The state of Texas licenses individuals as home inspectors, but most states do not; that means virtually anyone can operate as a home inspector. The American Society of Home Inspectors (ASHI) is a trade association for home inspectors. Membership is restricted to applicants with experience. Also, ASHI imposes continuing education requirements and a code of ethics on its members. Using a home inspector who is an ASHI member does not guarantee that you will get a good inspection, but he or she is likely to exhibit a level of professionalism that might not exist with a nonmember inspector. ASHI can also refer inspectors in your area if you are having difficulty finding someone qualified for the job.

Ask each inspector to describe the scope of his or her inspection. Some inspectors don't check roofs, others won't check out the drainage system. Most home inspectors will not check security systems, sprinkler systems, spas, wells, septic systems, swimming pools, environmental hazards, code violations, or building permit history. Plan to hire appropriate professionals to check any major systems not covered by the home inspector.

Find out what the inspectors charge, but don't make your final decision based solely on the fee. This is one area where you don't want to skimp. The consequences of a poor or incomplete inspection can be costly. It is not a good idea to rely on free inspections done by friends or relatives. And you should not inspect a property yourself, even if you have professional expertise, because you may be emotionally committed to buying. You need unbiased professional opinions about the condition of the property to make an informed decision about whether to buy it and how much to pay for it.

Make sure that the inspector you use has errors and omissions insurance that specifically pertains to his or her home inspection business. Inspectors, like anyone, can make mistakes. If your inspector misses a significant defect, you may be able to collect damages from the inspector, particularly if he or she has insurance to cover errors and omissions. Some contractors have errors and omissions insurance for their contracting business, but often the policies specifically exclude a contractor's liability for home inspections. ASHI members have home inspector's errors and omissions insurance available to them through their trade organization.

Many inspectors will complete either a written or a verbal report. It's a good idea to have the inspector prepare a written report of the inspection findings. Not only will it serve as a handy reference, it may help you in your further negotiations with the seller. Find out how long it will take to get a written report from the inspector after the inspection is complete. If it will take longer than a few days, you may want to use someone else. Also, make sure the inspector includes verbal consultations as a part of his or her service. You may need to get professional advice after you have consulted with other inspectors on any defects found during the general home inspection. Good inspectors make themselves available for phone consultations with their customers.

Your home inspection should be scheduled during daytime hours and the utilities at the property should be on. It's not a good idea to have a home inspected during bad weather. A clear, dry day is your best bet.

## Attending the inspection

Make sure that your home inspector will allow you to attend the general home inspection. Schedule the inspection at a time when you and your agent can be available and plan on spending a few hours. Some home inspectors will schedule an inspection on Saturday, if necessary. Bring a pad and pencil, tape measure, and flashlight. Also, bring any existing reports or seller disclosures for your inspector to review. You may want to bring a camera and tape recorder to help record your inspection.

Don't skip the inspection. It gives you the opportunity to ask the inspector about defects while you are at the property. If you are a first-time buyer and know little about construction, the written inspection report may read like a foreign language unless you have walked through the property with the inspector. Attending the on-site inspection is a wonderful learning experience. The inspector should be able to educate you about good home maintenance so that you know what you will need to do in the future to preserve your investment.

Some inspectors prefer to inspect a property by themselves alone, without the home buyers and their agent. They can get the job done faster and they are less likely to be distracted while they are inspecting. If this is the way your inspector prefers to work, plan to meet him or her at the property after the inspection is done for an in-person review. The inspector should walk you through the property and point out all the significant findings that will appear in the written report. This will give you the opportunity to ask any questions and to make sure that you understand what will appear in the report. You probably won't want to wait until you receive the written report to order additional inspections, so ask the inspector which additional reports he or she recommends. Ask for any home maintenance tips the inspector thinks you should be aware of, such as how to keep the roof in good condition.

Don't get discouraged when the inspector starts pointing out defects. All homes, even new ones, have defects of one kind or another. A growing problem with home inspections is that inspectors are increasingly fearful of being liable if they overlook defects. You may find that your inspector makes recommendations in the written report that were not mentioned at the on-site inspection. For example, the inspector may write that the fireplace should not be used until it is inspected by a qualified expert. This could mean that the chimney is dangerous. But the inspector might just be attempting to relieve himself or herself of further responsibility for the condition of the chimney. Talk to the inspector about any such statement. Have your inspector distinguish between insignificant flaws and major deficiencies. Ask him or her to prioritize recommended repairs so that you know which need to be remedied immediately and which can wait.

Your agent should arrange for the sellers' absence during the inspection. The sellers' inclination will probably be to stay around to answer any questions. But the sellers' presence can inhibit your investigations. You need to feel free to ask the inspector whatever you want without worrying about whether you are offending the sellers. Any questions you or the inspector have about the home that require the sellers' input can be dealt with later.

Home buyers moving long distances may have difficulty attending inspections. If it is impossible to attend the home inspection, try to find a friend or relative in the area who can attend for you. Have your stand-in call you after the inspection with a detailed report (perhaps the inspection can be tape recorded). Then have the audio tape and the written report express-mailed to you. Call the inspector directly if you have any questions or for a recap of the inspection.

### Further inspections

The home inspection may give you all the information you need to know about a property. Usually, however, defects will be uncovered that require further inspecting by a qualified contractor or engineer. Say the general inspector sees signs that the home has a drainage problem and recommends that you hire a drainage specialist. Or the inspector may think that the roof's condition is questionable and suggest you have a roofing contractor give an opinion. Your inspection contingency should be worded so that you are entitled to complete any inspections you deem necessary.

You should never skip an inspection just to save money. However, there are times when the cost of further inspections may be prohibitive. Suppose the general inspector suspects that uneven floors in a house might be related to a soil condition. An inspection and report from a soil engineer could cost $1,000 or more. If you cannot afford this but you want to buy the home if the soil condition is satisfactory, ask the seller to share the cost of hiring the soil engineer. A seller might agree to this to save the sale, particularly since another buyer is likely to have the same concern about the property.

Get the best recommendations you can for professionals to complete further inspections. You want reputable people who will not hike up the price because they know that the property is being sold. Avoid unscrupulous, out-of-work contractors who are looking for an employment opportunity. Always check references.

Although it is usually a good idea for the sellers to leave during the general inspection, it often helps if they are present for further investigations, especially regarding problems they were unaware of. Buyers may also want to attend further inspections; if a defect is in dispute buyers and sellers need to agree on a solution to keep the transaction moving forward. Usually, the more information both parties have, the better. It's a good idea to have both parties' agents present also to help keep matters on an even emotional keel.

*Jim and Penny had a termite inspection done when they listed their house for sale. The report showed a moderate amount of infestation that could be repaired for about $800. The buyers then ordered a second termite inspection, which turned up $18,000 worth of wood pest repair work. Both the buyers and sellers were disturbed by the huge discrepancy between the two reports, so they asked both termite inspectors to meet with them and their agents at the property to justify their findings. The high bidder claimed that the entire back wall of the two-story house had dry rot and needed to be replaced. The first inspector asked the sellers for permission to do test openings at several locations on the wall to determine if the wall was rotted. Each test opening revealed solid wood—no dry rot or infestation. The second inspector had based his opinion on one test probe. His probe passed through a void between two support beams; failing to hit solid wood, the inspector falsely assumed that the wall was shot, without performing further test probes. Chagrined, the second inspector revised his report in line with the other inspector's.*

Sometimes it is impossible to inspect a property without doing damage to it. Let's say the sellers have a termite report that recommends opening the finished ceiling beneath a shower to check for leakage and termite or dry rot infestation. Your purchase contract should give you permission to do invasive inspections, if necessary. It should also specify who will pay to correct damage created by such tests. The buyers often pay for such things as the cost of the further inspection and for repairing the ceiling after the inspection is done. The sellers are often responsible for repairing any pest damage that might be discovered during the inspection. If your contract does not cover a situation like this, make sure you have the seller's permission to do an invasive inspection, and a written agreement regarding sharing the costs involved, before the inspection is done.

## Termite inspections

Most pre-printed purchase contracts include a termite, or pest control, inspection clause. Often the clause requires the sellers to provide the buyers with a current pest control inspection report, done by a licensed structural pest control operator. The report may be broken down into two parts: one for "Section I" conditions and one for "Section II" findings. A Section I notation refers to any part of the structure where wood pest infection or infestation is present. Section II items are conditions deemed likely to lead to infection or infestation in the future, but where no active infestation or infection currently exists. Who pays for the report and for the work recommended in the report is negotiated. Sometimes local custom dictates who pays for what. In many areas, the custom is for the sellers to pay for the Section I repairs and for the buyers to take responsibility for the Section II items.

It's a good idea for buyers to have a wood pest inspection done as a condition of the purchase agreement. Many lenders require a notice from a licensed structural pest control operator stating that the property is free and clear of infestation before they will grant a mortgage.

This report is often referred to as a "termite" report, which is misleading. Termites are wood-destroying organisms, but they are not the only such pests that harm wood. Just because a home is free of active termite infestation does not mean that it should be given a clean bill of health. Some areas are more prone to termite problems than others, and there are various types of termites. Subterranean termites are prevalent in the San Francisco Bay Area, but they are not much of a problem in dryer parts of California where dry wood termites are the culprits. As you move north in this country, termites become less of a problem than in the south. They are virtually nonexistent in the most northern states where there are other destructive wood pests to watch out for, like carpenter ants.

Wood pest problems vary from one micro-environment to the next. Some areas have fungus and dry rot problems, others are prone to beetle infestation. Find out what kinds of wood pests are common in the area where you are buying. Make certain that the home you buy is carefully inspected for those pests. Ask your real estate agent or home inspector to recommend some good structural pest control inspectors who know the local area. If you are buying an older home, don't use a wood pest inspector who only has experience looking at newer homes. New homes generally have fewer wood pest problems and are easier to inspect.

**Don't use an out-of-area pest control operator who might not be familiar with local pest problems.**

### Normandy
*A picturesque home in the French Revival tradition incorporating many features of French architecture including: a steeply pitched hipped roof, French doors, a stucco exterior, louvered shutters, double-hung wood windows, and often featuring a forecourt. Some Normandy homes feature a conical tower.*

Sometimes a wood pest report calls for a "further inspection." Plan to have these further inspections completed during the inspection contingency time period. If the property has detached decks and auxiliary structures, like a detached garage, get these inspected. Sometimes sellers expect the buyers to accept any auxiliary structures in "as is" condition. If so, you'll want to know if any have wood pest problems. The buyer often pays the cost of these additional inspections, but it's better to know about any pest problems before closing.

If you are buying a home that has a stucco exterior, make sure to have test openings done if the inspector sees any suspicious signs that might indicate wood pest problems behind the finished walls. Old roofs and leaky gutters can cause water to leak inside the finished walls and rot out the concealed support beams. This problem can be expensive to fix. You may be able to negotiate for the sellers to pay for such repairs if they are discovered before closing.

Sellers often order a pest control report when they list their home for sale. If you make an offer on a home with an existing wood pest report and the sellers want you to accept their report, include a provision in the contract that states that the report is subject to your approval. Also, reserve the right to have another pest control inspection done at your expense if you find that the seller's report is incomplete. Have your general home inspector review the seller's pest control report. Although the home inspector may not be a licensed pest control operator, he or she should be able to tell you if the report is glaringly deficient.

---

**TALES FROM THE TRENCHES: EPISODE 13**
*Pete and Ginger bought a house and, like most buyers, they included an inspection contingency in the purchase contract. The sellers already had a current termite report. Pete and Ginger asked their home inspector to review the sellers' termite report to make sure that nothing was missed. The home inspector found some damage that was not mentioned in the report, so he recommended a second termite inspection. The second termite company agreed that the first company had overlooked some termite damage. When Pete and Ginger removed their inspection contingency, they did so with a condition that the sellers repair the damage that was missed. The sellers agreed to keep the transaction together.*

---

In some parts of the country, sellers hire structural pest control companies to periodically service their homes for wood pests. If this is the case with a home you are buying, ask for copies of the service records. Find out how often the home was serviced and what it cost. Check with neighbors and your real estate agent to see if other homeowners in the area have routine pest control treatments. What companies are most commonly used and how much do they charge? Before you hire a company to do routine treatment for you, make sure the company is aware of local problems.

Many homeowners who sell after years of ownership are shocked that they have thousands of dollars of termite repairs to complete before closing. To guard against this, have a wood pest inspection done every two to three years and take care of critical problems when they arise. Contracting with a pest control company for periodic chemical treatment may not be enough, especially in areas where dry rot is a problem. Leaky pipes, showers, tub walls, windows, gutters, and porches can lead to expensive dry rot problems. A good regime of home maintenance will help keep problems like dry rot from developing. Make repairs when necessary and practice preventive maintenance by keeping fixtures well-caulked and sealed. You will protect your investment and have less deferred maintenance to correct when you sell.

### Environmental Hazards

There are frightening tales about homeowners who discovered, only after they owned their homes for awhile, that their housing development was built on highly toxic landfill. In one case, tar oozed from barren soil, the water tasted like metal, and one neighbor after another developed a mysterious illness. Less notorious but worrisome to many home buyers are environmental hazards that might affect only a single household. Recent attention has focused on lead (present in house paint before 1978 and lead solder used in plumbing older homes), asbestos (an insulating and stiffening material used in older homes), radon (a gas emitted from decaying uranium in the soil beneath a house), formaldehyde (used in the manufacturing of many home building products), and leaky underground fuel storage tanks.

An environmental hazard on a residential property is a material found in the building products, the soil, the water, or the air, the exposure to which may pose a health risk. Since homeowners may occupy their home for years, they could experience a dangerous degree of exposure to a contaminant. But health is not the only issue. The cost of removing or abating a health threat can be enormous. Removing an abandoned heating oil tank that has not caused a contamination problem could cost from $2,000 to $5,000. If the surrounding soil is contaminated, the clean-up could cost more than $50,000. An additional concern is the effect that an environmental hazard might have on the value of the property. The stigma of being located on or next to a contaminated waste site could be so great that a home might not be salable at all.

Sellers should disclose knowledge of any environmental hazards on their property before a sale is completed. Sellers who intentionally conceal such defects may face criminal penalties. Many sellers, however, are not aware of any environmental hazards. But this does not mean the property is free of such hazards.

What can you do to minimize the likelihood of buying a property with an environmental hazard? Make sure that your inspection contingency allows you to inspect the property for environmental hazards. Ask the sellers if they are aware of any environmental hazards, especially if state or local laws do not require them to disclose this information. Real estate agents and home inspectors who have extensive experience in the area should be able to tell you about the kinds of environmental hazards other homeowners have encountered. For example, some areas of the country have high concentrations of radon, others do not. Hire an environmental contractor to visit the site and make an evaluation. Often, the only way to determine if contamination has occurred is to collect samples, and send them to a laboratory for analysis.

Federal law requires that a lead-based paint disclosure be made to buyers of properties built before 1978. Real estate agents must give buyers of such properties a federal lead hazard pamphlet that describes the hazards of lead-based paint. Buyers have up to ten days to have a lead-risk assessment done on the property, if they want one. During this ten-day period, the buyers can cancel (rescind) the contract based on the possibility of lead contamination. Some properties are exempt from this disclosure requirement, such as foreclosure sales. For more information about lead hazard disclosure requirements, contact a local branch of the U.S. Department of Housing and Urban Development (HUD) or the Environmental Protection Agency (EPA). State and local ordinances may require additional disclosures or abatement of environmental hazards when a home is sold. A knowledgeable real estate agent or real estate attorney should be able to tell you if there are any such ordinances.

For more information about environmental hazards in your area, contact a local environmental risk-screening expert or local waste management expert. To find out if a property is near a hazardous waste site, contact the Environmental Risk Information and Imaging Services (ERIIS) in Alexandria, Virginia. ERIIS is an environmental database reporting service that reports on known or suspected hazardous sites within the proximity of a property. A report costs $75; call 1-800-989-0403.

Don't attempt to abate contaminants yourself without seeking professional advice. In some cases, it is better to encapsulate a contaminant rather than remove it. For more information about environmental hazards in general, call the EPA Public Information Center at 1-202-260-7751.

# Existing reports and seller disclosures

You may have access to a report about a property's condition before you inspect it. Frequently, sellers order their own inspection reports when they list their home for sale. Some sellers order a wood infestation or termite report; others have a complete home inspection done. Local customs vary considerably regarding seller inspection reports. Depending on where you buy, you may have a lot of information about the property's condition—or very little. Some sellers don't order any reports at all.

A seller may order a report on a specific part of property, like the roof. If the sellers know that the roof needs replacing, it makes sense to have this information available to buyers before offers are made. Buyers can then factor the cost of the roof into the purchase price. Or they can ask the sellers to replace the roof as a condition of the sale. Having the report available in advance eliminates the need to renegotiate the roof replacement after the buyers complete their inspections.

Sellers often have copies of old inspection reports, either from inspections ordered during their ownership or when they purchased the property. You should ask for copies of all existing reports on the property, new and old. Look these over before making an offer, or at least before your general home inspection. You can then ask your inspector any questions you might have about the reports. It is almost always a good idea for buyers to have their own general home inspection done. Even if the sellers have a current home inspection report from a reputable home inspector, a second opinion can't hurt— especially when you consider the cost of buying a home.

Buyers often wonder whether they should rely on inspections that were ordered and paid for by the sellers. Reputable inspectors and contractors should give reliable opinions and estimates, but establish that the contractor or inspector is reputable. If a seller's report includes an estimate for work, find out if the contractor will complete the job for you at the same price. Also, find out how long the contractor will honor that price and have at least one other contractor bid the job to confirm that the seller's bid is reasonable.

Many states have seller disclosure laws that require sellers to make certain disclosures to buyers about the condition of their property. In some states, sellers are required to complete a state-mandated seller disclosure form that asks specific questions about the property. Other states do not have mandatory disclosures, but they have a voluntary seller disclosure. Some realty companies require sellers to complete a seller disclosure form as a condition of listing the property for sale, even though state law may not require it. Although state disclosure laws vary considerably, recently there has been a radical shift away from the concept of caveat emptor or "buyer beware," which used to be the home buying rule. Caveat emptor places the burden of discovering property defects on the buyer. In the current era of consumer awareness, "seller beware" might be the more appropriate admonition.

Sellers are usually required to disclose any known material facts that are not readily apparent to the home buyers, but this is not the case in every state. A material fact is one that affects a buyer's decision to buy or the price a buyer will pay. A leaky roof is an example of such a material fact. The sellers could have covered the telltale water stains on the ceiling when they painted the interior of the house before marketing it. In this case, the buyers would not know that the roof leaks unless the sellers told them. Depending on where you are buying, you may have to purchase "as is" and without a seller warranty to cover latent or hidden defects. Having a property thoroughly inspected is your best protection.

Determining what a material fact is and is not isn't always clear-cut. Sometimes an element of subjectivity is involved. Also, what is material to one buyer may not be to another.

*Ben sold a house in California, where a seller disclosure law has been in effect since 1987. He debated whether he needed to tell potential buyers that a cleaning lady had been raped in his house several years before. Ben, an attorney, was concerned that he might be held to a higher standard of disclosure than a nonattorney seller. So he decided to disclose the incident, since the new owners would ultimately find out about it because it was widely discussed in the neighborhood. Ben's disclosure was material to one buyer who decided not to buy the house. She was a single woman who was terrified of crime in general. However, the rape disclosure was of little concern to another set of buyers, who happily paid full price for the house.*

State law also varies on the issue of whether sellers have to disclose a property's infamous past, like a murder or other serious crimes. In the above example, the law was vague and the seller didn't want to take any chances. In New York state, however, sellers are not required to disclose if a murder, suicide, natural death, or felony occurred on the property. Nor does a New York home seller have to disclose the HIV status of a prior occupant. In California, home sellers are not required to disclose the HIV status of a past owner, but they must disclose a death on the property within the last three years. Consult a knowledgeable real estate attorney if you have any questions about seller disclosure requirements in your area. Also, find out the answers to all your questions about the condition of a property before closing, not after.

Real estate agents also have disclosure obligations. Agents are supposed to disclose known material facts about a property to buyers. They can even be held responsible for failing to disclose facts that they should have known but didn't. For example, a seller who was transferred out of the area years ago might not know that a shopping center development is planned across the street from his property. But his agent, who actively sells homes in the neighborhood, might reasonably be expected to know this. And, since this information could influence a buyer's decision to buy the home or the price a buyer would pay, it should be disclosed. A strong argument for using an agent who specializes in the area where you want to buy is that you are more likely to get disclosure on neighborhood conditions that could affect your home buying decision.

**Complete disclosure before closing tends to minimize after-closing litigation over property defects.**

Home buyers who are buying in a state that does not have a seller disclosure requirement should consider asking the sellers to complete a disclosure form like the sample provided in Appendix 2. Your real estate agent might have such a form if his or her brokerage company requires sellers to complete one. One way to get the seller to complete the form is to include a contingency in your purchase offer requiring them to do so within a certain number of days. Or simply ask the sellers to make a list of known defects. If there are multiple offers on the property, however, and seller disclosures are against local custom, you may not want to take this approach because it could make the sellers suspicious. When there are several offers on a property, often the "cleanest" offer—one with the fewest contingencies—wins the competition. If you feel uncomfortable asking the sellers to fill out a disclosure form, wait to raise the issue when you have a ratified contract. If the sellers still refuse to complete the form and you feel strongly after inspecting the property that it should be done, require it as a condition of removing your inspection contingency. Full disclosure is good protection for both buyers and sellers, although some sellers don't understand this.

# Red flags

A red flag is a term used in the home sale business to refer to a visual sign or indication that a property might have a defect. Your aim during the inspection phase of your home purchase is to discover a property's red flags, then to determine which indicate serious problems and which are of little concern. Cracks in wall surfaces are an example of a red flag. The cracking could indicate a serious problem, or it could be a cosmetic nuisance of no major significance. Cracking in the walls of an older home built with lath and plaster construction could be the result of routine settling, which may be nothing to worry about. But if the home is less than a year old, cracking in the wallboard could indicate a serious structural problem.

Experienced home buyers will be able to pick out some red flags on their own. Your real estate agent can also look for red flags. In California, real estate agents are required by state law to complete red flag inspections of the homes they sell. Even if your agent is not required by state law to do this, ask him or her to examine the property with you and point out any red flags. This sort of an inspection should never be a substitute for a general home inspection by a professional inspector. But a cursory red flag tour by the buyers and their agents is often a helpful aid to the more formal home inspection. It can help to pinpoint areas of concern so you can ask an expert. Red flags include cracks in foundations, walls, sidewalks, retaining walls, fireplaces and chimneys; uneven or sticking doors and windows; sloping floors; landslides and erosion; damp basements; water-stained basement floors and walls; out-of-level swimming pools; deteriorated roofs and decks; frayed electrical wires; sooty heat vents; and sump pumps in basements.

Identifying a red flag is the first step. Next is determining if a serious problem exists. A basement sump pump is a red flag. If the house you are buying has one, ask the owner why the basement needs a sump pump. The pump may have been installed to pump out a minor amount of water that runs into the basement from the outside stairwell during heavy rains. In this case, the sump pump may be an acceptable solution to a relatively minor problem. On the other hand, a sump pump may be needed to handle serious flooding that occurs every time it rains. In this case, the sump pump may not be an effective solution to what could be a much more serious drainage problem. A drainage specialist should be consulted to determine what sort of drainage system the home needs.

Another example of a red flag is the presence of black soot marks around the heating vents. The soot marks might indicate that the furnace has not been serviced recently and that the filter needs to be changed—a rather benign problem. But the black smudges could also be caused by a cracked heat exchanger, which is a serious problem. When the heat exchanger cracks, potentially deadly carbon monoxide fumes can escape into the living area of the home. A utility company would probably require that a furnace with a cracked heat exchanger be shut down until the heat exchanger is replaced.

A good home inspector will be able to point out a home's red flags and distinguish the structural problems from the cosmetic nuisances. If the red flag points to a problem which is beyond the home inspector's expertise, consult an appropriate specialist. Inspections might take time and cost money, but they will protect you.

# Resolving inspection issues

Your home inspection may reveal no significant defects. If so, you may feel comfortable removing your inspection contingency without making any inspection-related requests of the sellers. Or you might ask the sellers to correct the few insignificant defects. If the sellers agree, you can move on to other matters, like completing your financial arrangements and satisfying any remaining contract contingencies.

On the other hand, your home inspection could turn up significant defects. This is always disappointing, but keep in mind that few homes are free of defects. If the defects are correctable, you should plan to proceed with the purchase, as long as the price is right. Your next step is to determine what it will cost to fix the defects and who is going to pay for the repairs. It is quite common for buyers and sellers to go back to the bargaining table after the buyers complete their inspections.

There are several different approaches you can take. If time permits, you can collect repair estimates and bids from reliable, licensed contractors before you remove your inspection contingency, then remove it with a condition that the sellers complete specific repairs. Include copies of your contractors' estimates with your request. The sellers will either accept your proposal, reject it, or propose an alternate solution. If they won't do all of the work, they might offer to share the cost of repairs. Or they may agree to do only some of the repairs. The sellers might want to collect more estimates to see if the work can be done for less, so you should allow the sellers several days to think about your proposal.

Your purchase contract should specify what your options are if the sellers refuse to do any repair work. In most cases, you will probably have a choice to make. You can go ahead and buy the home, and pay for the repair work yourself. Or if the home is too expensive, considering the necessary repairs, you ought to have the right to withdraw from the deal and find another home to buy.

Sometimes the inspection contingency is due before the buyers have had a chance to collect repair estimates. One option is to ask the sellers to grant an extension for the inspection contingency so that bids can be collected. An another approach is to remove the inspection contingency with a condition that the sellers complete certain repairs, with mutually acceptable bids to follow within a certain number of days. Or the buyers might simply put the burden of repairing defects on the sellers. In this case, an addendum to the contract could specify that the sellers can use whomever they want to complete the work, as long as it is done by licensed contractors and with local building permits, if required.

Check the purchase contract to see if it includes a "seller warranty" clause. If it does, this may obligate the sellers to have the systems of their home in working order at closing. The seller may be responsible, according to the contract, for fixing certain defects discovered during the inspections. Also, many sellers feel responsible for repairing defects that fall into the category of "health and safety" issues, like dangerous electrical wiring. But regardless of what you ask the sellers to fix, expect that your requests could upset them. Many sellers have a strong sense of "pride of ownership." They may have a hard time accepting that what has been good enough for them is not good enough for you. It is unreasonable to expect the sellers to fix every defect your inspector uncovers or to upgrade their home to your specifications. So prioritize the list of defects, and concentrate on working out a satisfactory resolution to the biggest problems.

An issue common with inspections of older homes is building code violations. An older home may have been built to the code requirements of the time, but these may be out of date. Sellers should not be expected to bring an older home up to current code, unless local law requires this. However, the sellers may have done work to the property that is not code-complying. Even though building permits are usually required for renovations, sellers often overlook this to save money and the hassle of dealing with city inspectors. (It's better to take out permits when they are required. A local contractor should be able to tell you.) If you are planning further renovations of the property and you have the work done properly with a permit, a local building inspector may cite you for earlier noncode-complying work. This means that you might have to correct these old defects to satisfy building department requirements for your current renovations.

**TALES FROM THE TRENCHES: EPISODE 15**

*Diane bought a house that had been partially renovated by the previous owner. Most of the past renovation work had been done by licensed contractors but without city building permits. After several years, Diane had to replace the furnace. She hired a furnace contractor and had him take out the appropriate permits. When the city inspector came to inspect the furnace installation, he refused to pass the work because he found some old electrical work that did not meet current building code requirements. Diane was forced to pay to have some of the seller's renovations redone before the city inspector would sign off on the furnace permit.*

Sometimes inspections reveal that systems are not defective. They still serve their purpose but they could be at the end of their useful life. It may be unreasonable to expect a seller to pay the entire cost of a new system (such as a furnace) if the current one is still working; it's just old and inefficient. If the system is truly decrepit, you may be able to negotiate a credit or a price reduction from the seller to help pay for a new system some time in the future.

## Conflicting reports

There is a certain amount of subjectivity involved in the inspection process. One inspector may tell you that a system is at the end of its life, another may think it will last for years. One roofer might call for an entire new roof, while another might recommend repairs that will extend the life of the current roof. What do you do in a case where reputable and qualified inspectors give conflicting opinions? One approach is to get a third opinion. You should also talk personally to all the inspectors to find out the rationale for their opinions. If you and the sellers cannot agree on a resolution and you are committed to buying the property, ask the sellers to credit you an amount of money that you can apply toward fixing the defect in the manner you want.

## Seller credits for repairs

Prices for repair work can also differ considerably from one contractor to another. You certainly want enough money from the sellers to get the problem repaired correctly, but don't expect the sellers to pay Cadillac prices. Again, if you want to pay for a more expensive fix than the sellers are willing to pay, ask for a money credit. The benefit of this approach is that you will have control over hiring the contractors and overseeing the work. If you are planning to make changes to the property, you may be able to have defects corrected for less money if the work is done at the same time as other renovations. Suppose that the stall shower in one bathroom needs a new shower pan. The sellers agree to pay for this. You plan to totally remodel that bathroom, so it makes economic sense to take a credit for the shower work and apply this toward the renovation.

Most lenders want any credits from the sellers to be called a credit for the buyers' nonrecurring closing costs. There are limits to how much lenders will allow sellers to credit buyers at closing. Usually the amount of the closing cost credit cannot exceed 3 to 6 percent of the purchase price. Nonrecurring closing costs are those costs paid by the buyer on a one-time only basis, like mortgage points and transfer taxes. (Some lenders will allow a credit for recurrent closing costs, too; most won't.) The amount of a nonrecurring closing cost credit cannot exceed the actual amount of the buyers' nonrecurring closing costs. So even though the lender may allow a credit from the seller to the buyer for up to 6 percent of the purchase price, if the actual amount of the closing costs is less, the lender will only permit a credit for the lesser amount.

Complications may come up when the sellers agree to credit more money to the buyers than the lender will allow. Suppose the buyers negotiated a credit from the sellers for the entire amount of their nonrecurring closing costs at the beginning of the transaction. The buyers' inspections reveal that the roof is bad and needs to be replaced. This will cost an additional $5,000. It is pouring rain, so there is no way the roof can be replaced before closing. And to further complicate the issue, the lender will not allow the seller to increase the closing cost credit to cover this amount. What do you do?

One option is for the sellers to give the buyers a cashier's check at closing made payable to the roofing contractor. The check could be held by the buyers until the work is done. If the contractor requires partial payments during the course of the job, the sellers can write out several checks the buyers release to the contractor according to a schedule. The sellers in this case might want a release of liability statement signed by the buyers, which relieves them of responsibility for the work.

A lender may insist that you get some work completed before closing as a condition of doing the loan. The lender's appraiser may notice that the front porch is so deteriorated that it poses a pedestrian hazard. The lender might insist that this hazardous situation be corrected before closing. Occasionally, a lender will allow money (called holdbacks) to be held in an escrow or a trust account until work is completed. Most lenders, however, don't want to be bothered with this. A portfolio lender will usually be more lenient with holdbacks than a lender who is selling loans to an investor, such as Freddie Mac or Fannie Mae.

A caution about taking a credit from the seller in lieu of having defects repaired: Get the work done soon after closing. Many buyers take a credit for repairs, use the money for something else, and never get the work done. This is risky. Many defects will worsen over time and cost more to repair later.

## Locating property boundaries

The only way to locate property boundaries is with a property survey performed by a professional surveyor. In some states, a property is surveyed by a surveyor at the time of sale, either at the seller's or the buyer's expense. But this is not the practice everywhere. Buyers often close on a home purchase without knowing exactly where the property boundaries are. Sometimes they think they know where the boundaries lie, but later find out they are mistaken.

Buyers and their agents frequently make the assumption that perimeter fences demarcate property lines. This will only be the case if the seller had the property surveyed and had the fences built on the property line. Often sellers do not pay for a survey when they put in a fence. So the fence ends up where the sellers think the line is. Some sellers find it hard to say they don't know when buyers ask. They may guess at the boundary location, with the best of intentions, which can have unpleasant consequences for you if they guess wrong. Keep in mind that any representations made by the sellers or their agents about the location of property boundaries can only be approximate without a survey.

Failure to locate the boundaries accurately can have serious repercussions. Picture this: You buy a house that is a little too small for your needs, but it's located on a big, flat lot that will be easy to build on. You remodel, without a survey. Later, your neighbor sells his house and that buyer has the neighbor's property surveyed. It turns out that a portion of your addition is built on the neighbor's property. This is called an encroachment. Your neighbors may be able to sue you successfully for damages or force you to remove the part of the addition that encroaches on their property.

The home you are buying or a portion of it may already encroach on a neighbor's property. A title search, which is advisable, won't necessarily reveal an encroachment. (See Chapter 7 for more information about title searches.) Having the property professionally surveyed is the only way to tell. Sellers should disclose any encroachments they know about, but they are often not aware of any. A neighbor's fence could have been built a few feet over the property line. Or the seller's driveway could encroach a few feet on the neighbor's property. These conditions could have existed for years, unquestioned by previous owners.

Most buyers do not get surveys when they buy a home because they are expensive, ranging from several hundred to several thousand dollars, depending on how difficult the survey is to complete. A careful visual inspection of the property may help you decide if a survey is necessary. For example, a house that is built very close to neighboring properties could be a problem if you are thinking of adding on. But the cost of a survey is minimal if it keeps you out of an ugly legal dispute. If you cannot afford to pay for one and you only want to buy the property if you can ease your uncertainty about a possible encroachment, ask the sellers to provide a survey. Or negotiate to share the cost.

# The cost of home maintenance

Buyers often fail to account for the ongoing cost of keeping a home in good repair. Home maintenance involves a myriad of tasks: painting, caulking, and sealing; cleaning and repairing the roof, gutters, and downspouts; clearing clogged drains; tree trimming; routine system maintenance and repair (plumbing, heating, cooling, septic tank, swimming pool, hot tub, wells); gardening; and wood pest and termite repairs.

Some homes require more maintenance than others. Some need immediate attention because the previous owners deferred routine upkeep. A well-maintained older home will cost less to keep up than one that has been let go. New homes usually require less maintenance than older homes. But all homes ultimately need to be maintained to keep them in good shape.

One benefit of buying a condominium or townhouse is that many of the costs of routine maintenance are included in the monthly homeowner association dues. Precisely what is covered by the dues varies from one complex to the next, but covered expenses often include common-area landscaping and upkeep, exterior paint, roofs, and common-area facility upkeep of walks, pools, decks, club house, and tennis courts. Condo buyers are forced to budget for these home maintenance expenses because the association dues are mandatory.

Buyers of detached homes should budget for maintenance costs and take the attitude that home maintenance is mandatory. The value of your home investment will diminish if you let the property fall into disrepair. There is usually a direct correlation between property condition and market value: The better the condition, the more a buyer is willing to pay.

The cost of good home maintenance is usually low compared with the cost to remedy deferred maintenance. Cleaning and sealing roof gutters may cost several hundred dollars. Repairing damage to a corner of the house where gutters have leaked can cost a few thousand dollars (depending on how many stories are damaged).

Ask the sellers to itemize all major repairs they have made to the property, including the dates the work was completed and the contractor's name and phone number. (Keep detailed records of your own, once you buy a home.) Find out when the major systems were last serviced, by whom, and what it cost. Call contractors who have worked on the home recently and ask them if they anticipate any major expenses for additional repairs in the near future. If they do, find out the cost. Ask them how often routine maintenance should be done on the roof, drains, heater or boiler, and other systems and what this will cost. Ask the seller what preventative maintenance they complete each year. Are there drains that need clearing? Are there skylights that need periodic caulking or overhanging trees that need trimming? If so, how often? Preventative maintenance is the key to avoiding and forestalling major, expensive repairs.

After you have collected the maintenance information, establish a budget. Figure out what the routine upkeep will cost on an annual basis, or on a monthly basis if you are on a very tight budget. Then budget for big-ticket items that will need to be replaced. A new roof could cost $5,000 to $10,000; so can an exterior paint job, depending on the size of the home. If both the roof and the paint had to be done in one year, this could pose a financial hardship. If the roof needs to be done in five years and the paint in ten, plan to save a couple of thousand dollars a year so that you are not caught short of cash when the work needs to be done.

Many of the features buyers find so charming and appealing are expensive to maintain: French doors, woodframe windows, decks, large yards, lots of trees. Waterfront and view houses are not only more expensive to buy but usually require more maintenance because they are exposed to the weather. A high-maintenance home may be beyond your budget. It's best to find this out during your inspection contingency, when you can still withdraw from the contract, rather than years later when you cannot afford the upkeep.

# Dealing with breakdowns

## Home warranties

A home protection plan, also called a home warranty, is a service contract that covers the major systems and appliances of a home. If a home protection plan is issued at closing, most warranty companies will issue coverage without inspecting the property. Most protection plans cover the plumbing, heating, electrical and hot water systems, as well as built-in appliances and a freestanding stove and dishwasher, if they are included in the sale agreement. A standard policy with this kind of coverage costs in the range of $250 to $300 per year. Additional coverage for spa, washer, dryer, refrigerator, and air conditioning is available at additional cost. Some policies cover roof repairs but usually up to a limit of about $1,000. You may have to pay an extra fee for roof coverage. Contracts typically run for one year and most plans are renewable at the owner's option. Home protection plans are available in most states.

They work like this: When a malfunction covered by the warranty occurs, the home owner calls the warranty company and requests a service call. A service call (sometimes referred to as the deductible) costs the homeowner about $35 per visit. The warranty company assigns the call to a technician and the company absorbs the cost of the repair or replacement. Don't assume that you can call any contractor to fix a malfunction; most companies will not cover a claim unless their contractor completes the repairs.

Either the seller or the buyer can pay for a home protection plan; it's negotiable. Your real estate agent or the closing officer can order the coverage for you. If the sellers do not offer to pay for a home warranty and you want them to, include this request in writing in your purchase offer. Be specific about the coverage you want. For instance, if you expect the pool equipment to be covered, write this into your contract. Otherwise, the seller may only provide a standard coverage policy.

Seller coverage is also available to protect against system malfunctions that might occur during the listing period. The cost is charged on a per-diem basis (usually less than a dollar a day) and is usually paid for at closing. Seller coverage works the same as the buyer coverage: The homeowner pays a service charge and the warranty company pays for repairing or replacing covered systems.

A number of companies offer home warranty plans. Regardless of who pays for the policy, the buyers should request that the plan be one of their choice. Before selecting a plan, review sample contracts from various companies. You want a plan that promises to cover "pre-existing conditions" not known to the sellers or their agents at the time coverage takes effect. Pre-existing defects that the sellers are aware of are excluded from coverage.

Read the fine print carefully. Even though the electrical system is covered, a problem that is the result of a power outage or of wiring that is not up to current building code requirements might be excluded from coverage. Watch out for policy limitations, such as on furnace or boiler repairs. Many warranty companies limit the amount they will pay for repairs to furnace or boilers to $1,000 or $1,500.

A home protection plan should not be considered an alternative to having the property thoroughly inspected by licensed professionals. System defects discovered during the buyers' inspections will not usually be covered by a home protection plan unless the sellers signed up for seller's coverage. But if you are buying an older home and the inspections reveal that the systems are old, it might be worthwhile to make a home warranty a part of the transaction, even if you have to pay for it yourself.

There are home warranty plans available for a much higher price that cover new homes. These extended warranty plans often cover new homes for up to ten years and they are more comprehensive than the home warranties discussed above. But many of these plans and their effectiveness are controversial. There are exclusions from coverage and deductibles can be high. If a builder provides you with one, make sure it is not in lieu of the contractor providing his or her personal warranty on workmanship. Also, make sure you review the policy. You may want a real estate attorney to review it for you.

### Discovering defects after closing

It is extremely aggravating to move into a newly acquired home and discover that something is wrong with it. Perhaps the oven does not work or the roof leaks in the first heavy rain. Maybe you rip up the old wall-to-wall carpet and find that the hardwood floors underneath are damaged. What do you do? First, ask yourself if the defect was something you actually knew about before closing. Memories can fade quickly. Sometimes the reality or enormity of a problem does not sink in until you live in the home for a while. Let's say there is standing water in the basement during the first heavy rainstorm after you move in. You are shocked at the amount of flooding, but when you review your home purchase file, you find a disclosure from the sellers stating that the basement floods in heavy rains. Also, your general inspection report mentions watermarks on the foundation walls indicating that the basement has flooded in the past. You were forewarned about the problem.

But suppose you look in your file and you find no mention of a drainage problem at all. State laws differ regarding how far sellers need to go with their property disclosures. In many states, sellers are supposed to disclose latent material defects to buyers, those problems that would affect the buyers' decision to buy or the price they would be willing to pay. In this case, if the sellers knew about the drainage problem and did not tell you about it and there was no physical evidence of such a problem, you might have a legitimate legal claim against the sellers. Their agent could be liable as well if he or she knew about the problem but failed to inform you.

The inspectors might be liable if they failed to discover defects you hired them to find. Be aware that many home inspectors attempt to limit their liability. These limitations vary but could be as low as the amount of the inspection fee (usually several hundred dollars). Check the contract you signed with the inspector at the time the inspection was done; a liability limitation will probably be included there. If there is a limitation, check with a real estate attorney to see if it is enforceable. Something else to check into: Minor problems in older homes may be covered by a home protection plan, if one was purchased at closing.

Problems that develop in new homes may be covered under a contractor's warranty. Even if the contractor did not give you an explicit written warranty on workmanship, state law may provide protection. Call a knowledgeable real estate attorney if you need more information on a contractor's responsibilities to the consumer. New appliances, systems (such as furnace, air conditioning, plumbing) and roofing materials may be covered by manufacturers warranties. If the builder paid for an extended warranty plan for you from a third party, this may cover the defect. However, there are exclusions to coverage and the homeowner often has to pay a deductible.

Most people prefer to have the defect fixed without having to go to court, which can be expensive and time-consuming. Start by documenting the problem. Call in an inspector or licensed contractor with expertise to diagnose the problem and to make a bid for repair or replacement. Mail a copy of the diagnosis and bid to the sellers and their real estate broker. Write a letter to accompany these documents explaining the problem. Offer to resolve the issue amiably. If this does not work, call your attorney for advice. You may decide to use a small-claims court if the problem will be inexpensive to fix. A statute of limitations may apply, which sets a legal time limit for making a complaint. So raise the issue with the parties you suspect to be responsible as soon as you discover a problem.

# 6

# *Financing the Purchase*

## Selecting the right mortgage

Some buyers are overwhelmed by the variety of mortgage products available. To simplify matters, it helps to think of home mortgages as variations on one of three basic themes. A mortgage is either a fixed-interest rate loan, a variable-interest rate loan, or a loan that combines the features of both. Deciding which type loan is right for your home purchase will depend on what you can afford, how long you plan to own your home, how you expect your finances to change in the future, how comfortable you feel with a mortgage payment that changes periodically, and current interest rates.

### Fixed-rate mortgages

A fixed-rate mortgage has one interest rate for the entire term of the loan. Most fixed-rate mortgages are fully amortized loans, with equal monthly payments. A fully amortized loan is one where the amount borrowed (called the principal) and the interest are paid back completely over the term of the loan. Part of each monthly payment pays the interest owed for that month, the other part goes toward paying back a portion of the principal. At the end of thirty years, a thirty-year fixed-rate loan is paid off in full.

In the first year of paying back an amortized loan, the bulk of each monthly payment goes to interest and only a small amount goes toward principal. As the remaining loan balance declines over time, the amount of each payment toward the principal increases and the interest owed each month decreases. By paying back the principal, you build equity in your home and this amounts to an enforced savings plan. But your annual interest tax deduction declines over time as you pay off an amortized loan, because the amount you pay for interest each month goes down.

Fixed-rate loans are often the loan of choice for home buyers who are on a fixed income. It's easier to budget for your monthly living expenses when your mortgage payment is constant. If interest rates rise, your mortgage payment is not affected. But you also don't get the advantage of a lower interest rate, if rates drop, unless you refinance your mortgage. The interest rate on fixed-rate mortgages is usually higher than on adjustable-rate mortgages (ARMs). Fixed-rate loans are also harder to qualify for than ARMs because of their higher interest rates. A higher interest rate means a higher monthly payment and that requires more income to qualify.

Studies have shown that over time, borrowers who used ARMs saved money when compared to fixed-rate mortgage borrowers. This is because the interest rate on ARMs is often about 2 percent below fixed-rate mortgages, and because homeowners usually don't keep their mortgages for the full term of the loan. Most people refinance or move before they pay off their loan. If you look at the cost of borrowing alone, it probably doesn't pay to take a fixed-rate loan unless you plan to stay in your home for more than seven to ten years. But some buyers prefer fixed-rate mortgages because it gives them peace of mind. They would rather know how much their monthly payment will be each month, even if it's higher than with an ARM. The monthly payment on an ARM has the potential of going higher in the future if interest rates rise significantly.

When interest rates are below 8 percent, home buyers tend to favor fixed-rate loans, if they can qualify. When interest rates rise above 9 percent, buyers usually prefer ARMs, to save money and to make qualifying easier. Your decision may depend on what you can afford now and what you anticipate your income will be in the future. For example, if your income is moving upward, it may make sense to buy a more expensive home using an ARM if the home will better suit your needs for the long run. You can refinance later into a fixed-rate mortgage when your income rises.

> **The longer you plan to stay in your home, the more it makes sense to get a fixed-rate mortgage.**

A variation on the thirty-year fixed-rate mortgage is a fixed-rate loan that has payments amortized on a thirty-year basis, but the loan is due in less than thirty years. These short-term fixed-rate mortgages, often due in five, seven, or ten years, usually have a lower interest rate than conventional thirty-year fixed-rate loans. Part of the principal is repaid during the term of the loan, because the payments are amortized. But they are not fully amortized. The due date is far short of the thirty years it would take to pay the loan off completely. At the end of the five, seven, or ten years, a *balloon payment* is due. A balloon payment is a final loan payment that is larger than the preceding installment (monthly) payments and that pays the loan off completely. On a thirty-year loan due in seven years with a 9 percent interest rate, the borrower will owe approximately 93 percent of the original loan amount at the end of seven years. For a $200,000 loan, the borrower would have an approximate remaining loan balance of $186,000 after seven years.

# Home Loan Guide

| Loan type | Description | Characteristics |
|---|---|---|
| **Fixed-rate mortgage** | Fixed interest rate for the term of the loan. | More difficult to qualify for than ARM because of higher interest rate. Usually not assumable. |
| **Adjustable-rate mortgage (ARM)** | Interest rate and monthly payments fluctuate during the term of the loan. Interest rate = index + margin. ARMs come in many forms. | Often start with a "teaser," or discounted, rate, but a higher interest rate may be used for qualifying. Often assumable. |
| **Hybrid loan** | Combines features of fixed- and adjustable-rate mortgages. Some are fixed for a time and then convert to an ARM. "Two-steps" are fixed at one rate for one period and at another rate for a second period. | More difficult to qualify for than ARM, but easier than conventional fixed-rate mortgages. Interest rates usually higher than ARMs but lower than fixed-rate mortgages. |
| **30-year loan** | The loan's monthly payments are calculated to pay the loan off fully in 30 years. | Has a lower monthly payment than a 15-year loan with the same interest rate. |
| **15-year loan** | The loan's monthly payments are calculated to pay the loan off fully in 15 years. | Interest rate is usually lower than on a 30-year loan. But more difficult to qualify for than 30- year fixed because of higher monthly payment. |
| **Amortized loan** | A part of each monthly payment goes to pay back principal (the amount borrowed). | Higher monthly payments than on interest-only loans. |
| **Interest-only loan** | Monthly payments pay interest only. Has a balloon payment equal to the amount borrowed. | Lower monthly payments; more tax write-off; riskier. |
| **Balloon payment loan** | Has a final loan payment larger than the periodic (monthly) payment, which pays the loan off completely. | Riskier than fully amortized loans, which completely pay back the principal over loan term. |
| **Conforming loan** | Conforms to Fannie Mae or Freddie Mac loan criteria. In 1996, the Fannie Mae and Freddie Mac loan limit was $207,000. | Must qualify according to Fannie Mae or Freddie Mac guidelines. Interest rates are lower than on nonconforming loans. |
| **Jumbo loan** | Loan amount over the Fannie Mae or Freddie Mac conforming limit. | Interest rates are usually .25 to .50% higher than on conforming loans. |

Fixed-rate, interest-only loans are also available. The monthly payments are not amortized; they pay the interest owed only. The amount borrowed is not reduced at all during the term of the loan. At the end of the term of the loan, the borrower must make a balloon payment equal to the original loan amount. One attraction of an interest-only loan is that the entire amount of the monthly mortgage payment is tax deductible. Also, the payments are lower than they would be on an amortized loan, so it's easier to qualify. Many loans that sellers carry-back are interest-only loans.

Don't wait until the last minute to line up the money to pay back a loan that has a balloon payment.

If you decide to take an interest-only loan or a short-term fixed-rate loan with a balloon payment, don't wait until the last minute to line up the money necessary to pay back the debt. Keep an eye on interest rates. You may want to refinance earlier than the due date if interest rates drop considerably.

## Adjustable-rate mortgages (ARMs)

An adjustable-rate mortgage has an interest rate that changes during the term of the loan. Most ARMs are fully amortized, so they are paid off completely at the end of the loan term. But the monthly payments do not remain constant for the term of the loan. The interest rate and monthly payments on ARMs change from time to time to reflect changes in the cost of money in finance markets.

The interest rate on an ARM is tied to an index, which measures the lender's cost of borrowing money. The index varies with the lender and the loan product. The most commonly used indexes are Treasury Securities (T-Bills), Eleventh District Cost of Funds Index (COFI), Certificates of Deposit (CDs), and the London interbank offering rate (LIBOR).

The fully indexed interest rate on an ARM is calculated by adding a margin, which is the lender's profit, to the index. The margin will also vary with the lender and the mortgage product, but it's usually in the 2 to 3 percent range. (The margin may be quoted in terms of basis points. If so, 100 basis points equal 1 percent.) An ARM that is tied to a one-year Treasury Security (T-Bill), with a starting index of 3.6 percent and a 3 percent margin, will have a fully indexed interest rate of 6.6 percent.

An ARM with a six-month CD or LIBOR index will be more volatile than one with either a one-year Treasury Security average index or the COFI. A more volatile index responds more quickly to market changes in interest rates: it moves up more quickly when rates rise

The fully indexed interest rate on an ARM is equal to the index plus the margin.

and drops faster when rates decline. The longer the term of the index, the more the borrower is protected from short-term erratic interest rate fluctuations. For example an ARM with a six-month T-Bill index will be more volatile than one with a one-year T-Bill index.

Many ARM lenders offer loans with discounted initial interest rates called teaser rates. These initial rates are well below the fully indexed rate. Whether a teaser rate is a good deal depends on the other terms of the loan. Find out how long the rate will be in effect and what the rate will be at the first adjustment. If the teaser rate will be in effect only for a few months, you might be better off with an ARM that starts at a higher interest rate, but that has a lower margin. The margin will be with you for the life of the loan. The lower the margin, the lower your long-term financing costs. Also, keep in mind that even though a teaser rate will save you money for a time, it may not make loan qualification easier. Most lenders will use a 7.5 percent interest rate to qualify you unless the fully indexed rate is less.

How often the ARM interest rate adjusts and by how much differs with the loan product. Some ARMs permit only one interest rate adjustment a year while others allow biannual or monthly adjustments. Some ARMs have a limit on how high the interest rate can go at any one adjustment. Many ARMs also set a limit on how high the interest rate can go in one year, called an annual cap. The annual cap is often no more than 2 percent a year. Most ARMs also have limits on how high the interest rate can go over the loan term. These are called lifetime caps. They also vary, depending on the loan, but expect about 4 to 6 percent. Find out if the lifetime cap is based on the teaser rate or on the fully indexed interest rate.

**A lower margin may save you more money in the long run than a lower teaser rate will.**

Watch out for loans that permit the lender to warehouse, or shelve, uncharged interest. Warehousing occurs if lenders can charge their borrowers interest that they were unable to charge in the past because of an interest rate cap. Let's say that your loan cannot increase more than 2 percent a year, and interest rates rise 3 percent in one year. If the lender can warehouse interest, the 1 percent that was not chargeable can be charged in a future year when interest rates rise less than 2 percent. In this case, you could find yourself with a loan rate that rises even though industry rates have dropped. Warehousing is a loan feature you want to avoid, if you can.

Some ARMs have payment caps; others do not. An ARM with a payment cap will limit the amount that the monthly payment can increase at each interest rate adjustment, usually up to 7.5 percent of the previous payment amount. If the amount of interest owed exceeds the capped payment amount and the borrower chooses to pay only the minimum payment due, negative amortization can occur. Let's say that you have a $150,000 adjustable-rate mortgage with a 7.5 percent payment cap and a current interest rate of 6 percent. Your current monthly payment is $900, which pays the entire interest owed. This payment will be in effect for one year, then it will adjust if interest rates have changed. During the year, suppose the interest rate on your loan increases to 7.5 percent. Without a payment cap, your monthly payment would jump to $1,048.50. But since your loan has a payment cap, the maximum monthly payment the lender can require you to pay at the next adjustment will be only $967.50. Even though your payment is capped, you are not relieved of the responsibility for paying the additional interest due; payment is simply deferred and added to the remaining loan balance. When this happens, your loan balance increases rather than decreases each time you make a monthly payment. Since you are charged interest on the entire remaining loan balance, you end up paying interest on the deferred interest when you allow negative amortization to occur. You can, however, avoid this.

Lenders put limits on how much negative amortization they will allow before they will require that the loan be restructured with a new fully amortized payment schedule. ARMs with payment caps are usually re-amortized every five years or so, or when the remaining balance increases to 125 percent of the original loan balance. What happens then? Your monthly payment is not protected by the 7.5 percent cap and could jump dramatically.

Negative amortization can be particularly risky when property values are declining. You could end up with a loan balance that is higher than the market value of your property. Let's say your initial loan was for 90 percent of the purchase price. Following your purchase, you accumulated $5,000 of negative amortization, and the value of your property declined by 10 percent. If you were then transferred and had to sell your home, you would have to come up with additional cash out-of-pocket to close the sale.

You might wonder why anyone would want a loan that has a payment cap. If you found yourself in a situation where interest rates escalated at the same time as you experienced a financial downturn, you might welcome a payment cap. It can help keep your expenses to a minimum until your financial picture improves. Sometimes ARMs with payment caps and the possibility for negative amortization are tied to a low index or they have a low margin, which makes them good deals.

Most borrowers have an adverse reaction to negative amortization, yet an ARM shouldn't be avoided just for this reason. Even though an ARM has the possibility of negative amortization, you don't have to let this occur if you are diligent and disciplined. The lender gives you the option each month of making the "minimum payment due" based on your payment cap, or you can make a fully amortized (or an interest only) payment that will pay the entire amount of interest due at that time. That way, you can avoid negative amortization.

Warning: Be aware that some low teaser rates on ARMs expire after three months. Then the fully indexed rate goes into effect. If the ARM has a payment that is capped for the first year, you could get into negative amortization starting with the fourth month unless you increase the amount you pay to cover the rate increase when the teaser rate expires.

One benefit of ARMs is that they are usually assumable by a subsequent qualified buyer. Fixed-rate loans usually are not. If money is scarce or interest rates are high at the time you want to sell your home, the next buyer may be able to take over your loan through a procedure call assumption, discussed later in this chapter.

Some ARMs are convertible to a fixed-rate loan. Usually the borrower has only once chance to convert and only at a time that is pre-determined when the loan begins. You might pay a premium for the convertibility feature in the form of a higher interest rate on the ARM. Make sure that the fixed-rate loan you end up with is competitive and that you are not paying too much for a convertibility feature. You might be better off to simply refinance from an ARM to a fixed-rate loan if interest rates drop significantly in the future—particularly if the nonconvertible ARM offers a much lower interest rate.

### Hybrids

Hybrid home mortgages combine features of both fixed- and adjustable-rate mortgages. They provide borrowers with some of the security of fixed-rate loans at interest rates that are lower than thirty-year fixed rate loans. Numerous hybrid loan products are on the market. When you are shopping for these loans, make sure that you are comparing like loan products. Some are fixed at one interest rate for a number of years (usually three, five, seven, or ten), after which they convert to an ARM. Others, called two-step loans, are fixed for a time at one interest rate and then switch to another fixed rate for the remaining term of the loan. If a loan is designated as a 7/23, this means that it is fixed for seven years at an initial interest rate, then the interest rate is adjusted to a second rate for the next twenty-three years. This second rate may be higher than the current rate on a thirty-year fully amortized fixed-rate loan. But if you sell your home before the higher rate takes effect, the savings could be substantial.

Hybrid loans are often the loan of choice for borrowers who plan to stay in their homes for a relatively short period of time but who want the temporary security of stable monthly payments. Even if you select a mortgage that is fixed for seven years before it becomes an ARM and you stay for nine or ten years, you will probably save money when compared to the cost of a thirty-year fixed rate loan. If you only plan to stay for three to five years, you may be better off with an ARM than you would be with a hybrid if you consider the loan cost alone. Just make sure to find out how much the interest rate on a hybrid can increase when the rate adjusts. With some hybrid loans, the annual interest rate cap does not apply to the first rate adjustment, which occurs at the end of the fixed-rate period of the loan. The interest rate may go to the fully indexed rate at that time.

**The key to determining which loan is best for you is to consider how long you plan to stay in the house.**

## Selecting the loan term

Most home mortgages are due in thirty or fifteen years. Twenty-year and forty-year terms are also available for some loans. A thirty-year loan uses a monthly schedule that pays the loan off completely over thirty years. A fifteen-year loan is paid off in fifteen years, a twenty-year loan in twenty years, and a forty-year loan in forty years. The longer the term of the loan, the lower the monthly payments. The monthly payments on a thirty- or forty-year loan are lower than they are on fifteen- and twenty-year loans. Because of the lower monthly payments, thirty-year and forty-year loans are easier to qualify for. When interest rates drop, which makes qualifying for all types of loans easier, more buyers consider fifteen-year loans. When rates rise or when a borrower's qualifying ratios are marginal a thirty- or forty-year term is often the choice.

The primary advantage of a fifteen-year loan is that the amount of interest paid during the term of the loan is much less than it is on a thirty-year loan. The longer the term of the loan, the larger the total finance charge paid by the borrower. Also, fifteen-year home loans are usually offered at a lower interest rate than thirty-year loans—about one-quarter to one-half percent less. The total interest paid on a $100,000, fifteen-year fixed-rate loan at 7 percent is $61,789. On a $100,000 thirty-year fixed-rate loan at 7.5 percent, the interest paid will amount to $151,712.

A fifteen-year loan makes sense for someone who plans to retire within the next ten to fifteen years. It also makes sense for someone who is starting out with a low cash down but a large income and who anticipates trading up to a more expensive home in the future. A fifteen-year loan forces you to save money faster than with a thirty-year loan. Since you pay more money to principal in the early years of a fifteen-year loan compared to a thirty-year loan you build equity at a much faster pace. It takes twenty-four and a half years to pay down one half of a fixed-rate loan that's amortized over thirty years. If you do select a fifteen-year loan in order to obtain maximum equity buildup in the shortest period of time and you plan to trade-up soon, make certain that the lender won't charge a prepayment penalty (an extra charge for paying a loan off before a certain date). This would diminish your savings.

Despite the savings, a fifteen-year home loan does not make sense for everyone. The monthly payments are $228 per month more on a fifteen-year fixed-rate loan than they are on a thirty-year loan for each $100,000 financed at a 7.5 percent interest rate. Even if you can qualify at the higher monthly payment rate, you may feel more comfortable with a thirty-year loan if your future income is uncertain or if it fluctuates widely. An additional factor to consider is that a fifteen-year loan will usually provide less tax shelter. Mortgage interest payments are tax deductible; the higher the amount of interest paid, the larger the tax deduction (although some restrictions apply). However, even when you take the tax savings into account, a fifteen-year loan could cost you less in the long run.

One advantage of a thirty-year home loan is that it gives you more control over your finances. Barring explicit restrictions by the lender, borrowers can increase the amount they pay monthly to the lender and thereby decrease the amount of interest paid over the term of the loan. If you make one extra monthly payment per year, you can pay a thirty-year fixed-rate loan off in just twenty years. With a thirty-year loan, you can decide how much interest you ultimately pay, how much interest write-off and tax shelter you want, and how much over the minimum payment due you pay monthly. With a fifteen-year loan, however, you are locked into making higher monthly payments every month for the term of the loan, even during times when you may be cash-strapped. An attractive feature of the thirty-year loan is that it gives the borrower the flexibility to make higher monthly payments when it's affordable to do so, but it's not required.

Before you select any loan product, understand fully how it works. Fixed-rate mortgages are simple and straightforward when compared to ARMs or hybrid loan products, because the interest rate never changes. If you are considering an ARM or hybrid, have your loan originator show you how the loan works. Find out the worst-case scenario if interest rates do nothing but rise—although this is unlikely to happen—during the term of the loan. The true test of whether you understand your mortgage is if you can explain to someone else how and when your interest rate and payments will change in the future. If you can't do this, have your mortgage broker or loan agent work with you until you can.

> **Making one extra monthly payment per year will pay a thirty-year fixed-rate loan off in twenty years.**

# Shopping for a lender

There are many ways to find a lender. Buyers who are short on time will want to delegate as much of this part of the transaction as possible to someone else. If you have bought and sold homes previously and you have a good working relationship with a lender or mortgage broker, you may want to use this person's services again. Busy first-time buyers will want to hook up with someone sharp who can handle the financing arrangements for them. If you followed the home buyer's game plan outlined in Chapter 1, you will already be prequalified or preapproved for a loan by the time you need to find a lender. If so, and if you established a good rapport with the person who prequalified you, you may need to look no further, particularly if this person came highly recommended.

Buyers who have the time and who want to shop for the best value in town may want to talk to several mortgage people before committing to one. There's no obligation to use the person who prequalified you. Most buyers want the best interest rate they can get, so it's natural to place this at the top of your shopping list. But keep in mind that some companies that offer unbelievably low rates in comparison to the competition are fly-by-night operations that don't deliver as promised. Ask for references. Try to get the names and phone numbers of the last several people who got a loan through the individual you are considering working with. Call the references and ask if they were pleased with the service. Ask if their loan closed on time, on the terms promised, and if there were any unanticipated surprises.

Research your local banking connections to see if you might be able to get a better-than-market-rate mortgage. Sometimes credit unions offer good deals to their subscribers. Just make sure that your credit union routinely makes home loans. If not, their loan processing may be inefficient, which could delay your closing or contingency deadline. A personal banker may be able to arrange a mortgage for you, especially if there is something out-of-the-ordinary about your financing package. If your ratios are slightly off but your banker knows you are a good risk from years of past experience, the bank may make an exception for you when a conventional mortgage lender would not. A friend in the business may be able to pull a string or two for you. Just make sure that the person is in the home loan business and has a lot of experience doing home loans. Doing business with friends can be a tricky, because if the transaction does not go well, your friendship could be jeopardized.

To get a grasp on current interest rates, look in the real estate section of the local Sunday newspaper for a posting of mortgage offerings from a number of local lenders. Interest rates do vary from one location to the next, so look within your local marketplace. The Internet is another source of information about current interest rates, as are on-line services like America Online, Prodigy, and Compuserve. Keep in mind that rates can change weekly, and even daily with some lenders. The rates you see in the paper may be out-of-date by the time the papers hit the newsstands. But at least this will give you a feel for what the going interest rates are, and a basis for comparison as you shop for a lender.

You will need to make a decision about where you are going for your financing in a relatively short period of time. Your purchase contract should include a financing contingency, which may set a deadline for your loan approval. The deadline is often thirty days following the sellers' acceptance. You should start looking for a lender the day your contract is ratified, if you haven't already picked one out. The financing contingency may also specify a time for you to submit a loan application (usually five to seven days) and to provide a prequalification letter, if you don't already have one.

If the current demand for money is low, you may find lenders competing wildly for your business. At other times they can be swamped with loan applications. When interest rates are relatively high or the housing market is slow, you will find that lenders offer incentives in order to get your lending business. Some lenders will pay part of your closing costs. Others will overlook blemishes on your credit report. Adjustable-rate lenders slash their teaser rates to stimulate business.

Don't let sales gimmicks be the deciding factor when you select a home loan. A very low teaser rate on an ARM will only be in effect for a short time. This may save you some money in the short run, but find out how your monthly payments will be affected in the future when the teaser rate expires. You will have to live with the loan and refinancing can be costly. Consider the merits of the loan itself, not just an up-front incentive that is offered in exchange for your business.

### Interest rates, points, and the APR

When you call around looking for a lender, you will be quoted information on the cost of loans in terms of the interest rate and points. Points is a term used in the mortgage business to refer to the upfront loan origination fee. One point is equal to 1 percent of the loan amount. One and one half points charged for a $200,000 loan would be $3,000. The number of points charged will vary from lender to lender, and from one type of loan to another. They are usually paid at closing. Points are often higher for a fixed-rate loan than they are for an ARM for the same loan amount. There is usually an inverse relationship between the interest rate and the points charged on a loan: the lower the interest rate, the higher the points and vice versa. Often a single loan will have different pricing options depending on how many points you are willing to pay. A loan of $200,000 might be available for 7.25 percent on a thirty-year fixed loan, with one point paid at closing. The same loan might also be available with a 7.125 percent interest rate, and one-and-one-half points. Each one-half point you pay buys down the interest rate on the loan 1/8 percent.

**The lower the interest rate, the higher the points and vice versa.**

**One-half point buys down the interest rate 1/8 percent.**

On a purchase loan, the points are tax-deductible in the year of purchase. On a refinance loan, the points can only be written off incrementally over the term of the loan (1/30 each year on a thirty-year loan). Points cannot be written off entirely in the year you refinance. Unclaimed refinance points can be taken as a write-off in the year the home is sold or refinanced again. No-point loans are available, but the trade-off is a higher interest rate on the loan. If you are short on cash but can qualify for a higher interest rate, a no-point loan will significantly reduce the amount of your closing costs. If you are not cash-strapped, then paying higher points in exchange for a lower interest rate will make more sense the longer you plan to own your new home. The lower monthly payment will save you money in the long run. Homeowners who plan to refinance might prefer a low- or no-point loan with a higher interest rate.

The APR (Annual Percentage Rate) is a tool borrowers can use to compare the cost of different loans. The APR is the effective rate of interest on a mortgage when the upfront financing charges (points and other loan fees) are taken into account. So a loan with a 7 percent interest rate might have an APR of 7.5 percent when the points and loan fees are taken into account. In calculating the APR, it's assumed that you are paying for the loan fees over the term of the loan rather than as one lump sum at closing. Federal law requires lenders to disclose the APR to a prospective borrower within three days of receiving a loan application. But you can ask any lender you talk to for the APR on the different loans you are comparing.

The APR for an adjustable-rate mortgage (ARM) will only be approximate, because the interest rate on an ARM changes over time. When lenders compute the APR on an ARM, they assume that the loan will adjust to the current fully indexed rate and will stay at that rate for the remaining term of the loan. In reality, the index and interest rate fluctuate, so it's impossible to know exactly what the interest rate will be in the future. Therefore it's unlikely that the APR on an ARM will reflect the true cost of borrowing. The same warning applies to hybrid loans that are fixed for a time, and then convert to an ARM.

Although the APR on an ARM won't tell you how much the loan will cost you over time, you should ask your loan originator to give you a worst-case cost scenario. This will tell you what your monthly payments will be if the interest rate on the loan goes up the maximum allowed at each adjustment. Some buyers ask for a worst-case, best-case, and historically based scenario. A historical analysis will tell you how the loan might behave in the future based on how the index has fluctuated in the past. All three scenarios give a well-rounded picture of how an ARM might behave over time.

When you are shopping for rates and you are comparing the APR on fixed-rate loans, be sure to ask how long the interest rate quote is good for. The lowest interest rates are usually for loans that will close quickly. A loan that can close in ten days, which is very difficult to do, will probably have a lower interest rate than will one that has a closing date of forty-five days. Most buyers can't close within ten days, much less get a loan processed within ten days, so it's deceptive to quote a rate that is only good for ten days. But if you ask for the lowest possible rate, you might be given a ten-day quote. A reputable mortgage broker will probably quote you a thirty- or forty-five-day rate. Also, just because a lender gives you a quote, it doesn't mean that the rate is guaranteed (or locked in). You may have to submit a loan application before a rate can be locked in. Some lenders can't lock rates until the loan is approved. See below for more about lock-ins.

For all loans, make sure you are comparing apples to apples, not apples to oranges. There are many different loan products on the market, with different prices. The interest rate and points for ARMs may differ considerably depending on the particular features of the loan, like the index and the margin. Fixed-rate loan pricing also varies depending on when the loan is due. If you are looking for a thirty-year fixed-rate loan due in thirty years, make sure you are not being quoted a rate for a "thirty-year, due in seven" loan. A loan with payments amortized on a thirty-year schedule that is due in seven years should have a lower interest rate than a fully amortized thirty-year fixed-rate loan—but it will be due in seven, not thirty, years.

### Comparing lenders

Here is a list of questions to ask when shopping for a loan. (Some questions may not be relevant to your situation.)

## Lender comparison checklist

| Lender: | Loan agent: | Phone number: |
| --- | --- | --- |

What types of home loan programs do you offer? *(Not all lenders provide all loan programs.)*

What are your current interest rates?

How many points do you charge?

Do you charge any other up-front fees *(in addition to points)*? When are these fees paid?

Are any fees refunded if the loan is denied?

What are your qualifying ratios? *(Briefly review your financial situation and the terms of the sale with each lender to make sure there's a good chance you will be approved for a loan before you apply.)*

Do you require impeccable credit or are you flexible? Do you give a preferential interest rate for good credit?

What will the monthly payment be *(principal and interest)*?

Will mortgage insurance (MI) be required? If so, how much will it cost?

Will an impound account be required *(for property taxes and insurance)*? If so, how much will it cost?

Approximately how much cash will I need to close?

Can some or all of the cash required to close be a gift from a relative? If yes, how much?

Will you allow the sellers to credit money for my closing costs? If so, how much?

Is there a balloon payment? If so, when is it due and how much will it be?

Can I lock in an interest rate? When? For how long? What will it cost? Will you put the lock-in commitment in writing?

How long will it take to get a loan approved?

Does loan approval and processing occur locally? *(Processing a loan long distance can take longer.)*

Do you have ultimate underwriting authority? *(If a second investor's approval is required, this takes longer.)*

Do you give a written *(not verbal)* loan commitment?

Do your loans have prepayment penalties? If so, how much? When do they expire?

Are your loans assumable? If so, on what terms?

Do you require that termite work be completed by closing?

How long have you been in business?

Do you sell your loans or are you a portfolio lender? *(See below for more information about portfolio lenders.)*

Will you provide references of recent customers? *(Be sure to check references. You are looking for a loan you can live with from a lender who will process your loan efficiently.)*

## Shopping for an ARM

Determining which ARM is right for you will depend, in part, on how long you plan to stay in your home. A low initial interest rate and up-front fees will be more important if you plan to move again soon. The margin and lifetime cap will be less important because you will not be living with the loan for very long. If you plan to be in the home indefinitely, a lower margin is usually better than a lower starting interest rate. A lower lifetime cap will be important since you may be in your home long enough to actually see it go into effect.

An ARM that adjusts only once a year but that has a higher initial rate may cost you less than one that adjusts twice a year but has a lower start rate. ARMs that adjust only once a year also have the benefit of enabling you to prepare for monthly payment adjustments. Six-month adjustments can be harder to handle.

Some ARMs have prepayment penalties if you pay the loan off early. A prepayment penalty could wipe out any benefit you derived from a lower start rate or no points. Whether you will want to consider a loan that has an early payoff penalty will depend on how long you plan to stay in the home. If your move is permanent, a loan with a prepayment penalty that expires after three or so years may be a reasonable gamble.

As discussed above, the APR on an ARM can only be an approximation of the true cost of the loan over time. Rather than focus on the APR, you should take other factors into account when comparing ARMs (see next page for comparison worksheet). For instance, how long will the initial rate be in effect? What is the index? How often will adjustments take place? What is the annual cap (the maximum amount the interest rate can go up in a year)? What is the lifetime cap (the maximum rate over the life of the loan)? Does the loan have the potential for negative amortization? Is warehousing of interest a possibility?

## Mortgage broker or direct lender?

Mortgage brokers originate loans, but they do not lend money to borrowers. They shop the loan market to find loans that suit their borrower's needs; they search for the best interest rate and terms. In addition, mortgage brokers assemble the buyer's financial documentation, including verifications of the cash required to close (down payment and closing costs) and employment, and they submit the buyer's loan package to a specific lender for approval. The lender reviews the loan package to determine how risky it is (called underwriting), approves the loan, and issues the funds to the borrower at closing. The lender is the money source; the mortgage broker is an intermediary who brings the borrower and lender together.

You can get a mortgage either by going directly to a lender, if the lender deals with the public, or by working through a mortgage broker. When you go directly to a lender, that lender can only offer you that lender's loan products. If the lender doesn't have the type of loan you want, you have to go to another lender. Mortgage brokers, on the other hand, usually have access to many different loan products offered through

# ARM comparison worksheet

| Adjustable-rate mortgage feature | Loan #1 | Loan #2 | Loan #3 |
| --- | --- | --- | --- |
| Index<br>What is the current index rate?<br>How much has the index varied over the last several years? | | | |
| Margin | | | |
| Initial interest rate<br>How long is initial rate in effect?<br>Interest rate after 1st adjustment? | | | |
| What is the fully indexed rate? | | | |
| Points<br>Other loan origination fees? | | | |
| How often does the interest rate adjust? | | | |
| What is the annual interest rate cap? | | | |
| What is the lifetime interest rate cap? | | | |
| Is there a payment cap?<br>What is the payment cap? | | | |
| Is negative amortization possible?<br>When is the loan reamortized? | | | |
| Is there a prepayment penalty?<br>How much?<br>When does it expire? | | | |
| Is the loan assumable?<br>On the same loan terms?<br>What is the assumption fee? | | | |
| Is the loan convertible to a fixed-rate loan?<br>When?<br>To what interest rate?<br>What is the conversion fee? | | | |
| Is warehousing of unclaimed interest allowed? | | | |

many different lenders. If you are working with a mortgage broker, and you fail to qualify for one type of loan, the broker can quickly move your application to another lender with easier qualification requirements. On your own, it might take weeks to find another lender, make an application, and get approved.

Mortgage brokers can also arrange financing that you wouldn't otherwise have access to. The reason is that some lenders work only with mortgage brokers; they do not accept loan applications from individual borrowers. These are called wholesale lenders, and some of these loans have the best rates and terms available. Lenders who offer loans directly to the public are called retail lenders. Some retail lenders only offer retail loans. They won't accept loans that are brokered through a mortgage broker. Some lenders offer loans on both a wholesale basis, through mortgage brokers, and on a retail basis.

Mortgage brokers work on commission. They charge borrowers a fee (called points) for their loan brokering services. (One point is equal to one percent of the loan amount.) The lender also charges points. However, with a brokered loan, the lender's points are usually less than they would be if you went directly to the lender. When loans are originated without a mortgage broker, the lenders must do all of the loan processing, and they usually charge more for this. With a brokered loan, much of the lender's processing work is done by the broker, so the lender can offer lower points. Even though both the lender and mortgage broker charge points on a brokered loan, you should not have to pay more than you would if you were to go directly to the lender. For example, if you were to go directly to ABC Bank for a loan, you might pay 1½ points. But if you go through a mortgage broker, who brokers the loan through the wholesale lending department of ABC bank, you might pay ½ point to the lender at closing, and a point to the mortgage broker. Mortgage brokers who have good working relationships with a lender are sometimes given preferred status. A preferred status broker can get you better pricing from a lender than you can get by going to the lender directly. In addition to getting a broader range of services from a mortgage broker, you may actually get a better interest rate.

On a zero-point loan, the borrower is not charged points at closing. Instead, the mortgage broker is paid by the lender at closing in the form of a rebate, which is a percent of the loan amount. The lender's rebate pays the mortgage broker for originating and packaging the loan. The rebate is figured into the borrower's cost of the loan, usually in the form of a higher interest rate, so in a sense the borrower is paying this fee.

A prepayment penalty is often part of the pricing package on a zero-point loan. If the borrower pays the loan off before the penalty expires (usually in about three years), the lender collects an additional fee from the borrower. This enables the lender to recoup the costs of loan processing, or the rebate that was paid to the mortgage broker at closing. Prepayment penalties are illegal in some states.

One disadvantage of working with mortgage brokers is that they do not have control over the lenders they work with. When you deal directly with a lender, your loan agent can check with their underwriters to see if your package is likely to be approved.

Underwriters are employed by lenders to assign a degree of risk to borrower's loan packages. Lenders and their underwriters dictate the terms under which they will grant a loan; mortgage brokers have no control over this.

An experienced mortgage broker can take a lot of the hassle out of the loan approval process. Sometimes the difference between loan approval and denial depends on how the borrower's financial documentation is assembled or packaged for the lender. A savvy loan broker will be able to assess your financial situation and know what kinds of documentation you need to provide in order to get a loan approved, and approved promptly. With experience, mortgage brokers learn how to anticipate underwriters' objections. They can work with you to overcome any objectionable items before your package is submitted to underwriting for approval.

TALES FROM THE TRENCHES: EPISODE 16

*Dana and Rod made an offer to buy their first home. They made their offer contingent upon obtaining a loan for 90 percent of the purchase price within thirty days of acceptance. Like many first-time buyers, they were getting gift funds from Rod's parents for part of the down payment. Their financial picture was not dismal, but not great: they had a few late payments on charge accounts. Their income was good, but they were both self-employed, working on commission. They had made less money for the past several years, so their ratios were marginal. Two mortgage brokers worked with them, but they were denied by three lenders. One lender was willing to do the loan, but only if Dana and Rod made a 20 percent cash down payment, which was impossible for them. Finally, they hooked up with an experienced and talented mortgage broker who understood what the underwriters wanted to see. She talked to the seller's agent, who was impressed with her expertise. Based on her optimism that she could get the loan approved, the sellers granted an extension on the financing contingency. When Dana and Rod's loan package was presented to a lender by this mortgage broker, the late payments had been satisfactorily explained, the income-to-debt ratios were in line, and the loan was approved.*

As in any profession, some mortgage brokers are better than others. Interview mortgage brokers just as you would real estate agents. You want someone who instills confidence and someone who has a good track record. Although interest rates and points are a consideration in selecting a mortgage broker, service and trustworthiness are also important. A mortgage broker should be able to advise you about which kind of loan will work best for you. A good broker should help educate you about mortgage products. If the broker just seems interested in making a fast buck, go to someone else. Good brokers will be interested in building an ongoing relationship with you so that you will use their services again when you refinance or move. Check with friends who have purchased or refinanced a home recently for recommendations. If you are dealing with someone who wasn't referred to you, ask for the names and phone numbers of recent borrowers. Call them to find out if they were satisfied and if they'd use the broker again. Ask if they were satisfied with the loan they got. Some brokers will attempt to sell borrowers loans that are the easiest to get approved, even if these loans are not the borrower's choice. Be sure to let each broker you talk to know that you are talking to several brokers. A broker might be willing to give you a break on the points to get your business.

## Portfolio lender

A portfolio lender generates home loans that will become a part of that lender's own investment portfolio. Other lenders generate loans that are later sold to other investors. Lenders who sell their loans usually sell them on the secondary money market to Fannie Mae (Federal National Mortgage Association) or Freddie Mac (Federal Home Loan Mortgage Corporation), two organizations that purchase home loans at a discount and then resell them to investors.

Loans intended for sale to Freddie Mac or Fannie Mae must conform to rigid guidelines. Consequently, you will find it harder to qualify for these loans. The originating lenders are limited when it comes to bending the rules to accommodate an individual borrower. For example, the maximum loan amount is restricted and varies from one year to the next. In 1996, the limit was $207,000. Loans that conform to these limits are referred to as conforming loans. Loans in amounts that exceed the conforming loan limits are called jumbo loans. The qualifying criteria are often tougher on conforming loans than on jumbos, but the pricing (interest rate, fees, and points) is usually better. Jumbo loan rates are usually higher. Conforming rates tend to be the lowest rates available.

Portfolio lenders have more flexibility in qualifying borrowers. For example, Freddie Mac and Fannie Mae will not permit the entire down payment to be a gift if the borrower is applying for a 90-percent loan. A portfolio lender may allow this. Freddie Mac and Fannie Mae will not approve 80-10-10 financing without charging MI (mortgage insurance), but a portfolio lender often will. Portfolio lenders may be able to stretch the qualifying ratios if your income is shy of what is required for a Freddie Mac or Fannie Mae loan. Portfolio lenders frequently offer 90- and 95-percent loans that don't require separate mortgage insurance (MI). Many of these lenders self-insure for MI, the cost of which is usually built into the price of the loan in the form of a higher interest rate. This makes loan qualification easier because separate loan approval by an independent MI company is not required.

Portfolio lenders are not only more flexible in approving borrowers, they can be more liberal about property condition. A portfolio lender might be your only option if you need an "as is" loan to buy a property in its present condition. Some portfolio lenders will allow funds from the seller's proceeds to be held in an account so that termite or other repair work can be completed after closing. Freddie Mac and Fannie Mae lenders usually won't permit holdbacks for such work.

Although portfolio lenders can often work wonders for borrowers whose circumstances are out of the ordinary, this will not always be the case. Some portfolio lenders are enormous financial organizations. In some cases, this means less rather than more flexibility. Before submitting a loan application with a portfolio lender, sit down with a loan agent and review your particular home loan needs. Find out if the loan processing and underwriting will be completed by local people who are knowledgeable about local conditions, or if it will be handled elsewhere. Find out if appraisals are done by local professionals, and if loan will be funded locally.

One disadvantage of using portfolio lenders is that they usually offer a limited number of loan programs, and they can be more expensive. But if your loan qualification is marginal, this may be your only option. You can refinance into a better loan when your financial situation improves.

### Deciding how many points to pay

How many points you pay should depend on how long you intend to stay in your home and on what kind of loan you are getting. On an adjustable-rate mortgage (ARM), paying points to buy down the initial rate may be a waste of money because the initial or teaser rate is only in effect for a short time. If you are going to pay points for an ARM, use them to buy down the margin on the loan. The index fluctuates over time; the margin stays constant. The lower the margin, the lower your long-term financing costs.

A large percentage of today's borrowers aren't paying points because they don't perceive that they get much benefit in relationship to the up-front cost. The future value of money is a consideration. Many no-point loan proponents believe that tomorrow's dollars will be worth less than the dollar is today because of future inflation. So why pay thousands of today's valuable dollars for a lower interest rate when you can save the points, pay a higher interest rate (which is tax deductible), and repay your loan with tomorrow's less valuable dollars? Other considerations come into play. Buyers, particularly first-time buyers, are often short on cash to close. Taking a no-point loan is one way to keep closing costs to a minimum. The ability to write off points in the year of purchase is lost, but the higher interest rate on the loan is tax-deductible, in most cases.

The time-test is often the deciding factor. The longer you plan to stay in the home, the more it makes sense to pay points to buy down the interest rate (or the margin on an ARM). Ask your lender or mortgage broker to run a cost analysis for you to compare the relative costs of a loan with points as compared to one with no points. You may want to have several projections run: one with high points (2 or more), one with low points (.5 to 1.5) and one with zero points. Lenders usually offer several pricing options.

Here is why the length of time you plan to keep the loan is so important. Let's say that you are considering a $200,000 loan at 7.5 percent and two points and one at 8 percent with no points. You plan to stay in the house for seven years. If you take the 7.5 percent loan, you will pay $4,000 at closing in points and $1,398 per month (principal and interest). At the end of seven years you will have paid about $101,136 in interest. If you take the 8 percent loan, you will pay no points at closing and $1,468 per month. But at the end of seven years, you will have paid about $108,227 in interest. In this case, you would be better off paying the points for the lower interest rate.

To figure out how many points you should pay, calculate how long you would need to keep the loan to make it worth your while to pay points. Or, ask your loan agent to calculate this for you. Buyers who plan to stay put a short time, say three to five years, will probably save money with a no-point loan. Homeowners who are refinancing and who can't write the points off in one year, may also prefer a no-point loan.

## Prepayment penalties

A prepayment penalty is a fee that a borrower must pay when a loan is paid off early. Not all loans have prepayment penalties. In fact, prepayment penalties are illegal in a dozen or so states. Years ago, the term "prepayment penalty" carried a negative connotation. Borrowers typically pay a hefty fee (points) to originate a loan. Lenders who penalized borrowers by collecting another fee when the loan was paid off early were regarded by many as greedy and unscrupulous. So prepayment penalties disappeared from the lending scene in the mid-1980s. Now they are back in vogue, but they are not all bad. In fact, a loan with a prepayment penalty may actually save you money. Many no-point loans have prepayment penalties.

The amount of a prepayment penalty will vary from one lender to the next and from one loan to another. The most common prepayment penalty in today's marketplace is 2 percent of the remaining loan balance. Even loans with prepayment penalties usually allow the borrower to prepay up to 20 percent of the loan balance in any given year without penalty. Most of today's loans have prepayment penalties that expire in three years. But this also varies with the loan. Some loans have prepayment penalties that expire in two years; some expire in four years.

Here's how a prepayment penalty can save you money. Let's say you need a $200,000 mortgage. Your lender gives you a choice. You can either have an ARM that starts at 4.5 percent with a one point loan origination fee, no prepayment penalty, and a 2.4 percent margin. Or you can have a no-point ARM with a 4.5 percent start rate, a 2.65 percent margin and a prepayment penalty. The prepayment penalty is equal to 2 percent of the loan balance if you pay the loan off within the next three years. The zero-point loan, with a prepayment penalty, is the best deal if you plan to keep the loan for three or four years. However, if you paid the loan off during the first three years the prepayment penalty would more than wipe out any savings you received by not paying the one point.

You are financially better off taking the one-point loan option if you plan to stay with the loan longer than four years because you will benefit from the lower margin. The amount saved with the lower margin in the example is approximately $500 per year. This comparison assumes that the other features of the two loan programs are the same. If the lifetime cap on one loan option is much lower than on the other, this could influence your decision, particularly if you plan to stay in the home for a long time.

# Getting the loan approved

Both you and the property need to qualify for a mortgage. Your loan approval depends on your loan application, your supporting documentation, and your credit history. For the property to qualify, the appraisal must be acceptable, and title to the property must be clear of any defects unacceptable to the lender. Your lender or loan broker will take care of ordering the appraisal and credit report for you. You may have to pay for both of these at the time you apply for the loan. A credit report should cost about $25 to $50 for an individual or a married couple. The cost of an appraisal will vary depending on the location, the price, and the size of the property. It could be from $200 to $500, or more for very expensive properties.

Lenders usually require a seemingly endless amount of documentation to approve a mortgage. First, you will have to complete a loan application, a copy of which is included in Appendix 2. Some lenders or brokers will take your financial information from you at an initial meeting and complete the application for you. You will have to sign the application, however, which asks you to acknowledge that the information you included is true and correct. Knowingly falsifying a loan application is a federal crime. Also, it's risky. A certain number of loan applications are actually audited after closing. If you submit a fraudulent loan application and get caught, the lender can demand instant repayment of the entire loan. In addition, you could face criminal penalties.

To hasten the approval process, provide as much of your financial documentation as possible when you meet with the lender to complete the loan application. Most lenders need copies of W-2s for the last two years and copies of paycheck stubs for the last thirty days. They will need your employment history for the past two years, including addresses for verification, and an explanation in writing for any gaps in employment. Self-employed individuals will need to supply complete copies of their federal tax returns for the last two years, along with a year-to-date profit and loss statement and a current balance sheet. If you are incorporated or have partnership income you will need to supply copies of corporate or partnership federal tax returns for the last two years. You will need to provide rental, or lease, agreements and mortgage statements for any rental properties that you own.

In addition to verifying your income, the lender will need to verify the source of the funds needed to close (your down payment and closing costs) and your debts. Compile three months' worth of statements for all checking, savings, IRAs, stocks, money market funds, and other asset accounts with their addresses, account numbers, and balances. The lender wants to know not only where your money is, but how long it has been there and where it came from. If your parents are giving you part of the down payment money, they will need to provide a gift letter that stipulates that the money does not have to be repaid. If you are selling or have sold a home to buy another one, the lender will want a copy of the final closing statement (called a HUD-1) from the sale of that property. If the sale has not yet closed, you can usually provide this at closing.

Compile a list of all outstanding debts (credit cards, car payments, student loans, etc.) with addresses, account numbers, current balances, and payment amounts. Divorced borrowers will need to provide a final copy of their settlement agreement. And if you are receiving child support or alimony the lender will want you to verify the last twelve months of payments received.

Some lenders will approve home mortgages using alternative or minimum documentation. If you are applying for such a loan, you will have less paperwork to produce to get approved for the loan. But you still need to provide three months' worth of bank statements, W-2s for the last two years, paycheck stubs for the past thirty days, and the last two years' tax returns, if you are self-employed. The lender will confirm the rest of your financial picture (like verification of employment) by phone.

To approve your mortgage, the lender will need a copy of the purchase agreement. Your real estate agent should be able to provide a copy. If you are buying a condominium or cooperative, the lender will require information about the project such as copies of the Covenants, Conditions, and Restrictions (CC&Rs), the Articles of Incorporation, and the Bylaws. Usually the seller, your real estate agent, or an officer of the homeowner's association or cooperative board of directors can provide copies of the necessary documentation.

After you have completed a loan application and assembled the necessary documentation, your loan agent will submit the package, with the property appraisal and your credit report, to the underwriting department. The underwriter reviews the package to determine the level of risk involved in approving the loan. Sometimes, after a loan has been underwritten, it requires separate approval from an investor or a mortgage insurance company. This can add time to the approval process.

To increase your chances of a speedy approval, be completely candid with your loan originator about any aspect of your financial history that might be questionable. If your credit was shaky at some time in the past, this should be dealt with upfront. When you apply for a mortgage, a residential mortgage credit report (RMCR) is usually ordered. This is an in-depth credit report, and it takes a couple of days to get. Your loan agent or mortgage broker should review the RMCR credit report with you when it comes in to see if there are any surprises. Often credit blemishes can be remedied with the help of your loan originator.

## Disclosure of settlement costs

Federal law says you are supposed to receive a Truth-in-Lending disclosure statement within three days of submitting a home loan application. The purpose of the disclosure is to tell you the true cost of the financing you are applying for, as well as other pertinent information about the loan. The Truth-in-Lending statement shows the Annual Percentage Rate (APR), the total finance change, the amount financed, the total number of payments, the amount of the scheduled monthly payments, penalties for early pre-payment (if there are any), whether the loan is assumable, late payment charges, and insurance requirements.

Your mortgage lender is also required to give you a good-faith estimate of all closing costs within three days, along with a booklet entitled "Settlement Costs—A HUD Guide." Typical closing costs might include: loan origination fees; loan discount fees (another name for points); appraisal fee; credit report; inspection fee; mortgage broker fee; tax service fee (informs the lender that your property taxes are current); prorated interest (to cover interest you owe from closing to your first mortgage payment); mortgage insurance premium; hazard (homeowner's) insurance premium; cash reserves; settlement fee; abstract or title search; title examination; document preparation fee; title insurance; attorneys' fees; recording fees; city/county tax (called stamps); state tax; survey; and pest inspection. Not all of these charges will apply to every transaction and some might be paid for by the sellers, depending on where you buy.

Make sure that you understand the closing cost estimate and have your real estate agent review it for you to see if anything has been overlooked. For instance, if the mortgage lender isn't routinely doing loans in your area and you have a local transfer tax that is customarily paid by the buyer, this might not be included on the good-faith estimate.

Ask your loan agent or mortgage broker if there will be any other cash requirements, other than those included on the closing cost estimate. Will the lender require you to have extra cash reserves in the bank after closing? Will you have to fund an impound account? (An impound account is a fund set up by the lender for collection of money from the borrower to pay future property taxes, mortgage insurance, and hazard insurance.) Is the estimate for homeowner's insurance accurate? If you are receiving a credit from the sellers for some or all of your nonrecurring closing costs, this will reduce the amount of cash you will need at closing. Find out if the lender has any closing cost credit limitation. Make sure you know exactly how much cash you need to come up with to complete the purchase.

You may receive more than one Truth-in-Lending disclosure and good-faith estimate of closing costs. If you are working with a mortgage broker, you should receive one set of disclosures from the broker within three days of submitting your application. When the broker submits your loan application to a specific lender, you should receive another set of disclosures directly from the lender. The two disclosures may not be identical. Buyers often don't know which loan they want when they complete the loan application.

When the loan is submitted to the lender for approval, a specific loan is usually designated. Often, the initial disclosure from your broker is not for the loan you ultimately decide on. If you have questions about any of the disclosures your receive ask your mortgage broker or loan agent for an explanation. You should receive another Truth-in-Lending statement and good-faith estimate of closing costs at closing. This should be an accurate disclosure of the loan.

The federal regulation that requires a mortgage lender to give you a good-faith estimate of settlement charges within three days is called RESPA (Real Estate Settlement and Procedures Act). RESPA was enacted by Congress in 1974 in order to protect consumers who are obtaining "federally related" home loans from unscrupulous settlement practices. Many states followed up with similar state laws for consumer protection. Before RESPA, it was common practice in the real estate business for settlement service providers—such as real estate agents, title insurers, attorneys, lenders, mortgage brokers—to make agreements to refer customers to one another in exchange for referral fees (also called kickbacks). Typically, a service provider received a kickback or unearned fee in exchange for a mere phone call to refer the business. The cost of these unearned fees was passed along to the consumer in the form of higher settlement fees. RESPA prohibits many real estate settlement service providers from giving or receiving kickbacks when a federally related mortgage loan is involved, except if actual services are performed. Unearned fees, for services not actually performed, are usually prohibited. The penalties for violating the anti-kickback provision are fines of up to $10,000 and a year in jail or both. For more information about RESPA, contact the Department of Housing and Urban Development (HUD).

> **RESPA prohibits real estate settlement service providers from giving or receiving "kickbacks."**

## The property appraisal

An appraisal completed by a professional appraiser is required by most lenders before they will approve and fund a home loan. The lender selects the appraiser but the borrower usually pays the fee, either when the appraisal is ordered or at closing. Some lenders have their own in-house appraisers; others accept independent appraisals done by appraisers whose names appear on their lender-approved list.

> **An appraisal is an educated opinion of the market value of a property.**

An appraiser usually arrives at an opinion of market value by comparing the subject home with three others in the vicinity that are roughly similar and that have sold and closed within the past six months. The appraiser adjusts the value of the comparable properties in relationship to the subject property to account for their differences, such as large or small lot size. By so doing, the appraiser arrives at a market value price for the subject property. The appraiser will also determine the replacement cost value of the property. But the lender uses the market value to determine if the loan will be approved.

Appraisals are somewhat subjective, so they should ideally be done by someone who is knowledgeable about the area. Establishing value is easier in tract developments, where there is consistency in home size and amenities than in neighborhoods with variability in home size, style, and age. Appraisals are easier to do when prices are relatively stable, but harder to do when prices are rising or dropping.

In some cases, the appraisal will include information about similar properties that are currently for sale and others that have recently sold but aren't yet closed. In locations where property values have declined recently, lenders want to make sure that the value indicated by the sold properties isn't higher than the current list price of similar properties. In areas where values are increasing, the most recent pending sale information may be used to justify a higher market value than that indicated by the closed sales.

Appraisals cost in the range of $200 to $500 for properties in the $150,000 to $750,000 price range. To save money, buyers often want to wait to order the appraisal until the property has been thoroughly inspected to their satisfaction. This strategy requires careful planning if you want your loan to be approved on time. It can take weeks to get the appraisal report if the home finance market is very active. Find out from your mortgage broker or loan agent how long you can reasonably delay the appraisal and still get your loan approved on time. If lenders are jammed with applications and the system is backlogged, you may not want to risk delaying the appraisal, especially if there is a backup buyer waiting to buy the house if you don't complete the purchase. The best strategy is to schedule your home inspection as soon as possible after acceptance. Then schedule the appraisal for a day or two after your home inspection. That way, you can cancel the appraisal if inspection problems arise, but you can get it done promptly if you are going ahead with the purchase.

Ideally, the buyer's agent should meet the appraiser at the property and provide comparable sales information for the appraiser, particularly if the appraiser is from out of the area. The appraiser will inspect, photograph, and measure the home. If the home has been extensively remodeled, the appraiser may want copies of the relevant building permits. This can pose a problem if the sellers completed additions without building permits. An appraiser's assessment of the remodel is often satisfactory for the lender. Sometimes, however, the lender will require a statement from a licensed contractor that the work was done in a professional manner. After the appraiser has reviewed the comparable sales information, he or she prepares a fairly detailed written appraisal report.

According to the Federal Equal Credit Opportunity Act of 1991, borrowers who pay for an appraisal are entitled to a copy of it, if they ask for a copy within a reasonable period of time. The request should be made in writing to the lender, not to the appraiser. If you are having difficulty getting a copy of the appraisal on the home you are buying or refinancing, ask to speak to a supervisor at the lender's office. If you are using a mortgage broker, he or she should be able to get a copy for you. The appraisal provides valuable information about the property, in addition to its value. It will give you the square footage of the home and the lot size. Your insurance carrier will base your insurance quote on square footage, among other things. It's a good idea to keep the appraisal in a safe place for future reference.

When lenders evaluate your loan to determine if it can be approved, they look at the *loan-to-value* (LTV) ratio. The appraisal report on the property is used to establish the value for the LTV equation. Let's say you have agreed to pay $175,000 for a property and you have applied for a 90 percent loan in the amount of $157,500. If the property appraises for $175,000, then your LTV will be 90 percent. As long as your income-to-debt ratios are adequate and your credit is good, your loan should be approved. But, if the property appraises for $170,000, you have a problem. The lender may still be willing to give you a loan, but it might not be for the amount you need. The lender may only be willing to loan based on a 90 percent loan-to-value. Ninety percent of a $170,000 appraised value is only $153,000—$4,500 less than you need. If your purchase contract includes a contingency for the property to appraise for the purchase price, you can probably withdraw from the contract without risking your deposit. But if you do want to go ahead with the purchase, either you will have to come up with the additional cash required to close, or the sellers will have to lower their price. If the sellers won't lower their price, perhaps they will loan you the amount you are short, if the lender will permit this.

Another approach to use if your appraisal comes in low and you are convinced that it's a mistake is to ask the lender to review the appraisal. Have your real estate agent provide comparable sales information for the lender that supports the purchase price. A last resort is to take the loan package to a different lender. Portfolio lenders tend to be more lenient on their appraisals, particularly if they have their own in-house staff of appraisers. You may need to get an extension on your financing contingency from the sellers. They should be agreeable, under the circumstances, unless there is a backup offer from a large-cash down buyer.

When a buyer has a large cash down payment, a low appraisal is less of a problem. Suppose you are paying $175,000 for a home and you intend to make a $75,000 cash down payment. If the appraisal comes in at $170,000, and the lender will give you a loan at 80 percent loan-to-value, then you and the property will qualify for a loan in the amount of $136,000. You only need a loan for $100,000, so the low appraisal is only a problem if you object to buying a home that appraises a little low.

**Loan approval**

Mortgages are often approved with conditions, which must be satisfied either before the loan documents are drawn up, or before the loan can close. Some are easily satisfied, such as providing a legible copy of an addendum to the purchase contract. Or the lender might need verification of some of your financial documentation, such as a copy of the gift letter from your parents, a signed copy of your most recent tax returns, proof that you have paid down a charge card account, or proof that you have liquidated stock for part of your down payment. If the sellers are having termite work done as a part of the sale agreement, the lender might need a copy of the final completion notice before closing. Make sure to get a copy of the written loan commitment from the lender so that you can personally review the conditions before you remove your financing contingency from the purchase agreement. If you are confident that you can meet the loan conditions with no problem, go ahead and remove the contingency.

Sometimes, however, a loan condition will be something major that cannot be easily satisfied. The lender might want you to put more cash down, which you might not be able or willing to do. Or the lender might require a copy of a building permit for an addition to the home. Don't unconditionally remove your financing contingency unless you know that the conditions can be satisfied. Ask the sellers for an extension of the contingency, if necessary.

> **Get a written copy of the loan commitment from your lender before you remove the financing contingency from the purchase contract.**

The loan commitment should include the terms of the loan: the type of loan (fixed or ARM), interest rate, and points. It should also tell you when the loan commitment will expire. If not, ask your loan agent or mortgage broker to find out how long the commitment will be in effect. You will need to close the sale before the loan commitment expires. This date could be earlier than the closing date in your purchase agreement. If you need to get the loan commitment extended, do so before you remove the financing contingency. If the lender won't grant you an extension on the commitment, ask the sellers to close early as a condition of removing the financing contingency. If you close early, the sellers may need to rent back from you until the date agreed to in the contract.

# Coping with rejection

The first thing to do if your loan is turned down is to find out what the lender didn't like and if there is anything you can do to remedy the situation. Often a simple letter of explanation to the lender is all it takes to get a problem loan approved. Let's say you were in a car accident and hospitalized for several weeks. A letter explaining that this is why you had several late payments on your credit report would probably get your loan approved unless there were other problems.

All too often a lender's rejection is due to a bad credit report. This kind of rejection should never occur. If you paid to have your credit checked when you were prequalified for a loan, you should be aware of any credit problems long before your loan is submitted for approval. But even if you didn't get prequalified, your loan originator should have ordered a Residential Mortgage Credit Report (RMCR) when you completed your loan application. A diligent loan originator will work with borrowers to try to clear up credit problems before the loan is submitted to underwriting. But suppose your loan originator dropped the ball and didn't help you clean up a messy credit file. If you are turned down for a loan because of information supplied by a credit reporting agency, you are entitled to that information if you request it within thirty days of receiving a denial notice. It's possible that negative information on a credit report is inaccurate. Consumers Union, the publisher of Consumer Reports, found in a 1991 study that 19 percent of all credit reports had errors that were serious enough to result in a loan denial.

The RMCR is a compilation of your personal credit profile for the past seven years. This information is gathered from your files at the three main credit-reporting agencies: Equifax, Trans Union, and TRW. For a minimal charge, you can get copies of your report from these three agencies. You are entitled to a free copy if you were denied credit in the last sixty days. Contact the credit agency if you are having difficulty interpreting a report. If you spot any errors or if you dispute an item on a report, write a letter to the appropriate credit bureau.

*For a copy of your credit reports, contact:*

**EQUIFAX**
P. O. Box 740241
Atlanta, GA 30374-0241
1-404-885-8000

**TRW**
12606 Greenville Avenue
P.O. Box 749029
Dallas, TX 75374
1-214-235-1200

**TRANS UNION**
P.O. Box 3110
Fullerton, CA 92634
1-714-738-3800

The credit bureau is required to re-investigate the disputed information on your credit report and respond to you within a reasonable time (usually thirty days). If the information is incorrect or if it can't be confirmed within the thirty days, the disputed item must be dropped from your credit file. Even if the disputed information is confirmed to be accurate, you are entitled to have a written one-hundred-word statement explaining your side of the story added to your credit file. Whenever your credit is checked in the future, a creditor will see that you have disputed an item. Don't go overboard, though. A creditor might be suspicious of a credit report that's loaded with consumer dispute statements on numerous derogatory credit entries.

Countrywide Funding Corporation publishes a free manual entitled "Your Credit and You." This informative booklet gives detailed instructions about how to get copies of your credit reports, and how to dispute inaccurate information in your credit file, including sample letters to use when communicating with the credit agencies. Call the House America counseling center at 1-800-577-3732 for a free copy. It's a good idea to order copies of your credit reports from time to time to make sure they are accurate.

Adverse credit information is not supposed to be reported or included on your credit report after seven years. Make sure that any outdated derogatory entries are deleted from your credit file. An exception to the seven-year rule is bankruptcy information, which can be reported for ten years. Although a lender won't be thrilled to give you a loan if you recently went through bankruptcy, it won't automatically keep you from getting a mortgage. Lenders will want to see court-approved papers that confirm that your past creditors are satisfied with your debt-restructuring. They also like to see that you have re-established credit and that you are making your payments on time.

Many lenders are starting to use "credit scoring" as a basis for loan approval or denial. The score is a numerical summation of your credit history, based on your credit files at the credit reporting agencies. Errors in your files could cause a low credit score. Inquiries that have been made about your credit by creditors can have an effect on your overall credit score. Be protective of your Social Security number so that credit inquiries aren't made that you are not aware of. If you are denied a loan because of a low credit score, find out why it's low. You may need to write a letter of explanation to the lender or have an error in your file corrected before your loan will be approved. See below for more information about credit scoring.

Sometimes it's possible to appeal a loan denial, particularly if you can come up with a counterproposal to the lender that will increase the lender's comfort level. Suppose you have several blemishes on your credit record and the lender denies your application for an 80-percent loan. The same lender might be willing to give you a loan for 75 percent of the purchase price. If you don't have the additional 5 percent cash for a down payment, the seller might be willing to loan you the 5 percent rather than have the deal fall apart.

Buyers who have a bad credit history that can't be cleaned up sufficiently to satisfy most lenders may be able to find a lender who will approve the loan for a higher interest rate or higher loan origination fees. Ask a mortgage broker about B- or C-rated loans. A-rated loans have the best rates and terms, and they are offered to gold-plated buyers with squeaky-clean credit. You will have to pay a premium for a B or C loan, but you can refinance later after you have established a good repayment record. Try to avoid a pre-payment penalty if you can.

Sometimes loans are turned down because the lender runs out of money for the specific loan product you were applying for and the terms of a substitute loan are so strict that you can't qualify according to the new guidelines.

*Rene and Allen went to a mortgage broker to get a loan to buy their new home. The mortgage broker submitted their loan package to a lender, who said they would have no problem approving it. However, the lender changed policies before the loan was approved and the loan was denied. The mortgage broker immediately took a duplicate loan package to a portfolio lender, who approved the loan in two days. The terms of this loan were not as good as the first loan, but at least Rene and Allen knew they wouldn't lose the home they wanted because they couldn't get financing. After the loan was approved, the mortgage broker shopped the loan market further and found a third loan that was even better than either the first or second ones. Allen and Rene were approved without a hitch.*

First-time buyers who need 90- or 95-percent loans can run into problems with mortgage insurance (MI) approval. Most 90- and 95-percent loans require MI insurance to protect the lender in case the buyers default. MI usually involves a second approval process. It's possible for a loan to be approved by the lender but denied by the MI underwriters. Many portfolio lenders self-insure for MI so that separate MI approval isn't necessary. Portfolio lenders also tend to be more lenient on loan qualification in general. Keep this in mind if you need to switch lenders.

How a loan is packaged for the lender can make the difference between a loan's being approved or rejected. If your loan is rejected, make sure that your loan agent repackages your loan to address issues that didn't pass underwriting the first time, before the loan package is submitted to a second lender for approval.

# Credit scoring and streamlined lending

Financing your home purchase can be as easy as financing a car purchase—at least for some home buyers. For years, car dealers have found it profitable to offer in-house financing to their customers, allowing car buyers to avoid the bother of lining up car loans on their own. Some real estate companies are following the auto industry example by offering one-stop shopping to their home buyers. In some cases, it's possible to use one real estate office to find a home to buy, negotiate the purchase agreement, arrange the mortgage, line up homeowner's insurance, and handle the closing. With ever-increasing automation of the mortgage application and approval process, arranging a loan in-house can be done quickly. Often the consumer's loan application is entered directly into a computer that transfers the borrower's information electronically to a loan processing center. Or the loan applicant may have a televised meeting with a loan representative, negating the need for an in-person interview. A couple of days later, barring credit glitches, the borrower is preapproved for the loan.

Such streamlined loan origination is becoming popular throughout the mortgage industry as increased competition forces lenders to become more efficient loan processors. As lenders become more efficient, they can pass some of their cost savings on to consumers in the form of lower interest rates or lower processing costs. Some lenders are using artificial intelligence software programs to electronically underwrite loans. Others even accept loan applications directly from borrowers over the Internet, eliminating the need for an intermediary loan agent or mortgage broker.

Credit scoring is becoming more widespread because it enables lenders to objectively evaluate risk and make informed loan approval decisions quickly. This method has been used for speedy car loan and credit card approval for years. A credit score is derived from a model that analyzes a number of variables from a consumer's credit files to determine the likelihood that the applicant will repay the loan on time. The scoring system is developed from a statistical analysis of variables that historically have been reliable in predicting satisfactory loan repayment. Among factors considered are: delinquencies and late payments (both the frequency and severity), outstanding debt (the number of balances reported by creditors and the average balances), credit history, and types of credit in use (including installment loans and credit cards of all types).

**A credit score is the result of an analysis of your credit file data. It predicts how likely you are to repay a loan on time.**

Several companies provide credit scoring models used by lenders. One of the most widely used is the Fair, Isaac score which analyzes the interrelationship among about one hundred variables by gathering information from your credit files at the three national credit bureaus (TRW, Trans Union, and Equifax). Fair, Isaac scores range from about four hundred to nine hundred. The higher the score, the better the credit risk. Some credit scoring models work in a reverse fashion so that a higher score indicates a higher degree of risk.

If you have a Fair, Isaac score of 680, or higher, you are considered a premium-quality borrower and should qualify for speedy loan approval, and possibly for a preferential interest rate. Some lenders use your credit score to determine your interest rate: the higher the credit score, the lower the interest rate and vice versa.

Recently, both Freddie Mac and Fannie Mae approved using credit scores. In time, credit scores may be required universally in the home loan industry. This is good news for borrowers with excellent credit because their loans can be approved quickly with less hassle. Some lenders offer an alternate documentation loan approval process for their most credit-worthy borrowers. This approval procedure requires a minimum of financial documentation. However, for borrowers with a Fair, Isaac score of 620 or lower, automated underwriting may result in rejection. (If the lender you apply to requires a credit score as a condition of loan approval, your lender or mortgage broker can tell you your score.) Streamlined loan origination won't work for low credit-scorers, who will have to rely on conventional methods of working closely with a loan agent or mortgage broker to get a mortgage approved.

Credit scores are great equalizers. They discriminate on one factor only: the likelihood that you will repay a loan on time. There has been some controversy that credit scores might be biased against lower-income borrowers, but so far no evidence supports this claim. Also, since credit scores analyze a multitude of variables, one late payment or even a past bankruptcy need not keep you from getting a mortgage. One piece of credit information should not determine whether you get a good or bad score. It's the interaction of many credit variables that results in the score. In fact, the use of credit scoring might help someone with a bankruptcy or foreclosure get a mortgage, because it is an objective evaluation method that eliminates an individual loan underwriter's bias.

# Low-cash-down financing

### 90 percent financing

Many first-time buyers have difficulty saving enough cash for a 20 percent down payment. But they often have sufficient income to qualify for a loan amount equal to 90 percent of the purchase price. However, there are drawbacks: 90-percent financing is difficult to find for loan amounts over $400,000. And 90-percent loans typically require the borrower to pay mortgage insurance (MI) to protect the lender from a buyer default.

MI premiums vary with the type and amount of the loan but they can run about one-half to three-quarters of a percent of the loan amount for the first year of the loan. On a $200,000 fixed-rate loan for 90 percent of the purchase price, with an annual level plan, the MI premium would be about $1,240. MI premiums are often a bit lower for later years. The first year's mortgage insurance premium is often paid in advance at closing. Some lenders collect less than this amount at closing, which will reduce the amount of cash you will need to close. Unfortunately, MI premiums are not deductible from your income tax. (See Chapter 1 for more information about MI premiums.)

Many portfolio lenders self-insure for MI. Instead of charging a separate, non-tax-deductible fee for MI, they increase the interest rate on the loan to cover the self-insurance cost. Since borrowers can usually write off mortgage interest, the cost of self-insuring MI is tax deductible. But you may pay a higher margin on a 90-percent ARM loan from a portfolio lender and the points could be higher than they would be on a conforming 90-percent loan with separate MI. There is another disadvantage to a self-insured 90-percent loan. If you pay a separate monthly MI premium you can ask the lender to drop the MI when you have 20 percent equity in the property. When the MI is dropped, your monthly payments will go down. On a self-insured 90-percent loan you are stuck with the higher interest rate until you pay back the loan.

Closing costs are usually higher for 90-percent loans. In addition to the one-year prepaid MI premium (if it's required by your lender), 90-percent lenders usually require that an impound account be collected at closing to cover several month's worth of property taxes, hazard insurance, and MI premiums. You can usually avoid an impound account

To avoid an impound account on a 90-percent loan, increase your cash down payment slightly so that your loan amount is less than 90 percent (89.9 percent).

by increasing the amount of your cash down payment by a few hundred dollars to just slightly more than 10 percent of the purchase price. Most lenders want 90-percent borrowers to demonstrate that they have cash reserves in their bank account (or in a 401K pension plan or IRA account) to cover several months of their housing expense. Cash reserve requirements vary from lender to lender; some have the ability to waive the requirement altogether. Find out how much reserve cash you will need when you shop for your loan so that you aren't caught by surprise and short of the cash at closing.

### 80-10-10 financing

Some buyers prefer to create 90-percent financing by getting an 80-percent first mortgage and a 10-percent second mortgage. This is called 80-10-10 financing. The second mortgage can come from the seller or it can come from a conventional lender. In the past, 80-10-10 financing was attractive to first-time buyers who wanted to avoid MI. But on conforming loans, which are sold on the secondary money market to Freddie Mac and Fannie Mae, MI is now charged on 80-10-10 financing. To avoid MI, the first loan cannot exceed 75 percent of the purchase price. So, you would have to get a second for 15 percent of the price, or put an additional 5 percent cash down. The overall interest rate on 75-15-10 financing won't be as good as an 80-10-10 package because the interest on most second mortgages is higher than it is on most first mortgages. If the interest rate on a thirty-year fixed-rate conforming loan is 7.5 percent, the interest rate on the second mortgage might be 8.75 or 9 percent. A portfolio lender may waive MI on an 80-10-10 deal. Also, on non-conforming (jumbo) loans, 80-10-10 financing without MI is still available. Buyers who go the 80-10-10 (or 75-15-10) route can usually avoid an impound account.

80-10-10 financing is one way for high-income buyers to get around the upper loan limits on 90-percent loans. Let's say that you are buying a $500,000 house with 10 percent down. You can't find a 90-percent lender who will do a first mortgage for more than $400,000. If you break the financing up into a first mortgage of $400,000 and a second of $50,000, you create the 90-percent financing you need. If the seller can't carry a second for you, get a second mortgage from a conventional lender.

### 95-percent financing

Conventional lenders offer 95-percent financing to qualified buyers who have good credit. Conforming 95-percent loans are readily available in loan amounts up to a maximum of $207,000. Jumbo 95-percent loans for amounts over the conforming loan limits are also available, up to an upper loan limit of $300,000.

MI is required on 95-percent loans and for a higher premium than on 90-percent loans. You should expect to pay about .75 to .95 percent of the loan amount for the first year premium depending on the MI carrier, type of loan, and payment plan. Your housing expense-to-income ratio should be no higher than 28 percent; your overall debt-to-income ratio usually cannot exceed 36 percent. The 5 percent down must be your own money. However, most lenders will allow the seller to credit up to 3 percent of the purchase price to the buyer for nonrecurring closing costs. Interest rates are a little higher on 95-percent mortgages, and the lender will require full documentation of your financial situation for loan approval. You will also need good assets and enough extra cash savings after closing to cover your housing payments for several months.

Jumbo 95-percent financing is available up to a purchase price limit of about $625,000, using a combination of a first mortgage for 80 percent of the purchase price and a second mortgage for 15 percent. This is private investor financing, which is arranged through a portfolio lender. The pricing is very steep. If conforming fixed-rate pricing is at 7 percent, the interest rate on this first mortgage would be about 8 percent, and the interest rate on the second would be in the 11.5 to 12 percent range. Mortgage brokers can tell you more about this type of financing package.

In the past, financing options available for buyers with little cash for a down payment were limited mainly to government-assisted programs like Federal Housing Administration (FHA) loans, which are offered through the U.S. Department of Housing and Urban Development (HUD). FHA loans are available to buyers with approximately 4.5 percent cash down. Not only that, all of the down payment money can be a gift. And, the sellers can credit up to 6 percent of the purchase price toward the buyers' nonrecurring and recurring closing costs.

The FHA loan limit varies from one area of the country to the next. The base loan amount in 1996 was $78,660 for single-family residences. The upper loan limit was increased to $155,250 in 1996 for single-family residences in high-cost areas of the country, like San Francisco. There is no income limit, as there is with some low-down mortgage programs, and FHA is flexible on credit. In other words, your credit doesn't have to be impeccable to get an FHA loan. Even if you had a bankruptcy less than two years ago, you might qualify. FHA looks at your back-end ratio for loan qualification: Your overall debt cannot exceed 41 percent of your gross monthly income.

FHA loan processing used to be a nightmare, but it has improved in recent years. FHA loan approval is possible in thirty days. FHA loans also used to be loaded with restrictions, but that has eased somewhat. Previously, the buyer could not pay points. Now buyers can pay for their own points, appraisal, and credit report. But buyers are not allowed to pay other loan fees such as a document preparation fee or a tax service; these fees have to be paid by the sellers. The purchase price can be increased to cover these fees, as long as the property appraises. A termite report and notice of completion indicating that the work has been done are required by closing.

The interest rates may be slightly higher on FHA loans than on conventional loans—perhaps .25 percent higher on a thirty-year fixed-rate mortgage. But FHA loans are easier to qualify for than the 97-percent Fannie Mae loans discussed below. FHA loans are available through participating lenders or through a mortgage broker. For more information about FHA loans, call the local HUD office in your area.

### 97-percent financing

Fannie Mae has a 97-percent loan program, available in most states, for loan amounts up to $207,000. The 3-percent cash down payment must be the borrower's own funds. The seller can credit a maximum of 3 percent of the purchase price for the buyer's nonrecurring closing costs. Standard ratio guidelines are used to qualify the borrower. The front-end ratio usually cannot exceed 28 percent. Although in some cases front-end ratios higher than this are acceptable. The back-end ratio usually cannot exceed 36 percent. Good credit is required.

To qualify for this loan program, the borrower's income cannot exceed an income limit, which varies by location. The HUD median income chart is used to set the income limit for the area. The upper income limit is adjusted annually and cannot exceed 120 percent of the HUD median income for the area. If your income exceeds this limit, you would not be eligible for this program. An additional requirement for the 97-percent Fannie Mae loan program is that the borrower must complete a four-hour educational class on home loans and the home-buying process. These courses are often announced in the real estate section of the newspaper.

Only fixed-interest rate loans are available through this program and interest rates are the same as they would be on conventional conforming loans. 97-percent Fannie Mae loans are available through lenders who sell their loans to Fannie Mae, or through a mortgage broker. For more information about Fannie Mae loans, call 1-800-7-FANNIE.

Not all mortgage brokers or lenders originate FHA, VA, and 97-percent loans. Make sure that you work with a loan originator who knows what is required to get a low-cash down loan approved. Knowing how to get one of these loans approved quickly and with minimal hassle usually requires years of experience.

### 100-percent financing

GI or VA (Veterans Administration) loans require no cash down. But you must be an eligible veteran to qualify. The maximum VA loan amount is $203,000, and although the buyers don't need cash for a down payment, they may need cash for closing costs. Sellers can contribute up to 4 percent of the purchase price for the buyer's nonrecurring and recurring closing costs. Currently, only fixed-rate loans are available. In the past, the VA had an ARM program. Interest rates are competitive with conforming interest rates or slightly higher (perhaps .25 percent). To qualify, the borrower must have a certificate of eligibility from the Veterans Administration. A back-end ratio of up to 41 percent is used for loan qualification. And exceptions can be made on credit. For more information about GI loans, call 1-800-831-6515.

Conventional 100-percent financing is also available, at premium prices, from private-investor portfolio lenders. This financing is usually created with a first mortgage for 75 percent of the purchase price and a second mortgage for 25 percent. Loan limits vary, but the maximum sale price usually cannot exceed about $200,000 to $300,000. Interest rates on the first and second are exorbitant, so this type of financing should only be used if there is no other way to finance a home purchase. Qualifying for 100-percent financing requires standard debt-to-income ratios. Your front-end ratio should be around 33 percent. Your total debt-to-income ratio should be about 38 percent. Your credit must be impeccable. Some lenders have 100-percent financing programs at reasonable interest rates for borrowers who pledge a CD held with the same lender as collateral. The CD can be pledged by a relative of the borrower. A CD equal to 15 to 25 percent of the purchase price is usually required.

Buyers who decide to use any of the above low-cash down payment programs should get preapproved before making an offer to buy a home. This will alleviate the sellers' concern that it might be difficult to qualify for a mortgage with little or no cash down.

In addition to the low-cash down payment mortgage programs discussed above, most states have government loan programs to assist low-cash down, low-income, and first-time home buyers. Contact the housing development agency, housing authority, or housing finance authority in your state for information. Your state may have a first-time buyer program or a down payment assistance program. Many cities and counties also offer low-cash down and first-time buyer mortgage programs, such as the Mortgage Credit Certificate program. This program allows eligible home buyers to take about 20 percent of their annual mortgage payments as a tax credit against their federal income tax. The tax credit improves the borrower's ability to qualify and it reduces the effective interest on the loan by about 2 percent. Income and purchase price restrictions usually apply to most first-time buyer loan programs. A lender or mortgage broker who originates FHA, GI, or 97-percent loans should have information on low-down payment loans in your area. Or contact your city mayor's office or the local county housing office.

# Improving affordability

### Lock-ins

A lock-in (also called a rate-lock) is a commitment from a lender to loan you money at a specific interest rate. The lock-in commitment will be good for a certain period of time. If you cannot complete your home purchase or refinance during the rate lock period and interest rates rise, you will probably have to pay the higher interest rate. Some loans can be locked-in when you submit your loan application; others can only be locked-in when the loan is formally approved by the lender.

Lock-ins usually vary from fifteen to sixty days. You can lock-in an interest rate for up to 120 days with some lenders, but it's very expensive to do so. You pay for the privilege of a rate-lock. The amount you pay will vary with the lender, the type of loan (fixed- or adjustable-rate mortgage, purchase or refinance), the length of the lock-in, and current market conditions.

The shorter the rate-lock period, the lower the cost to lock-in. You might have to pay ½ point to lock-in a fixed-rate loan for thirty days, and ¾ point for a forty-five-day lock. On a no-point loan, you might pay ⅛ percent higher on the interest rate for a lock-in. Sometimes you have the option of either paying higher points for a lock-in or paying a higher interest rate on the loan. Some lenders require that a nonrefundable fee be paid at the time the rate is locked. Other lenders collect their lock fee at closing.

The alternative to locking in an interest rate is to let the rate float during the loan processing period. If interest rates rise before the lender finalizes your loan documents, you will pay a higher interest rate on your new loan than you would have if you had locked in the rate. If interest rates drop during the loan processing period, you will get a lower interest rate on your loan. Some lenders will allow you to lock-in with a "float down" option, for a price. This entitles you to the lower interest rate if rates drop after you lock-in. In very competitive financing markets, a lender might give you the benefit of a lower interest rate, even if it's lower than your locked rate, rather than lose your business. If you do lock-in, try to get a lock-in commitment in writing.

Ask your loan agent or mortgage broker if interest rates appear to be rising or falling before making the decision to lock-in a rate. If there is no threat of rising rates, you may be better off floating because it costs more to lock-in. But no one can guarantee which way rates will go and financing markets can change rapidly. Have your loan agent or mortgage broker call you every few days or so to let you know what rates are doing.

Once you lock-in a rate, you must make sure that your loan is approved and closed before the commitment expires. Get a completed loan application to your lender as soon as possible. Follow up to make sure that any additional documents required by the lender (employment and deposit verifications, for example) are sent without delay. Make sure that payoff demands from existing lenders are ordered on time. Existing loans that are secured against the property must be paid off before a new first mortgage can be secured against the property. If your lender won't lock-in a rate for you until your loan is approved and rates are jumping, it's imperative that you get the necessary financial documentation to the lender as soon as possible so the loan can be approved quickly. Lenders offering the most competitive interest rates are flooded with applications when interest rates rise. This backlog means it will take longer to get loans approved.

**If you lock-in an interest rate, get the commitment in writing from the lender.**

Some lenders have programs that allow you to lock-in a rate before you purchase a home. The parameters differ with the lender. But it's possible to get preapproved for a loan with an interest rate that is guaranteed for a period of time, usually thirty or sixty days. Then, once you have found the home and negotiated the purchase, the loan commitment can often be extended until closing. Depending on current financing market conditions, you may not have to pay an upfront fee for a prepurchase rate-lock. But double check and make sure the rate you are getting is competitive.

**Buy-downs**

With a buy-down loan program, funds are put into a subsidy account at closing and are used to pay part of the borrower's mortgage payment each month. The subsidy account can be funded by a builder, a seller, or the buyer. Buy-downs can be temporary (for a period of six months to three years), or permanent. The buy-down amount is usually quoted as points (one point is equal to one percent of the loan amount). Because of the lower initial mortgage payment, buy-downs make is easier for a buyer to qualify for a loan.

A common buy-down program is called a 3-2-1 buy-down. For the first year of the loan, the buyer pays an interest rate that is 3 percent below the note rate. The note rate is the ultimate interest rate the borrower will pay at the end of the buy-down period. During the second year, the interest rate is 2 percent below the note rate. The rate is 1 percent below the note rate for year three. Thereafter, the buyer pays the interest rate on the note.

The cost to buy down a rate is usually 1 point a year for each 1 percent decrease in the interest rate. The cost of a 3-2-1 buy-down will usually be 6 points paid to the lender at closing (3 points for the first year buy-down, 2 points for the second year, and 1 point for the third year).

In addition to paying an upfront charge to buy down the interest rate, the borrower usually agrees to pay a higher note rate than would be the case with a conventional mortgage. Let's say the going rate on a conventional thirty-year fixed-rate mortgage is 7.5 percent. On a 3-2-1 buy-down program, you might pay 5.5 percent for the first year, 6.5 percent for the second and 7.5 for the third. When the buy-down period is over, you might pay 8.5 percent for the remainder of the loan.

When interest rates rise, many home buyers turn from fixed- to adjustable-rate financing to make their home purchases more affordable. ARMs have initial interest rates that are even lower than the start rates on most buy-down loans. But at the end of the buy-down period for a buy-down loan, the interest rate is fixed for the remainder of the loan. The interest rate on an ARM can increase 4 to 6 percent over the term of the loan. A buy-down mortgage appeals to buyers who want the stability of a fixed-rate loan but who can't qualify at today's fixed rate.

Most lenders will allow you to design your own buy-down loan. That is, you can decide how long you want a lower interest rate, how much the rate will be reduced, and how often the interest rate will adjust (for example, every six months or annually). Most lenders are flexible regarding points. By increasing the points you pay, you can buy the interest rate down to a lower rate or you can buy it down for a longer time period. For fewer points, you get less of an interest rate reduction or the buy-down period is shorter. A buy-down can even be combined with a two-step mortgage for an even greater initial interest rate discount. A two-step loan has one interest rate that is in effect for a period of time (say seven years), and another rate that is in effect for the remainder of the loan (twenty-three years). Two-steps have lower initial interest rates than conventional thirty-year fixed-rate loans.

Buyers who don't intend to own their homes for very long will probably save money by taking an ARM rather than paying the cost to buy down an interest rate. Sometimes, however, a seller or builder may be willing to pay the upfront buy-down fee for you. When real estate markets slow, more sellers are willing to buy down a rate for a buyer. But if you can qualify for a loan without a buy-down, you may be better off negotiating a lower purchase price or a closing cost credit, rather than asking the seller for a buy-down concession.

### Graduated payment mortgages

A graduated payment mortgage (GPM) is another financing option that makes owning a home more affordable during the early years of ownership. With a GPM, the initial monthly payments are lower than they would be on a conventional mortgage. The lender qualifies the borrower at the lower initial payment, so the borrower is able to qualify for a larger mortgage. The monthly payment increases at predetermined intervals until it ends up at a payment amount that will fully amortize the remaining loan balance. To compensate for the lower initial monthly payments, the later monthly payments end up being higher than for a conventional mortgage.

Negative amortization is a feature of these mortgages because the low monthly payments during the early years of the loan do not fully pay the amount owed on the loan. GPMs can be risky in a declining market because while your loan balance grows in the initial years of lower monthly payments, the value of the property is dropping. GPMs make more sense when the real estate market is appreciating. Even though your loan balance increases initially, so does the property value. You can avoid negative amortization by making a lump-sum payment to the lender at closing to cover the amount of any deferred payments during the early years of the loan. Perhaps a seller or builder might be willing to make that payment for you as a part of your purchase negotiation. Another downside with GPMs is that they often carry a higher interest rate than a convention loan. However, GPMs are a consideration for buyers who anticipate a large income increase in the future and who don't want to wait to buy a home.

# Creative financing

Most buyers use a new mortgage from a third-party lending institution, such as a bank or savings and loan, to finance their home purchase. Any financing arrangement that deviates from this is called "creative financing." The most popular form of creative financing is seller or owner carry-back financing.

## Seller financing

With seller financing, the sellers agree to be the bank for the buyers. The property being sold becomes the security for the loan. If the sellers own their home free and clear of any existing mortgages, they can carry a first mortgage. If not, they can carry a mortgage in second position, either behind the buyer's new first mortgage or behind an already existing first mortgage on the property that the buyers assume.

One benefit of seller financing is that the buyers are able to bypass the red tape involved in qualifying for a new conventional loan. Sellers will want to check the buyer's credit history and financial statement, but the cumbersome loan qualification procedures required by a conventional lender are usually avoided. A purchase agreement that includes seller financing might include a contingency for the sellers to approve the buyer's financial statement and credit report within a certain number of days. Another benefit is that sellers usually don't charge points. The interest rate on a seller-carry mortgage, which is negotiable, will often be lower than it would be on a conventional loan. However, if interest rates are too low, sellers may be unwilling to carry financing because they can make a better return on their money elsewhere.

There are also benefits to sellers, not the least of which is making a sale possible. Sellers may also receive tax benefits, if they would otherwise owe capital gains tax when they sell. Sellers who carry financing for buyers may qualify for installment sale tax treatment by the IRS. An installment sale permits sellers to spread their capital gain tax liability over several years. For some sellers, carrying financing for a buyer is a good investment, with a higher rate of return than might be available elsewhere. Another benefit to the sellers is that they know the property against which the loan will be secured.

Some sellers who agree to carry financing will only do so in exchange for a higher sale price. This may be worth it if it enables you to a buy a home that would otherwise not be possible. But overpaying in a market where prices are declining is unwise. You may want to include a contingency in the purchase contract for the property to appraise. In this case, you may have to order and pay for an appraisal yourself.

Negotiating a seller financing agreement can be complicated. There is more to it than simply agreeing on the loan amount and the interest rate. Other negotiable factors include the term of the loan (when it's due), the amount of the monthly payment (interest only or amortized), the amount of the late-payment fee, whether the loan is due when the property is sold, and whether the loan will have a prepayment penalty (where legal). Ideally, buyers want the loan to be

> **Make sure that you don't overpay for a property in exchange for seller financing.**

assumable by a future credit-worthy buyer and to have no penalty for prepayment. Buyers may want to hire a real estate attorney to help negotiate the terms of a seller-financed loan, unless you have an agent who can assist you.

Since most sellers are not in a position to carry a loan for thirty years, many seller-financed loans have a balloon payment. Make sure that the term of your loan is long enough so that you don't get caught owing a large balloon payment before you are able to pay it. If the seller is carrying a second mortgage behind a new conventional first mortgage, the first lender will probably require that the seller's loan carry a term of at least five to seven years.

Sellers usually advertise the fact that they are willing to carry financing. But you may be able to uncover good candidates for owner-carry financing among sellers who aren't actively offering creative financing. Seniors who are retiring and who don't need all their cash at the close are good candidates. Other likely prospects are sellers who have been unable to sell for a long time and who don't need the proceeds from the sale to buy another home. A seller facing foreclosure, whose loan balance exceeds the asking price, is not a good candidate for seller financing. Owner-carry sellers usually need to have enough cash left from the sale of their home, after their mortgage and fees are paid, to make a loan.

## Assumptions

An assumption occurs when the buyers take over the seller's mortgage on the property at the time of purchase. Let's say a property sells for $125,000. The buyers make a $25,000 cash down payment and take over the existing mortgage on the property in the amount of $100,000. The buyers use the seller's mortgage to finance the purchase instead of getting a new mortgage. Loan assumptions become popular when money is tight and home loans are hard to find. Assumptions are also more common when interest rates are high, and during economic downturns.

Lenders require borrowers to undergo complete loan qualification to assume a loan. The process is the same as it is with a new mortgage, except that an appraisal may not be required. This reduces the upfront fees by several hundred dollars, and it can cut the qualification time down. An assumption should take no longer than twenty-one to thirty days. But if you are dealing with a loan servicing department that has no experience processing assumptions, formal approval can take six to eight weeks.

Not all home loans are assumable. Most ARMs are assumable by a qualified buyer. Most fixed-rate loans are not, with the exception of FHA and VA loans, which are assumable. The fee charged to complete an assumption on most conventional home loans is 1 percent of the remaining loan balance. The fee to assume an FHA loan is $500.

When interest rates rise, it may make sense, in some cases, to consider assuming the seller's mortgage. Before doing so, contact the lender to verify the terms of the loan and the remaining loan balance. Find out what is involved in completing an assumption and how long it will take. Make your purchase contract contingent upon your approval of the existing loan. Be sure to read the note (the document which is the promise to repay). Also, make sure that a statement of condition of the loan is ordered from the lender so you can verify the remaining loan balance and that the seller's payments are current.

An ARM that is several years old may have a lower margin than you can find on a new ARM today. A low margin will keep your interest rate down. However, you tend to find lower lifetime caps (maximum interest rate limits) on today's ARMs than were available in years past. You may not get the benefit of a teaser (discounted) rate if you take over the seller's loan, but remember that the teaser rate is only in effect for a short time period. If you do decide to assume the seller's low-margin ARM, make sure that the lender cannot change the margin on you. Some ARMs permit the lender to modify the terms of the loan if it is assumed by a subsequent buyer.

It is risky to take over a seller's existing mortgage without the lender's approval. If the note has a "due on sale" clause, it may not be assumable. Even if the note has a clause that permits assumptions under certain conditions, the lender probably has the right to call the loan due and payable immediately if it is taken over without permission.

**Ranch style**
*The ranch-style house is characterized by a one-story layout with features made for easy indoor-outdoor living and a casual lifestyle. These include a secluded rear yard, patios, terraces, and sliding glass doors.*

# 7
# *The Closing*

Closing occurs when all the terms and conditions of the purchase agreement have been met, and the sale transaction is complete. Closing practices vary considerably from one area to the next. In some places, a huge cast of characters assembles: buyers, sellers, buyers' and sellers' attorneys, their real estate agents, a closing agent, the buyers' loan agent, a title officer, and perhaps the even the sellers' mortgage representative. They all sit around a large table and sign closing documents, pass papers, and exchange checks. In other areas, the buyers and sellers may never meet. They sign papers separately before a third party— an escrow officer, settlement agent, attorney, or real estate broker—who handles the signing of documents and the exchange of funds. But regardless of where you buy, the closing of a home purchase transaction culminates when the sellers give the buyers marketable title to the property (in the form of a deed, or shares of stock in the case of a cooperative).

By the time your mortgage is approved, you will be nearing the end of your home purchase transaction, unless you are waiting for another property to sell. Most if not all of your contingencies will have been removed from the contract. You are heading toward home plate. However, a few more details need your attention before closing can occur.

## Title matters
### Deciding how to hold title
There are various ways to hold title to real property. The one you choose will depend primarily on whether you are buying by yourself or with others. It will also depend on estate planning considerations. If you are buying alone and you are unmarried, you will probably take title as the sole owner, which is called ownership in severalty. Holding title

# Closing checklist

| To complete before closing: | Deadline: | Completed? |
|---|---|---|
| **1** Determine how to hold title. Consult with attorney and/or accountant. | | |
| **2** Have current title to the property examined. | | |
| **3** Arrange for title insurance. | | |
| **4** Obtain homeowner's insurance (or insurance to cover personal possessions, liability, etc. if you are buying a condominium or cooperative). | | |
| **5** Donate, throw out, or sell what you don't need. | | |
| **6** Arrange for a mover. Get estimates from several movers. | | |
| **7** Review estimate of your closing (settlement) costs. | | |
| **8** Arrange to have down payment and closing cost money available for closing. | | |
| **9** Confirm that your loan documents will be ready on time. Try to get a copy to review before signing. | | |
| **10** Confirm that any required repairs/termite work will be completed before closing. | | |
| **11** Transfer utilities into your name at new address. | | |
| **12** Forward mail and subscriptions to new address. | | |
| **13** Complete a final walk-through inspection. | | |
| **14** Meet with the sellers to learn the idiosyncrasies of the home; get copies of operating and instruction manuals. | | |
| **15** Arrange to get keys and garage door openers. | | |
| **16** Review all the closing documents. | | |
| **17** Sign closing documents. | | |

in a living trust is becoming more common because of its estate planning advantages. So as a sole owner, your choices are really two: sole ownership or living trust.

When you buy property with others, the choice of how to hold title becomes more complicated. One option is tenancy in common. Tenants in common can have equal or unequal interests in the property. Each co-owner can transfer his or her ownership interest to another person without the consent of the other co-owners. At death, the co-owner's interest passes to his or her heir(s) or devisee(s), not to the other co-owner(s). A devisee is someone who is named in a will.

Another ownership option for two or more persons is joint tenancy. Joint tenants have an equal interest in the property. With joint tenancy all co-owners must join in a sale, or conveyance. At the time of death, the co-owner's interest passes to the survivor, not to the co-owner's heirs or devisees. This is called the right of survivorship. The last survivor owns the property in severalty.

In community property states (Arizona, California, Idaho, Louisiana, Nevada, New Mexico, Washington, Wisconsin), holding title as community property is an option. With community property, ownership interests are equal and written consent of the other party is required in order to convey to a third party. At death, half of the property belongs to the survivor in severalty and half goes to the decedent's heirs subject to court administration. Usually there is no right of survivorship. So instead of the descendant's one-half of the property automatically passing to the remaining spouse (the survivor), that half interest goes to the descendant's heirs. If the heir happens to be the spouse, then the entire property belongs to that spouse in severalty (as sole owner). But if the decedent left his or her half interest in the property to the children, for example, then the spouse would own half of the property and the other half would belong to the children, subject to court approval. (Arizona permits community property with the right of survivorship.)

Some states recognize tenancy by the entirety, which is a special form of ownership for married persons. With this form of ownership, both parties have an equal interest, and both are required to sell, or convey. But unlike community property, tenants by the entirety have the right of survivorship. When one spouse dies, the property automatically reverts to the other spouse who becomes the sole owner.

How you hold title to property has legal, tax, and estate planning ramifications that must be carefully explored before you take title, especially if you are buying with another person or persons. It is a good idea to see an attorney who is knowledgeable about estate planning, and to also consult a tax advisor.

The forms of ownership discussed above are the most common, but there are other methods of holding title, such as partnerships, corporations, and irrevocable trusts. Most people leave the decision of how to hold title until the last minute, and then don't get proper advice. Plan ahead and make sure you understand why your choice is the best one for you and your family.

Your lawyer may advise you to hold title in a living trust. If so, you will probably have to arrange for title to be transferred into the trust after closing. Why? Because most lenders won't lend to a trust, only to individuals or corporations. Also, lenders usually require that title to the property against which the loan is secured must be vested in the names of the people responsible for repaying the debt. Homeowners whose property is in a living trust usually have to transfer title to the property out of the trust to refinance their mortgage. Check with your real estate attorney if you want to hold title in trust, and also if your lender won't permit this form of ownership.

## Ensuring good title

Buying a home that has a messy title record is very risky. That's why it's so important to have the title to the property examined by a title insurance company, real estate attorney, or other title expert before you close. How title is checked varies from one locale to the next.

A title search should tell you the name of the legal owner, and it should also tell you how title to the property is held (joint tenancy or tenancy in common, for example). It should reveal any easements and restrictions affecting the property (such as CC&Rs—Covenants, Conditions, and Restrictions—or a common maintenance agreement for a shared driveway). Finally, it should give you the legal description of the property and tell you what, if any, liens (loans, judgments, property taxes, mechanics liens, IRS tax liens) are recorded against the property.

Most buyers assume that the person who signs the purchase contract as the seller has the right to sell the property and has the ability to pass title to the property to the buyer. But this is not always the case. Probate sales, which involve properties where an owner is deceased, can present problems. If the heirs have the legal power to sell the property, a sale can proceed. If they do not, a court proceeding may be necessary before the property can be sold. If the heirs are disputing with each other over who has the legal right to the property, the property might not be salable until the estate matters are settled.

Your purchase contract should include a contingency that allows you to inspect the title condition. If you discover a title defect (called a "cloud"), and the sellers can't remedy the situation by the closing date, your deposit should be returned to you and you should be released from the sale contract.

A "cloud" on the title may have been caused by a mistake made during an earlier title transfer. Suppose you are in contract to buy a home from a seller who bought the property years ago at a probate sale. A current title search reveals a deed transferring ownership from the estate of the past owner to the present owner. The title record also shows that the past owner had a wife who did not sign the deed when title was transferred. Since the wife did not transfer any interest she might have in the property, she (or her heirs) could make a claim to the property. You wouldn't want to take title to the property until this woman, or her heirs if she is deceased, relinquished any interest they might have.

When buyers take out a mortgage to buy a home, they are required to provide title insurance to protect the lender's interest in the property. Title insurance for the lender covers the loan amount only; it does not protect the buyers, their down payment, or any equity they might build up over time. Buyers can purchase title insurance for their own protection. It's purchased on a one-time-only basis, and is not transferable to the next owner. The cost is usually based on the purchase price: the higher the price of the home, the higher the title insurance premium. For example, in California, title insurance to cover the buyer of a $200,000 house is about $900; a concurrent lender's policy for a $160,000 loan is approximately $310. On a $500,000 house, title insurance for the buyer is about $1,565; lender's coverage for a $400,000 loan is about $485. Title insurance companies will usually give a discounted rate (called a short rate) if the title has been searched within the past year or two. Title insurance for the lender is usually required again when homeowners refinance. If you are buying a home where the owner refinanced recently, ask the title company if you qualify for a short-rate premium.

An abstract of title used in many areas of the country is a historical summary of a title search on a property. If the sellers provide an abstract, the buyers usually have their attorney review it and issue a certificate of title, which is a written opinion of the title condition. A certificate of title is not the same as title insurance. Even if title insurance is not customary where you are buying, it is wise to protect yourself by making your contract contingent on your getting title insurance coverage. Whether the buyer or seller pays for title insurance varies with local custom.

**Easements**

An easement is a right to use another person's property for a specific purpose. Easements are usually created by written agreement and they are more or less permanent. Easements generally "run with the land." This means that when the property is sold, the easement is acquired by the new owner with the property. The property you buy may be subject to an easement that has existed for many years through several owners.

A buyer might encounter two types of easements. One is an easement that benefits the property in question. The other is an easement that affects the property; that is, it benefits someone else. An example of the first is an easement for ingress and egress across a neighbor's property. Let's say you are buying in a rural area and the only way to get from the main road to the house is across a neighbor's property. Make certain before you buy the property that title to the property includes an easement for ingress and egress across the neighbor's property. A search of the title record should show whether such an easement exists.

In urban areas, neighbors often share driveways. In many cases, one neighbor has granted an easement to the other neighbor for use of a portion of his property, say a five-foot strip of land to be used for ingress and egress. Multiple owners are often involved in shared driveway situations, in which case easements may be granted between multiple parties. Ideally, in a situation like this, there should be a common maintenance agreement recorded against the properties involved, which specifies how and when the common driveway will be repaired, and how costs will be shared between co-owners/users.

A neighbor might have an easement for ingress and egress across the property you are buying. In this case, the easement affects the property and benefits someone else. A utility easement is another example. Utility easements are common. A title search will often reveal that there is a portion of the property reserved for utility companies (water, gas, electric, sewer, telephone, cable TV) to maintain their equipment. Because utility companies may need to dig up the easement to complete repairs, the property owner cannot build over the easement.

Buyers who only want to buy a specific property if they can modify it, such as putting in a swimming pool, should have a property survey completed as a condition of the purchase agreement. A surveyor can make sure that the proposed addition won't interfere with an easement.

Homeowners often landscape and build fences or decks over easements. This is risky because the improvements may have to be ripped out. Planting large trees over utility easements, particularly a sewer easement, isn't a good idea either. The tree roots might damage the underground facilities, and the property owner might be liable for the repairs.

A title search should show all easements that are recorded against the property. But the search may only list the easements; if a full description of any easement is not included, ask whoever is completing the title search to provide you with a detailed description.

TALES FROM THE TRENCHES: EPISODE 18

*Fran and Ted purchased a home on a large piece of property which afforded them the privacy they desired. They planned to fence the perimeter to keep deer and trespassers out. But when they put up the fence, they discovered they could not fence completely around their property because the neighbor had an easement that ran through their property. Ted contacted the neighbors to get permission to fence over the easement. The neighbors would only grant permission for a hefty fee. Fran and Ted had noticed there was an easement on the property when they reviewed the preliminary title report before closing. But they didn't pay attention to it, nor did they ask for a more detailed explanation of what it meant. If they had, they could have asked the seller to get permission from the neighbor to fence over the easement as a condition of the purchase. Or, at least they could have asked the seller to share in the cost of paying off the neighbor.*

There could also be unrecorded easements that affect a property. Several neighborhoods in Oakland, California, have houses built over underground culverts. The culverts were built decades ago to divert water from local creeks; they are part of the city's storm drain system. There are no written easements indicating that in some places the city system runs underneath houses, and the city disclaims any responsibility for any houses damaged if a culvert were to break. A buyer would want to know about this before closing a sale. One way to find out about unrecorded easements is to go to the planning department and look at maps of the underground sewer and storm drain systems. Another resource is people who live in the neighborhood. Talk to neighbors to find out if they are aware of any unrecorded easements that might affect the property you are considering buying. Ask sellers if they are aware of any such easements.

It is common to find utility wires running over a property, with no mention of a utility easement in the written title record. Even if it is not recorded, the easement could nonetheless be valid. Consult a real estate attorney if you have any questions about easements on a property you are buying.

# Homeowner's insurance

Before you can close a home purchase, your lender will require that you take out a hazard insurance policy. Usually the lender requires that the borrower carry hazard (or homeowner's) insurance to cover the amount of the mortgage, unless state law dictates otherwise. In California, for example, the lender cannot require you to carry insurance to cover the loan amount as long as you carry adequate replacement cost coverage. If you buy a home for $250,000 with a 90-percent loan, the amount of your mortgage is $225,000. The land, which presumably won't be destroyed in a fire, may be worth $50,000. If the dwelling has 1,500 square feet and the cost to rebuild is $125 per square foot, you may be adequately covered with a replacement cost insurance policy in the amount of $187,500 (1,500 square feet times $125 per square foot). Your lender should indicate the minimum acceptable coverage either in your conditional loan approval letter or in the lender's instructions to your settlement agent. The lender is named as loss payee on your homeowner's policy so that if the home burns down and you choose not to rebuild, the lender is paid back the amount you owe. Condominium buyers will need to have their lender added as a loss payee to the homeowner association's insurance policy. Your lender will probably also expect you to pay one year's premium in advance at closing. Even if you are paying all cash for a home, you are wise to insure it against loss.

Most buyers get a comprehensive homeowner's insurance policy, of which there are several varieties. In addition to covering the home in case of fire, a homeowner's policy covers such things as personal possessions, personal liability, vandalism, theft, water damage (except for flooding), and loss of the use of the dwelling. Insurance premiums can vary significantly from one company to the next, so shop around before making a choice. When making comparisons, be sure you receive quotes for equivalent coverage. Also, talk to people who recently made an insurance claim with a company you are considering. Did they receive prompt and dependable service? Be sure to check the financial rating of a company you are considering.

The Cadillac of insurance policies, in most cases, is a guaranteed replacement cost policy that will pay to rebuild your home even if the cost to rebuild exceeds your policy limit. This kind of coverage is not available everywhere, nor for all kinds of properties. With guaranteed replacement cost coverage, no deductions are made for depreciation (the decrease in value due to age and wear and tear). Some companies limit the amount they will pay on a claim to 125 or 150 percent of the policy's face value. Let's say you have guaranteed replacement cost coverage, with no limit on how much the insurance company will pay out on a claim. You are insured for $250,000, which your insurance carrier says is adequate to replace your home if it is destroyed in a fire. Subsequently, your home burns down. After getting bids to rebuild, you discover that it will cost $300,000 to rebuild. In this case, the insurance company will pay the full $300,000, even though you are insured for $50,000 less than this amount. If you have guaranteed replacement cost coverage with a cap of 125 percent of the policy amount, then the insurance company will pay up to a maximum of $312,500 (125 percent of $250,000), so you would still be fully covered. But if the cost to rebuild exceeded $312,500, you would have to pay the additional costs yourself.

Some insurance companies won't issue a guaranteed replacement cost policy on an older home. You may only be able to get replacement cost coverage, which will pay to rebuild your house if it's destroyed, but the coverage will be limited to the policy amount. If you are insured for $187,500, and your home is destroyed and costs $300,000 to rebuild, you will have to pay the difference. If you have replacement cost coverage limited to the policy amount, you must make sure that you have enough coverage to rebuild. Some insurance agents will want to sell you less than enough coverage to save you money on premiums. Do your homework and make sure that you have enough coverage. Ask a local builder or knowledgeable real estate agent how much it costs to rebuild per square foot in your area. This figure varies significantly from one location to the next. It also varies over time. Then find out the approximate square footage of the home you are buying. The easiest way to find the square footage is to ask for a copy of the appraisal report on the property that was completed by your mortgage lender. This will include a square footage figure. Multiply the two figures to arrive at the amount of coverage you need. You don't need to insure for the full purchase price, unless the replacement cost of the dwelling exceeds that amount. Remember, you don't need to insure the land.

New homes are usually cheaper to insure because all systems are new and in good working order. Also, new homes are built up to current code requirements. Insurance companies are much fussier about insuring older homes. Some won't insure homes that are older than a certain age. Some won't insure homes with electrical systems that are on fuses and not circuit breakers. Others won't insure older homes that have knob and tube wiring. You may be able to negotiate an agreement with an insurance carrier if you are buying an older home that needs electrical or earthquake retrofitting. Some carriers will give you coverage with a stipulation that you make required upgrades within thirty days to one year after the policy goes into effect. Or you may be able to negotiate with the sellers to have the required work completed before closing.

Insurance companies differ greatly on how they insure older homes. Most policies won't pay the cost to upgrade your home to meet current code requirements if you have to rebuild. However, if your home is destroyed, the city building department will require that you rebuild to current code. This will add additional cost. Ask the insurance carrier if you can purchase an endorsement, an attachment to an insurance policy that changes the coverage to the policy to cover the cost of code upgrades. You will pay a little more for a code upgrade endorsement, but it will cover some or all of the cost of code upgrades. It's probably worthwhile to get a code upgrade endorsement if you are buying an older home built according to an outdated building code.

Insurance policies have limitations on coverage. For instance, most policies won't cover loss from flooding, earthquakes, wind, or landslides. You may be able to purchase endorsements to cover such disasters. But you will need to research who offers what kinds of coverage and at what additional costs. Some companies won't insure for earthquakes unless the building is bolted to the foundation; others require more complete earthquake retrofitting. Flood insurance may be required by your lender if the home you are buying is in a flood-prone area. A federal government flood insurance policy can be purchased through the National Flood Insurance Program. For more information, call 1-800-638-6620.

To calculate how much personal property coverage you need, make a list of your possessions. It's a good idea to supplement the inventory with photographs or a videotape recording of valuable possessions. Keep this inventory up to date and keep it (including photos and videos) in a secure place, such as a safe deposit box. Most homeowner's insurance policies limit personal property coverage to 50 or 75 percent of the amount of insurance on the dwelling. If this is not enough, consider upgrading your personal property coverage. Also, find out if your possessions will be covered on a guaranteed replacement cost basis; some policies deduct for depreciation.

Condominium and cooperative buyers usually have insurance coverage provided through the homeowner's or cooperative shareholders association. This insurance probably won't cover your personal possessions, liability, or the interior of your dwelling unit. Make sure you understand exactly what is and is not covered by the association or cooperative policy, and arrange to get whatever additional coverage you will need to protect yourself. Also, make sure that your condo association or cooperative is carrying adequate coverage for the project. You may want to ask your attorney to review the policy for you. This policy will need reviewing and updating from time to time.

The amount of insurance coverage you need may change over time because of such things as improvements you make to the property, inflation, and changes in building costs. You may want to consider adding an "inflation guard clause" to your policy, which will automatically increase your coverage over time. Even if your policy has a built-in inflation guard, review your insurance coverage annually and upgrade when necessary. The cost to rebuild can change for many reasons, including the availability of materials and labor. The cost to rebuild after the 1991 Oakland firestorm skyrocketed because of a shortage of materials and a high demand for labor as hundreds of homeowners began rebuilding at once. Check with a contractor from time to time about any significant changes in the cost to rebuild in your area.

You can save money on homeowner's insurance by increasing the deductible amount on the policy. The deductible is the amount the homeowner pays on any given claim. How much you will save by increasing your deductible from $250 to $1,000 varies from one company to the next. But it could reduce your annual premium by as much as 25 percent. Discounts are also available for such things as a security system, dead bolt locks, and smoke alarms. Non-smokers, and homeowners older than fifty-five may be eligible for discounts.

Be prepared when you shop for insurance. Insurance representatives will want certain information about you and the property before they will tell you if they can write a policy and how much they will charge to insure. They will want to know your Social Security number, whether you have made insurance claims recently, the age and location of the home, and the age and condition of the plumbing and electrical systems. Some insurance carriers won't insure homes that have shake roofs or homes that are built on a slope. Some won't insure homeowners who have pit bull dogs because of potential liability. The insurance company will also want to be sure that you are a good risk. If you have a history of making claims against insurance companies or if you are frequently late paying your bills, you could be denied coverage.

Buyers often wait until the last minute to line up insurance coverage. This can be a mistake if the insurance carrier you have in mind refuses to insure your home. USAA, a highly rated company, probably won't insure your home if it is an older one with knob and tube wiring. Other companies will insure such a home, but to get the best coverage for the best price requires comparison shopping, which takes time. After recent disasters in California and Florida, homeowner's insurance became scarce when insurance carriers stopped writing new policies to limit their exposure.

If you are buying in an area where homeowner's insurance is difficult to obtain, be sure that you include a contingency in your purchase contract that allows you to find acceptable insurance coverage. Then start shopping for insurance as soon as you have a ratified contract. If you can't find insurance, you may be able to get coverage under the Fair Access Insurance Requirements plan, also called the FAIR plan, available in the following states: California, Connecticut, Delaware, Georgia, Illinois, Indiana, Iowa,

**If you are having trouble finding homeowner's insurance:**

- Call your auto insurance carrier and ask if homeowner's coverage is available.
- Promise to move your car insurance coverage to a new insurance carrier who will also give you homeowner's insurance.
- Find out if the seller's insurance policy is assumable by the buyer.
- Transfer your homeowner's insurance from your current home to the new home.
- See if your renter's insurance carrier will write a homeowner's policy for you.
- Try the FAIR plan if you are buying in a state that offers such coverage.
- Check with your state's department of insurance for a list of insurance carriers.
- Get recommendations from local real estate agents, real estate attorneys, title and escrow officers, and from friends in the area who have bought a home recently.

Kansas, Kentucky, Louisiana, Maryland, Massachusetts, Michigan, Minnesota, Missouri, New Jersey, New Mexico, New York, North Carolina, Ohio, Oregon, Pennsylvania, Rhode Island, Virginia, Washington, West Virginia, Wisconsin, and the District of Columbia. The FAIR plan assures the availability of insurance protection for high-risk areas. Contact the state's department of insurance for more information. For general information about homeowner's insurance, call the National Insurance Consumer Hotline at 1-800-942-4242.

# Selecting a mover

Don't wait until the last minute to hire a mover. Although it's possible to line up a mover as late as two weeks before you move, it's better to start the selection process a month or two in advance. During busy spring and summer months, peak season for the moving industry, it can take a couple of weeks just to get an appointment with a moving company representative.

Movers are listed in the Yellow Pages. But rather than shop blind, ask friends or colleagues who moved recently if they would recommend their mover. Your real estate agent may be able to suggest a good mover. If your move is a work-related transfer, your employer may have a working relationship with a reputable mover.

Use a licensed, bonded mover. Interstate movers are licensed by the Interstate Commerce Commission (ICC). You may want to get estimates from three licensed movers before making a choice. An estimator from each company should visit your home to examine the items you are moving before issuing an estimate. Verbal estimates are not binding, so make sure each mover gives you a written estimate. In most cases, you will want a "not to exceed" or "best price" estimate. This will limit your moving expense to the amount of the estimate. If the move ends up costing less than the estimated amount, you will pay the lower price.

A "nonbinding" estimate requires you pay the actual amount of the move above the estimated price. However, ICC regulations prohibit licensed movers from charging more than 10 percent above the amount of the original estimate. Thanks to recent deregulation in the moving industry, movers are able to offer discounts. Ask about these.

Price is an important factor when you pick a mover, but service can be equally important. Moving is stressful, even when it goes smoothly. Beware of a mover whose bid is way below all other bids. A low bid may mean someone is trying to buy your business or it can be a sign of inexperience. You are trusting a stranger with your personal belongings, so make sure you feel confident that you will get an acceptable level of service.

The ICC requires licensed movers to provide cargo insurance at no additional charge to the customer. This insurance will only pay 60 cents per pound per article. You may be wise to purchase more insurance through your mover. Or check with your homeowner's insurance carrier to see if you can purchase coverage for your goods while they are in transit. Find out each company's policy on damage that occurs to possessions that you pack yourself. Unless the box itself is damaged in the move, the mover may not be responsible for damage to the contents of the box if you did the packing.

Cut the cost of your move by throwing out, selling, or donating possessions you no longer want or need. Eliminate these items before the movers gives you estimates. A good mover can give you tips on how to save money on your move. Ask for advice about how to pack and how to stack boxes so they can be easily loaded. You may want to move valuables and houseplants yourself. Prepare an inventory of the items you are moving and label each box with your name and the address of your new home. Attach a copy of your inventory to the mover's estimate. Knowing in advance where you want your belongings put in your new home will hasten the unloading process.

If you are moving onto a narrow, windy street, let your mover know this in advance. It may affect the size of the truck chosen to move you. Also, make sure if you are moving into an area where street work is in progress that there will be easy access to your new home on moving day. If you are moving into a condominium or cooperative, check to see if there are any moving restrictions. Some condominiums and co-ops only permit owners to move in and out on certain days of the week, like a Saturday. You may need to make arrangements to use a freight elevator to move your possessions into the building.

**Reduce the cost of your move by eliminating possessions you no longer want before you move.**

Be sure to confirm ahead of time the payment type the movers will accept at your destination. Some movers will only take cash or a certified check (not a personal check). Others will take credit cards. The mover will ask you to sign a copy of the inventory to show that you received everything and that nothing was damaged in the move. Read any document you are asked to sign carefully and check your possessions for damage before signing.

## Preparing to move

Several weeks before you move, arrange to have the utilities at the new home transferred into your name as of the day you take possession. Your real estate agent should be able to provide you with the relevant phone numbers. If you are moving into a new area, the new utility company may require a security deposit unless you can provide a credit letter from your current utility company. You will also want to put in a change of address at your post office and change magazine subscriptions to your new address. Ask your doctor, dentist, and banker for recommendations of professionals to use in the new location if you are moving out of the area. Take care of routine doctor and dentist visits before you move and renew any critical drug prescriptions. If you are moving out of the area, make sure that you have enough cash or traveler's checks to tide you over. You may need to make special arrangements for moving pets. If you are moving to Hawaii or out of the country, your pet might have to go through a quarantine. Many cities have pet licensing requirements. You may need verification from a veterinarian that your animal has been vaccinated for rabies.

# Settling up

Most buyers get a mortgage to buy their home. The closing or settlement cannot occur until that loan is funded by the lender and all the buyers' cash for the down payment and closing costs is accounted for. At closing, the sellers' loans secured against the property must be paid off (unless the buyers are assuming the sellers' loan). Also, fees associated with the sale, such as the brokerage commission and transfer taxes, are paid. Title to the property is transferred into the buyers' names, and the buyers' new mortgage is recorded against the property. Funds are then dispersed: The sellers receive their proceeds, the various real estate settlement service providers (like agents and attorneys) receive their fees, and the closing costs associated with the transaction (like transfer taxes) are paid.

Although the mechanics of the actual closing vary from one location to the next, certain elements are common to all closings. The person who handles the closing (attorney, settlement agent, escrow officer, or real estate broker), prepares closing papers for the buyers and sellers to sign. One of the closing documents is a settlement statement or HUD-1 form. This form includes a cost accounting of the charges and credits associated with the property transfer. On the settlement statement, the buyers are given credit for any deposits they have made that apply toward the purchase price. If the sellers agreed to pay some of the buyers' closing costs, this amount will appear as a credit to the buyers. The buyers are also given credit for the amount of their new loan, because this will be applied to the purchase price. Buyer charges might include loan fees, transfer taxes, title fees, a hazard insurance premium, and impounds required by the lender. If you are paying mortgage points, which you plan to write off to reduce your income tax liability, your settlement statement (HUD-1) must clearly identify this amount of money as either "discount points," "loan discount," or "loan origination." The IRS requires that points be computed as a percent of the amount borrowed, not as a flat fee. And you must pay the points directly to the lender with your own funds. If you get audited by the IRS, you need to show that you paid for the points and that they were not simply subtracted from your mortgage amount. To be on the safe side, write a separate check for the points.

Property taxes are usually prorated to the closing date. If the sellers have paid property taxes that cover a time period when the buyers will have ownership to the property, the buyers reimburse the sellers for this amount. This would appear as a buyer charge on the settlement sheet. If the sellers owe taxes, they are collected at closing. If the taxes are not yet due, the amount collected from the sellers may appear as a credit to the buyers. The buyers will be responsible for paying the tax bill when it is due.

When a new loan is involved, the lenders will have certain requirements that must be met before the closing can occur. Typically, lenders require assurances that title to the property is clear. They also require hazard insurance, usually with proof that a one-year premium has been paid in advance. A lender may require an impound account (also called an escrow account) for the collection of funds to pay the buyers' property taxes and insurance. If so, the lender is supposed to provide you with an "initial escrow account" disclosure at closing. The lender will collect one-twelfth of your total property tax and insurance premiums per month. At closing, the lender will usually collect two months' worth of property taxes and hazard and mortgage insurance premiums to set up an impound or escrow account. The lender may require a larger property tax impound, depending on when the next property tax bill is due.

The loan documents will include the note, which is the promise to repay the loan, and the mortgage (or deed of trust, depending on the state in which you are buying), which is recorded against the property and makes the property the security for the loan. In addition, there will be loan disclosure statements, copies of your tax returns (which you will have to sign for the lender), your loan application, and numerous other documents. One document that lenders require gives the lender permission to obtain copies of the borrowers' tax returns directly from the IRS. Some loan files are randomly audited for fraud. You can restrict the lender's access to returns for the years used to qualify for the loan. Ask your settlement agent to take care of this for you.

Buyers are often surprised at the volume of papers they have to sign at closing. You may be frustrated because you may have to sign complicated and confusing documents you have never seen before. If possible, obtain copies of all your closing documents from the settlement agent before you sign the originals. Review them all to make sure that you understand everything. If there is any discrepancy between the loan you thought you were getting and what the loan papers indicate, call your loan agent or mortgage broker for an explanation. If there is anything in your closing package that you don't understand, talk to the escrow officer or closer, your loan agent, real estate agent, or attorney. Sometimes it is impossible to review your loan documents in advance. In this case, make sure that your loan agent or mortgage broker will be available, at least by phone and preferably in person. That way you can consult while you are signing documents if you have any questions.

**Get copies of all your closing documents to review in advance.**

Your closing funds will have to be in the form of a certified or cashier's check, or the funds can often be wired from your account to the closer's bank account. Find out exactly how much money you will need to close, and get detailed wiring instructions from the settlement agent. If there is any question about the amount of the money you will need to close, arrange to transfer more than enough. The excess will be returned to you at closing. Your signature may have to be notarized when you sign closing documents, so bring your driver's license or other acceptable proof of identification with you to the signing.

# The final walk-through inspection

Some buyers complete a final walk-through inspection of the property before closing to confirm it is in substantially the same condition as it was when the purchase contract was negotiated. If the seller agreed to complete repairs as a part of the purchase agreement, a final inspection enables the buyers to verify that the work has been done. The final walk-through also gives the buyers the opportunity to confirm that the seller's personal belongings and debris are being removed from the property, that tenants are gone, and that appliances the seller agreed to leave with the property have not been moved out by accident.

Although the final walk-through inspection is usually a buyer's right, it is usually not a contingency of the contract. This means that buyers cannot use the walk-through as a means of backing out of the contract at the last minute. The walk-through should be completed far enough in advance of closing, at least several days, so that the sellers have time to remedy any problems.

New homes are often sold before they are completed. During the final walk-through of a new home, you should make a list (called a punch list) of finishing details the builder still needs to complete. It's wise to have the builder sign a copy of your punch list. If the list is short, the builder probably won't have trouble completing the work by closing. If a substantial amount of work remains, you may want to delay closing until the work is done. Your lender may actually require this.

In addition to completing a final walk-through inspection, it's a good idea to schedule a meeting with the seller so that you can learn about the idiosyncrasies of your new home before you move in. Find out how to operate the irrigation, security, and lighting systems. Ask the seller to leave any operating manuals and warranties for you. Inquire about routine maintenance items the sellers feel are necessary to keep the house in top condition. For example, is there a sewer pipe that will back up unless you call out a rooting service once a year? How often do the gutters need cleaning? Is there an area of the roof or a skylight that needs routine caulking? Are there underground drains that need periodic clearing? Are there areas around the foundation that require caulking?

Ask the sellers to provide you with a list of tradespeople that have worked on the home, such as a roofer, painter, handyman, plumbing and heating contractor, electrician, chimney sweep, and pest control operator. Such a list is valuable because the tradespeople are familiar with the property. It's often hard to find a good gardener. If the seller's gardener is willing to stay on and work for you, be sure to get his or her name and phone number. Buyers of new homes should ask the builder who they should call when they find defects that need correcting. If you are moving into a completely new community, ask the sellers to introduce you to a few of your new neighbors. If you don't have an opportunity to meet with the sellers personally before closing, ask them to leave you a note detailing any relevant information.

The sellers should remove all their personal possessions from the property before they turn it over to you. They should take away any debris and have the property in broom-swept condition when you take possession, unless you agreed otherwise. If you see that the sellers have not done this when you do the final walk-through inspection, let the sellers know through your agent that a condition of the closing is that the sellers abide by the contract.

You may want to ask the sellers to leave any matching paint behind. If they don't have extra paint, ask for the paint color and brand, unless you plan to change the colors when you move in. By the way, the best time to paint, re-carpet, and refinish floors is before you move your possessions in. The work will progress more quickly if the home is vacant and it will probably cost you less than if you have the work done while you are living there.

Some buyers don't complete a final walk-through inspection. They operate on good faith that the sellers will comply with the terms of the contract, and that they will deliver a home that has been maintained, is free of debris, and is broom-clean. But if you have ever heard a horror story about buyers taking possession of a home that was a mess, you will want to exercise your right to do a final inspection.

## Pre-closing property damage

The purchase contract should specify what will happen if the property you are buying is damaged or destroyed before you become the new owner. Damage could be as minor as a broken window caused by a misthrown ball. Or the home could be totally destroyed by fire caused by an electrical storm. The purchase contract may require that the sellers bear the "risk of loss" if the home is destroyed before closing. If so, the buyers may have an automatic way out of the contract if they choose to take it. If they choose to cancel the contract, their deposit money should be returned to them. However, the "risk of loss" clause could oblige the buyers to proceed with the transaction, provided the sellers repair the damage.

Even if the sellers bear the risk of loss, the contract may provide several options for buyers who want to proceed with the purchase of a property that is totally or partially destroyed before closing. For example, the contract could require the sellers to repair damage if the destruction is equal to or less than a predetermined percentage of the property's value (say 1 or 10 percent). Or the contract could give the buyers the right to buy the property in its "as is" condition at the price agreed to in the contract. In this case, the sellers might be required to pay the buyers a predetermined percent of the property's value. In addition, the sellers might be obliged to transfer their rights to any insurance claims to the buyers. Buyers in this situation should check with the sellers' insurance carrier about the assignability of claim rights. They should also make sure there is enough insurance money to repair the damage; the seller's insurance coverage may be inadequate. Another option is for the buyers to buy the damaged property "as is" but at a reduced price to compensate for the destruction.

Minor damage, such as a broken window, could be a sellers' responsibility. But, again, the contract should indicate who is responsible. A "condition of property" clause is common in some residential purchase agreements. Such a clause usually requires the sellers to maintain the property until closing. This means that the sellers are required to keep the property in substantially the same condition it was in when the buyers agreed to buy it. Some contracts include "seller warranty" clauses. These clauses vary from one contract to the next, but basically require the sellers to have the property systems (plumbing, heating, roof, etc.) in working order at closing. If a pipe bursts or an appliance breaks before closing, the sellers have to fix it at their expense.

In some states, unless the contract indicates otherwise, the buyers bear the risk of loss to the property, not the sellers. This means that the buyers have to complete the purchase and pay the full contract price, even if the property is totally destroyed. Consult a real estate attorney if you have any questions about the "risk of loss" clause in the contract.

When buyers take early possession of a property, they may become responsible for damage that occurs to the property between the time they move in and closing. If the buyers move in before closing, there should be a written early occupancy agreement that specifically states who is responsible for any damage that might occur. Also, the seller's hazard insurance coverage should stay in effect until title transfers to the buyers. During the interim occupancy period, the buyers will need renter's insurance coverage for their personal possessions and liability.

## Maintaining your investment

Homes that are maintained in top condition hold their value better than homes that are left to deteriorate. One of the first things you should do after you settle into your new home is to establish a home maintenance routine. The best way to preserve the investment you make in a home is to keep it well-maintained.

Study the inspection reports you ordered or received when you bought the home. Make a list of all repairs the sellers didn't complete before closing that still need fixing. If it's impossible to complete all the repairs at once, prioritize and complete those that need the most urgent attention. The inspector who examined the property for you may be willing to help you prioritize the list if you feel too inexperienced to do this yourself. Don't make the mistake of indefinitely postponing needed repairs until small problems develop into major projects. If you received a credit from the sellers at closing in lieu of having a defect repaired, schedule this work as soon as possible. Often buyers use such a credit to pay for some of their closing costs and then neglect to get the repair work done. Sometimes buyers purchase a property "as is" with respect to termite work or other deferred maintenance. Don't be lulled into a false sense of security that just because your lender didn't require the work to be done before closing you don't have to get it done at all.

Make a thorough examination of your home each year before the rainy season begins. Patch and seal voids and cracks in the exterior to keep water out. Make sure doors and windows are watertight. Have the roof checked for needed repairs, clean gutters and downspouts, and make sure water coming off the roof is directed away from the foundation. Check under the house during the rainy season to see if water accumulates and look for standing water around the exterior of the foundation. Call a drainage expert, if necessary, to make recommendations about how you can improve the drainage system.

Make sure your furnace and fireplace are in good repair. Replace batteries in smoke detectors and recharge fire extinguishers on a regular basis. If you were not successful in getting the sellers' recommendations of tradespeople to work on the property, ask your real estate agent to recommend reliable professionals to you. If you are using people that don't come highly recommended, make sure you check their references.

Plan to have termite inspections done every few years and take care of minor problems promptly. Keep bathroom and kitchen tile and fixtures well caulked and sealed. Repair all plumbing leaks. Painting and sealing is an important part of home maintenance. However, the mere thought of painting the entire interior of your home may cause you to procrastinate indefinitely. So that the job doesn't become too overwhelming, plan to paint one room of your home each year. The same approach can work for exterior painting: Paint one side of the house a year. One side may get more exposure than the others and will need paint more often. Set up a regime to paint that side twice as often as you paint the others. Sticking to a good home maintenance program will also make it easier for you to get your home ready to market when you decide to sell and move on.

Townhouse and condominium owners worry less about home maintenance than single-family residential owners do because many of the exterior maintenance chores are taken care of by the homeowner's association. However, even with a homeowner's association, individual-unit owners may be responsible for their own roof, drainage system, deck, bathroom, kitchen, and interior repairs. Check with the homeowner's association to determine who is responsible for what repairs. You will want to take an active interest in how common area repairs are handled by the homeowner's association. Those areas need to be well maintained to preserve your investment.

Keep a log of all the improvements and repairs you complete during your period of ownership. This will come in handy when you sell and can show new buyers your regime of good home maintenance.

**Farmhouse**
*Features typical of the farmhouse style are pitched roofs, clapboard wood siding, large verandas or porches, and double-hung wood windows. Farm-houses often have traditional charm, but they are as maintenance-free as possible.*

# Strategies for Repeat Home Buyers

# 8

Most first-time buyers eventually become repeat home buyers. They outgrow their starter homes and need something larger. Later in life, empty-nesters often decide to trade down to smaller, low-maintenance homes. New jobs and lifestyle changes can create the need to sell one home and buy another. So that your next move, and future moves, will be sane and economically sound, avoid these ten repeat home buyer mistakes.

## Ten common repeat home buyer mistakes

☐ *Buying a new home before you sell your old one.*
The temptation may be great to buy a replacement home first. That way you'll know where you're going and how much you will pay. You won't have to worry about being left out in the cold if your home sells quickly and you have nowhere to go. However, the financial risks of buying first are great. It is usually better to endure the inconvenience of moving to an interim rental—which rarely happens—than it is to end up owning two homes when you only want one.

Of course, there are exceptions to every rule. If you can financially and emotionally afford to own two homes, it is sometimes better to buy the replacement home first. Suppose you, your family, and your pets are bursting out of your tiny two-bedroom, one-bath bungalow. It may be easier to sell the old place without you and your menagerie in it. And, it will probably be easier on the family. This is the more expensive and riskier way to go and most people cannot afford to do it this way. Even many of those who can afford it should not take the risk.

☐ *Listing your home based on the price you would like to get rather than on market value.*
Market value determines the price of your home, not wishful thinking. A buyer won't pay more for your home just because you think you need more to buy your next home. Find out the market value of your current home first, then find out what price home you can afford to buy.

☐ *Failing to get a termite report (or other indicated reports) before listing your home for sale.*
Sellers are often required to pay for eliminating wood pest infestation when they sell their home. They may also be asked to correct other defects. Sellers who know the condition of their home before they sell it are in a better position to negotiate a firm sale.

☐ *Putting a home on the market before it is spruced up.*
Most buyers buy homes through real estate agents. Agents, like buyers, remember what they see and their first impressions are lasting ones. If a property looks messy when it hits the market, that is how the agents will remember it. It's difficult to get agents to come back later to take another look at a home after the fix-up-for-sale work has been completed. Most people lack the vision to imagine what a property will look like fixed up. It's usually better to delay marketing a home until it is spruced up for sale. Agents are most excited about showing and selling homes that are in mint condition.

☐ *Refusing to reduce a list price that is too high for the market.*
Because it's hard to be objective about the value of your home, get a professional opinion before setting a list price. Overpriced listings often take a long time to sell. And they frequently sell for less than if they were priced right to begin with. It's natural to want to get the most money possible when you sell. Competitive pricing is the way to achieve that result. If you find that your list price is too high for the market, reduce your price sooner, not later. Letting a property stay on the market overpriced usually costs you money in the long run.

☐ *Refusing to counter a low offer.*
Sellers want to sell high; buyers want to buy low. A low offer from well-qualified buyers is better than no offer at all. A high offer from unqualified buyers can lead to disaster. The price buyers offer is not the most important part of their offer, if they are willing to negotiate. Sometimes buyers don't know the top price they will pay for a property until they are in the midst of a negotiation, when the buyers' resolve to buy the property is solidified. This can positively affect the price they will pay.

☐ *Being present when the home is shown to prospective buyers.*
One way to discourage buyers from buying your home is to be home during showings. For buyers to decide to buy a home, they first must discover and discuss all of its flaws.

Buyers are reluctant to say anything negative about a home in the seller's presence. Have your real estate agent contact the buyers' agent to learn what prospective buyers think of the home.

☐ *Listing with a contingency to find a replacement home.*
This is like saying that your home might be for sale. Serious buyers make offers on homes that are definitely for sale. Sellers who want to minimize their chances of having to move twice should list their homes with a provision that they may need a long closing, or that they may need to remain in possession and rent-back the property for a time after closing. Sellers who choose to buy their replacement home first might want to list the old home contingent upon the successful closing of the new home. More buyers will be receptive to this type of condition because the sellers will have already found and negotiated the purchase of their new home.

☐ *Setting up a complicated showing procedure that discourages showings.*
A home that can't be shown can't be sold. The easier it is to show a home, the more often it will be shown, and the quicker it will be sold. There is usually a direct correlation between the number of showings a home receives and the time it takes to sell.

☐ *Refusing to do anything to get your home ready to sell.*
The way most people live in their homes is usually very different from the way a home should look when it goes on the market. People who want to buy a home must be able to envision themselves living there. Most sellers have to de-clutter and clean their homes, at the very least. Often there's quite a bit more work that should be done before a home is shown to prospective buyers. To get top dollar when you sell a car, it's wise to have it detailed so that it shows at its shiny best. The same concept applies to selling homes. Buyers pay a premium for homes they can move right into, without having to do a lot of work. Properties that are in the best condition sell fastest, and for the most money.

# Strategies for repeat home buyers

The repeat buyer's game plan is more complicated than the home buyer's game plan described in Chapter 1. Regardless of whether you are trading up to a larger home, trading down to a smaller one, or trading even, the process is twice as complex as it was the first time you bought. It involves two real estate transactions: the sale of your existing home and the purchase of your replacement home. You'll have the best results if you go about the move in a systematic fashion with a well-thought-out game plan. Although the process is more complex, repeat buyers have the benefit of experience. They have bought and owned at least one home, so the fear of the unknown should not be as paralyzing a problem as it was the first time around.

The home buying process as described in chapters 1 through 7 of this book applies to the repeat home buyer, too. This chapter will deal primarily with coordinating the sale of your existing home with the purchase of a new one.

**Remodel or move?**

Homeowners who like their current home but who need more space often look into remodeling before deciding whether to move. Before you spend a lot of time and effort planning a major remodel, analyze the character of your neighborhood. If it is made up entirely of small starter homes, it may not be wise to add a sizable addition to your home. You probably won't recoup your investment if you end up with the most expensive home on the block. A small house located in the midst of larger houses might be a good candidate for remodeling as long as it can be done within a reasonable budget. However, if a major addition cannot be done without creating an architectural nightmare, you are better off moving.

The next step is to make a wish list of all the things you need in a home that you don't already have. Then get a recommendation of a good architect and set up a consultation. Discuss the feasibility of creating the additional space or amenities you need. It may be immediately obvious that what you want to do is impossible. More likely, however, you will be told that what you want to do might be possible. Find out if municipal building restrictions could affect completion of the project. If the project is definitely feasible, then you need to get a rough estimate of what it will cost.

A contractor won't be able to give you a firm price without a set of drawings to work from. But architectural drawings are expensive, particularly if you never use them. Interview several contractors and get ballpark estimates from each for the remodel you have in mind. If you decide to go ahead with the job, you can have detailed plans drawn and get firm bids from contractors later.

To guard against overimproving your home for the neighborhood, have a real estate agent prepare a comparative market analysis (CMA) for you. You will actually need two CMAs: one to determine the market value of your home in its present condition, and one to give you the market value of homes in the neighborhood that are similar to what your home would be like after a remodel. Then take the ballpark cost to remodel and add it to the present market value of your home. If the projected value of your remodeled home is more than the value of the larger comparables, it does not make good economic sense to go ahead. However, if the comparable homes sell for much

# Remodel or move analysis

| Property description | Remodel project #1 | Remodel project # 2 |
|---|---|---|
| **1** Value of the home in its present condition: 2 bedrooms, 1½ bathrooms, no family room (based on comparable sales): | $200,000 | $200,000 |
| **2** Projected value of the home after the remodel is complete: 3 bedrooms, 2½ bathrooms, family room (based on comparable sales): | $350,000 | $300,000 |
| **3** Cost of improvements: | $110,000 | $110,000 |
| **4** Value of the home in its present condition plus the cost of improvements: | $310,000 | $310,000 |
| **5** Subtract #4 from #1: | +$40,000 | -$10,000 |
| **6** Conclusion: If #5 is a positive number, the remodel makes sense financially. The larger the number, the better. If #5 is a negative number, the remodel may be a mistake financially. | Remodel makes sense financially. | Remodel may be a mistake financially. |

more than the current value of your home plus the cost to remodel, renovating may be an excellent investment.

Don't assume that a future buyer will pay you back for the improvements you put into your home. A buyer will only pay market value for your home. If you put more into it than is warranted in terms of market value, you will be overimproving for the neighborhood, and you probably will not recoup your investment. Be aware that remodels almost always run over budget. Also keep in mind that you are not working with firm bids at this point. It's tempting once you are involved in the remodel process to keep adding to the list of things you want changed. This increases costs, through no fault of your contractor.

An important factor to take into account when deciding whether to remodel or move is how much it will cost you to buy a new home. Have a real estate agent show you several replacement home possibilities so that you can get a feel for the kind of available housing, as well as how much it will cost.

A final consideration, which shouldn't be taken lightly, is the hassle factor involved in remodeling; it can be enormous. Kitchen and bathroom remodels are particularly difficult. During a redo, the home is always dirty, there is constant disruption, it takes longer than you plan, and it takes time away from other endeavors—like work. But the results can be extremely gratifying. And if you work with good people who do quality work and you plan carefully, it may cost less to remodel than to move.

## Buy or sell first?

Homeowners who decide not to remodel their current home but to buy a new one have to decide whether to buy or sell first. Buying the replacement home first makes sense to many people for several reasons. It may take a long time to find the home you want. If you sell your current home first, you could end up with nowhere to go. You might feel pressured to buy a mediocre replacement home so you don't have to move to an interim rental. If you buy first, you know exactly where you are going and when. You know how much the new home will cost and what will be included in the price. If a washer, dryer, and refrigerator are included, you can throw in your appliances in the sale of your home to sweeten the deal. Sounds peachy. But buying first can be very risky.

When you buy the new home before selling the old one, you are locked into paying a certain price, regardless of how much your old home sells for. If you sell for $10,000, $20,000, or $30,000 less than you think you will, the sellers you are buying from probably won't take less for their home just because you miscalculated. Granted, it's easier to establish market value in some markets than it is in others. Predicting an ultimate selling price is more certain in a relatively uniform tract development than it is in a neighborhood with extreme variability in home size and styles. But real estate markets can change quickly and unpredictably. You could buy your replacement house during an upbeat market cycle. Within the few weeks it takes to get your home ready to sell, market conditions might change. If the real estate market slumps, it will take longer to sell and you could sell for less than you thought.

---

**TALE FROM THE TRENCHES: EPISODE 19**

*Todd and Jennifer intended to sell their existing home before buying a replacement home. But one Sunday, by accident, they discovered the home they knew they wanted. They went ahead and bought it without a contingency for the sale of their home. It took them about a month to get their existing home ready to put on the market. In that time, the real estate market stalled and property values declined. It took more than four months and several price reductions for Todd and Jennifer to sell their house. Jennifer worried incessantly and lost sleep most nights during this ordeal. They ended up selling for $50,000 less than they had anticipated, which they were able to afford, but only after liquidating other investments.*

---

Most homeowners can't afford to buy a replacement home before selling their existing home. If part of your cash down payment for the new home is coming from the sale of your current home, you will either have to sell it first or borrow against your equity. Qualifying to carry several home loans at once is beyond most home buyers' financial capability. If you buy first and your existing home doesn't sell in time, you could end up owning two properties and two mortgage payments—three if

# Strategies for repeat home buyers

| | Strategy | Advantages | Disadvantages |
|---|---|---|---|
| 1 | Buy replacement home first. | You know where you will be moving and how much you will be paying. | You don't know how much you will net from the sale of your home, or how long it will take to sell. Owning two homes is a possibility. Qualifying for a mortgage may be difficult. Requires liquid cash for down payment. |
| 2 | Buy replacement home first with a contingency for the sale of your current home. | Same as #1, but you minimize many of the risks. | Many sellers won't accept contingent sale offers. The best homes sell without this contingency. Poor bargaining position. |
| 3 | Buy replacement home first using a swing loan (interim financing) for the down payment. | Same as #1. Enables you to compete against non-contingent sale buyers because you can buy without having your home sold. | High financial risk, especially if your home takes a long time to sell and/or sells low. High carrying costs. Qualifying for financing is more difficult. Swing loans are often due in six months. |
| 4 | Buy replacement home first using a line of credit secured on your current home for the down payment. | Same as #1 and #3. | Less financial risk than #3 because credit lines usually don't have short due date. High carrying costs. Some lenders don't permit use of line of credit for home purchase. |
| 5 | Buy replacement home first with an employee buy-out (for transferees), or a new home where builder will take your home in trade. | Same as #1. | You will probably have to discount the price of your home in exchange for turning the risks of sale over to someone else. |
| 6 | Sell current home first. | You know how much cash you will net from the sale. Eliminates financial risk. | You may have to go to an interim rental if you can't find a replacement home to buy in time. |
| 7 | Sell current home first with a contingency to find a replacement home. | Same as #6. You don't have to move if you don't find a replacement home. | Few buyers will accept this contingency. You may have to discount your price. |
| 8 | Sell current home first with a long closing and/or a rent-back option. | Same as #6. Reduced chance of having to move to an interim rental. | Buyers who need a quick close and possession won't be able to accommodate you. |

you also borrowed the down payment money. Even if you can qualify, you might not want to carry this high a debt load. At the very least, it's extremely stressful to carry two homes at once when you only want one.

### Buying before you sell

Let's say you have the cash for a 10- or 20-percent cash down payment and you have sufficient income to qualify for the new mortgage before selling your current home. Even though you can qualify for a large mortgage, you may want to lower your mortgage amount by investing the proceeds from the sale of your existing home in the replacement home. If so, you may want to consider this strategy: Structure the financing of the new home so that when the old home sells, you can pay down the mortgage on the new home and be left with a more manageable loan amount. For example, suppose you want to buy a $300,000 house with a 20-percent down payment of $60,000. Your mortgage amount would be $240,000, which keeps your monthly payments at a comfortable level. But without having your current home sold, you only have $30,000 cash available, plus enough extra for closing costs and several months of double mortgage payments. Instead of putting 20 percent down, you put 10 percent down, and apply for a 90-percent loan ($270,000). Your monthly payments will be higher than you ultimately want, but the financing can be structured so that you'll lower your monthly payments later when your current home is sold.

Buyers who prefer a fixed interest rate should consider getting two mortgages—a first and a second—to finance the purchase of the replacement home rather than one loan. With this strategy, the first mortgage would be for the ultimate loan amount you want after you sell your existing home. The second mortgage would be for the balance you need to close the sale. When your old home sells, you can pay off the second mortgage. Using the above example, rather than getting a 90-percent first mortgage, you would get an 80-percent first and a 10-percent second. When the old house sells, the proceeds can be used to pay off the second mortgage, leaving you with an 80-percent first mortgage. Make sure that the second does not have a prepayment penalty. To keep your payments low while you own two homes, get a second that has payments amortized over thirty years, or interest-only payments.

You may be wondering why you wouldn't simply get one large first mortgage, instead of two, to finance the purchase. Then, when the old home sells, you could pay the first mortgage down to the desired loan amount. But you wouldn't want to take this approach because when you make a large principal paydown on a fixed-rate mortgage, you reduce the term of the loan but the monthly payments stay the same. So if your aim is to end up with lower monthly payments, you will be better off with a first and a second mortgage. When you pay the second mortgage off, you are relieved of that monthly obligation, and your monthly payments will be reduced.

Buyers who prefer adjustable-rate financing can get one large adjustable-rate first mortgage to finance the purchase of the new home (for 90 percent of the purchase price, in the above example). When the old home sells, you can make a large principal paydown. In this case, your monthly payments would go down. The monthly payment on an adjustable-rate mortgage (ARM) changes periodically to reflect interest rate adjustments. If you make a large principal paydown on an ARM, your monthly payment will be lowered at the next ARM adjustment because ARMs are re-amortized with each interest rate adjustment.

Be warned: 90-percent mortgages often require MI. You can ask for the lender to drop the MI after you have 20-percent equity in the property. Be aware that some lenders have additional requirements you must meet before you can drop MI, such as making no late payments for a couple of years.

## Interim financing

Repeat buyers often need to use the equity in their existing home for a down payment on a new home. The equity is the difference between the property value and the loans secured against it. To close on the new home, the equity needs to be converted to cash. One way to do this is to use interim financing (also called "swing" or "bridge" financing).

An interim loan is a short-term loan, usually due in six months, which is made against the equity in the home being sold. The money generated from this loan is used for a down payment on the next home. One problem with interim financing is the short term of the loan. If you use this financing strategy, make sure the lender will grant you an extension if you need it.

Many repeat buyers cannot qualify for a swing loan. The monthly carrying costs can be significant, including the principal, interest, taxes, and insurance (PITI) on the home being purchased, as well as the PITI on the home that is being sold, and the monthly payment on the interim loan. The interim loan could be an interest-only loan, which lowers carrying costs a bit. Some interim loans don't require monthly payments; the payments accrue and are due at the end of the loan. Sometimes lenders will factor in rental income on one of the two properties, which also lowers the buyer's monthly debt load. If you need rental income from one of the two properties to qualify for the interim loan, the lender will usually want a copy of a bona fide rental agreement.

Make sure that the term of an interim loan will give you more than enough time to sell your home.

Most lenders will not allow borrowers to borrow 100 percent of their equity. They usually limit the loan amount to 70 to 80 percent of the appraised value of the property, minus the amount of the loans already secured against the property. Let's say the home you are selling appraises for $150,000. Your remaining mortgage balance is $75,000. If the lender will only lend up to 75 percent of the appraised value of the property minus the amount of the existing loans on the property, the maximum you will be able to borrow is $37,500. (75 percent of $150,000 is $112,500, minus the $75,000 mortgage equals $37,500.)

Some repeat buyers use an equity line of credit, usually secured against the home they are selling, for their interim financing. With an equity line of credit, you and your property are approved for a maximum loan amount. After the credit line is approved and recorded against your property, you can draw funds as you need them, up to the approved loan amount. If you have a line of credit for up to $50,000 and you haven't used any of this, you have $50,000 that can be applied toward the down payment on the replacement home. The lender for the mortgage on the replacement home will need to know the source of your down payment funds. If the lender thinks that you are too highly leveraged, you may not be able to qualify using this financing strategy. Also, be aware that some equity lines have a restriction in the note that prohibits borrowers from using the credit line to buy another home.

Sellers who don't need all their cash at closing might be willing to provide you with interim financing. They could carry a short-term second loan secured against the home they are selling to you, which would be due upon the sale of your home. This should be less expensive than obtaining interim financing from a conventional lender.

### Selling with a contingency to find a home

To avoid the cost and risk of owning two homes, why not sell your existing home contingent upon finding a suitable replacement home? One reason is that most top listing agents won't market a listing on these terms because most buyers want to buy homes from sellers who are sincere about selling. Also, it's hard to get the best price for a home when it's only provisionally for sale.

When a home is listed with a contingency for the sellers to find a replacement home, it may not be for sale at all. If the sellers are unable to find a new home, they do not have to go through with the sale of their home. They have the right to back out. Buyers often avoid these listings because they might wait in vain for unreasonable sellers to find an acceptable replacement home at the right price. Meanwhile, the buyers could miss out on other homes while they wait for the sellers to make a move.

If you do find buyers who will allow you to have a contingency to find a home, you may have to give the buyers a break on the price as a concession for the contingency. Highly motivated sellers usually sell without this restriction because they realize it may jeopardize their ability to successfully market their home for the best possible price, and because they rightfully fear that it will scare off motivated buyers.

Buyers who do agree to buy a house with such a contingency will want to include a "kick-out" clause in the contract that allows the buyers to withdraw at some point. A kick-out clause can be structured in several ways. For example, it might give the sellers a period of time to find another home, say thirty days. After that time, the contract could be voided at the buyers' option. This way, if the sellers drag their feet, the buyers can get out of the contract when they find another home they like better.

The kick-out clause could allow the buyers to withdraw from the contract at any time up until the sellers notify the buyers that they have found another home and that they are removing their contingency from the contract. Most sellers, however, will want buyers to commit to remaining in contract for some period of time before a kick-out clause goes into effect. The buyers might not want to start incurring costs associated with the purchase—for inspections and financing—until they know the sellers are going through with the sale. This could pose problems because sales can fall apart if defects are discovered during inspections or if the buyers can't get financing. The sellers should offer to reimburse the buyers the amount of their financing and inspection fees if the sale doesn't close because the sellers fail to find another home.

In a hot seller's market, where there is a shortage of homes for sale, sellers will have more success with a contingency to find a replacement home, especially if their home is exceptional and in high demand. But don't even consider this strategy unless you are selling in a very low-inventory market.

> **Listing your home with a contingency to find a replacement home can jeopardize your ability to sell.**

## Buying contingent on selling your home

A contingent sale offer is an offer to purchase that includes a contingency for the buyers to sell their home. If the buyers sell their home, they are usually obliged contractually to complete the purchase of the new home. If their home does not sell, however, they don't have to go through with the purchase and their deposit money is returned to them.

Sellers often won't accept contingent sale offers because the buyers have a legitimate way out of the contract if their home doesn't sell. The sellers can wait in vain for an event that may never occur. Suppose the buyers are unrealistic about the market value of their home and they price it too high for the market? Overpriced listings don't sell no matter how good the market is. If the sellers have an urgent need to sell their home, a contingent sale offer may be out of the question.

The best homes usually don't sell with contingent sale contracts because a healthy demand exists for these homes. In a multiple-offer situation, where several buyers are bidding against one another, the offers with the fewest contingencies are the strongest contenders. Most sellers will even accept a lower price from buyers who don't have to make their offer contingent upon selling another property.

You may find a home that you like well enough to buy that isn't selling quickly. If the sellers are tired of waiting for an offer, they might entertain one that is contingent on the sale of your property. The first thing you should do in this situation is find out why the home isn't selling. Is there something wrong with it that would make it unacceptable to you, or is it just a slow market? The home may not be selling because it is priced too high. You may be able to buy it with a contingent sale provision, but you will probably have to pay more for it than you would if you could make a contingency-free offer.

Sellers willing to consider a contingent sale offer will probably want the purchase contract to include a release clause which permits the sellers to continue to offer their home for sale in the hopes that another buyer will make an offer. If this happens, the sellers accept the second offer in backup position. The backup offer will only become the primary offer if you cannot remove your sale contingency from the contract within a specified time period.

A release clause can specify any time period mutually agreed to by the buyers and sellers. The most common is seventy-two hours (called a seventy-two-hour release clause). If and when the sellers accept a backup offer, they then notify the primary buyers that the seventy-two-hour clock is ticking. If the primary buyers cannot remove their sale contingency within seventy-two-hours they must withdraw and let the second buyers buy the property. In this case, the first buyers get their deposit money back but they lose the property. Not only is it heartbreaking to lose a home under these circumstances but it can also be costly. Contingent sale buyers usually incur fees for inspections and financing of the new home, which can run into the hundreds of dollars.

The best approach to take with a contingent sale offer, if you can find sellers who are receptive, is to specify in the contract that the release clause will not go into effect for a set period of time—say, two or three weeks. This gives you a chance to get your home sold before the release clause kicks in. For this strategy to work, your home must be ready to put on the market. It must be priced to sell. You should also make sure there is a decent demand for the kind of home you are selling.

Be aware that there are other problems with contingent sale offers from the buyers' standpoint. Until your home is sold and the buyers have completed their inspections, it's difficult to know exactly how much money you will net from the sale. Sellers often find themselves renegotiating the purchase price downward because of defects discovered during inspections. You could end up selling for less than you counted on.

It's also risky to make an offer that is not contingent on the sale of your home when in fact you need to sell in order to buy. And it's risky to remove a sale contingency if your home is not sold, even if you receive

**Until your home is sold and the inspection contingency is removed, it's hard to know exactly how much you will net from the sale.**

a seventy-two-hour notice from a seller who has accepted a backup offer. It's disappointing to let the home go to another buyer but at least your deposit isn't at risk. Many of the release clauses specify that you can't just remove the sale contingency if your home isn't sold. You must be able to show that you have the financial means to close without having sold your home.

The best contingent sale strategy is to market your home and find a buyer for it before you make an offer on a replacement home. Ideally, you would wait to buy another home until your buyers are prequalified and the inspection contingency is removed from your contract. Sellers who won't accept offers contingent on the sale of another property will often agree to an offer contingent on the closing of a home sale that is already under contract (pending). You will have the best chance convincing sellers to accept your contingent-on-closing offer if you can show that the major contingencies in your sale agreement have been removed.

## Selling with a rent-back option

One of the best strategies for a repeat home buyer is to list your current home for sale with a provision that you may need a long closing and/or a rent-back. A rent-back allows you to rent your current home back from the buyers for a time after closing. With this approach, you eliminate the financial risk of owning two homes and you don't discourage potential home buyers. You may lose a buyer who must have possession by a certain date, but that will only be the case if another suitable home for that buyer comes up. Most buyers will grant sellers a rent-back. Even though it may be inconvenient, at least the buyers know they have bought a home and can avoid dealing with sellers who have a contingency to find a replacement home.

You may not have to rent back from the buyers if the closing period is long enough, such as ninety days. But in a rising interest rate environment, the buyers may prefer to close earlier to preserve a low interest rate. Repeat buyers who are buying in a very competitive marketplace and who can't buy before they sell their existing home may find that they need to actually close on their current home before they can compete with other buyers in the home buying market. A short closing—thirty days, or so—with a rent-back works well in this situation. In thirty days the sellers have cash from their sale and they are relieved of their mortgage obligation. They can make a noncontingent offer on another home with cash in hand, and they don't have to worry about trying to qualify to own two homes at once.

With a rent-back, it's customary for the sellers to pay a rent equal to the buyers' principal, interest, taxes, and insurance (PITI), prorated on a per diem basis. The amount you pay to rent back your home from the buyers may be considerably higher than your cost of ownership. You also lose your tax write-off because you will be paying rent, not interest. And if the market is appreciating rapidly, you will lose out on appreciation until you find and buy a replacement home. But the equity from your home can be invested for the short term, so you will earn interest on your money. Just make sure that your money will be liquid in time to close on another home when you find it.

The rent-back strategy is a safe and convenient way to make a trade move. It's a small price to pay for financial security and the convenience of not having to make an interim move. You should plan to give the buyers a thirty-day notice before vacating so that they can make plans to move in. For more information about rent-backs, see Chapter 4.

### Buy-outs

Homeowners who are transferred may be offered moving assistance from their employers. Some employers or their relocation companies actually offer to buy the transferee's home, enabling the relocating employee to settle into a new location quickly. There are many different relocation buy-out programs; generally, they work like this: the transferee's home is appraised by several appraisers. Based on the appraisals, the relocation company makes an offer to purchase the home at a certain price. The transferee then has a period of time during which the offer must be accepted—perhaps sixty days from the time the purchase offer is made. Transferees often complain that relocation buy-out prices are low. It's understandable that the price would be conservative; the employer or relocation company has to take on all the risk of selling the property.

Some new home builders offer to take your current home in trade if you buy a new home from them. Also some real estate companies advertise that they will guarantee the sale of your home. Like the relocation buy-out programs, you should not expect to get top price for your home if you give it to someone else in lieu of selling it yourself.

## Timing your move: When is the best time to sell?

The best time to buy is at the low point of a market cycle when prices are down and the market is poised for a turnaround. The best time to sell is after a big run-up in prices, ideally when inventories of houses for sale are low and buyers are competing to buy at premium prices. Buyers usually have more flexibility in timing their home purchase than sellers do in deciding when to sell. Transfers come regardless of what the housing market is doing. So do divorce, death, and childbirth. But let's say you do have the luxury of being able to sell when you want to. How can you time your sale advantageously?

Local economic factors have a strong influence on real estate activity. If business is booming and unemployment is low, more people will be looking to fill their housing needs. It is generally easier to sell during an economic upturn than it is during a recession. There is a direct correlation between interest rates on home loans and affordability. When housing is more affordable, more buyers can qualify for home mortgages. High interest rates can price buyers out of the market and put a damper on real estate sales activity. Low interest rates usually stimulate home sales, except during an economic downturn. Home buyers need to have jobs and the confidence that they will continue to have jobs, regardless of how low interest rates might be.

Consumer confidence has been the most reliable indicator of real estate sales activity in recent years. When the confidence index is high, home sales tend to pick up. When confidence drops, home sales activity also drops. Consumers feel good about making large purchases when they feel good about their jobs and the economy in general.

Supply and demand affect real estate as they do any economic activity. When the local inventory of homes for sale is high and few buyers are looking, the market tends to favor buyers. A seller's market is one in which the inventory is relatively low, which means there is less competition from other sellers. When low inventory combines with high buyer demand, sellers are in the driver's seat. Homes often sell with multiple offers, sometimes for more than the list price.

The time of year affects some real estate markets more than others. Typically, spring is the most active market, followed by fall. The winter months can be slow because of the weather. Home sales can also stagnate during the summer months when vacationing takes priority over home buying. But economic factors can stimulate real estate sales during what would otherwise be a slow time of year. For example, a large drop in interest rates might pick up a stale summer market. Other factors, like a change in the tax laws, can bring a sleepy real estate market alive.

Repeat buyers are sellers and buyers at the same time. Timing may work to your advantage as a seller, but may not work equally as well for you as a buyer. If you are making a trade-up move, the best time to sell may not be when the market is exclusively favoring sellers. It's easier to sell in a seller's market and you are likely to sell for more money. But it may also be difficult to find a home to buy because of low inventory. Also, you could pay an inflated price because of heavy buyer demand. If you are selling for a high price, you will probably pay a high price on your replacement home if you are buying and selling in the same market. If you are trading from a less expensive home to a more expensive home, you might be better off selling and buying in a soft market. You will sell for less than you would in a strong seller's market, but you'll pay less for a more expensive home. This could put you dollars ahead. Suppose you sell a $200,000 house to buy a $300,000 house. If you wait for prices to appreciate 10 percent before you make your move you will sell for $20,000 more, but pay $30,000 more.

You are better off trading down from a more expensive home to a less expensive one in a seller's market. You will pay more for the smaller home than you would in a buyer's market but you will sell the more expensive home for more. Cash-wise, you will come out dollars ahead. It's the reverse of the above example. Let's say you sell for $400,000 in a hot seller's market. Five years earlier, the market value of your home was only $350,000 and you could have purchased your replacement home for only $200,000. Today, you will have to pay $225,000 for the same home. You pay $25,000 more but you sell for $50,000 more, so you are $25,000 ahead.

When the market is declining, you may be better off financially to wait to buy your replacement home. You have two years within which to reinvest to defer paying tax on your gain. (See page 246 for more information about capital gain tax.) You could rent for awhile and buy your replacement home in an even lower market. However, it is difficult to predict when prices, like interest rates, will turn upward or downward. Finding the right home is certainly an important part of the equation—as important to some buyers as trying to time your move to be perfectly in synch with the market. If you are selling one home to buy another of roughly equal value, it doesn't matter if the market is flat or robust because you trade even.

Regardless of whether you are selling to trade up to a more expensive house or down to one that costs less, it is ideal to sell when there is enough market activity so that you can be assured of a sale within three to four months. The right price will help in any market. See page 244 for more information about pricing your home to sell.

## Selecting a listing agent

Choosing an agent to represent you as a seller in the sale of your home is similar to selecting an agent as a buyer (discussed in Chapter 2). You want a local market specialist who has a lot of experience selling homes like yours. He or she should have an excellent reputation, both with other local real estate agents and with previous sellers he or she has represented. He or she should be hardworking and honest, professional, and someone you can relate to well. If you had a good experience working with the agent who sold you your home and that agent is still active in the business, he or she is an obvious choice. Just make sure that the agent is a strong listing agent. With the advent of buyer brokerage, you will find more agents specializing and working only with buyers and never with sellers. If the agent who sold you your home is an exclusive buyer's agent, ask him or her to recommend a good listing agent to you.

Many prospective home sellers interview several agents before selecting one to represent them. If you choose this route, select the three best agents you can find in your area. Some sellers are reluctant to use a top-producing agent who sells a lot of homes. But remember, agents get to be good agents through years of experience. You should use an agent who is working full-time selling real estate and who has a good track record. The busiest agents sell the most property. The point of listing your home for sale is to sell it quickly and for the highest price possible.

**Don't list with an out-of-area agent.**

In addition to finding an agent with the stellar attributes in Chapter 2, you need to be concerned with marketing expertise when you select a listing agent. Ask each agent you interview to prepare a Comparative Market Analysis (CMA) for you. A CMA should provide you with the appropriate comparable sales information so you can list at the right price. It should also describe a marketing proposal, a specific plan of how the agent intends to sell your home. Even if you are satisfied with the agent who sold you your home or with someone who comes highly recommended, and you do not plan to interview several agents, you should ask for a CMA that includes a marketing proposal.

Your listing agent should be a straightforward, no-nonsense professional who will level with you about current market conditions and how to get the best price possible for your home. An agent who just tells you what you want to hear is not doing you a service. Some agents have difficulty speaking candidly to sellers; they are often afraid they will hurt sellers' feelings by suggesting that the decor needs updating or that the home needs de-cluttering. Sometimes agents can't bear to tell sellers their home is worth less than they had hoped for. Yet property condition and proper pricing are both vital to a successful home sale.

> **You should expect your listing agent to:**
> - Prepare a comparative market analysis and marketing proposal.
> - Give your property the broadest marketing exposure possible.
> - Prepare a descriptive brochure about your property, with a color photograph or artist's rendering of the home if possible.
> - List your property on the Multiple Listing Service and on the Internet.
> - Hold a broker's open house for local real estate agents as soon as possible after the property is listed for sale.
> - Keep you informed on local market conditions.
> - Follow up on showing activity and give you feedback from agents who showed your home to potential buyers.
> - Send you copies of weekly advertisements and other marketing materials.
> - Tell you how you can improve the marketability of your home, including reducing the price if market conditions suggest it.
> - Be available to consult regularly with you.

**TALES FROM THE TRENCHES: EPISODE 20**

*Teri listed her home for sale with an agent she met by calling a local realty office. She didn't interview several agents and she didn't check references. Teri asked her listing agent if she should do anything to fix up her house for sale. She had lived there for more than twenty years and hadn't redecorated in a long time. The agent said, "No, do nothing. The buyers will want to redo the house according to their own taste." He also suggested a list price that was about $50,000 too high for the market. When the listing expired, Teri took the house off the market for a few months. During that time, she had about $30,000 of termite work done. She also called a top-producing agent who sold a lot of property in the neighborhood. The second agent recommended that Teri repaint, de-clutter, and spruce the house up for sale. The second agent also recommended a lower list price based on recent comparable sales. Teri took the second agent's advice and received multiple offers within two weeks of listing her home for the second time.*

Some home sellers wonder whether it's better to list with a big company or a small company. A recent study completed by two real estate experts from Penn State's Smeal School of Business concluded that the size of the company had no impact on how fast listings sell. The same study found that listing your home with agents who only sell their own listings is not a good idea. Go with an agent who sells multiple listings. The study also showed that you are likely to sell your home faster if you list with an agent who is selling a lot of homes.

**Usually, the ideal time period for a listing agreement is ninety days.**

Under normal circumstances, a ninety-day listing agreement is what you want. If you and the agent are getting along and you are satisfied with the job the agent is doing, you can renew the listing at the end of ninety days, if necessary. A top agent should be content with a ninety-day listing. However, if you have a very unusual or expensive home that will take a long time to sell or will require a lot of advertising, you should be ready to commit to a longer listing. An agent who is going to spend a lot of money marketing your home will want to know that he or she has a good chance of selling it.

It's tempting to give your listing to the agent who gives you the highest listing price for your home. This can be a big mistake. Some agents intentionally overprice to get listings, then suggest price reductions to get the listing down to the market price. This can cost sellers money because listings are most marketable when they are new on the market. It's hard to sell for the best price after several price reductions.

Sellers often wonder if they should use the same agent to sell the old home and buy the new one. The answer will depend on various factors. If you want to move to a different market area, you should definitely use two agents: One to list your current home and another to find your next home. But if you are moving to a replacement home within the same area, you may want to use one agent for both transactions, particularly if the agent can represent you as a seller's agent in one transaction and as a buyer's agent in the other. Coordinating the two transactions is easier and may also save you money if you use one agent. An agent who is getting two commissions may be willing to negotiate on commission. Real estate commissions are, by law, negotiable. See Chapter 2 for more information about commissions and agency relationships.

# Fixing up your home to sell

The first thing you need to do if you are serious about selling is to stop thinking of your home as "home" and start visualizing it as a commodity that you want to sell. This is one of the most difficult aspects of the home selling process because our identities are usually reflected in our homes. But to be a successful seller you must detach yourself emotionally from your home. You need to be brutally honest with yourself about how your home must look to sell it for a price you will accept. Property condition and appearance play a much bigger part in today's home sales than they did in the run-away seller's market of the late 1980s when even rundown fixer-uppers sold at a premium. Today's buyers discount the price of homes that appear to need a lot of work, if they're willing to buy them at all.

Ask your agent to go through your home with you and make a list of what should be done to get it ready to market. If it's impossible to do everything on the list, have your agent prioritize for you. You don't have to spend a fortune readying your home for sale. In fact, you shouldn't. You should concentrate on cost-effective improvements that will give you a good return on your investment. If your kitchen is out of date, it's impractical to do a major renovation for sale, but it does make sense to do cosmetic enhancements because kitchens are important to most buyers. To freshen up the kitchen, consider painting old cabinets, replacing a worn linoleum floor, adding new counters, and perhaps new light fixtures—particularly if the kitchen is dark.

Paint is the least expensive and fastest improvement you can make to a home. A neutral color scheme may seem boring but it is a safe bet from a resale standpoint. If your decor is acceptable but grimy, try cleaning first. But if your home is painted in strong colors, repaint using neutral colors, such as off-white or beige before you market your home. The same goes for floor coverings: Stick to neutral linoleum and carpet. It's always a good idea to get advice from your agent or a decorator who specializes in fix-up-for-sale before investing in your cosmetic makeover to be sure the improvements will enhance the marketability of your home.

**Make cost effective fix-up-for-sale improvements that will give you a good return on your investment.**

**Painting is one of the most economical improvements you can make to your home.**

A lot of what needs to be done to get a home ready to sell doesn't cost a dime but takes time. Most of us feel good living in our cozy surroundings with all our personal possessions. However, too many belongings make it difficult for buyers to see the home and imagine themselves living there. One of the most important things you can do is to de-clutter, which means to remove the excess from your home. Some homeowners rent storage space if their own storage space is limited. It's quite common for homeowners to have too much furniture, from a showing standpoint. A lot of furniture in a room can make it appear smaller than it is. When showing a home for sale, the bigger it looks, the better. Move pieces out to create a more spacious impression. The easiest way to create more space is to throw out, donate, or sell what you no longer need. It makes no sense to move unwanted items.

> **De-cluttering is the least expensive fix-up-for-sale improvement you can do. It costs nothing but time.**

When you finish de-cluttering and neutralizing, your home will no doubt look sterile to you. But remember: The sleek look sells. Make sure that kitchen counters and bathrooms are clear of almost everything. This is one of the more difficult parts of the home fix-up process. Ideally, you should put away everything you need for a comfortable day-to-day existence, like toothbrushes and toothpaste tubes, the coffee maker, and refrigerator art. Put kitchen and bathroom essentials into plastic bins that can be stored in cabinets. That way you can quickly get what you need when you need it, and stash it away again just as quickly when you know your home is going to be shown. In addition to the untidy essentials, put away your personal collections. Buyers can easily be distracted by your things: picture galleries, figurines, or a collection of baseball hats. By depersonalizing, you force buyers to concentrate on your home.

The way your home presents itself from the street (the "curb appeal") is very important. First impressions are lasting. A front gate hanging on a hinge, a dripping front faucet, and peeling trim paint can cause buyers to wonder what else is wrong with your home. You want to convey the impression that your home is well maintained. If you have limited resources available for fix-up, start with the front. Some buyers won't go into a home that doesn't look inviting from the outside. Make sure the yard is tidy, broken fence posts are fixed, peeling paint is removed and repainted, and overgrown bushes and trees are trimmed. For more about curb appeal, see Chapter 3.

After you finish with the front, go through the house and fix other known defects, many of which you have probably lived with for years. An irony of the fix-up-for-sale process is that most people's homes have never looked as good as they do when they are offered for sale. As you labor through this very critical endeavor, remember that you are doing it to sell your home faster and for more money.

Pet odors can kill a sale, particularly if the buyer is allergic or doesn't like animals. If you have lived with pets for years, you may be unaware of any odors. If so, ask a friend you can trust and who has a good sense of smell to give your home the sniff test. Pet stores carry products that can help remove pet odors from carpets; use the unscented varieties. Also, if you smoke, don't smoke inside your home while it's on the market.

Cleanliness is next to godliness when it comes to selling homes. The interior of your home should gleam and windows should be washed inside and out. Hire help, if necessary. And plan to keep your home this way during the marketing period. Hire a cleaning person or service to come once a week if you are a very busy person who doesn't already have help. Organize cleaning supplies in a plastic container in one area, so that you can easily grab them for a freshening-up at a moment's notice. Your agent should be able to recommend painters, gardeners, haulers, contractors, handymen, cleaning crews, and window washers to help you with fix-up-for-sale chores.

## Staging

Staging is a relatively new concept in the residential resale industry. It was borrowed from new-home builders who decorate models to help sell their houses. Staging can involve minimal effort on the part of a seller, such as rearranging furniture to show a home off to advantage. For some sellers, however, it's a major production involving hiring a fix-up-for-sale decorator who rents a home full of furniture, complete with plants and decorative art work. But homes that are staged for sale tend to sell faster and for a higher price than competing listings that have not been staged. You may find more demand and possibly multiple buyers for a well-staged home.

Ask your agent if your home needs staging. If so, your agent may be able to help you if he or she has expertise in home decorating. If not, your agent should be able to recommend someone who can assist you with staging. Vacant homes are more difficult to sell. You should consider having an empty home staged with furniture before it goes on the market.

**Homes that have been staged for sale tend to sell faster and for more money.**

Fresh flowers are a nice touch inside. Outside, use flowering plants at the front entry for added color and to show off the yard. Don't forget to paint the front door so that it looks fresh and inviting. Buyers like homes that are cheerful and bright. Light is very important to most home buyers. Open curtains and drapes, unless the outlooks are poor. Consider buying window coverings that let light through but that cover windows with unsightly views or that look directly onto neighbors' homes. Leave lights on when the home is shown, even when the sun is shining. Add lighting to rooms that are dark or increase the wattage of light bulbs, if the fixtures will allow it. Also, make sure that the heating or cooling system is set at a comfortable temperature.

Small staging efforts can make a big difference, such as buying a new shower curtain to replace the old one that's mildewed. If you have a yard, patio, or deck, put out deck furniture to show that the space is usable; it then becomes an extension of the living area of the home and adds value in the buyers' mind. Likewise, an unused cubbyhole can be turned into usable space with a little staging. An extra large walk-in closet can become a computer room. A sun room can be transformed into a den or home office with minimal furnishing.

When you sell a home, you are selling a fantasy. Even though the buyers won't live in your home the way it looks in its staged-for-sale condition, they will be attracted to it because it presents a lifestyle they aspire to. Good furnishing and decor pay off. Buyers pay more money for homes that look livable and inviting, even though the furnishings will be moved out with the sellers. By staging your home, you are attempting to fulfill a buyer's dream of how the perfect home should look.

### Pre-sale inspections

Inspections are one of the main reasons home sale transactions fall apart. Something unanticipated is discovered during the home inspection process, and the buyers and sellers cannot agree on a remedy. For example, in December 1995, the sale of a four-year-old, multimillion dollar property in Northern San Diego county fell apart because of an inspection. The buyer brought in a team of inspectors to report on the property's condition.

# Fix-up-for-sale checklist

| Fix-up checklist | Recommended work | Estimated cost |
|---|---|---|
| **Exterior:** | | |
| Yard clean up | | |
| Repair fences, patios, decks | | |
| Exterior paint | | |
| Enhance the front entry | | |
| Stage the yard | | |
|    (with colorful plants and outdoor furniture) | | |
| **Interior:** | | |
| Repair defects and deferred maintenance | | |
| Remove furniture | | |
| Paint | | |
| Change floor coverings, refinish floors | | |
| Improve lighting | | |
| Change window coverings | | |
| De-clutter | | |
| Update the kitchen | | |
| Update the bathroom(s) | | |
| Rearrange furniture | | |
| Store excess belongings | | |
| Stage the home | | |
| Professional cleaning, including windows and carpets; treat for odors | | |

The roofer said the roof needed repairs at a cost of $450,000. This shocking news so concerned the buyer that he immediately backed out of the deal. He figured that if there was that much work needed on a relatively new home, what else might be wrong?

The sellers sued the roofer. Further investigations revealed that the first roofer was correct; the roof had been improperly installed. The repair estimates varied but they were all considerably less than the "deal-killing" bid. Would the sellers be better off if they had ordered a home inspection before they marketed their home? Undoubtedly, yes. The home inspector would have brought their attention to the faulty roof. The sellers could have consulted roofers before marketing their home to get estimates for repairs. Then they could have marketed the home, disclosing the roof's condition, along with the repair estimates. Or they could have had the repair work done before the house was listed for sale.

There is a lot of psychology involved in a home sale. Buyers who are aware of a problem upfront can process this information before making an offer. They can factor the cost into their offer, or ask the sellers to take care of the problem. Buyers often have mixed feelings of excitement and trepidation when they enter into an agreement to buy a home. The impact of an unexpected "bad" report can diffuse any excitement and enhance their fear to the point that they want nothing to do with the property.

Sellers who decide that a presale home inspection is the way to go should ask their agent for the names of several home inspectors who are well-known and respected in the local real estate community. Interview these inspectors until you find one who you think will give you a thorough, objective, and accurate inspection. One reason for using an inspector who has a good track record and name recognition locally is that you want the buyers and their agent to feel comfortable with your inspector. This will add credibility to your report. Your agent should make the report readily available to other agents so their buyers can review it before they make an offer. Make sure that your home inspector will return to the property with the buyers to review the inspection report with them. There will probably be an additional charge for this, but it should be considerably less than the cost of the original inspection. Also, encourage the buyers to have their own inspector look at the property. A seller's report is not meant to replace buyers' inspections; it's to uncover defects in advance so that they don't become deal-breakers. (See Chapter 5 for more information about home inspections.)

In addition to a general home inspection, you should order a presale wood pest (termite) inspection, depending on where you are selling. Ask your agent what inspections are typically ordered before marketing homes in your area. If it's customary for sellers to have a presale termite inspection, then follow local custom. If your roof is at the end of its life and your agent thinks that this could be a concern to prospective buyers, have a presale roof inspection done.

It's often a good idea to offer a home protection plan for the buyer as a part of your sale. You might also want to order seller home protection plan coverage if the systems and appliances in your home are old. See Chapter 5 for more information about home protection plans. Home protection plans are not available in all states.

## Pricing to sell

Why shouldn't you list your home for a high price? Buyers will offer less and a high price can always be reduced later if the home doesn't sell. This seems like a great rationale for overpricing. However, listing at a price that is too high for the market can end up costing you money in the long run. The homes that sell for the most money and that sell the fastest are those priced close to the expected selling price. Overpriced listings tend to take longer to sell. When they do sell, they often sell for less than they would have if they were priced right to begin with.

A home is most marketable when it is new on the market. Real estate agents and buyers anxiously await new listings. There is often a rush to see new listings, because if the home is special and priced right it could sell quickly. Serious buyers don't want to risk losing out on a great property. But if the home doesn't sell quickly, the showing activity usually drops off.

One of the first questions buyers ask before they make an offer is how long the home has been on the market. If it has been on the market for months without a price reduction, buyers often wonder if the sellers are unrealistic about their price. They sometimes shy away from making an offer altogether. Sellers don't understand why buyers don't make offers on overpriced listings. One reason is that today's home buyers are busy; they don't want to waste precious time with a seller who may be unreasonable. Also, today's home buyers are well-educated about the market. They usually know home values better than sellers do, because they look at so many properties before they buy.

To make sure that your home comes on the market priced competitively, ask your agent to prepare a comparative market analysis (CMA) for you. This will give you the market value of homes similar to yours that have sold and closed recently. The more recent the sale, the more relevant it will be. Sales older than six months will probably be out of date. Also, ask to see a list of pending sales—those that have an accepted offer, but have not yet closed. You will also want information about recent expired listings and currently available listings. Find out how long it took for the pending and closed sales to sell. Did any bring in multiple offers? This will tell you how active the market is in your area. Expired listings usually didn't sell because they were priced too high for the market.

The currently available listings will be your competition when you are on the market. You should keep the price of competing listings in mind when you set your list price. But don't give too much significance to your neighbors' list price, particularly if their home is listed at a price that is too high for the market. The pending and closed sales are usually your most reliable indicators of current market value. The exception is when the market is appreciating rapidly. In this case, even the recent closed sales might be out of date. The most recent pending sales will be your most reliable indicators of current market value.

Finding out what your home is likely to sell for is the first part of the pricing exercise. Once you know this, you need to decide on a listing price that will sell your home in the least amount of time for the highest price possible. To set an accurate price, find out how much sellers in your area are having to discount their price to sell. To determine this, divide the selling price of the comparable sales by their list price at the time of sale. Many real estate agents have computerized market evaluation programs that automatically calculate this figure for you. Usually, in price ranges up to about $750,000, homes sell for within 95 to 98 percent of the list price. In the higher price ranges, you may find homes selling, on average, for about 10 percent less than the list price. Use the discounting information as a pricing guide when you set the list price of your home. If homes similar to yours are selling for 97 percent of the list price, your house should be listed for no more than 3 percent above what you expect it to sell for. Listing higher than this may price you out of your market. (See Chapter 3 for more about understanding pricing.)

Sellers often fear that they will price their home too low and lose out on money that should rightfully be theirs. But in reality it's almost impossible to sell your home too low, as long as you fully expose it to the market before you accept an offer. If your list price is too low, you are likely to receive multiple offers. Market forces will push the price up. The key is to get maximum exposure. Don't sell your home to the first person who walks through the front door without first exposing it to the local real estate community.

One way to confirm that your list price is accurate for the market is to ask your agent to collect selling price opinions, called REVs (Realtor Estimate of Value), from the agents who preview your home at the broker open house. Have your agent do this anonymously. Agents object to putting a suggested price on the back of their business cards for fear of offending a seller. Take a look at the average of the price opinions. If the agent's price opinions indicate that you are priced too high, adjust the price immediately so that agents don't lose interest in showing your property.

The market is constantly changing. You must keep current on how changes in the market are affecting the market value of your home. Your agent should keep you informed and let you know about new listings that are competition for your home and about new comparable sales as they occur. If homes similar to yours are coming on the market at lower prices, you will need to adjust your price accordingly. If you haven't received an offer within four to six weeks and the showing activity has dropped off, lower your asking

**Agents don't like to show over-priced listings because they fear that they will lose credibility with their buyers.**

price by about 5 percent. Make a price reduction that makes a strong statement. Small price reductions have little impact. If your agent doesn't suggest a price reduction, ask him or her to drop the price. Some agents have difficulty being candid with sellers about the price of their home, particularly if the sellers are losing money.

---

**TALES FROM THE TRENCHES: EPISODE 21**

*Dan and Julie listed their condo for sale at the price their Realtor suggested. After several weeks of little showing activity and no offers, Julie called her agent and told her to lower the price. The agent reluctantly agreed, but thought that Julie was being too hasty. After another three weeks of no action, Julie told her agent to drop the price again. This time the agent vehemently disagreed. She was sure that Julie was pricing her condo under market value. Julie insisted on the reduction and within one week she had an all-cash offer that closed two weeks later. At the time, the agent felt that Dan and Julie sold too low. But the market continued to decline. If they had waited longer to lower their price, they would have sold for even less.*

---

Ask your agent to follow up on all showings of your home and to report back to you with information about the agents' and buyers' reactions. This is a vital part of a successful home sale. If your agent is not accustomed to providing this customer service, let him or her know that this is what you expect. You and your agent should work together as a team to achieve a satisfactory sale.

# Tax issues

Tax laws favor homeowners who sell one home and use the proceeds to purchase another. The IRS will let you defer paying tax on gain that you have realized on your home sale if you buy or build a new principal residence of equal or greater value within twenty-four months of the sale. This is called the rollover residence replacement rule. You must close on the replacement home within twenty-four months of closing the sale of your current home. The IRS is rigid on this deadline, unless you were in military service or working abroad when your home sold.

Even if you buy or intend to buy a replacement home within twenty-four months, you must report the sale of your home to the IRS. If you do not buy a replacement home within this time frame, you will have to pay the IRS tax on your gain. You may also owe state tax, depending on where you live. In IRS terms, gain is the difference between the amount you realize from the sale of your home and your adjusted cost basis. Briefly, the adjusted cost basis is the price you paid for your home plus the cost of any improvements you made and minus any depreciation you claimed as a tax deduction (for a home office, for instance). Capital improvements can be used to adjust the basis upward so improvements help to offset gain that is reported at the time of sale. This is why you should be sure to keep good home improvement records.

Many costs of the sale, like the brokerage commission, are deducted from the gross selling price to arrive at the amount realized from the sale. If you paid $100,000 for your home and you made capital improvements in the amount of $20,000, your adjusted cost basis is $120,000. If you sell for $175,000 and your deductible costs of sale are $20,000, the amount realized from the sale is $155,000. In this case, you have realized $35,000 of taxable gain. If you buy a replacement home for $180,000 within twenty-four months, you can defer paying tax on the gain until some time in the future. When you carry gain forward from one home into another, it reduces the cost basis of the new home. Using the above example, your adjusted cost basis of the new home at the time of purchase will be $145,000, not $180,000. (Subtract the $35,000 deferred gain from the $180,000 purchase price.) If you sell this home for $250,000 in ten years and you make no improvements to the property, you will have $105,000 of gain to report, not including any deductible costs of sale ($250,000 minus $145,000). The tax picture can get complicated if you have deferred gain from several homes. Be sure to consult a knowledgeable tax advisor if you have any questions about how a move from one primary residence to another will affect you tax-wise. The rollover residence replacement rule can only be used once in a twenty-four-month period, but there is no limit on how many times you can roll gain from one primary residence to the next. At some point you have to pay tax on your gain if you sell and do not reinvest in another residence within twenty-four months.

Homeowners who are fifty-five or older can take an added tax benefit when they sell their primary residence. They are permitted a one-time exemption of $125,000 on their capital gain liability. Several restrictions apply. The homeowner (or one of the owners, in the case of a husband and wife) must be age fifty-five or older on the day the sale closes. And the homeowner must have owned and lived in the residence for three of the last five years. This tax break enables homeowners fifty-five and older to trade down to a smaller home and receive a huge tax break. The $125,000 gain exclusion can be used only once in a lifetime. You don't have to use it as soon as you are fifty-five, so make sure that you use it judiciously. Also, be aware that a married couple can only take one exemption. If you are remarrying and your new spouse has already taken the one-time exemption, you may want to sell your home and claim your one-time exemption before you marry. If you wait to sell later, you will lose your exemption because you married someone who already claimed it (this is called the "tainted spouse" rule). Congress is considering changing the tainted spouse rule and other aspects of the tax code. Because the tax code is always subject to revisions, it's wise to consult a knowledgeable tax advisor about the tax ramifications of any home sale or purchase.

Homeowners younger than fifty-five can trade down to a less expensive home and defer paying tax on the gain if they make sufficient capital improvements to the new home within the twenty-four month replacement period. For IRS purposes, the cost of the new home is the price you paid, plus the capital improvements you made within that critical time period. If you trade down to a less expensive home and you don't make improvements to it, you will owe tax on that portion of gain that you do not reinvest in your replacement home. You will be allowed to defer tax on the portion of gain that you reinvest. Keep records of all improvements and copies of all settlement sheets. Some of the costs associated with buying and selling a home can be used to adjust your cost basis, which can save you tax dollars.

The tax code is complex. The above explanation is a simplified summary to alert you to potential tax benefits available when you move from one home to another, and to encourage you to consult qualified tax advisors so you don't make a costly mistake.

**Dutch Colonial**
The most characteristic feature of a Dutch Colonial is a steeply pitched gambrel roof with eaves that project and flare outward. They usually have at least two stories.

# Amortization Schedule

The amortization schedule is used to determine the monthly principal and interest payment for any loan amount given an interest rate and loan term. To use the schedule, read down the far left column of the table until you find the loan amount in question, then read across the page to the appropriate interest rate and amortization period (fifteen- or thirty-year). Monthly principal and interest payments for loan amounts not provided on the chart are computed by dividing a loan amount into smaller amounts and adding the corresponding monthly payment figures. For example, to find the monthly principal and interest payment on a thirty-year loan in the amount of $105,000 with an interest rate of 8 percent, add $733.76 (the monthly payment on a $100,000 loan with an 8-percent interest rate and a 30-year due date) to $36.69 (the monthly payment on a $5,000 loan with an 8-percent interest rate and a thirty-year due date) for a total of $770.45. Likewise, the monthly principal and interest payment on a $150,000 loan with an 8.5-percent interest rate and a fifteen-year due date is $1,477.11. This figure was calculated by adding $984.74 (the monthly payment on a $100,000 loan with an 8.5-percent interest rate and a fifteen-year due date) to $492.37 (the monthly payment on a $50,000 loan with an 8.5-percent interest rate and a fifteen-year due date).

# 4.00% - 4.75% Interest Rates

| Interest Rate | 4.00% | | 4.25% | | 4.50% | | 4.75% | |
| Term (years) | 15 | 30 | 15 | 30 | 15 | 30 | 15 | 30 |
|---|---|---|---|---|---|---|---|---|
| $ **1,000** | 7.40 | 4.77 | 7.52 | 4.92 | 7.65 | 5.07 | 7.78 | 5.22 |
| **2,000** | 14.79 | 9.55 | 15.05 | 9.84 | 15.30 | 10.13 | 15.56 | 10.43 |
| **3,000** | 22.19 | 14.32 | 22.57 | 14.76 | 22.95 | 15.20 | 23.33 | 15.65 |
| **4,000** | 29.59 | 19.10 | 30.09 | 19.68 | 30.60 | 20.27 | 31.11 | 20.87 |
| **5,000** | 36.98 | 23.87 | 37.61 | 24.60 | 38.25 | 25.33 | 38.89 | 26.08 |
| **6,000** | 44.38 | 28.64 | 45.14 | 29.52 | 45.90 | 30.40 | 46.67 | 31.30 |
| **7,000** | 51.78 | 33.42 | 52.66 | 34.44 | 53.55 | 35.47 | 54.45 | 36.52 |
| **8,000** | 59.18 | 38.19 | 60.18 | 39.36 | 61.20 | 40.53 | 62.23 | 41.73 |
| **9,000** | 66.57 | 42.97 | 67.71 | 44.27 | 68.85 | 45.60 | 70.00 | 46.95 |
| **10,000** | 73.97 | 47.74 | 75.23 | 49.19 | 76.50 | 50.67 | 77.78 | 52.16 |
| **20,000** | 147.94 | 95.48 | 150.46 | 98.39 | 153.00 | 101.34 | 155.57 | 104.33 |
| **30,000** | 221.91 | 143.22 | 225.68 | 147.58 | 229.50 | 152.01 | 233.35 | 156.49 |
| **40,000** | 295.88 | 190.97 | 300.91 | 196.78 | 306.00 | 202.67 | 311.13 | 208.66 |
| **50,000** | 369.84 | 238.71 | 376.14 | 245.97 | 382.50 | 253.34 | 388.92 | 260.82 |
| **60,000** | 443.81 | 286.45 | 451.37 | 295.16 | 459.00 | 304.01 | 466.70 | 312.99 |
| **70,000** | 517.78 | 334.19 | 526.59 | 344.36 | 535.50 | 354.68 | 544.48 | 365.15 |
| **80,000** | 591.75 | 381.93 | 601.82 | 393.55 | 611.99 | 405.35 | 622.27 | 417.32 |
| **90,000** | 665.72 | 429.67 | 677.05 | 442.75 | 688.49 | 456.02 | 700.05 | 469.48 |
| **100,000** | 739.69 | 477.42 | 752.28 | 491.94 | 764.99 | 506.69 | 777.83 | 521.65 |

# 5.00% – 5.75% Interest Rates

| Interest Rate | 5.00% | | 5.25% | | 5.50% | | 5.75% | |
|---|---|---|---|---|---|---|---|---|
| Term (years) | 15 | 30 | 15 | 30 | 15 | 30 | 15 | 30 |
| $ 1,000 | 7.91 | 5.37 | 8.04 | 5.52 | 8.17 | 5.68 | 8.30 | 5.84 |
| 2,000 | 15.82 | 10.74 | 16.08 | 11.04 | 16.34 | 11.36 | 16.61 | 11.67 |
| 3,000 | 23.72 | 16.10 | 24.12 | 16.57 | 24.51 | 17.03 | 24.91 | 17.51 |
| 4,000 | 31.63 | 21.47 | 32.16 | 22.09 | 32.68 | 22.71 | 33.22 | 23.34 |
| 5,000 | 39.54 | 26.84 | 40.19 | 27.61 | 40.85 | 28.39 | 41.52 | 29.18 |
| 6,000 | 47.45 | 32.21 | 48.23 | 33.13 | 49.03 | 34.07 | 49.82 | 35.01 |
| 7,000 | 55.36 | 37.58 | 56.27 | 38.65 | 57.20 | 39.75 | 58.13 | 40.85 |
| 8,000 | 63.26 | 42.95 | 64.31 | 44.18 | 65.37 | 45.42 | 66.43 | 46.69 |
| 9,000 | 71.17 | 48.31 | 72.35 | 49.70 | 73.54 | 51.10 | 74.74 | 52.52 |
| 10,000 | 79.08 | 53.68 | 80.39 | 55.22 | 81.71 | 56.78 | 83.04 | 58.36 |
| 20,000 | 158.16 | 107.36 | 160.78 | 110.44 | 163.42 | 113.56 | 166.08 | 116.71 |
| 30,000 | 237.24 | 161.05 | 241.16 | 165.66 | 245.13 | 170.34 | 249.12 | 175.07 |
| 40,000 | 316.32 | 214.73 | 321.55 | 220.88 | 326.83 | 227.12 | 332.16 | 233.43 |
| 50,000 | 395.40 | 268.41 | 401.94 | 276.10 | 408.54 | 283.89 | 415.21 | 291.79 |
| 60,000 | 474.48 | 322.09 | 482.33 | 331.32 | 490.25 | 340.67 | 498.25 | 350.14 |
| 70,000 | 553.56 | 375.78 | 562.71 | 386.54 | 571.96 | 397.45 | 581.29 | 408.50 |
| 80,000 | 632.63 | 429.46 | 643.10 | 441.76 | 653.67 | 454.23 | 664.33 | 466.86 |
| 90,000 | 711.71 | 483.14 | 723.49 | 496.98 | 735.38 | 511.01 | 747.37 | 525.22 |
| 100,000 | 790.79 | 536.82 | 803.88 | 552.20 | 817.08 | 567.79 | 830.41 | 583.57 |

# 6.00% - 6.75% Interest Rates

| Interest Rate<br>Term (years) | 6.00%<br>15 | 30 | 6.25%<br>15 | 30 | 6.50%<br>15 | 30 | 6.75%<br>15 | 30 |
|---|---|---|---|---|---|---|---|---|
| $ 1,000 | 8.44 | 6.00 | 8.57 | 6.16 | 8.71 | 6.32 | 8.85 | 6.49 |
| 2,000 | 16.88 | 11.99 | 17.15 | 12.31 | 17.42 | 12.64 | 17.70 | 12.97 |
| 3,000 | 25.32 | 17.99 | 25.72 | 18.47 | 26.13 | 18.96 | 26.55 | 19.46 |
| 4,000 | 33.75 | 23.98 | 34.30 | 24.63 | 34.84 | 25.28 | 35.40 | 25.94 |
| 5,000 | 42.19 | 29.98 | 42.87 | 30.79 | 43.56 | 31.60 | 44.25 | 32.43 |
| 6,000 | 50.63 | 35.97 | 51.45 | 36.94 | 52.27 | 37.92 | 53.09 | 38.92 |
| 7,000 | 59.07 | 41.97 | 60.02 | 43.10 | 60.98 | 44.24 | 61.94 | 45.40 |
| 8,000 | 67.51 | 47.96 | 68.59 | 49.26 | 69.69 | 50.57 | 70.79 | 51.89 |
| 9,000 | 75.95 | 53.96 | 77.17 | 55.41 | 78.40 | 56.89 | 79.64 | 58.37 |
| 10,000 | 84.39 | 59.96 | 85.74 | 61.57 | 87.11 | 63.21 | 88.49 | 64.86 |
| 20,000 | 168.77 | 119.91 | 171.48 | 123.14 | 174.22 | 126.41 | 176.98 | 129.72 |
| 30,000 | 253.16 | 179.87 | 257.23 | 184.72 | 261.33 | 189.62 | 265.47 | 194.58 |
| 40,000 | 337.54 | 239.82 | 342.97 | 246.29 | 348.44 | 252.83 | 353.96 | 259.44 |
| 50,000 | 421.93 | 299.78 | 428.71 | 307.86 | 435.55 | 316.03 | 442.45 | 324.30 |
| 60,000 | 506.31 | 359.73 | 514.45 | 369.43 | 522.66 | 379.24 | 530.95 | 389.16 |
| 70,000 | 590.70 | 419.69 | 600.20 | 431.00 | 609.78 | 442.45 | 619.44 | 454.02 |
| 80,000 | 675.09 | 479.64 | 685.94 | 492.57 | 696.89 | 505.65 | 707.93 | 518.88 |
| 90,000 | 759.47 | 539.60 | 771.68 | 554.15 | 784.00 | 568.86 | 796.42 | 583.74 |
| 100,000 | 843.86 | 599.55 | 857.42 | 615.72 | 871.11 | 632.07 | 884.91 | 648.60 |

# 7.00% – 7.75% Interest Rates

| Interest Rate | 7.00% | | 7.25% | | 7.50% | | 7.75% | |
|---|---|---|---|---|---|---|---|---|
| Term (years) | 15 | 30 | 15 | 30 | 15 | 30 | 15 | 30 |
| $ 1,000 | 8.99 | 6.65 | 9.13 | 6.82 | 9.27 | 6.99 | 9.41 | 7.16 |
| 2,000 | 17.98 | 13.31 | 18.26 | 13.64 | 18.54 | 13.98 | 18.83 | 14.33 |
| 3,000 | 26.96 | 19.96 | 27.39 | 20.47 | 27.81 | 20.98 | 28.24 | 21.49 |
| 4,000 | 35.95 | 26.61 | 36.51 | 27.29 | 37.08 | 27.97 | 37.65 | 28.66 |
| 5,000 | 44.94 | 33.27 | 45.64 | 34.11 | 46.35 | 34.96 | 47.06 | 35.82 |
| 6,000 | 53.93 | 39.92 | 54.77 | 40.93 | 55.62 | 41.95 | 56.48 | 42.98 |
| 7,000 | 62.92 | 46.57 | 63.90 | 47.75 | 64.89 | 48.95 | 65.89 | 50.15 |
| 8,000 | 71.91 | 53.22 | 73.03 | 54.57 | 74.16 | 55.94 | 75.30 | 57.31 |
| 9,000 | 80.89 | 59.88 | 82.16 | 61.40 | 83.43 | 62.93 | 84.71 | 64.48 |
| 10,000 | 89.88 | 66.53 | 91.29 | 68.22 | 92.70 | 69.92 | 94.13 | 71.64 |
| 20,000 | 179.77 | 133.06 | 182.57 | 136.44 | 185.40 | 139.84 | 188.26 | 143.28 |
| 30,000 | 269.65 | 199.59 | 273.86 | 204.65 | 278.10 | 209.76 | 282.38 | 214.92 |
| 40,000 | 359.53 | 266.12 | 365.15 | 272.87 | 370.80 | 279.69 | 376.51 | 286.56 |
| 50,000 | 449.41 | 332.65 | 456.43 | 341.09 | 463.51 | 349.61 | 470.64 | 358.21 |
| 60,000 | 539.30 | 399.18 | 547.72 | 409.31 | 556.21 | 419.53 | 564.77 | 429.85 |
| 70,000 | 629.18 | 465.71 | 639.00 | 477.52 | 648.91 | 489.45 | 658.89 | 501.49 |
| 80,000 | 719.06 | 532.24 | 730.29 | 545.74 | 741.61 | 559.37 | 753.02 | 573.13 |
| 90,000 | 808.95 | 598.77 | 821.58 | 613.96 | 834.31 | 629.29 | 847.15 | 644.77 |
| 100,000 | 898.83 | 665.30 | 912.86 | 682.18 | 927.01 | 699.21 | 941.28 | 716.41 |

# 8.00% - 8.75% Interest Rates

| Interest Rate | 8.00% | | 8.25% | | 8.50% | | 8.75% | |
|---|---|---|---|---|---|---|---|---|
| Term (years) | 15 | 30 | 15 | 30 | 15 | 30 | 15 | 30 |
| $ 1,000 | 9.56 | 7.34 | 9.70 | 7.51 | 9.85 | 7.69 | 9.99 | 7.87 |
| 2,000 | 19.11 | 14.68 | 19.40 | 15.03 | 19.69 | 15.38 | 19.99 | 15.73 |
| 3,000 | 28.67 | 22.01 | 29.10 | 22.54 | 29.54 | 23.07 | 29.98 | 23.60 |
| 4,000 | 38.23 | 29.35 | 38.81 | 30.05 | 39.39 | 30.76 | 39.98 | 31.47 |
| 5,000 | 47.78 | 36.69 | 48.51 | 37.56 | 49.24 | 38.45 | 49.97 | 39.34 |
| 6,000 | 57.34 | 44.03 | 58.21 | 45.08 | 59.08 | 46.13 | 59.97 | 47.20 |
| 7,000 | 66.90 | 51.36 | 67.91 | 52.59 | 68.93 | 53.82 | 69.96 | 55.07 |
| 8,000 | 76.45 | 58.70 | 77.61 | 60.10 | 78.78 | 61.51 | 79.96 | 62.94 |
| 9,000 | 86.01 | 66.04 | 87.31 | 67.61 | 88.63 | 69.20 | 89.95 | 70.80 |
| 10,000 | 95.57 | 73.38 | 97.01 | 75.13 | 98.47 | 76.89 | 99.94 | 78.67 |
| 20,000 | 191.13 | 146.75 | 194.03 | 150.25 | 196.95 | 153.78 | 199.89 | 157.34 |
| 30,000 | 286.70 | 220.13 | 291.04 | 225.38 | 295.42 | 230.67 | 299.83 | 236.01 |
| 40,000 | 382.26 | 293.51 | 388.06 | 300.51 | 393.90 | 307.57 | 399.78 | 314.68 |
| 50,000 | 477.83 | 366.88 | 485.07 | 375.63 | 492.37 | 384.46 | 499.72 | 393.35 |
| 60,000 | 573.39 | 440.26 | 582.08 | 450.76 | 590.84 | 461.35 | 599.67 | 472.02 |
| 70,000 | 668.96 | 513.64 | 679.10 | 525.89 | 689.32 | 538.24 | 699.61 | 550.69 |
| 80,000 | 764.52 | 587.01 | 776.11 | 601.01 | 787.79 | 615.13 | 799.56 | 629.36 |
| 90,000 | 860.09 | 660.39 | 873.13 | 676.14 | 886.27 | 692.02 | 899.50 | 708.03 |
| 100,000 | 955.65 | 733.76 | 970.14 | 751.27 | 984.74 | 768.91 | 999.45 | 786.70 |

# 9.00% - 9.75% Interest Rates

| Interest Rate | 9.00% | | 9.25% | | 9.50% | | 9.75% | |
|---|---|---|---|---|---|---|---|---|
| Term (years) | 15 | 30 | 15 | 30 | 15 | 30 | 15 | 30 |
| $ 1,000 | 10.14 | 8.05 | 10.29 | 8.23 | 10.44 | 8.41 | 10.59 | 8.59 |
| 2,000 | 20.29 | 16.09 | 20.58 | 16.45 | 20.88 | 16.82 | 21.19 | 17.18 |
| 3,000 | 30.43 | 24.14 | 30.88 | 24.68 | 31.33 | 25.23 | 31.78 | 25.77 |
| 4,000 | 40.57 | 32.18 | 41.17 | 32.91 | 41.77 | 33.63 | 42.37 | 34.37 |
| 5,000 | 50.71 | 40.23 | 51.46 | 41.13 | 52.21 | 42.04 | 52.97 | 42.96 |
| 6,000 | 60.86 | 48.28 | 61.75 | 49.36 | 62.65 | 50.45 | 63.56 | 51.55 |
| 7,000 | 71.00 | 56.32 | 72.04 | 57.59 | 73.10 | 58.86 | 74.16 | 60.14 |
| 8,000 | 81.14 | 64.37 | 82.34 | 65.81 | 83.54 | 67.27 | 84.75 | 68.73 |
| 9,000 | 91.28 | 72.42 | 92.63 | 74.04 | 93.98 | 75.68 | 95.34 | 77.32 |
| 10,000 | 101.43 | 80.46 | 102.92 | 82.27 | 104.42 | 84.09 | 105.94 | 85.92 |
| 20,000 | 202.85 | 160.92 | 205.84 | 164.54 | 208.84 | 168.17 | 211.87 | 171.83 |
| 30,000 | 304.28 | 241.39 | 308.76 | 246.80 | 313.27 | 252.26 | 317.81 | 257.75 |
| 40,000 | 405.71 | 321.85 | 411.68 | 329.07 | 417.69 | 336.34 | 423.75 | 343.66 |
| 50,000 | 507.13 | 402.31 | 514.60 | 411.34 | 522.11 | 420.43 | 529.68 | 429.58 |
| 60,000 | 608.56 | 482.77 | 617.52 | 493.61 | 626.53 | 504.51 | 635.62 | 515.49 |
| 70,000 | 709.99 | 563.24 | 720.43 | 575.87 | 730.96 | 588.60 | 741.55 | 601.41 |
| 80,000 | 811.41 | 643.70 | 823.35 | 658.14 | 835.38 | 672.68 | 847.49 | 687.32 |
| 90,000 | 912.84 | 724.16 | 926.27 | 740.41 | 939.80 | 756.77 | 953.43 | 773.24 |
| 100,000 | 1014.27 | 804.62 | 1029.19 | 822.68 | 1044.22 | 840.85 | 1059.36 | 859.15 |

# 10.00% – 10.75% Interest Rates

| Interest Rate | 10.00% | | 10.25% | | 10.50% | | 10.75% | |
|---|---|---|---|---|---|---|---|---|
| Term (years) | 15 | 30 | 15 | 30 | 15 | 30 | 15 | 30 |
| $ 1,000 | 10.75 | 8.78 | 10.90 | 8.96 | 11.05 | 9.15 | 11.21 | 9.33 |
| 2,000 | 21.49 | 17.55 | 21.80 | 17.92 | 22.11 | 18.29 | 22.42 | 18.67 |
| 3,000 | 32.24 | 26.33 | 32.70 | 26.88 | 33.16 | 27.44 | 33.63 | 28.00 |
| 4,000 | 42.98 | 35.10 | 43.60 | 35.84 | 44.22 | 36.59 | 44.84 | 37.34 |
| 5,000 | 53.73 | 43.88 | 54.50 | 44.81 | 55.27 | 45.74 | 56.05 | 46.67 |
| 6,000 | 64.48 | 52.65 | 65.40 | 53.77 | 66.32 | 54.88 | 67.26 | 56.01 |
| 7,000 | 75.22 | 61.43 | 76.30 | 62.73 | 77.38 | 64.03 | 78.47 | 65.34 |
| 8,000 | 85.97 | 70.21 | 87.20 | 71.69 | 88.43 | 73.18 | 89.68 | 74.68 |
| 9,000 | 96.71 | 78.98 | 98.10 | 80.65 | 99.49 | 82.33 | 100.89 | 84.01 |
| 10,000 | 107.46 | 87.76 | 109.00 | 89.61 | 110.54 | 91.47 | 112.09 | 93.35 |
| 20,000 | 214.92 | 175.51 | 217.99 | 179.22 | 221.08 | 182.95 | 224.19 | 186.70 |
| 30,000 | 322.38 | 263.27 | 326.99 | 268.83 | 331.62 | 274.42 | 336.28 | 280.04 |
| 40,000 | 429.84 | 351.03 | 435.98 | 358.44 | 442.16 | 365.90 | 448.38 | 373.39 |
| 50,000 | 537.30 | 438.79 | 544.98 | 448.05 | 552.70 | 457.37 | 560.47 | 466.74 |
| 60,000 | 644.76 | 526.54 | 653.97 | 537.66 | 663.24 | 548.84 | 672.57 | 560.09 |
| 70,000 | 752.22 | 614.30 | 762.97 | 627.27 | 773.78 | 640.32 | 784.66 | 653.44 |
| 80,000 | 859.68 | 702.06 | 871.96 | 716.88 | 884.32 | 731.79 | 896.76 | 746.79 |
| 90,000 | 967.14 | 789.81 | 980.96 | 806.49 | 994.86 | 823.27 | 1008.85 | 840.13 |
| 100,000 | 1074.61 | 877.57 | 1089.95 | 896.10 | 1105.40 | 914.74 | 1120.95 | 933.48 |

# 11.00% - 11.75% Interest Rates

| Interest Rate | 11.00% | | 11.25% | | 11.50% | | 11.75% | |
|---|---|---|---|---|---|---|---|---|
| Term (years) | 15 | 30 | 15 | 30 | 15 | 30 | 15 | 30 |
| $ 1,000 | 11.37 | 9.52 | 11.52 | 9.71 | 11.68 | 9.90 | 11.84 | 10.09 |
| 2,000 | 22.73 | 19.05 | 23.05 | 19.43 | 23.36 | 19.81 | 23.68 | 20.19 |
| 3,000 | 34.10 | 28.57 | 34.57 | 29.14 | 35.05 | 29.71 | 35.52 | 30.28 |
| 4,000 | 45.46 | 38.09 | 46.09 | 38.85 | 46.73 | 39.61 | 47.37 | 40.38 |
| 5,000 | 56.83 | 47.62 | 57.62 | 48.56 | 58.41 | 49.51 | 59.21 | 50.47 |
| 6,000 | 68.20 | 57.14 | 69.14 | 58.28 | 70.09 | 59.42 | 71.05 | 60.56 |
| 7,000 | 79.56 | 66.66 | 80.66 | 67.99 | 81.77 | 69.32 | 82.89 | 70.66 |
| 8,000 | 90.93 | 76.19 | 92.19 | 77.70 | 93.46 | 79.22 | 94.73 | 80.75 |
| 9,000 | 102.29 | 85.71 | 103.71 | 87.41 | 105.14 | 89.13 | 106.57 | 90.85 |
| 10,000 | 113.66 | 95.23 | 115.23 | 97.13 | 116.82 | 99.03 | 118.41 | 100.94 |
| 20,000 | 227.32 | 190.46 | 230.47 | 194.25 | 233.64 | 198.06 | 236.83 | 201.88 |
| 30,000 | 340.98 | 285.70 | 345.70 | 291.38 | 350.46 | 297.09 | 355.24 | 302.82 |
| 40,000 | 454.64 | 380.93 | 460.94 | 388.50 | 467.28 | 396.12 | 473.65 | 403.76 |
| 50,000 | 568.30 | 476.16 | 576.17 | 485.63 | 584.09 | 495.15 | 592.07 | 504.70 |
| 60,000 | 681.96 | 571.39 | 691.41 | 582.76 | 700.91 | 594.17 | 710.48 | 605.65 |
| 70,000 | 795.62 | 666.63 | 806.64 | 679.88 | 817.73 | 693.20 | 828.89 | 706.59 |
| 80,000 | 909.28 | 761.86 | 921.88 | 777.01 | 934.55 | 792.23 | 947.31 | 807.53 |
| 90,000 | 1022.94 | 857.09 | 1037.11 | 874.14 | 1051.37 | 891.26 | 1065.72 | 908.47 |
| 100,000 | 1136.60 | 952.32 | 1152.34 | 971.26 | 1168.19 | 990.29 | 1184.13 | 1009.41 |

# 12.00% - 12.75% Interest Rates

| Interest Rate | 12.00% | | 12.25% | | 12.50% | | 12.75% | |
|---|---|---|---|---|---|---|---|---|
| Term (years) | 15 | 30 | 15 | 30 | 15 | 30 | 15 | 30 |
| $   1,000 | 12.00 | 10.29 | 12.16 | 10.48 | 12.33 | 10.67 | 12.49 | 10.87 |
| 2,000 | 24.00 | 20.57 | 24.33 | 20.96 | 24.65 | 21.35 | 24.98 | 21.73 |
| 3,000 | 36.01 | 30.86 | 36.49 | 31.44 | 36.98 | 32.02 | 37.47 | 32.60 |
| 4,000 | 48.01 | 41.14 | 48.65 | 41.92 | 49.30 | 42.69 | 49.95 | 43.47 |
| 5,000 | 60.01 | 51.43 | 60.81 | 52.39 | 61.63 | 53.36 | 62.44 | 54.33 |
| 6,000 | 72.01 | 61.72 | 72.98 | 62.87 | 73.95 | 64.04 | 74.93 | 65.20 |
| 7,000 | 84.01 | 72.00 | 85.14 | 73.35 | 86.28 | 74.71 | 87.42 | 76.07 |
| 8,000 | 96.01 | 82.29 | 97.30 | 83.83 | 98.60 | 85.38 | 99.91 | 86.94 |
| 9,000 | 108.02 | 92.58 | 109.47 | 94.31 | 110.93 | 96.05 | 112.40 | 97.80 |
| 10,000 | 120.02 | 102.86 | 121.63 | 104.79 | 123.25 | 106.73 | 124.88 | 108.67 |
| 20,000 | 240.03 | 205.72 | 243.26 | 209.58 | 246.50 | 213.45 | 249.77 | 217.34 |
| 30,000 | 360.05 | 308.58 | 364.89 | 314.37 | 369.76 | 320.18 | 374.65 | 326.01 |
| 40,000 | 480.07 | 411.45 | 486.52 | 419.16 | 493.01 | 426.90 | 499.53 | 434.68 |
| 50,000 | 600.08 | 514.31 | 608.15 | 523.95 | 616.26 | 533.63 | 624.42 | 543.35 |
| 60,000 | 720.10 | 617.17 | 729.78 | 628.74 | 739.51 | 640.35 | 749.30 | 652.02 |
| 70,000 | 840.12 | 720.03 | 851.41 | 733.53 | 862.77 | 747.08 | 874.19 | 760.69 |
| 80,000 | 960.13 | 822.89 | 973.04 | 838.32 | 986.02 | 853.81 | 999.07 | 869.35 |
| 90,000 | 1080.15 | 925.75 | 1094.67 | 943.11 | 1109.27 | 960.53 | 1123.95 | 978.02 |
| 100,000 | 1200.17 | 1028.61 | 1216.30 | 1047.90 | 1232.52 | 1067.26 | 1248.84 | 1086.69 |

# 13.00% – 13.75% Interest Rates

| Interest Rate | 13.00% | | 13.25% | | 13.50% | | 13.75% | |
|---|---|---|---|---|---|---|---|---|
| Term (years) | 15 | 30 | 15 | 30 | 15 | 30 | 15 | 30 |
| $ 1,000 | 12.65 | 11.06 | 12.82 | 11.26 | 12.98 | 11.45 | 13.15 | 11.65 |
| 2,000 | 25.30 | 22.12 | 25.63 | 22.52 | 25.97 | 22.91 | 26.30 | 23.30 |
| 3,000 | 37.96 | 33.19 | 38.45 | 33.77 | 38.95 | 34.36 | 39.45 | 34.95 |
| 4,000 | 50.61 | 44.25 | 51.27 | 45.03 | 51.93 | 45.82 | 52.60 | 46.60 |
| 5,000 | 63.26 | 55.31 | 64.09 | 56.29 | 64.92 | 57.27 | 65.75 | 58.26 |
| 6,000 | 75.91 | 66.37 | 76.90 | 67.55 | 77.90 | 68.72 | 78.90 | 69.91 |
| 7,000 | 88.57 | 77.43 | 89.72 | 78.80 | 90.88 | 80.18 | 92.05 | 81.56 |
| 8,000 | 101.22 | 88.50 | 102.54 | 90.06 | 103.87 | 91.63 | 105.20 | 93.21 |
| 9,000 | 113.87 | 99.56 | 115.36 | 101.32 | 116.85 | 103.09 | 118.35 | 104.86 |
| 10,000 | 126.52 | 110.62 | 128.17 | 112.58 | 129.83 | 114.54 | 131.50 | 116.51 |
| 20,000 | 253.05 | 221.24 | 256.35 | 225.15 | 259.66 | 229.08 | 263.00 | 233.02 |
| 30,000 | 379.57 | 331.86 | 384.52 | 337.73 | 389.50 | 343.62 | 394.50 | 349.53 |
| 40,000 | 506.10 | 442.48 | 512.69 | 450.31 | 519.33 | 458.16 | 525.99 | 466.05 |
| 50,000 | 632.62 | 553.10 | 640.87 | 562.89 | 649.16 | 572.71 | 657.49 | 582.56 |
| 60,000 | 759.15 | 663.72 | 769.04 | 675.46 | 778.99 | 687.25 | 788.99 | 699.07 |
| 70,000 | 885.67 | 774.34 | 897.22 | 788.04 | 908.82 | 801.79 | 920.49 | 815.58 |
| 80,000 | 1012.19 | 884.96 | 1025.39 | 900.62 | 1038.65 | 916.33 | 1051.99 | 932.09 |
| 90,000 | 1138.72 | 995.58 | 1153.56 | 1013.20 | 1168.49 | 1030.87 | 1183.49 | 1048.60 |
| 100,000 | 1265.24 | 1106.20 | 1281.74 | 1125.77 | 1298.32 | 1145.41 | 1314.99 | 1165.11 |

# 14.00% - 14.75% Interest Rates

| Interest Rate | 14.00% | | 14.25% | | 14.50% | | 14.75% | |
|---|---|---|---|---|---|---|---|---|
| Term (years) | 15 | 30 | 15 | 30 | 15 | 30 | 15 | 30 |
| $ 1,000 | 13.32 | 11.85 | 13.49 | 12.05 | 13.66 | 12.25 | 13.83 | 12.44 |
| 2,000 | 26.63 | 23.70 | 26.97 | 24.09 | 27.31 | 24.49 | 27.65 | 24.89 |
| 3,000 | 39.95 | 35.55 | 40.46 | 36.14 | 40.97 | 36.74 | 41.48 | 37.33 |
| 4,000 | 53.27 | 47.39 | 53.94 | 48.19 | 54.62 | 48.98 | 55.30 | 49.78 |
| 5,000 | 66.59 | 59.24 | 67.43 | 60.23 | 68.28 | 61.23 | 69.13 | 62.22 |
| 6,000 | 79.90 | 71.09 | 80.91 | 72.28 | 81.93 | 73.47 | 82.95 | 74.67 |
| 7,000 | 93.22 | 82.94 | 94.40 | 84.33 | 95.59 | 85.72 | 96.78 | 87.11 |
| 8,000 | 106.54 | 94.79 | 107.89 | 96.37 | 109.24 | 97.96 | 110.60 | 99.56 |
| 9,000 | 119.86 | 106.64 | 121.37 | 108.42 | 122.90 | 110.21 | 124.43 | 112.00 |
| 10,000 | 133.17 | 118.49 | 134.86 | 120.47 | 136.55 | 122.46 | 138.25 | 124.45 |
| 20,000 | 266.35 | 236.97 | 269.72 | 240.94 | 273.10 | 244.91 | 276.50 | 248.90 |
| 30,000 | 399.52 | 355.46 | 404.57 | 361.41 | 409.65 | 367.37 | 414.75 | 373.34 |
| 40,000 | 532.70 | 473.95 | 539.43 | 481.87 | 546.20 | 489.82 | 553.00 | 497.79 |
| 50,000 | 665.87 | 592.44 | 674.29 | 602.34 | 682.75 | 612.28 | 691.25 | 622.24 |
| 60,000 | 799.04 | 710.92 | 809.15 | 722.81 | 819.30 | 734.73 | 829.50 | 746.69 |
| 70,000 | 932.22 | 829.41 | 944.01 | 843.28 | 955.85 | 857.19 | 967.75 | 871.13 |
| 80,000 | 1065.39 | 947.90 | 1078.86 | 963.75 | 1092.40 | 979.64 | 1106.00 | 995.58 |
| 90,000 | 1198.57 | 1066.38 | 1213.72 | 1084.22 | 1228.95 | 1102.10 | 1244.25 | 1120.03 |
| 100,000 | 1331.74 | 1184.87 | 1348.58 | 1204.69 | 1365.50 | 1224.56 | 1382.50 | 1244.48 |

# 15.00% - 15.75% Interest Rates

| Interest Rate | 15.00% | | 15.25% | | 15.50% | | 15.75% | |
|---|---|---|---|---|---|---|---|---|
| Term (years) | 15 | 30 | 15 | 30 | 15 | 30 | 15 | 30 |
| $ 1,000 | 14.00 | 12.64 | 14.17 | 12.84 | 14.34 | 13.05 | 14.51 | 13.25 |
| 2,000 | 27.99 | 25.29 | 28.33 | 25.69 | 28.68 | 26.09 | 29.03 | 26.49 |
| 3,000 | 41.99 | 37.93 | 42.50 | 38.53 | 43.02 | 39.14 | 43.54 | 39.74 |
| 4,000 | 55.98 | 50.58 | 56.67 | 51.38 | 57.36 | 52.18 | 58.05 | 52.98 |
| 5,000 | 69.98 | 63.22 | 70.84 | 64.22 | 71.70 | 65.23 | 72.57 | 66.23 |
| 6,000 | 83.98 | 75.87 | 85.00 | 77.07 | 86.04 | 78.27 | 87.08 | 79.48 |
| 7,000 | 97.97 | 88.51 | 99.17 | 89.91 | 100.38 | 91.32 | 101.59 | 92.72 |
| 8,000 | 111.97 | 101.16 | 113.34 | 102.76 | 114.72 | 104.36 | 116.10 | 105.97 |
| 9,000 | 125.96 | 113.80 | 127.51 | 115.60 | 129.06 | 117.41 | 130.62 | 119.22 |
| 10,000 | 139.96 | 126.44 | 141.67 | 128.45 | 143.40 | 130.45 | 145.13 | 132.46 |
| 20,000 | 279.92 | 252.89 | 283.35 | 256.89 | 286.80 | 260.90 | 290.26 | 264.92 |
| 30,000 | 419.88 | 379.33 | 425.02 | 385.34 | 430.20 | 391.36 | 435.39 | 397.39 |
| 40,000 | 559.83 | 505.78 | 566.70 | 513.78 | 573.60 | 521.81 | 580.52 | 529.85 |
| 50,000 | 699.79 | 632.22 | 708.37 | 642.23 | 717.00 | 652.26 | 725.65 | 662.31 |
| 60,000 | 839.75 | 758.67 | 850.05 | 770.68 | 860.39 | 782.71 | 870.78 | 794.77 |
| 70,000 | 979.71 | 885.11 | 991.72 | 899.12 | 1003.79 | 913.16 | 1015.92 | 927.23 |
| 80,000 | 1119.67 | 1011.56 | 1133.40 | 1027.57 | 1147.19 | 1043.61 | 1161.05 | 1059.69 |
| 90,000 | 1259.63 | 1138.00 | 1275.07 | 1156.01 | 1290.59 | 1174.07 | 1306.18 | 1192.16 |
| 100,000 | 1399.59 | 1264.44 | 1416.75 | 1284.46 | 1433.99 | 1304.52 | 1451.31 | 1324.62 |

# Glossary

**Abstract of title**
A historical summary of the proceedings and recorded documents affecting the title to a property. Prepared by an attorney or title insurance company.

**Acceleration clause**
Gives the lender the right to call all sums owed to the lender due and payable immediately upon the occurrence of a specific event, such as sale of the property or delinquent repayment.

**Addendum**
An attachment to a purchase contract or escrow instructions. Used to make changes or additions.

**Adjustable-rate mortgage (ARM)**
A mortgage with an interest rate subject to change during the term of the loan.

**Agency**
The legal relationship between a buyer or seller (who are called principals) and his or her agent. Agents owe loyalty to their principals.

**Agency disclosure**
A disclosure made by real estate agents to the buyers or sellers that describes the real estate agent's duties and responsi-bilities, along with the types of agency relationships that can exist in a real estate transaction. Required in most states, although the specific form of the disclosure varies.

**Amortized loan**
A loan that is paid off in full by periodic payments of principal and interest over a fixed period of time.

**Appraisal**
An opinion about the value of a property based on a factual analysis.

**Appreciation**
The increase in the value of property (the opposite of depreciation).

**APR**
Annual Percentage Rate.

**Arbitration**
A process whereby the parties resolve a dispute before a mutually accepted neutral, disinterested person such as a retired judge. In the case of binding arbitration, the arbitrator's decision is final and the parties usually give up both the rights to appeal and to a trial. Arbitration is less formal, faster, and less expensive than a court trial.

**ARM**
Adjustable-rate mortgage.

**Assumption**
An agreement whereby the buyers take on the liability for repayment of an existing loan on a property they are purchasing. Usually requires the lender's approval.

**Attorney-in-fact**
Someone who is authorized to act as an agent for another person under a power of attorney.

**Back-end ratio**
A borrower's monthly debt (including housing expense) divided by the borrower's gross monthly income. Used by lenders in qualifying borrowers for a mortgage.

**Backup offer**
An offer to buy a property that is accepted in secondary position, subject to the collapse of the primary offer. There can be more than one backup offer, in which case they are ranked backup offer #1, backup offer #2, and so on.

**Balloon payment**
A final payment on an installment debt that is significantly larger than the other periodic (monthly) payments. Loans with interest-only payments rather than fully amortizing payments have a balloon payment due at maturity.

**Beneficiary statement**
A statement issued by the lender stipulating pertinent information about the loan such as the remaining loan balance, interest rate, and monthly payment. Requested from the lender when a buyer is assuming the loan.

**Binder**
Another term for purchase agreement.

**Buy-down**
A payment made to the buyer's lender, often by the seller, to reduce the buyer's interest rate on a new loan for a specified period of time.

**Buyer's agent**
An agent who represents and owes allegiance to the buyer in a real estate transaction.

**Capital gain**
Generally the difference between the original cost and the selling price of a capital asset, such as real property, adjusted to allow for deductible expenses. Capital gain is subject to taxation. Capital gain tax liability on a primary residence can be deferred under certain circumstances.

**CC&Rs**
Abbreviation for Covenants, Conditions, and Restrictions, which describe restrictive limitations that apply to a property. Usually found in planned community developments, such as condominiums.

**CDs**
Certificates of Deposit.

**Certificate of title**
An attorney's opinion as to the condition of the title to a property.

**Closing**
The successful completion of a real estate transaction or refinance, including the transfer of documents and disbursement of funds.

**Closing costs**
Miscellaneous fees and expenses that buyers and sellers incur in a real estate sale.

**CMA**
Comparative market analysis.

**COFI**
Eleventh District Cost of Funds Index.

**Condominium** (also called condo)
A type of ownership in a multiunit structure; a buyer acquires exclusive ownership rights to the interior space of an individual unit and shared ownership rights to the common areas.

**Conforming loan**
A loan in an amount that does not exceed the Fannie Mae/Freddie Mac limit. This limit changes annually and was $207,000 in 1996. Conforming loans usually carry the best interest rates and terms, but they often have the most stringent qualifying criteria. A conforming loan is a loan that is packaged for sale on the secondary mortgage market.

**Contingency**
A condition that must be met before a contract becomes binding, such as an inspection or financing contingency.

**Contingent sale offer**
An offer to purchase a property that is dependent on the sale of another property.

**Cooperative** (also called co-op)
A type of corporate ownership of real estate where the shareholders are entitled to use common areas; they lease their individual dwelling units from the corporation. Tax laws permit co-op shareholders to deduct mortgage interest and property taxes paid by the corporation with certain restrictions.

**Cosigner**
A second person who signs a note with the primary borrower and is equally responsible for repaying the loan.

**Counter offer**
An offer in response to an offer (as opposed to an acceptance).

**Credit report**
A record of a person's credit history, including current credit balances on outstanding loans and charge cards with credit limits, repayment terms, late payments, and defaults. The three major credit reporting agencies are TRW, Trans Union, and Equifax.

**Credit scoring**
A numerical score derived from an analysis of numerous variables from a borrower's credit file data. These variables, such as delinquencies, late payments, outstanding debt, and credit history have been historically reliable in predicting loan repayment. Credit scoring is used by some lenders to objectively evaluate the risk of granting a loan and to make loan approval decisions quickly.

**CRB**
Certified Residential Broker.

**CRS**
Certified Residential Specialist.

**Deed**
A written document used to transfer title to real property.

**Deed of trust**
A legal document, used instead of a mortgage in many states (such as Mississippi, Missouri, Montana, Texas, Colorado, Utah, and California), by which the borrower pledges a piece of real property as a guarantee for repayment of a loan.

**Default**
Failure to fulfill a promise or perform a legal duty.

**Depreciation**
The decrease in the value of property (the opposite of appreciation).

**Dormer**
A window that projects through a sloping roof.

**Dual agency**
One broker represents both the buyer and seller in a real estate transaction. Dual agency can also exist if two agents working for the same broker represent both the buyer and seller in a transaction. Dual agency must be disclosed and agreed to by both the buyers and sellers to be legal. Dual agency is illegal in some states.

**Due-on-sale clause**
A clause in a real estate loan stating that the amount owed to the lender is all due and payable when title to the property is transferred to a new owner.

**Easement**
One party's right, privilege, or interest to land that belongs to another party.

**Encroachment**
Building improvements that are wholly or partly on an adjacent property that belongs to someone else.

**Encumbrance**
Anything that limits the title to real property, including liens, easements, or restrictions of any kind.

**EPA**
Environmental Protection Agency.

**Equity**
The current value of a property, less any liens secured against it.

**Escape clause**
A clause in a purchase contract that allows one party to withdraw from the contract under certain terms and conditions. Also called a release clause or kick-out clause.

**Escrow**
The deposit of the funds, documents, and instructions required to complete a real estate purchase with a neutral third party until all the terms of the purchase contract have been mutually fulfilled, at which time title to the property is transferred and the escrow is said to be closed.

**Escrow account**
Another term for an impound account.

**Exclusion**
An item of real property that is not included in the sale (such as a dining room light fixture). Also, an individual who is an exception from the listing agreement. If the owners sell to the exclusion, a real estate commission is not owed to the real estate broker.

**Facilitator**
Someone who represents neither the buyer nor the seller but who is employed to help the buyer and seller reach agreement. A mediator who does not advocate for either party. Also called a transaction broker in some locations.

**FAIR Plan**
Fair Access Insurance Requirements Plan.

**Fannie Mae**
Federal National Mortgage Association (FNMA). A private corporation that buys and sells mortgages at a discount.

**Fee simple**
Absolute ownership of real property with complete power to sell the property. At death, title passes to the owner's heirs.

**FEMA**
Federal Emergency Management Agency.

**FHA**
Federal Housing Administration. A government agency within the Department of Housing and Urban Development (HUD) that administers mortgage programs.

**FHLMC**
Federal Home Loan Mortgage Corporation. See Freddie Mac.

**Fiduciary**
A person acting in a relationship of trust and confidence, as between a principal (buyer or seller) and an agent.

**First deed of trust, or first mortgage**
A deed of trust or mortgage that has priority over all other voluntary liens secured against a property.

**Fixed-rate mortgage**
A loan secured against real property that has a constant interest rate for the term of the loan.

**Fixture**
Personal property that is attached to real property and is therefore treated as real property, such as plumbing and light fixtures. Fixtures transfer with real property, unless specifically excluded from the sale.

**FNMA**
Federal National Mortgage Association. See Fannie Mae.

**Foreclosure**
A procedure whereby a property that is pledged as collateral for a debt is sold to pay that debt when the borrower defaults on payments or terms.

**Freddie Mac**
Federal Home Loan Mortgage Corporation (FHLMC). An organization that purchases loans from banks and other loan originators.

**Front-end ratio**
A borrower's monthly housing expense (principal, interest, taxes, insurance, and mortgage insurance and homeowner's association dues, if applicable) divided by the borrower's gross monthly income. Used by lenders to qualify borrowers for mortgages.

**FSBO**
(pronounced Fizzbo) "For Sale by Owner." A property offered for sale without the assistance of a real estate broker.

**Gable roof**
A pitched roof commonly used on a number of American housing styles. The two sloping sides of the roof create a triangular shape where they meet at the top (ridge) of the roof.

**Gambrel roof**
A variety of a pitched roof. Each side of the roof slopes twice, the lower slope being the steeper of the two. Often seen on Dutch-style homes.

**Gift letter**
A letter from parents who give money to their children for all or part of a down payment. Most lenders require that the letter state that the money is a gift and does not have to be repaid.

**Graduated payment mortgage** (GPM)
A mortgage that has lower monthly payments in the early years. Payments increase over the term of the loan at predetermined intervals until they are sufficient to fully amortize the loan.

**GRI**
Graduate Real Estate Institute.

**Hip roof**
A pitched roof with two sloping sides; the two ends of the roof are also sloped. Introduced in America by French colonists.

**Homeowner's association**
An organization of homeowners in a condominium complex or planned unit development which manages the common areas and/or enforces restrictions in the CC&Rs (Covenants, Conditions, and Restrictions).

## Homeowner's policy

An insurance policy available to homeowners for a premium that provides coverage for the home and its contents in the case of damage or loss due to common disasters, such as fire. Coverage also usually includes theft, vandalism, loss of use, and liability.

## Home protection plan

An insurance policy to insure buyers and sellers against defects in a home they are buying or selling (usually in heating, electrical, and plumbing systems). Also called a home warranty. Available in most states.

## HOW

Home Owner's Warranty.

## HUD

Department of Housing and Urban Development.

## ICC

Interstate Commerce Commission.

## Impound account

An account set up by a lender for the collection of funds from the borrower to pay for future property taxes, mortgage insurance, and homeowner's insurance premiums. These funds are usually collected with the mortgage payment. Often required when the loan amount is for 90 percent or more of the purchase price. Also called an escrow account.

## Installment sale

A tax term used to refer to a sale in which the seller carries financing for the buyer to spread capital gain liability over a number of years.

## Interim loan

Also called a swing or bridge loan. A temporary, short-term loan that enables a homeowner to liquidate the equity in

one home before it is sold to make a cash down payment on another home. Can also refer to a construction loan.

## IRED

International Real Estate Directory.

## Jumbo loan

A loan in an amount that exceeds the Fannie Mae and Freddie Mac conforming loan limit which, in 1996, was $207,000. The conforming loan limit is adjusted annually. Jumbo loans usually have higher interest rates than conforming loans.

## Junior loan (or lien)

Any mortgage, deed of trust, or other lien against a property that is of lesser priority than the first mortgage or deed of trust, such as a second deed of trust or a second mortgage.

## Lease option

A lease giving the lessee the option to purchase the property at the specific price and terms set forth in the option agreement.

## Lessee

One who contracts to rent a property; a tenant.

## Lessor

An owner who enters into an agreement to rent to a tenant; a landlord.

## Leverage

The use of borrowed money and a small amount of cash to purchase a property or investment to maximize the return per dollar of equity invested.

## LIBOR

London interbank offering rate.

## Lien

A type of encumbrance that makes a property the security for a debt or obligation.

**Liquidated damages**
A predetermined sum, agreed to by the parties in a contract, to be considered as full damages if a certain event occurs, such as the breaching of a contract.

**Listing agreement**
An employment contract between a property owner and an agent authorizing the agent to perform certain services involving the property.

**Loan-to-value ratio** (LTV)
The percentage of a property's appraised value that a lender may be willing to loan to a borrower. The amount is the loan amount divided by the appraised value. Sometimes, the higher the LTV ratio, the higher the interest rate charged on the loan. Also, mortgage amounts with an LTV higher than 80 percent often require that the borrower pay mortgage insurance.

**Lock-in**
A commitment from a lender to guarantee a specific interest rate to a prospective borrower for a certain period of time. If the borrower's loan is not closed by the deadline, the interest rate is no longer guaranteed.

**Loss payee**
A clause in a homeowner's policy stating the priority of claims in the event that the property is destroyed. Lenders and sellers carrying financing for the buyer will usually be named as loss payees and will be paid the amounts owed to them before the buyer is paid.

**Market value**
The highest price a willing buyer would pay and a willing seller would accept for a property that is exposed on the open market for a reasonable period of time, assuming that both buyer and seller are well-informed and neither party is acting under undue pressure.

**Material fact**
A fact that is not known to, or readily observable by, the buyer which materially affects the value or desirability of a property.

**Mechanic's lien**
A lien created by statute that exists against real property in favor of persons who have performed work or provided materials for the purpose of improving that property.

**Mediation**
A voluntary process whereby parties work with one or more professional mediators to resolve disputes. If an agreement cannot be reached, the parties may pursue other forms of dispute resolution.

**MLS**
Multiple Listing Service.

**MMIS**
Mortgage Market Information Services.

**Mortgage**
Technically, a legal document that creates a lien on real property as security for repayment of a debt or obligation. The term is commonly used to refer to a home loan; it is often used interchangeably with "deed of trust" (although a mortgage and a deed of trust are different legal instruments).

**Mortgage insurance** (MI)
Insurance paid for by the borrower to protect the lender in case the borrower stops repaying the mortgage. Often required when the amount of the mortgage exceeds 80 percent of the purchase price. (Also called private mortgage insurance—PMI.)

**Multiple listing**
A listing taken by a member of an organization of real estate brokers with a provision that all members will have an opportunity to find a buyer for the property, thus ensuring wider market exposure for the seller.

**NAR**

National Association of Realtors.

**Negative amortization**

A condition that occurs when the monthly payments on a loan are insufficient to pay the interest accruing on the principal balance. The unpaid interest is added to the remaining principal due.

**Nonrecurring closing costs**

Closing costs that are paid on a one-time-only basis, such as title insurance or points.

**Notary public**

One who has the authority to take the acknowledgments of persons signing documents, such as deeds, contracts, and mortgages. Also, someone before whom affidavits are sworn.

**Note**

A signed written document acknowledging a debt and promising repayment on specific terms and conditions. When concerning real property, the note is secured by a deed of trust or mortgage.

**Payoff demand**

A written request for a lender to provide exact figures of the amount owed by the borrower to pay the loan off in full.

**Personal property**

Property that is movable; that is not permanently attached to real property.

**PITI**

Abbreviation for Principal, Interest, Taxes, and Insurance; prorated on a monthly basis, the monthly housing expense.

**PMI**

See mortgage insurance.

**Points**

The loan origination fee charged by the lender. One point is equal to one percent of the loan amount.

**Portfolio lender**

A lender that originates loans for its own portfolio, as opposed to a lender that packages loans to be sold on the secondary money market (to Freddie Mac or Fannie Mae).

**Power of attorney**

A legal document authorizing a person to act as an agent for the person granting the power of attorney. A power of attorney can be general or specific (as in specific to the purchase or sale of a property).

**Preliminary title report**

Also called a prelim. A report issued by a title insurance company before the completion of a real estate sale or loan transaction. Indicates the condition of the title.

**Prepayment penalty**

A charge paid by a borrower to a lender if the loan is paid off before its maturity or before a specified date. The loan agreement (note) must contain a provision stating that such a charge applies. Illegal in some states.

**Proration**

To allocate between buyer and seller their proportionate share of obligations that have been paid or that are due, such as property taxes, insurance premiums, interest, rental amounts. Prorations are usually made to the closing date.

**PUDs**

Planned unit developments.

**Purchase contract**

An agreement between the buyer and seller that sets forth the terms and conditions of the sale.

**Quitclaim deed**

A deed that relinquishes, without warranty, any interest in a property that the grantor may have.

**REO**

Real Estate Owned.

**Real property**
Land and anything that is permanently attached to it such as a house, trees, shrubs, and fences.

**Reconveyance**
A legal document commonly used when a debt is satisfied or paid in full. The lender conveys the property back to the equity owner, free of the debt.

**Recording**
Placing a document on file with a designated public official (usually the County Recorder) for everyone to see. Recording is governed by statute, and signatures on legal documents usually must be notarized before the documents can be recorded.

**Recurring closing costs**
Costs paid at closing that will be paid again on an on-going basis, such as hazard insurance, interest, property taxes, or mortgage insurance.

**Red flag**
Anything seen at a visual inspection of a property that might indicate a problem.

**Refinance**
To pay off an existing loan on a property and replace it with another loan.

**Rescind**
To cancel, terminate, or withdraw an offer or contract.

**RESPA**
Real Estate Settlement and Procedures Act.

**REV**
Realtor Estimate of Value.

**RMCR**
Residential Mortgage Credit Report.

**RIN**
Realtor Information Network.

**Seller disclosure**
A seller's statement of the condition of a property, including such things as known defects that would not be visible to the buyer. Many states require sellers to complete a disclosure statement at the time of sale.

**Seller financing**
A loan on real property, secured by a first (or junior) deed of trust that a seller carries for a buyer. The seller is the lender rather than a conventional lender.

**Seller warranty**
A clause in a purchase agreement which states that the property will be in a certain condition at closing.

**Seller's agent**
An agent who represents the seller exclusively in a real estate transaction.

**Settlement**
The same as closing.

**Short sale**
The proceeds from the sale of a property are insufficient to pay off the loan(s) secured against the property. The lender(s) must agree to accept less than the balance owed for the sale to close.

**Single agency**
One real estate broker represents one principal in a real estate transaction—either the buyer or seller, but not both.

**Specific performance**
A legal action to compel the performance of a contract requirement.

## Statement of identity

Also called statement of identification. A confidential form that a title company requires the buyer and/or seller to complete as a condition of issuing title insurance to ensure that liens and judgments of record do not apply to the individuals in question.

## Statute of limitation

A legal limit on the time period within which a court action must be initiated.

## Tax lien

A lien that attaches to real property if the property owner fails to pay property or income taxes when they are due.

## Tax service

A service, usually paid for by the borrower, that notifies the lien holder if the borrowers fail to keep their property taxes current.

## Termite report

An inspection report of a structure completed by qualified personnel to determine the presence of termites and other wood-destroying organisms.

## Title

Evidence of ownership and right to real property.

## Title cloud or defect

An outstanding claim, or encumbrance, against the property that affects the owner's title and prevents the owner from delivering marketable title to a new owner.

## Title insurance

Insurance issued by a title company to protect a property owner from loss caused by imperfect title.

## Transfer tax

A tax charged upon the sale of a property.

## Underwriting

The technical analysis completed by a lender to ensure that a contemplated loan is a sound investment.

## VA

Veterans Administration.

## Vesting

The manner in which title of ownership to a particular property is held.

## Waiver

To release a right to require something, such as waiving a contingency in a purchase contract.

## Zoning

The act of a governing authority specifying how property in specific areas can be used.

# Appendix 1

## Guide to closing costs

Closing costs vary from one area to the next. Who pays which fee is often governed by local custom, but it may also be negotiable. When sellers have difficulty selling, they may be willing to pay some of the buyers' closing costs. In a seller's market, there may be no room for negotiating the closing costs. Some of the fees listed on page 275 do not apply to all areas. For instance, in some places, properties are rarely surveyed as a part of the sale; in other places, properties are almost always surveyed. See the "Guide to local real estate custom and practice" for information on finding out what fees apply in your area.

Many closing fees are dependent on the purchase price: the higher the price, the higher the fee. Also, even though the buyer may usually pay a fee, sellers sometimes agree to credit buyers some money at closing to help pay for their closing costs. Such a credit will reduce the amount of the buyers' closing costs. Be aware that lenders restrict how much they will permit a seller to credit to a buyer at closing (discussed in more detail in Chapter 1).

An asterisk (*) marks nonrecurring closing costs, which are paid by buyer only once, at closing. Many lenders will allow sellers to credit buyers only for their nonrecurring closing costs. Recurring closing costs are paid by buyers repeatedly. Many lenders will not allow credits from sellers to buyers for their recurring closing costs.

| Closing costs | Approximate cost | Who usually pays? |
| --- | --- | --- |
| **Mortgage points*** (Also called loan origination, or discount, fee.) | 1 to 2 points, each point equaling 1 percent of the loan amount. One point on a $100,000 loan is $1,000. (No-point loans are available.) | Buyer. |
| **Credit report*** | $50 per person or married couple. | Buyer. |
| **Property appraisal*** | Varies, from about $200 up. | Varies; usually buyer. |
| **Flood certification*** (Lender requirement.) | Approximately $70. | Buyer. |
| **Tax service*** (Lender requirement.) | Approximately $70. | Buyer. |
| **Mortgage document preparation and miscellaneous fees** (such as an appraisal review)* | Varies, from a few hundred dollars up. | Buyer. |
| **Assumption fee*** (If buyer is assuming existing loan[s].) | Varies; often 1 percent of loan amount(s). | Buyer. |
| **Proration of interest** (Lender collects interest to cover the period from closing to the first regular monthly payment date.) | Depends on closing date: interest to cover from 1 to 30 days. | Buyer. |
| **Mortgage insurance (MI) premium** (To cover the lender in case the buyer defaults. Usually required on first mortgages for more than 80 percent of the purchase price.) | Varies. Some MI programs require a full year's MI premium paid at closing (from about .05 to 1 percent of the loan amount). Others only require 2 months' MI premiums to be paid at closing. | Buyer. |
| **Impounds** (Usually required when the loan amount is 90 percent or more of the purchase price.) | 2 months of hazard insurance, property taxes, and mortgage insurance. More may be required, depending on when property taxes are due. | Buyer. |
| **Title search or abstract*** (This fee may be included in attorney's fee.) | Varies. | Varies; buyer or seller. |

| | | |
|---|---|---|
| **Title insurance for buyer*** | Varies with purchase price. | Varies; buyer, seller, or shared. |
| **Title insurance for lender*** | Varies with loan amount. | Usually the buyer. |
| **Surveyor's fee*** | Varies; often not done. | Varies; buyer or seller. |
| **Real estate brokerage commission*** | Varies; often 5 to 7 percent of sale price. | Seller, in a conventional sale. Some buyers' agents' fees may be paid by buyer. |
| **Attorneys' fees*** (Not part of all home sale transactions.) | Varies: usually from a few hundred dollars to 1 percent of sale price. | Buyer and seller usually pay their own attorney fees. |
| **Hazard insurance** | Varies. Most lenders require first-year premium to be paid at closing. | Buyer. |
| **Property taxes, rents** | Varies. | Buyer and seller usually pay their prorated share based on the closing date. |
| **Assessments** | Varies; may be none. | Varies; sometimes negotiable or prorated. |
| **Prepayment penalty on existing mortgage(s)** | Varies; often none. | Seller. |
| **Liens against the property** | Varies; may be none. | Seller. |
| **Homeowner's association dues** | Varies; may be none. | Buyer and seller usually pay their prorated share based on the closing date. |
| **Homeowner's association transfer fee*** | Varies (state law may limit the fee); may be none. | Often the seller, but negotiable. |
| **Escrow or settlement preparation fee*** | Varies: usually at least several hundred dollars. | Varies; buyer, seller, or shared. |
| **Miscellaneous document preparation, notary recording fees*** | Varies; about $100 to $200. | Buyers and sellers each usually pay for their own respective documents. |
| **Transfer taxes*** | Varies. | Varies; sometimes shared. |
| **Home inspection fees*** | Varies; about $200 to $500. | Buyer. |
| **Home inspection repairs*** | Varies; may be none. | Buyer, seller, or shared. |
| **Termite inspection fee*** | Varies; about $100 to 200. | Buyer or seller. |
| **Termite repair work*** | Varies; may be none. | Often seller, but negotiable. |
| **Home warranty*** | Varies; from about $250 up. Available in most states. | Negotiable. |

(Note: A lender might not consider inspection or termite repairs paid by the buyers as non-recurring closing costs.)

# Guide to contract contingencies

The following is a guide to the contingencies most commonly used in real estate purchase contracts. A contingency is a condition that must be met before the sale is completed. Contingencies should have a time period for completion (either a specific date or a number of days following the date the contract is accepted by the buyer and seller). Contingency time periods are negotiable. The time periods suggested in the chart below are approximate; they may vary given the circumstances of a particular purchase contract. If a contingency cannot be satisfied, the contract is usually canceled and the buyer's deposit is returned.

| Contract contingency | Time period | Conditions that suggest including contingency in the purchase contract: |
|---|---|---|
| Financing | 30 days | If the buyers need to get a mortgage(s) to complete the purchase. |
| Prequalification, preapproval | 5 to 15 days | If the buyers aren't already prequalified or preapproved when they make an offer. |
| Property to appraise for the purchase price | 30 days | If the buyers want confirmation from a professional that they are not paying too much. |
| Assumption | 30 days | If the buyers are assuming the sellers' mortgage(s). |
| Approval of existing note(s) | 30 days | If the buyers are assuming the sellers' mortgage(s). (Gives the buyers the opportunity to read and approve the note.) |
| Seller approval of buyer's financial statement and credit report | 7 to 14 days | If the sellers are carrying financing for the buyers. (Gives the sellers the right to approve the buyers' creditworthiness.) |
| Buyer to provide verification of funds required to close | 7 to 14 days | If the buyers are paying all cash, with no mortgage. (When the buyer gets a mortgage, the lender verifies the funds.) |
| Inspections | 10 to 14 days | If the property has not been inspected by licensed professionals of the buyers' choice before the buyers make an offer. |

| | | |
|---|---|---|
| **Pest control inspection** | 10 to 14 days | If the property has not been inspected by a pest control (termite) inspector acceptable to buyers before the buyers make an offer. |
| **Approve condition of title to the property, property taxes, bonds, and assessments** | Within 10 days of receipt | Should always be included. |
| **Approval of CC&Rs (for condominiums, common interest developments) or cooperative documents** | Within 10 to 14 days of receipt | If buying a condominium, cooperative, or a home in any common-interest development. |
| **Seller disclosures** | Varies with state law | If buying in a state where seller disclosure is required. |
| **Compliance with local laws** | Varies with local law | If buying in an area where local law requires compliance when a property transfers. |
| **Flood hazard, earthquake fault or seismic hazard zone disclosure** | 7 days | If the property is located in one of these zones. |
| **Lead disclosure** | 10 days | If the property was built before 1978. |
| **Probate sale** | Varies | If the sale is subject to court confirmation. |
| **Contingent sale** | Varies: often 30-60 days | If the buyer must sell a property in order to complete the purchase. |
| **Insurance** | 15 to 30 days | If homeowner's insurance is difficult to get in your area. |
| **Review of the contract by attorney or accountant** | 5 to 10 days | If buyers or sellers need professional advice before proceeding. |
| **Buyer approval of repairs completed by seller** | Varies | If buyers need to confirm that work has been completed satisfactorily. |
| **Buyer approval of finishing details or specifications** | Varies | If home is under construction and not completed by the time a purchase contract is entered into. |

# Guide to local real estate custom and practice

The specifics of how homes are bought and sold vary considerably from one area to the next. State and local laws pertaining to home sales also vary. The following checklist will help you to find out the details of how homes are bought and sold in your area, or any area.

| Ask a local real estate professional: agent, attorney, escrow officer, or settlement agent: | Local custom, law, or practice |
| --- | --- |
| Whom do real estate agents represent (seller, buyer, both, neither, or does it vary)? | |
| Is there an agency disclosure law? | |
| Who pays the agent commission? | |
| How much does this usually cost? | |
| Do attorneys participate in the transaction? | |
| What do they do? | |
| How much do they charge? | |
| Who writes the purchase contract (real estate agent, attorney)? | |
| How are offers presented to the sellers? | |
| How are multiple offers handled? | |
| Who handles the money and closing details (escrow, attorney, broker)? | |
| Approximately how much will my closing costs be? | |
| Are there local transfer taxes? | |
| If so, who pays them and how much do they cost? | |
| Who checks title to the property? | |
| Who pays? How much does it cost? | |
| What size good-faith deposit is typical? | |
| Are seller disclosures required? | |
| If so, what's specifically required? | |

What kinds of inspections do most buyers get?

How much do these cost?

When are homes usually inspected (before or after contract is ratified)?

Are there local environmental hazards or soils problems (radon, slides)?

Are there local earthquake or flood zones?

Are there local point-of-sale ordinances or compliance requirements (retrofitting, asbestos removal)?

Do most buyers get termite reports?

Who pays for the inspection report?

Who pays for corrective work?

Are properties surveyed during the sale?

If so, who pays? How much?

Is hazard insurance hard to get? Are any endorsements recommended (such as for code upgrade or earthquake damage)?

How are closings handled (do I need to attend)?

# Appendix 2

NCR (No Carbon Required)

# STANDARD RESIDENTIAL PURCHASE AGREEMENT
## FOR RESALE PROPERTY

### DEFINITIONS

*BROKER* includes cooperating brokers and all sales persons. *DAYS* means calendar days unless otherwise specified. *DATE OF ACCEPTANCE* means the date Seller accepts the offer or the Buyer accepts the counter offer. *DELIVERED* means personally delivered or transmitted by facsimile machine, pursuant to Item 34, or mailed by deposit in U.S. mail, postage prepaid. In the event of mailing, delivery will be deemed to have been made on the fifth day following the date of mailing. *DATE OF CLOSING* means the date title is transferred. *TIME LIMITS* for contingencies are shown in bold print. *TERMINATING THE AGREEMENT* means that both parties are relieved of their obligations and all deposits will be returned to Buyer less expenses incurred by or on account of Buyer to date of termination. *PROPERTY* means the real property and any personal property included in the sale.

**AGENCY RELATIONSHIP CONFIRMATION.** The following agency relationship is hereby confirmed for this transaction and supersedes any prior agency election:

LISTING AGENT: _____ is the agent of (check one):
(Print Firm Name)

☐ the Seller exclusively; or ☐ both the Buyer and the Seller.

SELLING AGENT: _____ (if not the same as the Listing Agent) is the agent of (check one):
(Print Firm Name)

☐ the Buyer exclusively; or ☐ the Seller exclusively; or ☐ both the Buyer and the Seller.

**Note:** *This confirmation DOES NOT take the place of any AGENCY DISCLOSURE form which may be required by law.*

_____ hereinafter designated as BUYER, offers to purchase the real property situated in _____, County of _____, State of _____,
described as _____

FOR THE PURCHASE PRICE OF $_____ (_____ dollars) on the following terms and conditions:

☐ Buyer does ☐ Buyer does not intend to occupy the property as his/her residence.

**1. FINANCING TERMS AND LOAN PROVISIONS.**

**A.** $_____ **DEPOSIT (EARNEST MONEY)** evidenced by ☐ Check, or ☐ Other: _____
held uncashed until acceptance and one business day thereafter deposited with: _____

**B.** $_____ **ADDITIONAL CASH DEPOSIT** to be placed in escrow _____ within _____ days after acceptance, ☐ upon receipt of loan commitment per Item 2, ☐ Other: _____

**C.** $_____ **BALANCE OF CASH PAYMENT** needed to close, not including closing costs.

**D.** $_____ **NEW FIRST LOAN:** ☐ CONVENTIONAL, ☐ FHA, ☐ VA, ☐ Other financing acceptable to Buyer:

☐ FIXED RATE: For _____ years, interest not to exceed _____%, payable at approximately $_____ per month,
with the balance due in not less than _____ years.

☐ ARM: For _____ years, initial interest rate not to exceed _____%, with initial monthly payments of
$_____ and maximum lifetime rate not to exceed _____%.

☐ OTHER TERMS: _____
Loan origination fee not to exceed _____%, plus $_____ paid by ☐ Buyer, ☐ Seller.
Discount Points paid by Seller not to exceed _____%. Discount Points paid by Buyer not to exceed _____%.

*RAGT MEETS PLAIN LANGUAGE™ GUIDELINES.*

E. $ _____ PMI, FHA-MIP, VA Funding Fee, if any, to be ☐ financed, ☐ paid in cash at closing. Appraisal fee to be paid by ☐ Buyer, ☐ Seller.

In the event of FHA or VA financing, the clause FHA FINANCING or VA FINANCING (Items 8 and 9, respectively) is made a part of this Agreement.

**EXISTING FINANCING:** ☐ **FIRST LOAN,** ☐ **SECOND LOAN:**
☐ **ASSUMPTION OF,** ☐ **SUBJECT TO** existing loan of record:
☐ FHA, ☐ VA, ☐ CONVENTIONAL, ☐ PRIVATE, ☐ FIXED RATE, ☐ ARM, ☐ OTHER: _____
payable at $ _____ per month, with interest currently at _____ %, interest rate to be adjusted not to
exceed _____ %. Other terms: _____

Held by: _____ Date balance due: _____

All charges related to assumption will be paid by Buyer. Assumption Fee, if any, not to exceed _____ %.
☐ **ASSUMPTION OF LOAN WITH RELEASE OF LIABILITY:** Buyer will assume Seller's Potential Indemnity
Liability to the U.S. Government for the repayment of the loan.
☐ **ASSUMPTION OF VA LOAN WITH SUBSTITUTION OF ENTITLEMENT:**

**Paragraph 1-E** is conditioned upon Buyer's approval of terms of said loan pursuant to Item 5, **EXISTING LOANS.** Any net differences between the approximate balances of encumbrances shown above, which are to be assumed or taken "subject to," and the actual balances at close of escrow will be adjusted in ☐ Cash,
☐ Amount of note to Seller, ☐ Other: _____

F. $ _____ **SELLER FINANCING:** ☐ **FIRST LOAN,** ☐ **SECOND LOAN,** ☐ **THIRD LOAN,** secured by the property.
☐ Seller Financing Addendum, P.P. Form 131, is attached and made a part of this Agreement.

G. $ _____ **OTHER FINANCING:** _____

H. $ _____ **TOTAL PURCHASE PRICE** (not including closing costs).

2. **LOAN APPROVAL.** Conditioned upon Buyer's ability to obtain a commitment for new financing, as set forth above, from a lender or mortgage broker of Buyer's choice, and/or consent to assumption of existing financing provided for in this Agreement, **within _____ days after acceptance.** Buyer will in good faith use his/her best efforts to qualify for and obtain the financing and will complete and submit a loan application **within five (5) days after acceptance.** Buyer ☐ will, ☐ will not provide a prequalification letter from lender or mortgage broker within _____ **days after acceptance.**

In the event a loan commitment or consent is obtained but not timely honored without fault of Buyer, Buyer may terminate this Agreement.

3. **BONDS AND ASSESSMENTS.** In the event there is a bond or assessment which has an outstanding principal balance and is a lien upon the property, such principal will be ☐ paid by Seller, or ☐ assumed by Buyer. In the event of assumption, said obligation(s) ☐ will, ☐ will not be credited to Buyer at close of escrow. This Agreement is conditioned upon both parties verifying and approving in writing the amount of any bond or assessment **within ten (10) days after receipt** of the preliminary title report.

In the event of disapproval, the disapproving party may terminate this Agreement.

4. **PROPERTY TAX.** Within five (5) days after acceptance, Seller will deliver to Buyer for his/her approval a copy of the latest property tax bill. Buyer is advised that the property may be reassessed upon change of ownership which may result in a tax increase. Buyer should make further inquiry at the office of the taxing authority. **Within ten (10) days after receipt** of the tax bill, Buyer will approve or disapprove the tax bill in writing. In the event of disapproval, Buyer may terminate this Agreement.

Buyer [ _____ ] [ _____ ] and Seller [ _____ ] [ _____ ] have read this page.

Rev. by _____
Date _____

Page 1 of 5

FORM 101-R.1 (4-95) COPYRIGHT © 1991, 1995, BY PROFESSIONAL PUBLISHING. 122 PAUL DRIVE, SAN RAFAEL, CA 94903 (800) 288-2006 FAX (415) 472-2069

🏛 **PROFESSIONAL PUBLISHING**

Property Address _____

**5.** **EXISTING LOANS.** Seller will, **within three (3) days after acceptance,** provide Buyer with copies of all notes, deeds of trust, or mortgages to be assumed or taken subject to. **Within five (5) days after receipt** Buyer will notify Seller in writing of his/her approval or disapproval of the terms of the documents. Approval will not be unreasonably withheld. **Within three (3) days after** acceptance, Seller will submit a written request for a current Statement of Condition on the above loan(s). Seller warrants that all loans will be current at close of escrow.

**6.** **PREPAYMENT.** Seller will pay any prepayment charge imposed on any existing loan paid off at close of escrow. Buyer will pay the prepayment charge on any loan which is to remain a lien upon the property after close of escrow. Seller is encouraged to consult his/her lender regarding prepayment provisions.

**7.** **DUE ON SALE CLAUSE.** If the note and deed of trust or mortgage for any existing loan contains an acceleration or Due on Sale clause, the lender may demand full payment of the entire loan balance as a result of this transaction. Both parties acknowledge that they are not relying on any representation by the other party or Broker with respect to the enforceability of such a provision in existing notes and deeds of trust or mortgages, or deeds of trust or mortgages to be executed in accordance with this Agreement. Both parties have been advised by Broker to seek independent legal advice with respect to these matters.

**8.** **FHA FINANCING.** In the event of FHA financing, it is expressly agreed that notwithstanding any other provisions of this Agreement, the Buyer will not be obligated to complete the purchase of the property or to incur any penalty by forfeiture of earnest money deposits or otherwise, unless Buyer has been given, in accordance with HUD, FHA or VA requirements, a written statement by the Federal Housing Commissioner, Veterans Administration, or a Direct Endorsement Lender, setting forth the appraised value of the property of not less than the amount specified in this contract as the purchase price. Buyer will have the privilege and option of proceeding with consummation of the Agreement without regard to the amount of the appraised valuation. The appraised valuation is arrived at to determine the maximum mortgage the Department of Housing and Urban Development will insure. HUD does not warrant the value nor the condition of the property. Buyer should satisfy himself/herself that the price and condition of the property are acceptable.

**9.** **VA FINANCING.** In the event of VA financing, it is expressly agreed that, notwithstanding any other provisions of this Agreement, the Buyer will not incur any penalty by forfeiture of earnest money or otherwise be obligated to complete the purchase of the property, if the contract purchase price or cost exceeds the reasonable value of the property established by the Veterans Administration. Buyer will, however, have the privilege and option of proceeding with the consummation of this Agreement without regard to the amount of the Reasonable Value established by the Veterans Administration. Escrow Fee to be paid by Seller.

**10.** **DESTRUCTION OF IMPROVEMENTS.** If the improvements of the property are destroyed, materially damaged, or found to be materially defective as a result of such damage prior to close of escrow, Buyer may terminate this Agreement by written notice delivered to Seller or his/her Broker, and all unused deposits will be returned. In the event Buyer does not elect to terminate this Agreement, Buyer will be entitled to receive, in addition to the property, any insurance proceeds payable on account of the damage or destruction.

**11.** **EXAMINATION OF TITLE.** In addition to any encumbrances assumed or taken "subject to," Seller will convey good and marketable fee simple title to the property subject only to: [1] real estate taxes not yet due; and [2] covenants, conditions, restrictions, rights of way and easements of record, if any, which do not materially affect the value or intended use of the property.
    Within three (3) days after acceptance, Buyer will order a Preliminary Title Report and copies of CC&Rs and other documents of record if applicable. **Within ten (10) days after receipt,** Buyer will report to Seller in writing any valid objections to title contained in such report (other than monetary liens to be paid upon close of escrow). If Buyer objects to any exceptions to the title, unless Seller will use due diligence to remove such exceptions at his/her own expense **before close of escrow.** If such exceptions cannot be removed before close of escrow, this Agreement will terminate, unless Buyer elects to purchase the property subject to such exceptions. If Seller concludes he/she is in good faith unable to remove such objections, Seller will so notify Buyer **within ten (10) days after receipt** of said objections. In that event Buyer may terminate this Agreement.

**12.** **EVIDENCE OF TITLE,** in the form of ☐ a policy of Title Insurance, ☐ Certificate of Title, ☐ Other: _____
    paid by _____

*RACT MEETS PLAIN LANGUAGE™ GUIDELINES.*

13. **PRORATIONS.** Rents, real estate taxes, interest, payments on bonds and assessments assumed by Buyer. Homeowners association fees will be prorated as of the date of recordation of the deed. Security deposits, advance rentals, or considerations involving future lease credits will be credited to Buyer.

14. **CLOSING.** Full purchase price to be paid and deed to be recorded ☐ on or before _____ ☐ within _____ days after acceptance. Both parties will deposit with an authorized escrow holder, to be selected by Buyer, all funds and instruments necessary to complete the sale in accordance with the terms of this Agreement. ☐ Where customary, signed escrow instructions to be delivered to escrow holder within _____ days after acceptance. Escrow fee to be paid by _____ ☐ Transfer tax(es), if any, to be paid by _____ Homeowner association transfer fee to be paid by _____
THIS PURCHASE AGREEMENT TOGETHER WITH ANY ADDENDA WILL CONSTITUTE JOINT ESCROW INSTRUCTIONS TO THE ESCROW HOLDER.

15. **PHYSICAL POSSESSION.** Physical possession of the property, with keys to all property locks, alarms, and garage door openers, will be delivered to Buyer (*check one*):
☐ On the date of recordation of the deed, not later than _____ ☐ A.M.; ☐ P.M.;
☐ On the _____ day after recordation, not later than _____ ☐ A.M.; ☐ P.M.
In the event possession is to be delivered **after recordation**, Seller agrees to pay Buyer in escrow, as a day-to-day tenant, for the period from recordation until the date specified above (or any lesser sum in proportion to the actual date possession is delivered) either ☐ $ _____ per day, or ☐ the sum of Buyer's principal, interest, taxes and insurance (PITI) and homeowners dues, if any, for said period.
Seller understands that unless a separate written rental or lease agreement has been signed by the parties, continued occupancy beyond the date specified above constitutes a breach of this Agreement.

16. **FIXTURES.** All items permanently attached to the property, including light fixtures and bulbs, attached floor coverings, all attached window coverings, including drapes, window hardware, window and door screens, storm sash, combination doors, awnings, TV antennas, burglar, fire, smoke and security alarms (unless leased), pool and spa equipment, solar systems, attached fireplace screens, electric garage door openers with controls, outdoor plants and trees (other than in movable containers), are included in the purchase price free of liens, EXCLUDING: _____

17. **MAINTENANCE.** Seller covenants that any existing heating, air-conditioning, electrical, solar, septic system, gutters and downspouts, sprinkler, and plumbing systems including well, sewer, water heater, pool and spa systems, as well as built-in appliances and other mechanical apparatus will be in working order on the date possession is delivered. Seller will replace any cracked or broken glass including windows, mirrors, shower and tub enclosures. Double pane windows with damaged seals, and damaged door and window screens will be replaced. Shower pans and enclosures will be free of leaks. Until possession is delivered, Seller will maintain all structures, landscaping, grounds, and pool. Seller agrees to deliver the property in a neat and clean condition with all debris and personal belongings removed. The following items are specifically excluded from the above: _____
Buyer and Seller understand and acknowledge that Broker will not in any circumstances be liable for any breach in this clause. Seller's obligations under this provision are not intended to create a warranty with respect to the condition of the property to be maintained, or to create an obligation upon the Seller to repair any item that may fail after possession is delivered.

18. **PERSONAL PROPERTY.** The following personal property, on the premises when inspected by Buyer, is included in the purchase price and will be transferred to Buyer free of liens and properly identified by a Bill of Sale at **close of escrow**. No warranty is made as to the condition of the property: _____

Buyer [ _____ ] [ _____ ] and Seller [ _____ ] [ _____ ] have read this page.

Page 2 of 5        FORM 101-R.2 (4-95)        COPYRIGHT © 1991, 1995, BY PROFESSIONAL PUBLISHING, 122 PAUL DRIVE, SAN RAFAEL, CA 94903        (800) 288-2006        FAX (415) 472-2069

Rev. by _____
Date _____

**PROFESSIONAL PUBLISHING**

*THE FORM OF THIS CONT*

Property Address _____

**19. SELLER'S PROPERTY DISCLOSURE STATEMENT. Seller** ☐ will, ☐ will not provide Buyer a completed Seller's Property Disclosure Statement. (P.P. Form 110.11–110.13 may be used unless another form is mandated by state law.)

☐ Buyer has received and read the completed Property Disclosure Statement.

☐ Seller will provide to Buyer the completed Property Disclosure Statement within _____ **days after acceptance.**

Buyer and Seller agree that any new reports or other documents received by Buyer after receipt of the Property Disclosure Statement are automatically deemed an amendment to the Statement. If any disclosure or a material amendment of any disclosure is delivered after the execution of an offer to purchase, Buyer will have **three (3) days** after delivery in person **or five (5) days** after deposit in the mail to terminate his/her offer by delivery of a written notice of termination to Seller or Seller's Agent.

Seller agrees to hold all Brokers in the transaction harmless and to defend and indemnify them from any claim, demand, action or proceedings resulting from any omission or alleged omission by Seller in his/her Property Disclosure Statement or supplement.

**20. SUPPLEMENTAL DISCLOSURE STATEMENTS. Seller** will provide the following supplemental disclosure statements to Buyer:

☐ P.P. FORM 110.90, STANDARD DISCLOSURES AND DISCLAIMERS, ☐ P.P. FORM 110.72, NOTICE RE: SEPTIC SYSTEMS, ☐ P.P. FORM 110.61, HAZARDOUS MATERIALS ADDENDUM, ☐ Other: _____

**21. SAFETY BOOKLETS.** By initialling below, Buyer acknowledges receipt of the following booklets or disclosures:

[    |    ] Lead Based Paint Disclosure

[    |    ] _____

[    |    ] _____

**22. ACCESS TO PROPERTY. Seller** agrees to provide reasonable access to the property to Buyer and inspectors, appraisers, and all other professionals representing Buyer.

**23. WALK-THROUGH INSPECTION.** Buyer will have the right to conduct a walk-through inspection of the property within _____ **days prior to close of escrow,** to verify Seller's compliance with the provisions under Item 16, FIXTURES, Item 17, MAINTENANCE, and Item 18, PERSONAL PROPERTY. Utilities are to remain turned on until the walk-through is completed. This right is not a condition of this Agreement.

**24. COMPLIANCE WITH LOCAL LAWS. Seller** will comply with any local laws applicable to the sale or transfer of the property, including but not limited to: Providing inspections and/or reports for compliance with local building and permit regulations, including septic system inspection reports; compliance with minimum energy conservation standards; and compliance with water conservation measures. All such inspections and reports will be paid by _____. If Seller does not agree within _____ days after receipt of report to pay the cost of any repair or improvement required to comply with such laws, Buyer may terminate this Agreement.

**25. OPTIONAL PROVISIONS.** The provisions in this Item 25, if initialled by Buyer are included in this Agreement.

**25-A.** [    |    ] **PEST CONTROL INSPECTION.** Within _____ **days after acceptance,** ☐ Buyer, ☐ Seller, will obtain at his/her expense a current written report of an inspection by a licensed structural pest control operator of the main building (excluding the roof covering), and all attached structures plus the following:

The inspector will be requested to provide a separate report for: **"Section 1"**—Any portion of the structure(s) where infestation or infection is evident, and **"Section 2"**—Where conditions are present which are deemed likely to lead to infestation or infection, but where no infestation or infection exists at this time.

Work recommended under Section 1 of the report will be paid by Seller. Work recommended under Section 2 of the report will be paid by ☐ Buyer, ☐ Seller, ☐ Other: _____

Work to be performed at Seller's expense may be performed in whole or in part by the Seller; provided that, upon completion of Seller's work but before the area has been closed up, the property is reinspected by a licensed structural pest control operator at Seller's expense who certifies that the inspected property is free of evidence of active infestation or infection. As soon as they are available, copies of inspection reports, certifications, or other proof of completion of the work will be delivered to Brokers of Buyer and Seller, who are authorized to receive the documents on behalf of their principals.

*CONTRACT MEETS PLAIN LANGUAGE™ GUIDELINES.*

Funds for work to be done at Seller's expense after close of escrow will be held in escrow and disbursed by the escrow holder upon receipt of a certification by a licensed structural pest control operator that the property is free of evidence of active infestation or infection.

**25-B. [____] [____] SUBJECT TO BUYER'S APPROVAL OF EXISTING PEST CONTROL REPORT. Within 24 hours after acceptance,** Seller will furnish Buyer a copy of the existing pest control report dated _____ by _____. Seller agrees to pay for work, if any, recommended in said report, or perform the work himself/herself as stated in Item 25-A. **Within fifteen (15) days after acceptance,** Buyer will notify Seller in writing of approval or disapproval of the report. In case of disapproval, Buyer may terminate this Agreement.

**25-C. [____] [____] WAIVER OF PEST CONTROL INSPECTION.** Buyer has satisfied himself/herself about the condition of the property and agrees to purchase the property without the benefit of a structural pest control inspection. Buyer acknowledges that he/she has not relied upon any representations by either the Broker or the Seller with respect to matters that would normally be covered in a pest control inspection.

**25-D. [____] [____] INSPECTIONS OF PHYSICAL CONDITION OF PROPERTY.** Buyer will have the right to retain, at his/her expense, licensed experts including but not limited to engineers, geologists, architects, contractors, surveyors, and structural pest control operators to inspect the property for any structural and nonstructural conditions, including matters concerning roofing, electrical, plumbing, heating, cooling, electrical appliances, well, septic system, pool, boundaries, geological and environmental hazards, toxic substances including asbestos, formaldehyde, radon gas, lead-based paint, and any items listed in Item 17. MAINTENANCE Buyer, if requested by Seller in writing, will promptly furnish, at no cost to Seller, copies of all written inspection reports obtained. Buyer will approve or disapprove in writing all inspection reports obtained within _____ days after acceptance. In the event of Buyer's disapproval, Buyer may terminate this Agreement.

**25-E. [____] [____] MAINTENANCE RESERVE.** Seller agrees to leave in escrow a maintenance reserve in the amount of $_____. If, in the reasonable opinion of a qualified technician, any of the equipment listed under Item 17, MAINTENANCE, is not in working order, Buyer will furnish Seller a copy of the technician's inspection report and/or submit written notice to Seller of non-compliance of any of the terms under Item 17, MAINTENANCE, **within seven (7) days after occupancy is delivered.**

In the event Seller fails to. make the repairs and/or corrections **within (5) days after receipt of said report or notice,** Seller authorizes the escrow holder to disburse to Buyer against bills for such repairs or corrections the sum of such bills, not to exceed the amount reserved. Said reserve will be disbursed to Buyer or returned to Seller **not later than fifteen (15) days after date occupancy is delivered.**

**25-F. [____] [____] HOME PROTECTION CONTRACT,** paid for by [ ] Buyer, [ ] Seller, will become effective upon close of escrow for not less than one year at a cost not to exceed $_____. The Brokers have informed both parties that such protection programs are available, but do not approve or endorse any particular program. Unless this provision is initialled, Buyer understands that such a protection plan is waived.

**25-G. [____] [____] COMMON INTEREST DEVELOPMENT DISCLOSURE.** The property is a condominium, planned development, stock cooperative, community apartment project or other common interest development. **Within fifteen (15) days after acceptance,** Seller, at his/her expense, agrees to provide to Buyer the management documents and current financial statements, including reserve analysis, of the homeowner's association. **Within five (5) days after receipt,** Buyer will notify Seller in writing of approval or disapproval of the documents and information. In case of disapproval, Buyer may terminate this Agreement.

Any delinquent assessments including penalties, attorney's fees, and other charges that are or could become a lien on the property will be credited to Buyer at close of escrow.

Buyer [_____] [_____] and Seller [_____] [_____] have read this page.

Page 3 of 5

FORM 101-R.3 (4-95)   COPYRIGHT © 1991, 1995, BY PROFESSIONAL PUBLISHING, 122 PAUL DRIVE, SAN RAFAEL, CA 94903   (800) 288-2006   FAX (415) 472-2069

Rev. by _____
Date _____

**PROFESSIONAL PUBLISHING**

Property Address: _____

**25-H.** [____] [____] **FLOOD HAZARD ZONE.** Buyer has been advised that the property is located in a special flood hazard area designated by the Federal Emergency Management Agency (FEMA). It will be necessary to purchase flood insurance in order to obtain any loan secured by the property from any federally regulated financial institution or a loan insured or guaranteed by an agency of the U.S. Government. The purpose of the program is to provide flood insurance at reasonable cost. For further information consult your lender or insurance carrier.

**25-I.** [____] [____] **EARTHQUAKE FAULT OR SEISMIC HAZARD ZONE DISCLOSURES.** The property is situated in a Earthquake Fault Zone or Seismic Hazard Zone. Construction or development of any structure for human occupancy may be restricted. No representations on the subject are made by Seller or Broker. Buyer may make further independent inquiries at appropriate governmental agencies concerning the use of the property. Within **seven (7) days after acceptance**, Buyer will notify Seller in writing of satisfaction or dissatisfaction of said inquiries. In case of dissatisfaction Buyer may terminate this Agreement.

**25-J.** [____] [____] **PROBATE/CONSERVATORSHIP SALE.** This is a Probate Sale subject to court approval at which time the court may allow open competitive bidding. An "AS IS" Addendum (P.P. Form 101-AI) [____] is, [____] is not attached and made a part of this Agreement.

**25-K.** [____] [____] **RENTAL PROPERTY.** Buyer to take property subject to rights of parties in possession on leases or month-to-month tenancies. **Within seven (7) days after acceptance**, Seller will deliver to Buyer for his/her approval copies of the following documents: existing leases and rental agreements with tenants estoppel certificates, any outstanding notices sent to tenants, a written statement of all oral agreements with tenants, existing defaults by Seller or tenants, claims made by or to tenants, a statement of all tenants deposits held by Seller, a complete statement of rental income and expenses, any service and equipment rental contracts with respect to the property which run beyond close of escrow. Seller warrants all of this documentation to be true and complete.

Within **seven (7) days after** receipt of documents, Buyer will notify Seller in writing of approval or disapproval of the documents. In case of disapproval, Buyer may terminate this Agreement. During the escrow period of this transaction Seller agrees that no changes in the existing leases or rental agreements will be made, nor new leases or rental agreements longer than month to month entered into, nor will any substantial alterations or repairs be made or undertaken without the written consent of the Buyer.

Security deposits, advance rentals, or considerations involving future lease credits will be credited to Buyer in escrow.

**25-L.** [____] [____] **RENT CONTROL ORDINANCE.** Buyer is aware that a local ordinance is in effect which regulates the rights and obligations of property owners. It may also affect the manner in which future rents can be adjusted.

**25-M.** [____] [____] **SMOKE DETECTORS.** Smoke detectors will be installed at expense of Seller in accordance with applicable laws.

**25-N.** [____] [____] **TAX DEFERRED EXCHANGE (INVESTMENT PROPERTY).** In the event that Seller wishes to enter into a tax deferred exchange for the property, or Buyer wishes to enter into a tax deferred exchange with respect to property owned by him/her in connection with this transaction, each of the parties agrees to cooperate with the other party in connection with such exchange, including the execution of such documents as may be reasonably necessary to complete the exchange; provided that: (a) the other party will not be obligated to delay the closing; (b) all additional costs in connection with the exchange will be borne by the party requesting the exchange; (c) the other party will not be obligated to execute any note, contract, deed or other document providing for any personal liability which would survive the exchange; and (d) the other party will not take title to any property other than the property described in this Agreement. It is understood that a party's rights and obligations under this Agreement may be assigned to a third party intermediary to facilitate the exchange. The other party will be indemnified and held harmless against any liability which arises or is claimed to have arisen on account of the exchange.

**26.  CONTINGENT ON SALE.** (Please check one of the following):

A. [ ] **CONTRACT IS NOT CONTINGENT** upon the sale or close of any property owned by Buyer.

B. [ ] **CONTRACT IS CONTINGENT** on Buyer accepting an offer for his/her property at _____. within _____ days after acceptance of this contract, and that sale closing on or before _____. Seller will have the right to continue to offer the property for sale. If Seller accepts a bonafide written offer from a third party, Seller will give Buyer written notice of that fact. **Within 72 hours of receipt of the notice**, Buyer will waive the contingency on

*IGT MEETS PLAIN LANGUAGE™ GUIDELINES.*

the sale and close of his/her property, or this Agreement will terminate without further notice. Upon waiver of the contingency, Buyer warrants that funds needed to close escrow will be available and Buyer's ability to obtain financing is not contingent upon the sale and/or close of any property.

27. **DEFAULT.** In the event Buyer defaults in the performance of this Agreement (unless Buyer and Seller have agreed to liquidated damages), Seller may, subject to any rights of Broker, retain Buyer's deposit to the extent of damages sustained and may take such actions as he/she deems appropriate to collect such additional damages as may have been actually sustained. Buyer will have the right to take such action as he/she deems appropriate to recover such portion of the deposit as may be allowed by law. In the event that Buyer defaults, unless Buyer and Seller have agreed to liquidated damages, Buyer agrees to pay the Broker(s) any commission that would be payable by Seller in the absence of such default.

28. **MEDIATION OF DISPUTES.** If a dispute arises out of or relates to this Agreement or its breach, by initialling in the "agree" spaces below the parties agree to first try in good faith to settle the dispute by voluntary non-binding mediation before resorting to court action or arbitration, unless the dispute is a matter excluded under Item 29—ARBITRATION.

[     ] Buyer agrees          [     ] Buyer does not agree
[     ] Seller agrees         [     ] Seller does not agree

29. **ARBITRATION OF DISPUTES.** Any dispute or claim in law or equity arising out of this Agreement will be decided by neutral binding arbitration in accordance with prevailing law and applicable court rules. Judgment upon the award rendered by the arbitrator may be entered in any court having jurisdiction. The parties will have the right to discovery.

The parties agree that the following procedure will govern the making of the award by the arbitrator: (a) a Tentative Award will be made by the arbitrator within 30 days following submission of the matter to the arbitrator; (b) the Tentative Award will explain the factual and legal basis for the arbitrator's decision as to each of the principal controverted issues; (c) the Tentative Award will be in writing unless the parties agree otherwise; provided, however, that if the hearing is concluded within one day, the Tentative Award may be made orally at the hearing in the presence of the parties. Within 15 days after the Tentative Award has been served or announced, any party may serve objections to the Tentative Award. Upon objections being timely served, the arbitrator may call for additional evidence, oral or written argument, or both. If no objections are filed, the Tentative Award will become final without further action by the parties or arbitrator. Within 30 days after the filing of objections, the arbitrator will either make the Tentative Award final or modify or correct the Tentative Award, which will then become final as modified or corrected.

The following matters are excluded from arbitration: (a) a judicial or non-judicial foreclosure or other action or proceeding to enforce a deed of trust or mortgage; (b) an unlawful detainer action; (c) the filing or enforcement of a mechanic's lien; (d) any matter which is within the jurisdiction of a probate court, or small claims court; or (e) an action for bodily injury or wrongful death. The filing of a judicial action to enable the recording of a notice of pending action, for order of attachment, receivership, injunction, or other provisional remedies, will not constitute a waiver of the right to arbitrate under this provision.

**NOTICE:** By initialling in the ["agree"] space below you are agreeing to have any dispute arising out of the matters included in this "Arbitration of Disputes" provision decided by neutral arbitration, and you are giving up any rights you might possess to have the dispute litigated in a court or jury trial. By initialling in the ["agree"] space below you are giving up your rights to discovery and appeal. If you refuse to submit to arbitration after agreeing to this provision, you may be compelled to arbitrate under state law. Your agreement to this arbitration provision is voluntary.

We have read and understand the foregoing and agree to submit disputes arising out of the matters included in this "Arbitration of Disputes" provision to neutral arbitration.

[     ] Buyer agrees          [     ] Buyer does not agree
[     ] Seller agrees         [     ] Seller does not agree

Buyer [_____] [_____] and Seller [_____] [_____] have read this page.

Rev. by _____
Date _____

Page 4 of 5

FORM 101-R.4 (4-95)   COPYRIGHT © 1991, 1995, BY PROFESSIONAL PUBLISHING, 122 PAUL DRIVE, SAN RAFAEL, CA 94903   (800) 288-2006   FAX (415) 472-2069

**PROFESSIONAL PUBLISHING**

THE FORM OF THIS CONTRACT

Property Address

**30. ATTORNEY FEES.** In any action or proceeding involving a dispute between Buyer and Seller arising out of the execution of this Agreement or the sale, the prevailing party will be entitled to receive from the other party a reasonable attorney fee to be determined by the court or arbitrator.

**31. ADDITIONAL TERMS AND CONDITIONS.**

_____

_____

_____

_____

_____

_____

_____  (Buyer's Broker)

**32. EXPIRATION OF OFFER.** This Offer will expire unless acceptance is delivered to Buyer or to _____
on or before _____ ☐ A.M. ☐ P.M., _____, 19____.

**33. COUNTERPARTS.** This Agreement may be executed in one or more counterparts, each of which is deemed to be an original.

**34. FAX TRANSMISSION.** The facsimile transmission of a signed copy of this offer or any counter offer to the other party or his/her Broker, followed by faxed acknowledgment of receipt, will constitute delivery.

**35. CONDITIONS SATISFIED/WAIVED IN WRITING.** Each condition or contingency, covenant, approval or disapproval will be satisfied according to its terms or waived by written notice delivered to the other party or their Broker.

**36. TIME.** Time is of the essence of this Agreement; provided, however, that if either party fails to comply with any contingency in this Agreement within the time limit specified, this Agreement will not terminate until the other party delivers written notice to the defaulting party requiring compliance **within 24 hours** after receipt of notice. If the party receiving the notice fails to comply **within the 24 hours,** the non-defaulting party may terminate this Agreement without further notice.

**37. SURVIVAL.** The omission from escrow instructions of any provision in this Agreement will not waive the right of any party. All representations or warranties will survive the close of escrow.

**38. ENTIRE AGREEMENT.** This document contains the entire agreement of the parties and supersedes all prior agreements or representations with respect to the property which are not expressly set forth. This Agreement may be modified only in writing signed and dated by both parties. **Both parties acknowledge that they have not relied on any statements of the real estate Agent or Broker which are not expressed in this Agreement.**

A real estate broker or agent is qualified to advise on real estate. If you have any questions concerning the legal sufficiency, legal effect, insurance, or tax consequences of this document or the related transactions, consult with your attorney, accountant or insurance advisor.

The undersigned Buyer acknowledges that he/she has thoroughly read and approved each of the provisions of this Offer and agrees to purchase the property for the price and on the terms and conditions specified. Buyer acknowledges receipt of a copy of this Offer.

Buyer _____  Date _____ Time _____

Buyer _____  Date _____ Time _____

## ACCEPTANCE

Seller accepts the foregoing Offer and agrees to sell the property for the price and on the terms and conditions specified.

**NOTICE: The amount or rate of real estate commissions is not fixed by law. They are set by each Broker individually and may be negotiable between the Seller and Broker.**

39. **COMMISSION.** Seller agrees to pay in cash the following real estate commission for services rendered, which commission Seller hereby irrevocably assigns to Broker(s) from escrow:

_____ % of the accepted price, or $ _____, to the listing Broker: _____, and
_____ % of the accepted price, or $ _____, to the selling Broker: _____,
without regard to the agency relationship. Escrow instructions with respect to commissions may not be amended or revoked without the written consent of the Broker(s).

If Seller receives liquidated damages upon default by Buyer, Seller agrees to pay Broker(s) the lesser of the amount provided for above or one half of the liquidated damages after deducting any costs of collection, including reasonable attorney fees.

Commission will also be payable upon any default by Seller, or the mutual rescission by Buyer and Seller without the written consent of the Broker(s), which prevents completion of the purchase. This Agreement will not limit the rights of Broker and Seller provided for in any existing listing agreement.

In any action for commission the prevailing party will be entitled to reasonable attorney's fees.

40. **PROVISIONS TO BE INITIALLED.** The following items must be "agreed to" by both parties to be binding on either party. In the event of disagreement, Seller should make a counter offer.
Item 28. MEDIATION OF DISPUTES
Item 29. ARBITRATION OF DISPUTES

Seller acknowledges receipt of a copy of this Agreement. Authorization is given to the Broker(s) in this transaction to deliver a signed copy to Buyer and to disclose the terms of purchase to members of a Multiple Listing Service, Board or Association of REALTORS® at close of escrow.

41. **SUBJECT TO:** _____

Seller _____ Date _____ Time _____
Seller _____ Date _____ Time _____

Buyer acknowledges receipt of a copy of the completed Agreement.

Buyer _____ Date _____ Time _____
Buyer _____ Date _____ Time _____
Date

Rev. by _____
Date _____

**PROFESSIONAL PUBLISHING**

FORM 101-R.5 (4-95)    COPYRIGHT © 1991, 1995, BY PROFESSIONAL PUBLISHING, 122 PAUL DRIVE, SAN RAFAEL, CA 94903    (800) 288-2006    FAX (415) 472-2069

THE FORM OF THIS CONTR

## COUNTER OFFER

In response to the Offer concerning the property located at _____

made by, _____, Buyer, dated _____

**the following Counter Offer is submitted:**

_____

_____

_____

_____

_____

_____

_____

_____

_____

_____

_____

_____

_____

_____

_____

_____

_____

_____

_____

**OTHER TERMS:** All other terms to remain the same.

**RIGHT TO ACCEPT OTHER OFFERS:** Seller reserves the right to accept any other offer prior to Buyer's written acceptance of this Counter Offer. Acceptance shall not be effective until a copy of this Counter Offer, dated and signed by Buyer, is received by _____, the Agent of the Seller.

**EXPIRATION:** This Counter Offer shall expire unless written acceptance is delivered to Seller or his/her Agent on or before _____ ☐ AM ☐ PM, on _____, 19____

Seller _____ Date _____ Time _____

Seller _____ Date _____ Time _____

## ACCEPTANCE

The undersigned Buyer accepts the above Counter Offer.

Buyer _____ Date _____ Time _____

Buyer _____ Date _____ Time _____

Receipt of acceptance is acknowledged.

Seller _____ Seller _____

Rev. by _____
Date _____

FORM 101-A (11-94)    COPYRIGHT © 1989, 1994 BY PROFESSIONAL PUBLISHING, 122 PAUL DR., SAN RAFAEL, CA 94903    (800)288-2006    FAX (415)472-2069

**PROFESSIONAL PUBLISHING**

# SELLER'S PROPERTY DISCLOSURE STATEMENT
(Including the main structure and any out buildings)

Property address: _____

Seller's name: _____

This form supplements any statutory form and is designed to give the Buyer additional information regarding the property. The following representations are made by the Seller(s) and are NOT representations of the Agent(s), if any. This information is a disclosure and is not intended to be part of any contract between the Buyer and Seller.

## 1. TITLE AND ACCESS.

| | | Yes | No | Unknown |
|---|---|---|---|---|
| 1.1 | Is property currently leased? | ☐ | ☐ | ☐ |
| 1.2 | Does anyone have a first right of refusal to buy, option, or lease? | ☐ | ☐ | ☐ |
| 1.3 | Has a Notice of Default been recorded against the property? | ☐ | ☐ | ☐ |
| 1.4 | Any bonds, assessments, or judgments which are liens upon the property? | ☐ | ☐ | ☐ |
| 1.5 | Can the bonds, if any, be paid off without an interest penalty charge? | ☐ | ☐ | ☐ |
| 1.6 | Any boundary disputes, or third party claims affecting the property (rights of other people to interfere with the use of the property in any way)? | ☐ | ☐ | ☐ |

## 2. ENVIRONMENTAL.

Are you aware of any of the following with respect to the property?

| | | Yes | No | Unknown |
|---|---|---|---|---|
| 2.1 | Any excessive noises from airplanes, trains, trucks, freeways, etc.? | ☐ | ☐ | ☐ |
| 2.2 | Any pet odors or contamination? | ☐ | ☐ | ☐ |
| 2.3 | Any other odors from animals, industry, or toxic waste? | ☐ | ☐ | ☐ |
| 2.4 | Formaldehyde emitting materials, especially urea-formaldehyde foam insulation? | ☐ | ☐ | ☐ |
| 2.5 | Asbestos insulation, fireproofing, or ceilings? | ☐ | ☐ | ☐ |
| 2.6 | Underground fuel storage tank? | ☐ | ☐ | ☐ |
| 2.7 | Elevated radon levels on the property? | ☐ | ☐ | ☐ |
| 2.8 | Elevated radon levels in the neighborhood? | ☐ | ☐ | ☐ |
| 2.9 | Use of lead-base paint on any surfaces? | ☐ | ☐ | ☐ |
| 2.10 | Contamination of well or other water supply? | ☐ | ☐ | ☐ |
| 2.11 | Any past or present flooding or drainage problems on adjacent properties? | ☐ | ☐ | ☐ |
| 2.12 | Any standing water after rainfalls? | ☐ | ☐ | ☐ |
| 2.13 | Any sump pumps in basement or crawl space? | ☐ | ☐ | ☐ |
| 2.14 | Any active springs? | ☐ | ☐ | ☐ |
| 2.15 | Is property located wholly or partially within Flood Hazard Area, as determined by the Federal Emergency Management Agency? | ☐ | ☐ | ☐ |
| 2.16 | Is the property located in an Earthquake Fault Zone or Seismic Hazard Zone? | ☐ | ☐ | ☐ |
| 2.17 | Any earthquake weaknesses? | ☐ | ☐ | ☐ |
| 2.18 | Is there any fill on the property (compacted or otherwise)? | ☐ | ☐ | ☐ |
| 2.19 | Any sinkholes or voids on or near the property? | ☐ | ☐ | ☐ |
| 2.20 | Any depressions, mounds, or soft spots? | ☐ | ☐ | ☐ |
| 2.21 | Any pending real estate development in your area (such as condominiums, planned unit developments, subdivisions, or property for commercial, industrial, sport, educational, or religious use)? | ☐ | ☐ | ☐ |
| 2.22 | Any federal or state areas once used for military training purposes within one mile of the property? | ☐ | ☐ | ☐ |
| 2.23 | Are there traces of concrete, metal, or asphalt indicating prior commercial or | ☐ Yes | ☐ No | ☐ Unknown |

| | | Yes | No | Unknown |
|---|---|---|---|---|
| 2.24 | industrial use? | ☐ | ☐ | ☐ |
| 2.25 | Is the property in the proximity of former, current or proposed mines or gravel pits? | ☐ | ☐ | ☐ |
| 2.26 | Is the property in the proximity of former or current waste disposal sites? | ☐ | ☐ | ☐ |
| 2.27 | Are there ravines or earth embankment that may indicate former dumping? Are there pipelines carrying oil, gas, or chemicals underneath or adjacent to the property? | ☐ | ☐ | ☐ |
| 2.28 | Are there pipeline rights-of-way or easements over or adjacent to the property? | ☐ | ☐ | ☐ |
| 2.29 | Is there discoloring of soil or vegetation? | ☐ | ☐ | ☐ |

## 3. STRUCTURAL

| | | Yes | No | Unknown |
|---|---|---|---|---|
| 3.1 | Approximate age of the house: _____ | | | |
| 3.2 | Are there any structural additions or alterations to the property completed, during the term of your ownership, or that of a prior owner, without an appropriate permit or other authority for construction from a public agency having jurisdiction? | ☐ | ☐ | ☐ |
| 3.3 | Are there any violations of government regulations, ordinances, or zoning laws regarding this property? | ☐ | ☐ | ☐ |
| 3.4 | Is there any excessive setting, slippage, sliding, or other soil problems, past or present? | ☐ | ☐ | ☐ |
| 3.5 | Are any retaining walls cracking or bulging? | ☐ | ☐ | ☐ |
| 3.6 | Is the swimming pool out of level? | ☐ | ☐ | ☐ |
| 3.7 | Are there any problems with driveways, walkways, sidewalks, patios (such as large cracks, potholes, raised sections)? | ☐ | ☐ | ☐ |
| 3.8 | Are there any significant cracks in any of the following: ☐ foundations, ☐ exterior walls, ☐ interior walls, ☐ ceilings, ☐ fireplaces, ☐ chimneys, ☐ decks, ☐ slab floors, ☐ garage floors? | ☐ | ☐ | ☐ |
| 3.9 | Are there any slanted floors? | ☐ | ☐ | ☐ |
| 3.10 | Are there any distorted door frames (uneven spaces between doors and frames)? | ☐ | ☐ | ☐ |
| 3.11 | Are there any sticking windows? | ☐ | ☐ | ☐ |
| 3.12 | Are there any sagging exposed ceiling beams? | ☐ | ☐ | ☐ |
| 3.13 | Are any structural woodmembers (including mudsills) below soil level? | ☐ | ☐ | ☐ |
| 3.14 | Is the crawl space, if any, below soil level? | ☐ | ☐ | ☐ |

## 4. ROOF, GUTTERS, DOWNSPOUTS (Indicate "UKN" if answer is unknown)

| | | Yes | No | Unknown |
|---|---|---|---|---|
| 4.1 | Type of roof: ☐ Tar and Gravel, ☐ Asphalt Shingle, ☐ Wood Shingle, ☐ Tile, ☐ Other _____ Age of roof. _____ | | | |
| 4.2 | Has roof been resurfaced? _____ If so, what year? _____ | ☐ | ☐ | ☐ |
| 4.3 | Is there a guarantee on the roof? _____ For how long? _____ By whom? _____ | ☐ | ☐ | ☐ |
| 4.4 | Has roof ever leaked since you owned the property? _____ If so, what was done to correct the leak? _____ ☐ Explanation attached. | ☐ | ☐ | ☐ |
| 4.5 | Are gutters and downspouts free of holes and excessive rust? | ☐ | ☐ | ☐ |
| 4.6 | Do downspouts empty into drainage system or onto splash blocks? | ☐ | ☐ | ☐ |
| 4.7 | Is water directed away from structure? | ☐ | ☐ | ☐ |

Seller(s) Initials [_____] [_____]

FORM 110.11 (5-95)   COPYRIGHT © 1991, 1995, BY PROFESSIONAL PUBLISHING, 122 PAUL DR., SAN RAFAEL, CA 94903   (800) 288-2006   FAX (415) 472-2069

**PROFESSIONAL PUBLISHING**

Property Address _____

## 5. PLUMBING SYSTEM (Indicate "UKN" if answer is unknown)

5.1 Source of water supply: ☐ Public, ☐ Private Well. If well water, when was water sample last checked for safety? _____ Result of test: _____ Condition: _____ Sufficient water during late summer? _____ ☐ Explanation attached.

5.2 Well water pump: Date installed: _____

5.3 Are water supply pipes copper or galvanized? _____

5.4 Are you aware of below normal water pressure in you water supply lines (normal is 50 to 70 lbs.)? _____

5.5 Are you aware of excessive rust stains in tubs, lavatories and sinks? _____

5.6 Are you aware of water standing around any of the lawn sprinkler heads? _____

5.7 Are there any plumbing leaks around and under sinks, toilets, showers, bathtubs, and lavatories? _____ If so, where? _____ ☐ Explanation attached.

5.8 Pool: age: _____ Pool heater: ☐ Gas, ☐ Electric, ☐ Solar. ☐ Pool Sweep? _____ Date of last inspection: _____ By whom? _____ Regular maintenance? _____ By whom? _____

5.9 Hot Tub/Spa: _____ Date of last inspection: _____ Redwood. Capacity: _____ Is septic tank in working order?

5.10 ☐ City sewer, ☐ Septic Tank: ☐ Fiberglass, ☐ Concrete, ☐ Redwood. Capacity: _____

## 6. ELECTRICAL SYSTEM

| | | | | |
|---|---|---|---|---|
| 6.1 | 220 Volt? | ☐ Yes | ☐ No | ☐ Unknown |
| 6.2 | Is the electrical wiring copper? | ☐ Yes | ☐ No | ☐ Unknown |
| 6.3 | Are there any damaged or malfunctioning receptacles? | ☐ Yes | ☐ No | ☐ Unknown |
| 6.4 | Are you aware of any damaged or malfunctioning switches? | ☐ Yes | ☐ No | ☐ Unknown |
| 6.5 | Are there any extension cords stapled to baseboards or underneath carpets or rugs? | ☐ Yes | ☐ No | ☐ Unknown |
| 6.6 | Does outside TV antenna have a ground connection? | ☐ Yes | ☐ No | ☐ Unknown |
| 6.7 | Are you aware of any defects, malfunctioning, or illegal installation of electrical equipment in or outside the house? | ☐ Yes | ☐ No | ☐ Unknown |

## 7. HEATING, AIR CONDITIONING, OTHER EQUIPMENT

| | | | | |
|---|---|---|---|---|
| 7.1 | Is the house insulated? | ☐ Yes | ☐ No | ☐ Unknown |
| 7.2 | Type of Heating System: _____ | | | |
| 7.3 | Is furnace room or furnace closet adequately vented? | ☐ Yes | ☐ No | ☐ Unknown |
| 7.4 | Are fuel-consuming heating devices adequately vented to the outside, directly or through a chimney? | ☐ Yes | ☐ No | ☐ Unknown |
| 7.5 | Is heating equipment in working order? | ☐ Yes | ☐ No | ☐ Unknown |
| 7.6 | Is solar heating in working order? | ☐ Yes | ☐ No | ☐ Unknown |
| 7.7 | Is air conditioning in working order? | ☐ Yes | ☐ No | ☐ Unknown |
| 7.8 | Does fireplace have a damper? | ☐ Yes | ☐ No | ☐ Unknown |
| 7.9 | Provision for outside venting of clothes dryer? | ☐ Yes | ☐ No | ☐ Unknown |
| 7.10 | Is water heater in working order? | ☐ Yes | ☐ No | ☐ Unknown |
| 7.11 | Is water heater equipped with temperature pressure relief valve, which is a required safety device? | ☐ Yes | ☐ No | ☐ Unknown |

| | | | |
|---|---|---|---|
| 7.12 | Is electric garage door opener in working order? | ☐ Yes ☐ No ☐ Unknown |
| 7.13 | Is burglar alarm in working order? | ☐ Yes ☐ No ☐ Unknown |
| 7.14 | Are smoke detectors in working order? | ☐ Yes ☐ No ☐ Unknown |
| 7.15 | Are lawn sprinklers or drip irrigation in working order? | ☐ Yes ☐ No ☐ Unknown |
| 7.16 | Is water softener in working order? | ☐ Yes ☐ No ☐ Unknown |
| 7.17 | Is sump pump in working order? | ☐ Yes ☐ No ☐ Unknown |
| 7.18 | Is any of the above equipment in need of repair or replacement or illegally installed? | ☐ Yes ☐ No ☐ Unknown |

## 8. BUILT-IN APPLIANCES

8.1 Are you aware of any built-in appliances that are in need of repair or replacement? ........ ☐ Yes ☐ No

## 9. CONDOMINIUMS–COMMON INTEREST DEVELOPMENTS

9.1 Please check the availability of copies of the following documents:
☐ CC&Rs or Declaration, ☐ Association Bylaws, ☐ Articles of Incorporation or Association, ☐ Subdivision Report, ☐ Current Financial Statement, ☐ Regulations currently in force, ☐ Minutes of Board Meetings.

9.2 Does the Condominium Declaration contain any resale restrictions? ........ ☐ Yes ☐ No ☐ Unknown

9.3 Does the Homeowners Association have the first right of refusal? ........ ☐ Yes ☐ No ☐ Unknown

9.4 Please check occupancy restrictions imposed by the association:
☐ Children, ☐ Pets, ☐ Storage of recreational vehicles or boats on driveways or in common areas, ☐ Advertising or for sale signs, ☐ Architectural or decorative alterations subject to association approval, Other:

9.5 In case of a conversion, have you an engineer's report on the condition of the building and its equipment? ........ ☐ Yes ☐ No

9.6 Monthly/annual association dues: $ _____ What is included in the association dues?

9.7 Are you aware of any contemplated future dues increases or special assessments? ........ ☐ Yes ☐ No
If so, give details: _____ ☐ Explanation attached.

9.8 Are you aware of any pending or threatened litigation either by or against the Homeowners Association? ........ ☐ Yes ☐ No

9.9 Are all dues, assessments, and taxes current? ........ ☐ Yes ☐ No ☐ Unknown

9.10 I shall provide a statement from the Condominium Homeowners Association documenting the amount of any delinquent assessments, including penalties, attorney's fees, and any other charges provided for in the management documents to be delivered to Buyer. ........ ☐ Yes ☐ No

9.11 Security: ☐ Intercom, ☐ Closed circuit TV, ☐ Guards, ☐ Electric gate, Other:

9.12 Does each unit have its own designated parking spaces? ........ ☐ Yes ☐ No ☐ Unknown

9.13 Is sound proofing adequate? ........ ☐ Yes ☐ No ☐ Unknown

9.14 Property Management Co.

Seller(s) Initials [_____] [_____]

Page 2 of 3
FORM 110.12 (5-95)   COPYRIGHT © 1991, 1995, BY PROFESSIONAL PUBLISHING, 122 PAUL DR., SAN RAFAEL, CA 94903   (800) 288-2006   FAX (415) 472-2069

PROFESSIONAL PUBLISHING

Property Address _____

## 10. OWNERSHIP

10.1 Are you a builder or developer? ................................. ☐ Yes ☐ No
10.2 Are you a licensed real estate agent? ......................... ☐ Yes ☐ No
10.3 Have all persons on the title signed the listing agreement? ....... ☐ Yes ☐ No
10.4 Please list all persons on the title who are not U.S. citizens: _____

## 11. PERSONAL PROPERTY INCLUDED IN THE PURCHASE PRICE

11.1 The following items of personal property are included in the purchase price: _____

_____

11.2 Are there any liens against any of these items? _____ If so, please explain: _____

_____

## 12. HOME PROTECTION PROGRAM

12.1 Do you want to provide a Home Protection Program at your expense? ................. ☐ Yes ☐ No

## 13. REPORTS

13.1 Have you received or do you have knowledge of any of the following inspection reports or repair estimates made during or prior to your ownership?

| REPORT | YES | NO | BY WHOM? | WHEN? | REPORT AVAILABLE? |
|---|---|---|---|---|---|
| Soils/Drainage | | | | | |
| Geologic | | | | | |
| Structural | | | | | |
| Roof | | | | | |
| Pest Control | | | | | |
| Well | | | | | |
| Septic | | | | | |
| Pool/Spa | | | | | |
| Heating | | | | | |
| Air Conditioning | | | | | |
| House Inspection | | | | | |
| Energy Audit | | | | | |
| Radon Test | | | | | |
| City/County Inspection | | | | | |
| Notice of Violation | | | | | |

## 14. OTHER DISCLOSURES

In addition to the disclosures made above, the following matters may materially affect the value or desirability of the property:

_____

_____

_____

_____

_____

_____

_____

_____

_____

_____

_____

_____

_____

_____

_____

_____

_____

_____

**Seller certifies that the above information is true and correct to the best of the Seller's knowledge as of the date signed by the Seller.**

Seller _____ Date _____ Seller _____ Date _____

**Receipt acknowledged:**

Buyer _____ Date _____ Buyer _____ Date _____

Page 3 of 3
FORM 110.13 (5-95)    COPYRIGHT © 1991, 1995, BY PROFESSIONAL PUBLISHING, 122 PAUL DR, SAN RAFAEL, CA 94903    (800) 288-3006    FAX (415) 472-2069

PROFESSIONAL PUBLISHING

# Uniform Residential Loan Application

This application is designed to be completed by the applicant(s) with the lender's assistance. Applicant(s) should complete this form as "Borrower" or "Co-Borrower", as applicable. Co-Borrower information must also be provided (and the appropriate box checked) when □ the income or assets of a person other than the "Borrower" (including the Borrower's spouse) will be used as a basis for loan qualification or □ the income or assets of the Borrower's spouse will not be used as a basis for loan qualification, but his or her liabilities must be considered because the Borrower resides in a community property state, the security property is located in a community property state, or the Borrower is relying on other property located in a community property state as a basis for repayment of the loan.

## I. TYPE OF MORTGAGE AND TERMS OF LOAN

| Mortgage Applied for: | □ VA | □ Conventional | □ Other: | Agency Case Number | | Lender Case No. |
|---|---|---|---|---|---|---|
| | □ FHA | □ FmHA | | | | |

| Amount | Interest Rate | No. of Months | Amortization Type: | □ Fixed Rate | □ Other (explain): |
| $ | % | | | □ GPM | □ ARM (type): |

## II. PROPERTY INFORMATION AND PURPOSE OF LOAN

Subject Property Address (street, city, state, & ZIP)            No. of Units

Legal Description of Subject Property (attach description if necessary)            Year Built

| Purpose of Loan | □ Purchase | □ Construction | □ Other (explain): | Property will be: | □ Primary Residence | □ Secondary Residence | □ Investment |
| | □ Refinance | □ Construction-Permanent | | | | | |

**Complete this line if construction or construction-permanent loan.**

| Year Lot Acquired | Original Cost | Amount Existing Liens | (a) Present Value of Lot | (b) Cost of Improvements | Total (a + b) |
| | $ | $ | $ | $ | $ |

**Complete this line if this is a refinance loan.**

| Year Acquired | Original Cost | Amount Existing Liens | Purpose of Refinance | Describe Improvements | □ made | □ to be made |
| | $ | $ | | | Cost: $ | |

Title will be held in what Name(s)            Manner in which Title will be held            Estate will be held in:
□ Fee Simple
□ Leasehold (show expiration date)

Source of Down Payment, Settlement Charges and/or Subordinate Financing (explain)

## III. BORROWER INFORMATION

| | Borrower | | | | | Co-Borrower | | |
|---|---|---|---|---|---|---|---|---|
| Borrower's Name (include Jr. or Sr. if applicable) | | | | | Co-Borrower's Name (include Jr. or Sr. if applicable) | | | |

| Social Security Number | Home Phone (incl. area code) | Age | Yrs. School | Social Security Number | Home Phone (incl. area code) | Age | Yrs. School |
|---|---|---|---|---|---|---|---|

| □ Married | □ Unmarried (include single, divorced, widowed) | Dependents (not listed by Co-Borrower) no. | ages | □ Married | □ Unmarried (include single, divorced, widowed) | Dependents (not listed by Borrower) no. | ages |
| □ Separated | | | | □ Separated | | | |

Present Address (street, city, state, ZIP) ☐ Own ☐ Rent _____ No. Yrs.

**If residing at present address for less than two years, complete the following:**

Former Address (street, city, state, ZIP) ☐ Own ☐ Rent _____ No. Yrs.

Former Address (street, city, state, ZIP) ☐ Own ☐ Rent _____ No. Yrs.

Present Address (street, city, state, ZIP) ☐ Own ☐ Rent _____ No. Yrs.

Former Address (street, city, state, ZIP) ☐ Own ☐ Rent _____ No. Yrs.

Former Address (street, city, state, ZIP) ☐ Own ☐ Rent _____ No. Yrs.

## IV. EMPLOYMENT INFORMATION

| Borrower | Co-Borrower |
|---|---|
| Name & Address of Employer ☐ Self Employed — Yrs. on this job | Name & Address of Employer ☐ Self Employed — Yrs. on this job |
| — Yrs. employed in this line of work/profession | — Yrs. employed in this line of work/profession |
| Position/Title/Type of Business — Business Phone (incl. area code) | Position/Title/Type of Business — Business Phone (incl. area code) |

**If employed in current position for less than two years or if currently employed in more than one position, complete the following:**

| Name & Address of Employer ☐ Self Employed — Dates (from - to) | Name & Address of Employer ☐ Self Employed — Dates (from - to) |
|---|---|
| — Monthly Income $ | — Monthly Income $ |
| Position/Title/Type of Business — Business Phone (incl. area code) | Position/Title/Type of Business — Business Phone (incl. area code) |

| Name & Address of Employer ☐ Self Employed — Dates (from - to) | Name & Address of Employer ☐ Self Employed — Dates (from - to) |
|---|---|
| — Monthly Income $ | — Monthly Income $ |
| Position/Title/Type of Business — Business Phone (incl. area code) | Position/Title/Type of Business — Business Phone (incl. area code) |

Freddie Mac Form 65   10/92

Page 1 of 4

Fannie Mae Form 1003   10/92

## V. MONTHLY INCOME AND COMBINED HOUSING EXPENSE INFORMATION

| Gross Monthly Income | Borrower | Co-Borrower | Total | Combined Monthly Housing Expense | Present | Proposed |
|---|---|---|---|---|---|---|
| Base Empl. Income * | $ | $ | $ | Rent | $ | |
| Overtime | | | | First Mortgage (P&I) | | $ |
| Bonuses | | | | Other Financing (P&I) | | |
| Commissions | | | | Hazard Insurance | | |
| Dividends/Interest | | | | Real Estate Taxes | | |
| Net Rental Income | | | | Mortgage Insurance | | |
| Other (before completing, see the notice in "describe other income," below) | | | | Homeowner Assn. Dues | | |
| | | | | Other: | | |
| Total | $ | $ | $ | Total | $ | $ |

\* Self Employed Borrower(s) may be required to provide additional documentation such as tax returns and financial statements.

**Describe Other Income** *Notice*: Alimony, child support, or separate maintenance income need not be revealed if the Borrower (B) or Co-Borrower (C) does not choose to have it considered for repaying this loan.

| B/C | | Monthly Amount |
|---|---|---|
| | | $ |
| | | |
| | | |

## VI. ASSETS AND LIABILITIES

This Statement and any applicable supporting schedules may be completed jointly by both married and unmarried Co-Borrowers if their assets and liabilities are sufficiently joined so that the Statement can be meaningfully and fairly presented on a combined basis; otherwise separate Statements and Schedules are required. If the Co-Borrower section was completed about a spouse, this Statement and supporting schedules must be completed about that spouse also.

Completed [ ] Jointly [ ] Not Jointly

| ASSETS | Cash or Market Value | Liabilities and Pledged Assets. List the creditor's name, address and account number for all outstanding debts, including automobile loans, revolving charge accounts, real estate loans, alimony, child support, stock pledges, etc. Use continuation sheet, if necessary. Indicate by (*) those liabilities which will be satisfied upon sale of real estate owned or upon refinancing of the subject property. | | |
|---|---|---|---|---|
| Description | | | | |
| Cash deposit toward purchase held by: | $ | **LIABILITIES** | Monthly Payt. & Mos. Left to Pay | Unpaid Balance |
| | | Name and address of Company | $ Payt./Mos. | $ |
| ***List checking and savings accounts below*** | | | | |
| Name and address of Bank, S&L, or Credit Union | | | | |
| | | Acct. no. | | |
| | | Name and address of Company | $ Payt./Mos. | $ |
| Acct. no. | $ | | | |
| Name and address of Bank, S&L, or Credit Union | | | | |
| | | Acct. no. | | |

Acct. no.

Name and address of Bank, S&L, or Credit Union

$

Acct. no.

Name and address of Bank, S&L, or Credit Union

$

Acct. no.

Stocks & Bonds (Company name/number & description)

$

$

Life insurance net cash value

$

Face amount: $

**Subtotal Liquid Assets**

$

Real estate owned (enter market value from schedule of real estate owned)

$

Vested interest in retirement fund

$

Net worth of business(es) owned (attach financial statement)

$

Automobiles owned (make and year)

$

Other Assets (itemize)

$

**Total Assets a.**

$

---

Name and address of Company

$ Payt./Mos.

$

Acct. no.

Name and address of Company

$ Payt./Mos.

$

Acct. no.

Name and address of Company

$ Payt./Mos.

$

Acct. no.

Name and address of Company

$ Payt./Mos.

$

Acct. no.

Name and address of Company

$ Payt./Mos.

$

Acct. no.

Alimony/Child Support/Separate Maintenance Payments Owed to:

$

Job Related Expense (child care, union dues, etc.)

$

**Total Monthly Payments**

$

**Total Liabilities b.**

$

Freddie Mac Form 65   10/92

Page 2 of 4

Fannie Mae Form 1003   10/92

# VI. ASSETS AND LIABILITIES (cont.)

**Schedule of Real Estate Owned** (If additional properties are owned, use continuation sheet.)

| Property Address (enter S if sold, PS if pending sale or R if rental being held for income) | Type of Property | Present Market Value | Amount of Mortgages & Liens | Gross Rental Income | Mortgage Payments | Insurance, Maintenance, Taxes & Misc. | Net Rental Income |
|---|---|---|---|---|---|---|---|
| | | $ | $ | $ | $ | $ | $ |
| | | | | | | | |
| | | | | | | | |
| Totals | | $ | $ | $ | $ | $ | $ |

List any additional names under which credit has previously been received and indicate appropriate creditor name(s) and account number(s):

| Alternate Name | Creditor Name | Account Number |
|---|---|---|
| | | |

---

## VII. DETAILS OF TRANSACTION

| | |
|---|---|
| a. Purchase price | $ |
| b. Alterations, improvements, repairs | |
| c. Land (if acquired separately) | |
| d. Refinance (incl. debts to be paid off) | |
| e. Estimated prepaid items | |
| f. Estimated closing costs | |
| g. PMI, MIP, Funding Fee | |
| h. Discount (if Borrower will pay) | |
| i. Total costs (add items a through h) | |
| j. Subordinate financing | |
| k. Borrower's closing costs paid by Seller | |
| l. Other Credits (explain) | |
| m. Loan amount (exclude PMI, MIP, Funding Fee financed) | |
| n. PMI, MIP, Funding Fee financed | |

## VIII. DECLARATIONS

If you answer "yes" to any questions a through i, please use continuation sheet for explanation.

| | Borrower Yes | Borrower No | Co-Borrower Yes | Co-Borrower No |
|---|---|---|---|---|
| a. Are there any outstanding judgments against you? | ☐ | ☐ | ☐ | ☐ |
| b. Have you been declared bankrupt within the past 7 years? | ☐ | ☐ | ☐ | ☐ |
| c. Have you had property foreclosed upon or given title or deed in lieu thereof in the last 7 years? | ☐ | ☐ | ☐ | ☐ |
| d. Are you a party to a lawsuit? | ☐ | ☐ | ☐ | ☐ |
| e. Have you directly or indirectly been obligated on any loan which resulted in foreclosure, transfer of title in lieu of foreclosure, or judgment? (This would include such loans as home mortgage loans, SBA loans, home improvement loans, educational loans, manufactured (mobile) home loans, any mortgage, financial obligation, bond, or loan guarantee. If "Yes," provide details, including date, name and address of Lender, FHA or VA case number, if any, and reasons for the action.) | ☐ | ☐ | ☐ | ☐ |
| f. Are you presently delinquent or in default on any Federal debt or any other loan, mortgage, financial obligation, bond, or loan guarantee? If "Yes," give details as described in the preceding question. | ☐ | ☐ | ☐ | ☐ |
| g. Are you obligated to pay alimony, child support, or separate maintenance? | ☐ | ☐ | ☐ | ☐ |
| h. Is any part of the down payment borrowed? | ☐ | ☐ | ☐ | ☐ |
| i. Are you a co-maker or endorser on a note? | ☐ | ☐ | ☐ | ☐ |
| j. Are you a U.S. citizen? | ☐ | ☐ | ☐ | ☐ |
| k. Are you a permanent resident alien? | ☐ | ☐ | ☐ | ☐ |
| l. Do you intend to occupy the property as your primary residence? If "Yes," complete question m below. | ☐ | ☐ | ☐ | ☐ |

o. Loan amount (add m & n)

p. Cash from/to Borrower
(subtract j, k, l & o from i)

m. Have you had an ownership interest in a property in the last three years?

(1) What type of property did you own–principal residence (PR), second home (SH), or investment property (IP)?

(2) How did you hold title to the home–solely by yourself (S), jointly with your spouse (SP), or jointly with another person (O)?

## IX. ACKNOWLEDGMENT AND AGREEMENT

The undersigned specifically acknowledge(s) and agree(s) that: (1) the loan requested by this application will be secured by a first mortgage or deed of trust on the property described herein; (2) the property will not be used for any illegal or prohibited purpose or use; (3) all statements made in this application are made for the purpose of obtaining the loan indicated herein; (4) occupation of the property will be as indicated above; (5) verification or reverification of any information contained in the application may be made at any time by the Lender, its agents, successors and assigns, either directly or through a credit reporting agency, from any source named in this application, and the original copy of this application will be retained by the Lender, even if the loan is not approved; (6) the Lender, its agents, successors and assigns will rely on the information contained in the application and I/we have a continuing obligation to amend and/or supplement the information provided in this application if any of the material facts which I/we have represented herein should change prior to closing; (7) in the event my/our payments on the loan indicated in this application become delinquent, the Lender, its agents, successors and assigns, may, in addition to all their other rights and remedies, report my/our name(s) and account information to a credit reporting agency; (8) ownership of the loan may be transferred to successor or assign of the Lender without notice to me and/or the administration of the loan account may be transferred to an agent, successor or assign of the Lender with prior notice to me; (9) the Lender, its agents, successors and assigns make no representations or warranties, express or implied, to the Borrower(s) regarding the property, the condition of the property, or the value of the property.
**Certification:** I/We certify that the information provided in this application is true and correct as of the date set forth opposite my/our signature(s) on this application and acknowledge my/our understanding that any intentional or negligent misrepresentation(s) of the information contained in this application may result in civil liability and/or criminal penalties including, but not limited to, fine or imprisonment or both under the provisions of Title 18, United States Code, Section 1001, et seq. and liability for monetary damages to the Lender, its agents, successors and assigns, insurers and any other person who may suffer any loss due to reliance upon any misrepresentation which I/we have made on this application.

Borrower's Signature                Date

X

Co-Borrower's Signature                Date

X

## X. INFORMATION FOR GOVERNMENT MONITORING PURPOSES

The following information is requested by the Federal Government for certain types of loans related to a dwelling, in order to monitor the Lender's compliance with equal credit opportunity, fair housing and home mortgage disclosure laws. You are not required to furnish this information, but are encouraged to do so. The law provides that a Lender may neither discriminate on the basis of this information, nor on whether you choose to furnish it. However, if you choose not to furnish it, under Federal regulations this Lender is required to note race and sex on the basis of visual observation or surname. If you do not wish to furnish the above information, please check the box below. (Lender must review the above material to assure that the disclosures satisfy all requirements to which the Lender is subject under applicable state law for the particular type of loan applied for.)

### BORROWER

I do not wish to furnish this information

Race/National Origin:
- American Indian or Alaskan Native
- Asian or Pacific Islander
- Black, not of Hispanic origin
- White, not of Hispanic Origin
- Hispanic
- Other (specify)

Sex:
- Female
- Male

### CO-BORROWER

I do not wish to furnish this information

Race/National Origin:
- American Indian or Alaskan Native
- Asian or Pacific Islander
- Black, not of Hispanic origin
- White, not of Hispanic Origin
- Hispanic
- Other (specify)

Sex:
- Female
- Male

To be Completed by Interviewer

This application was taken by:
- face-to-face interview
- by mail
- by telephone

Interviewer's Name (print or type)

Interviewer's Signature                Date

Interviewer's Phone Number (incl. area code)

Name and Address of Interviewer's Employer

Freddie Mac Form 65   10/92

Page 3 of 4

Fannie Mae Form 1003   10/92

## Continuation Sheet/Residential Loan Application

Use this continuation sheet if you need more space to complete the Residential Loan Application. Mark **B** for Borrower or **C** for Co-Borrower.

Borrower:

Co-Borrower:

Agency Case Number:

Lender Case Number:

I/We fully understand that it is a Federal crime punishable by fine or imprisonment, or both, to knowingly make any false statements concerning any of the above facts as applicable under the provisions of Title 18, United States Code, Section 1001, et seq.

| Borrower's Signature: | Date | Co-Borrower's Signature: | Date |
| --- | --- | --- | --- |
| X | | X | |

Freddie Mac Form 65   10/92

Page 4 of 4

Fannie Mae Form 1003   10/92

## A. Settlement Statement

**U.S. Department of Housing and Urban Development**

OMB Approval No. 2502-0265

**B. Type of Loan**

1. ☐ FHA 2. ☐ FmHA 3. ☐ Conv. Unins.
4. ☐ VA 5. ☐ Conv. Ins.

6. File Number

7. Loan Number

8. Mortgage Insurance Case Number

**C. Note:** This form is furnished to give you a statement of actual settlement costs. Amounts paid to and by the settlement agent are shown. Items marked "(p.o.c.)" were paid outside the closing; they are shown here for informational purposes and are not included in the totals.

D. Name and Address of Borrower

E. Name and Address of Seller

F. Name and Address of Lender

G. Property Location

H. Settlement Agent

Place of Settlement

I. Settlement Date

| J. Summary of Borrower's Transaction | | |
|---|---|---|
| 100. Gross Amount Due From Borrower | | |
| 101. Contract sales price | | |
| 102. Personal property | | |
| 103. Settlement charges to borrower (line 1400) | | |
| 104. | | |
| 105. | | |
| Adjustments for items paid by seller in advance | | |
| 106. City/town taxes | to | |
| 107. County taxes | to | |
| 108. Assessments | to | |
| 109. | | |
| 110. | | |
| 111. | | |
| 112. | | |
| 120. Gross Amount Due From Borrower | | |

| K. Summary of Seller's Transaction | | |
|---|---|---|
| 400. Gross Amount Due To Seller | | |
| 401. Contract sales price | | |
| 402. Personal property | | |
| 403. | | |
| 404. | | |
| 405. | | |
| Adjustments for items paid by seller in advance | | |
| 406. City/town taxes | to | |
| 407. County taxes | to | |
| 408. Assessments | to | |
| 409. | | |
| 410. | | |
| 411. | | |
| 412. | | |
| 420. Gross Amount Due To Seller | | |

| 200. Amounts Paid By Or In Behalf Of Borrower | | | 500. Reductions In Amount Due To Seller | | |
|---|---|---|---|---|---|
| 201. Deposit or earnest money | | | 501. Excess deposit (see instructions) | | |
| 202. Principal amount of new loan(s) | | | 502. Settlement charges to seller (line 1400) | | |
| 203. Existing loan(s) taken subject to | | | 503. Existing loan(s) taken subject to | | |
| 204. | | | 504. Payoff of first mortgage loan | | |
| 205. | | | 505. Payoff of second mortgage loan | | |
| 206. | | | 506. | | |
| 207. | | | 507. | | |
| 208. | | | 508. | | |
| 209. | | | 509. | | |
| Adjustments for items unpaid by seller | | | Adjustments for items unpaid by seller | | |
| 210. City/town taxes | to | | 510. City/town taxes | to | |
| 211. County taxes | to | | 511. County taxes | to | |
| 212. Assessments | to | | 512. Assessments | to | |
| 213. | | | 513. | | |
| 214. | | | 514. | | |
| 215. | | | 515. | | |
| 216. | | | 516. | | |
| 217. | | | 517. | | |
| 218. | | | 518. | | |
| 219. | | | 519. | | |
| 220. Total Paid By/For Borrower | | | 520. Total Reduction Amount Due Seller | | |
| 300. Cash At Settlement From/To Borrower | | | 600. Cash At Settlement To/From Seller | | |
| 301. Gross Amount due from borrower (line 120) | | | 601. Gross amount due to seller (line 420) | | |
| 302. Less amounts paid by/for borrower (line 220) | ( | ) | 602. Less reductions in amt. due seller (line 520) | ( | ) |
| 303. Cash  ☐ From  ☐ To Borrower | | | 603. Cash  ☐ To  ☐ From Seller | | |

HUD-1 (3-86)
RESPA, HB 4305.2

Previous Edition Is Obsolete

# *Index*

Home protection plans, 21, 72–73, 126, 157–58, 244
HomeScout, 95
Home showings, 222–23
Home warranties. *See* Home protection plans
House America Counseling Center, 188
HOW. *See* Home Owner's Warranty
HSH Associates, 97
HUD (Housing and Urban Development)
    FHA loans through, 193
    Internet address of, 94
    median income chart, 194
HUD-1 settlement statement, 13, 181, 214, 302–3

**I**

Impound accounts, 182, 191–92
Indexes
    for ARMs, 163
    differences among, 163–64
Inman News Features, 97
Inspection, 138–59
    buyer's attending, 141–42
    of condominiums, 80
    conflicting reports, 153
    contingency, 61, 120–21, 138, 146, 151–52
    of cooperatives, 85
    cost of, 138
    discovering defects after closing, 158–59
    environmental hazards, 146–47
    existing reports and seller disclosure, 147–50
    failure to, 8
    final walk-through, 126, 216–17
    further, 142–43, 145
    general, 139–42
    liability of inspectors, 140, 159
    locating property boundaries, 154–55
    of new homes, 68
    presale, 243–44
    punch list, 216
    red flags, 150–51
    resolving issues from, 151–54
    scheduling, 141
    selecting inspectors, 139–41
    seller credits for repairs, 153–54
    of short sale properties, 87
    termite, 143–46, 219
    time for, 65
    of townhouses, 80
Installment sales, 199
Insurance
    amount of, 211
    for condominiums, 82, 210
    for cooperatives, 86, 210
    deductibles, 211
    discounts, 211
    flood, 210
    homeowner's, 208–12
    information on the Internet, 97
    limitations on, 210
    mortgage, 23–24, 177, 189, 191, 193
    title, 206

Insurance News Network, 97
Interest
    proration of, 12, 121
    warehousing, 164
Interest rates
    changes in, 33–34
    information on the Internet, 97, 169
    lock-ins, 195–97
    points vs., 170
    teaser, 164, 165, 170
International Real Estate Directory (IRED), 95, 96
International style, 51
Internet
    agents on, 92, 96
    computer equipment required, 94
    financing information on, 97, 169
    FSBO on, 97
    information about buying real estate on, 94
    insurance information on, 97
    loan applications over, 190
    newspapers on, 96–97
    real estate companies on, 96
    search engines, 94–95
IRED. *See* International Real Estate Directory

**K**

Kickbacks, 183

**L**

Lead-based paint, 147
Lease options, 89–91
Lenders
    bait-and-switch, 9
    comparison checklist, 172
    mortgage brokers vs. direct lenders, 173, 175–77
    portfolio, 177–78, 191
    retail, 175
    shopping for, 9, 168–80
    wholesale, 175
Leverage, 28–29
LIBOR. *See* London interbank offering rate
Listing agreements, 238
Listing Link, 95
Living trusts, 205
Loans. *See also* Financing; Interest rates; Lenders
    adjustable-rate, 19, 162, 163–66, 171, 173, 174,
        200–201
    amortization schedule, 249–61
    amortized, 160, 162
    application for, 180–86
    approval of, 186
    APR, 170–71
    assumable, 166, 200–201
    back-end ratio, 17, 18
    balloon payments, 161, 162, 163, 200
    B- and C-rated, 188
    buy-down, 197–98
    conforming, 162, 177
    co-signing, 24
    credit scoring, 188, 189–91